THE PARADISE
OF THE HOLY FATHERS
VOLUME II
CONTAINING
THE COUNSELS OF THE HOLY MEN AND THE QUESTIONS & ANSWERS OF THE ASCETIC BRETHREN GENERALLY KNOWN AS THE SAYINGS OF THE FATHERS OF EGYPT

ST. MACARIUS THE GREAT

THE PARADISE OR GARDEN OF THE HOLY FATHERS BEING HISTORIES OF THE ANCHORITES RECLUSES MONKS COENOBITES AND ASCETIC FATHERS OF THE DESERTS OF EGYPT BETWEEN A.D. CCL AND A.D. CCCC CIRCITER COMPILED BY *ATHANASIUS* ARCHBISHOP OF ALEXANDRIA: *PALLADIUS* BISHOP OF HELENOPOLIS: SAINT *JEROME* AND OTHERS ⒞ NOW TRANSLATED OUT OF THE SYRIAC WITH NOTES & INTRODUCTION BY *ERNEST A. WALLIS BUDGE* M.A: L^{ITT}.D: D.L^{IT}: KEEPER OF THE ASSYRIAN & EGYPTIAN ANTIQUITIES IN THE BRITISH MUSEUM

ST. NECTARIOS PRESS
SEATTLE, WASHINGTON
1984

Published by

St. Nectarios Press
10300 Ashworth Avenue North
Seattle, Washington 98133-9410

Reprinted 1984 from the original edition of
Chatto & Windus, London, 1907.

ISBN 0-913026-56-5

Printed in Singapore

And again, we begin, by the power of our Lord, the Third (sic) Part with the Counsels of the Holy Old Men, and the Questions and the Answers [which they gave] to the Brethren

ST. ARSENIUS THE GREAT

Book the First

Chapter i. Of Flight from Men, and of Silent Contemplation, and of Dwelling continually in the Cell, [a work] which was composed by Bishop Palladius for the Prefect Lausus

WHEN Abbâ Arsenius was in the palace, he prayed to God, and said, "O Lord, direct me how to live"; and a voice came to him, saying, "Arsenius, flee from "men, and thou shalt live."

2. And when Arsenius was living the ascetic life in the monastery, he prayed to God the same prayer, and again he heard a voice saying unto him, "Arsenius, flee, keep silence, "and lead a life of silent contemplation, for these are the fun-"damental causes which prevent a man from committing sin."

3. A certain man said that there were once three men who loved labours, and they were monks. The first one chose to go about and see where there was strife, which he turned into peace; the second chose to go about and visit the sick; but the third departed to the desert that he might dwell in quietness. Finally the first man, who had chosen to still the contentions of men, was unable to make every man to be at peace with his neighbour, and his spirit was sad; and he went to the man who had chosen to visit the sick, and he found him in affliction because he was not able to fulfil the law which he had laid down for himself. Then the two of them went to the monk in the desert, and seeing each other they rejoiced, and the two men related to the third the tribulations which had befallen them in the world, and entreated him to tell them how he had lived in the desert. And he was silent, but after a little he said unto them, "Come, let each of us go and fill a vessel "of water"; and after they had filled the vessel, he said unto them, "Pour out some of the water into a basin, and look "down to the bottom through it," and they did so. And he said unto them, "What do ye see?" and they said, "We see "nothing." And after the water in the basin had ceased to move, he said to them a second time, "Look into the water," and they looked, and he said unto them, "What do ye see?" And they said unto him, "We see our own faces distinctly"; and he said unto them, "Thus is it with the man who dwell-"eth with men, for by reason of the disturbance caused by "this affair of the world he cannot see his sins; but if he live

II-1a

" in the peace and quietness of the desert he is able to see God
" clearly."

4. On one occasion Abbâ Ammon came during the season
of winter to Abbâ Sisoes, and he saw that the old man was
grieved because he had left the desert; and Abbâ Ammon
said unto him, " Why art thou distressed, O father ? For what
" wast thou able to do in the desert in thine old age? " And
the old man Sisoes looked at him fiercely, and said, "What
" sayest thou to me, Ammon? Are not the mere thoughts of the
" freedom which is in the desert better for us [than living out
" of it] ? "

5. There were two brethren in the desert who were the
equals of each other in the spiritual life, and they led a life of
ascetic self-denial, and performed the exalted works which
belong to spiritual excellence. And it happened that one of
them was called to be the head of a habitation of the brethren,
but the other remained in the desert, where he became a man
perfect in self-denial. And he was held by God to be worthy of
the gift of healing those who were possessed of devils, and he
knew beforehand the things which were about to happen, and he
made whole the sick. Now when he who had become the head of a
habitation of brethren (i.e., a coenobium, or monastery) heard
these things, he decided in his mind that his fellow monk must
have acquired these powers suddenly, and he lived a life of
silence and ceased from converse with men for three weeks,
and he made supplication unto God continually that He would
shew him how the monk in the desert wrought these mighty
works, while he had not received even one of the gifts which
he had. And an angel appeared and said unto him, " He who
" dwelleth in the desert maketh supplication to God both by
" night and by day, and his pain and anxiety are for our
" Lord's sake ; but thou hast care for many things, and thou
" hast converse with many, and the consolation and encou-
" ragement of the children of men must be sufficient for thee."

6. Abbâ Arsenius on one occasion went to the brethren in
a certain place where there were some reeds growing, and
the wind blew upon them, and they were shaken. And the old
man said, " What is this rustling sound ? " and they said
unto him, " It is that caused by the reeds which are being
" shaken by the wind." And he said unto them, " Verily I say
" unto you, if the man who dwelleth in silence heareth but the
" twittering of a sparrow, he shall not be able to acquire that
" repose in his heart which he seeketh; how much less then
" can ye do so with all this rustling of the reeds about you? "

7. A certain brother came to Abbâ Arsenius, and said unto
him, " My thoughts vex me, and say, ' Thou canst not fast

4

" ' and thou art not able to labour, therefore visit the sick,
" ' which is a great commandment.' " Then Abbâ Arsenius,
after the manner of one who was well acquainted with the war
of devils, said unto him, " Eat, drink, and sleep, and toil not,
" but on no account go out of thy cell "; for the old man knew
that dwelling constantly in the cell induceth all the habits of the
solitary life. And when the brother had done these things for
three days he became weary of idleness, and finding a few palm
leaves on the ground, he took them and began to split them
up, and on the following day he dipped them in water and began to work (i.e., to weave baskets); and when he felt hungry
he said, " I will finish one more small piece of work, and then
" I will eat." And when he was reading in the Book, he said,
" I will sing a few Psalms and say a few prayers, and then I
" shall eat without any compunction." Thus little by little, by
the agency of God, he advanced in the ascetic life until he
reached the first rank, and received the power to resist the
thoughts and to vanquish them.

8. When Abbâ Sisoes was dwelling in the mountain of Abbâ
Anthony, the man who used to minister unto him departed
and remained away for a period of ten months and did not
come [back] to him, and he saw no man. And afterwards, as
he was walking in the mountains, he saw a man hunting wild
animals, and the old man said to him, " Whence comest thou?
" And how long hast thou been here?" And the man said unto
him, " Father, I have been in this mountain eleven months,
" and I have seen no man except thyself." Then the old man
having heard these things went into his cell, and smote upon
his face, and said, "Behold, O Sisoes, well mayest thou think
" that thou hast done nothing, for thou hast not made thyself
" even like unto this man who is in the world, and is not a
" monk."

9. I once asked Abbâ Sarmâtâ a question, and said unto him,
" What shall I do, O my father, for I do nothing which the
" monks do ? On the contrary, I am negligent, and I eat, and
" drink, and sleep, and I think many filthy thoughts, and my
" mind is ever disturbed, and I depart from one work to an-
" other, and from one group of thoughts to another. What
" shall I do, then ? For I am troubled, and my soul is little."
And Abbâ Sarmâtâ said unto him: " Sit thou in thy cell, and
" whatsoever thou canst do, that do, and trouble not thyself.
" For I wish thee to do now a little, even as did Abbâ An-
" thony in the mountain, and I believe that by sitting in [thy]
" cell for the sake of the Name of God, thou also wilt be found
" in the same place as Abbâ Anthony."

10. On one occasion the brethren went up from Scete to go

5

to Abbâ Anthony, and having embarked in a boat to journey
to him, they found [there] a certain old man, who was
also going to visit him, and they were not acquainted with
him. And as they were sitting in the boat, they spake now and
again a word of the Fathers, or a word from the Book, or
they talked about the work of their hands; and the old man
listened unto all they said, but held his peace. Then, having
crossed the ferry, the old man was found to be going also to
Abbâ Anthony. And when they had all arrived at the place
where he was, he said unto them, "Ye found excellent com-
"pany in this old man"; and to the old man himself he said,
"Thou didst find excellent brethren to travel with thee, O
"father." And the old man said, "They are excellent brethren,
"but they have no door to their house, and whosoever wisheth
"can go into the stable, and untie the ass, and go whither-
"soever he pleaseth on him." Now this he said because they
uttered every word which came into their mouths.

11. A certain brother asked Abbâ Sisoes, saying, "Father,
"how was it that thou didst leave Scete where thou wast
"with Abbâ Macarius, and didst come here?" And the old man
said unto him, "When Scete began to be filled [with monks]
"I heard that Abbâ Antonius had fallen asleep, and I came to
"the mountain here, and found that this place was quiet, and
"I lived here for a little time." The brother said unto him,
"How long hast thou been here?" and the old man said,
"Behold, I have been here seventy years this day."

12. They used to say concerning Abbâ Theodore and Abbâ
Luk that they passed fifty years with disturbed minds, and
were troubled the whole time about changing their place [of
abode]; and they said, "Behold, we will change in the winter";
and when the winter arrived, they said, "We will change in
"the summer"; and thus they did unto the end of their lives.

13. A certain father came to Abbâ Arsenius, and he knocked
at the door, and the old man opened unto him thinking that
it was his servant [who had knocked]; and when he saw who
it was, he cast himself upon his face, and the father entreated
him, saying, "Stand up, O father, that I may give thee the
"salutation of peace." But Arsenius disputed with him, saying, "I will not stand up until thou hast departed"; and
though he entreated him to do so often he would not stand
up, and the father left him and departed.

14. Abbâ Battimion said, "When I went down to Scete
"they gave me some apples to take to the brethren, and when
"I had knocked at the door of Abbâ Abhîlâ, he said to me
"when he saw me, 'If these apples had been of gold I would
"'not have wished thee to knock at my door; and moreover, do

6

" 'not knock at the door of any other brother'; so I returned
" and placed the apples in the church and departed."

15. They said concerning Abbâ Sisoes that when the church
began [to fill] he fled quickly to his cell, and, [though] the
brethren said, " He hath a devil," he was performing the
work of God.

16. Abbâ Joseph said to Abbâ Nestîr, " What shall I do
" with my tongue, for I cannot conquer it?" Abbâ Nestîr said
unto him, " If thou talkest wilt thou have relief from this
" [trouble]?" And he said unto him, " Nay." The old man said
unto him, " If then thou hast no relief when thou talkest, why
" dost thou talk?" Abbâ Joseph said unto him, " What shall
" I do? For I cannot stand against it." The old man said unto
him, " Wilt thou have relief then?" and he said unto him,
" Nay." The old man said unto him, " If thou canst not gain
" relief by talking, then hold thy peace."

17. A certain brother went to Abbâ Poemen on the second
Sunday in the Fast of Forty Days and repeated unto him his
thoughts, and sighing over what the old man had told him,
he said unto him, " I had almost kept myself from coming here
" to-day"; and the old man said, " Why?" Then the brother
said, " I said in my mind, Peradventure during the fast the
" door will be closed against thee"; and Abbâ Poemen said
unto him, " We do not learn to shut a door made of wood,
" but to close the door of the tongue."

18. When a certain brother in Scete was going to the harvest, he went to Abbâ Moses, the Black, and said unto him,
" Father, tell me what I shall do; shall I go to the harvest?"
and Abbâ Moses said unto him, " If I tell thee, wilt thou be
" persuaded to do as I say?" And the brother said unto him,
" Yea, I will hearken unto thee." The old man said unto him,
" If thou wilt be persuaded by me, rise up, go, and release
" thyself from going to the harvest, and come unto me, and I
" will tell thee what thou shalt do." The brother therefore
departed and obtained his release from his companions, as the
old man had told him, and then he came to him. And the old
man said unto him, " Go into thy cell and keep Pentecost, and
" thou shalt eat dry bread and salt once a day [only], and after
" thou hast done this I will tell thee something else to do later
" on"; and he went and did as the old man had told him, and then
came to him again. Now when the old man saw that he was
one who worked with his hands, he shewed him the proper
way to live in his cell; and the brother went to his cell, and
fell on his face upon the ground, and for three whole days and
nights he wept before God. And after these things, when his
thoughts were saying unto him, " Thou art now an exalted

7

"person, and thou hast become a great man," he used to con-
tradict them, and set before his eyes his former shortcomings,
[and say], "Thus were all thine offences." And again, when
they used to say to him, "Thou hast performed many things
"negligently," he would say, "Nevertheless I do small ser-
"vices for God, and He sheweth His mercy upon me." And
when by such means as these the spirits had been overcome,
they appeared unto him in the form of corporeal creatures, and
said unto him, "We have been vanquished by thee"; and he
said unto them, "Why?" and they said unto him, "If we
"humble thee, we are raised up by thee to an exalted posi-
"tion, and if we exalt thee we are accounted by thee for
"humility."

19. There was a certain brother in the monastery who worked
hard, and the brethren who were in Scete heard about him,
and came to see him, and they entered into the place where
he used to work; and having received them, and saluted them,
he turned round and began to work again. And when the brethren saw what he did, they said unto him, "John gave thee
"the garb of the monk, and made thee a dweller in a mona-
"stery, but he did not teach thee to receive a blessing (*literally*,
"prayer) from the brethren, or to give one, or to say to them,
"'Pray ye,' or, 'Sit ye down.'" And John said unto them,
"Nay, a sinner is not sufficient for these things."

20. Abbâ Anthony said, "As a fish when it is lifted up out
"of the water dieth, even so doth the monk who tarrieth out-
"side his cell."

21. They tell the story of a certain brother who came to
Scete to see Abbâ Arsenius, and who went into the church
and entreated the clergy to take him to see him; and the clergy
said unto him, "Refresh thyself a little, and thou shalt see
"him." And the brother said unto them, "I will eat nothing
"before I meet him and see him"; and when the clergy heard
this they sent a brother with him to shew him Abbâ Arsenius,
because his cell was some distance away. And when they had
arrived there, they knocked at the door and went inside, and
having saluted him, and prayed, they sat down and held their
peace; and the brother who was from the church answered
and said, "I will depart, pray ye for me." But when the other
brother saw that he possessed not freedom of speech with the
old man, he said unto the brother from the church, "I also
"will go with thee," and they departed together.

Then he entreated him, saying, "Take me also to Abbâ
"Moses who was a thief," and when they went to him, the
old man received them with joy, and having refreshed them
greatly he dismissed them in peace. And the brother who had

brought the visitor to Abbâ Moses said unto him, "Behold,
"I brought thee to a man from a foreign land, and to an
"Egyptian, which of the two pleaseth thee?" And he answered
and said unto him, "The Egyptian who hath just received me,
"and refreshed me." And when one of the old men heard what
had happened, he prayed to God, and said, "O Lord, shew
"me this matter; one fleeth from the world for Thy Name's
"sake, and another receiveth and is gracious for Thy Name's
"sake." And behold, suddenly there appeared unto him on
the river two great boats, and lo, Abbâ Arsenius and the
Spirit of God were travelling in silence in the one, and Abbâ
Moses and the angels of God were in the other, and they were
feeding the monk with honey from the comb.

22. A certain brother asked Abbâ Poemen a question, saying, "If I see something done, dost thou wish me to tell it
"abroad?" The old man said unto him, "It is written, 'Who-
"'soever shall declare a matter incorrectly, it is a disgrace to
"'him and [a subject for] mockery.' And if thou art asked,
"speak; and if thou art not asked, hold thy peace."

23. On one occasion there was an assembly in a great church,
and all the old men were asked in a body, "What striving is
"the mightiest against the monks?" And they all agreed that
there was none stronger than that which would make a man
leave his cell and depart, for when this striving is overcome,
all the rest can quite easily be brought low.

24. They say concerning Abbâ Âpôs, who afterwards became Bishop of Oxyrhyncus, that when he was a monk he laboured with great toil in the ascetic life, and that he was
moved every hour by Divine Grace, but that after he became
Bishop, though he wished to perform the same labours, he
was not able to do so. And he cast himself before God, and
made supplication unto Him, saying, "Peradventure, O my
"Lord, it is because of the Bishopric that Thou hast removed
"Thy grace from me," and it was said unto him, "It is not
"so, but formerly thou wast in the desert, and there were no
"men there, and God took care of thee; here, however, thou
"art in a portion of the world which is inhabited, and men care
"for thee."

25. A certain brother from the Cells soaked some palm
leaves in water, and then sat down to weave ropes, and his
mind said unto him, "Go and visit such and such a brother";
and he pondered on the matter, and said, "I will go after a
"few days." And again his mind said unto him, "Supposing
"thou shouldst die, what wilt thou do? for thou wouldst not
"see thy brother"; and once again he satisfied his mind by
saying, "I will go after such and such a time." Now when the

summer had come, he said within himself, "To-day is not the
" right time for going," and again he said to his mind, " As
" soon as thou hast cut off the end of the palm leaves it will
" be time for thee to go"; and he said to himself, " I will
" finish these leaves, and then I will go." And once again his
mind urged him and said, "The weather is beautiful to-day,"
and he rose up straightway and left the palm leaves soaking
in the water, and he picked up a cloak and ran off on his way.
Now he had as a neighbour a certain old man who used to see
visions, and as soon as this man saw the brother running, he
cried out, and said unto him, " Prisoner, prisoner, come
"hither"; and when he had gone in the old man said unto
him, " Go back to thy cell," and the brother went back, and
he related unto him the whole story of his war. And having
entered his own cell, he offered up repentance unto God, and
the devils cried out with a loud voice, saying, " Thou hast
" vanquished us, thou hast vanquished us, O monk." Now he
had a palm-leaf mat under him, and it was charred as if it had
been burned in the fire, and the devils vanished like smoke;
then straightway the brother perceived their wiles, and he
gave thanks unto God.

26. Abbâ Poemen said: A certain brother asked Abbâ Sîmôn,
and said, "If I go out from my cell, and I find a brother ab-
" sorbed and immersed in matters unnecessary for salvation,
" shall I associate myself also with him? And supposing also
" that I should find him laughing, and that I also should laugh,
" when I have gone into my cell again shall I not be forgiven
" my relaxation?" And the old man said unto him, "What
" dost thou wish? Dost thou mean that having gone out of thy
" cell and having found a man who was laughing, and laughed
" with him, and having found a man who was talking, and
" talked with him, thou canst go back to thy cell and find thy-
" self as thou wast before thou didst go out?" And the brother
said unto him, "If not, how then?" Then the old man answered and said unto him, "It is right for thee to keep a care-
" ful watch both within and without."

27. An old man said, "One man is thought to be silent, and
" yet his heart judgeth and condemneth others, and the man
" who acteth thus speaketh continually; another man speak-
" eth from morning till evening, and yet keepeth silence, that
" is to say, he speaketh nothing which is not helpful."

28. There were two excellent brethren in the Cells, and they
were held to be worthy to see things of mystery, and each one
of them saw the might which was sent down by God upon his
brethren. Now it happened that one of them came on Friday to
the coenobium, and as he was outside, he saw that some of the

brethren were eating from the morning [upwards], and he said
unto them, "Is it possible that ye eat at this time on Friday?
"And do ye usually hold a congregation at the turn of the
"day?" And as his brother looked upon him, he saw that the
might of God was going away from him, and he was grieved,
for he was accustomed to see it upon him. And when they had
come to their own cell he said unto him, "What hast thou
"done, O my brother? Or what thoughts hast thou had? For
"I do not see upon thee as usual the might of God." And the
brother made answer and said, "I know not; I do not feel
"that I have any filthy thoughts in me, and I do not perceive
"in my soul that any evil act hath been committed by me."
His brother said unto him, "Peradventure some vain and
"empty word hath gone forth from thy mouth." Then that
brother recalled the matter to his mind, and said, "Yea,
"yesterday I saw certain men outside the coenobium eating,
"and I said unto them, 'Do ye eat at this time on Friday?'
"This then is my sin. But I entreat thee to labour with me
"for two weeks, and thou and I will beg God to forgive me."
And they did even as he had said, and after two weeks his
brother saw that might which is of the goodness of God come
upon him as usual.

29. The old men used to say about the blessed Abbâ Arsenius, and Abbâ Theodore of Parmê, that they possessed in a
far greater degree than many monks a hatred of the admiration of men; Abbâ Arsenius was never pleased at meeting and
conversing with a man, and Abbâ Theodore, even though he
was willing to meet a man, was as sharp as a sword in his
conversation.

30. Abbâ Macarius said unto the brethren when the service
in the church was ended, "Flee ye, O brethren"; and one of
the old men said, "Father, whither can we flee farther than
"this desert?" Then Macarius laid his hand upon his mouth,
saying, "Flee in this manner," and straightway he went to
his cell and, shutting the door, sat down.

31. Abbâ Poemen said:—Abbâ Moses asked Abbâ Zechariah
a question when he was about to die, and said unto him,
"Father, is it good that we should hold our peace?" And
Zechariah said unto him, "Yea, my son, hold thy peace."
And at the time of his death, whilst Abbâ Isidore was sitting
with him, Abbâ Moses looked up to heaven, and said, "Re-
"joice and be glad, O my son Zechariah, for the gates of heaven
"have been opened."

32. A brother asked an old man, saying, "What is humi-
"lity?" And the old man answered and said unto him, "That
"thou payest not back evil for evil." That brother said unto

him, "And supposing that a man cannot attain to this mea-
" sure, what must we do?" The old man said unto him, "Let
" us flee and follow after silence."

33. And an old man said, "Lay hold upon silence. Look
" carefully into and scrutinize the manner in which thou train-
" est thyself, both when thou art lying down, and when thou
" art standing up. Meditate upon the fear of God, and be not
" afraid of the attack of sinners. Consent not to everything.
" Be swift to hear and slow to believe."

34. An old man said: "The man, who hath learned by expe-
" rience the sweetness of the quietness which is in his cell,
" doth not flee from meeting his neighbour because he is as one
" who despiseth him, but because of the fruits which he pluck-
" eth from silence."

35. Abbâ Moses used to say, "The man who fleeth from the
" world is like unto ripe grapes, but he who dwelleth among
" the attractions of the children of men is like unto sour
" grapes."

36. An old man said: "Human care and worry and anxiety
" about the things of the body destroy the faculties of know-
" ledge and expression in a man, and leave him like unto a
" piece of dry wood."

37. They used to say about Abbâ Nastîr that the old man
was like unto the serpent which Moses made for the healing
of the people (Numbers xxi, 9 ff.), and that he was perfect in
all spiritual excellences, and that, although he kept silence, he
healed every man.

38. A certain brother asked an old man a question, and said
unto him, "Father, what shall I do? For, although my body
" is in my cell, my thoughts wander about into every place,
" and because of this they vex me greatly, saying, 'Thou hast
" ' no benefit whatsoever, for though thy body is shut up in the
" ' cell, thy thoughts wander and are scattered abroad.' And
" they bring me to despair, and counsel me to go back to the
" world as one who has not the ability to acquire the rule of
" life which is proper for the ascetic monk." The old man said
unto him, " Thou must know, O my son, that this is an attack
" of Satan, but go, and continue to abide in thy cell, and go
" not out of it at any time, and pray to God that He may give
" thee the power to endure patiently, and then thy mind shall
" collect itself in thee. For the matter is like unto that of a
" she-ass which hath a sucking foal. If she be tied up, how-
" ever much the foal may gambol about or wander hither and
" thither, he will come back to her eventually, either because
" he is hungry, or for other reasons which drive him to her;
" but if it happen that his mother be also roaming about

"loose, both animals will go to destruction. And thus is it in
"the matter of the monk. If the body remain continually in its
"cell, the mind thereof will certainly come back to it after all
"its wanderings, for many reasons which will come upon it,
"but if the body as well as the soul wander outside the cell,
"both will become a prey and a thing of joy to the enemy."

39. A certain brother belonging to a habitation of brethren
said to Abbâ Bessarion, "What shall I do?" The old man
said unto him, "Keep silence, and consider thyself to be
"nothing."

40. Abbâ Moses besought Abbâ Zechariah, saying, "Speak
"a word of consolation to the brethren"; and Zechariah took
his cloak, and placed it under his feet, saying, "Except a man
"die thus he cannot be a monk."

41. Abbâ Poemen said, "The rule of the monk is this—to
bear at all times his own blame."

42. Abbâ Poemen said, "If thou holdest thyself in thine
"own sight to be of no account, thou mayest dwell where
"thou pleasest, and find rest."

43. The same old man used to say, "A man will be always
"tripped up by that thing which he will not cut off from him-
"self."

44. Abbâ Alônîs said, "If a man will only remember that
"which is written, 'Thou shalt be justified by thy words, and
"shalt be condemned by thy words' (St. Matthew xii, 37), he
"would know that it is right to hold his peace."

45. Abbâ Poemen said, "If thou wishest to acquire the
"power to keep silence, think not and say not within thyself
"that thou art doing the works of spiritual excellence, but say,
"'I am not even worthy to speak.'"

46. Abbâ Anthony said, "He who liveth in the desert is free
"from three kinds of spiritual attacks, that is to say, those
"which arise through the ears, speech, and sight; he hath only
"one kind to fight, namely, that of the heart."

47. Abbâ Alônîs said, "Unless a man saith in his heart,
'Only God and myself exist in this world,' he will not find
"rest."

48. Abbâ Sisoes used to say, "It is well for a man to dwell
"in his cell, and if he suffer with patient endurance he will
"find blessings of every kind."

49. A certain brother asked Abbâ Panbô (Pambo), "Is it a
"good thing for a man to praise his neighbour?" Saith the
old man, "It is a much better thing for a man to hold his peace."

50. Abbâ Poemen said, "In all the labour which cometh
"upon a man, his victory is only assured when he holdeth his
"peace."

51. A certain brother said unto an old man, "If a brother
"bringeth unto me news from the outer world, dost thou wish
"me to tell him not to bring it to me?" The old man said unto
him, "Nay," and the brother said unto him, "Why?" The old
man said unto him, "Because not even we are able to flee
"from this. For having told our neighbour that he must not
"do this, we ourselves afterwards may be found doing the
"very same thing." And that brother said unto him, "What
"then is the right [course of action]?" Then the old man said
unto him, "If we take upon ourselves to hold our peace, the
"example alone will be sufficient to make our neighbour do
"the same."

52. The blessed Theophilus, Archbishop of Alexandria, once
went with a certain judge to Abbâ Arsenius, and begged the
old man to let him hear some saying from him; and the old man
held his peace for a little, and then answered him, and said,
"If I speak a word to you will ye observe it?" And they promised to keep it. The old man said unto them, "In whatsoever
"place ye hear that Arsenius is, come not nigh thereunto."

53. Abbâ Macarius said unto Abbâ Arsenius, "Why fleest
"thou from us?" And the old man said unto him, "God know-
"eth that I love you, but I cannot be both with God and with
"men. The thousands and ten thousands of beings who are
"above have only one will, but men have many wills: I can-
"not, therefore, leave God and be with men." And the old
man was always uttering these words, "Arsenius, for this
"thou didst go forth." And he used to say thus: "I have
"many times repented that I spoke, but that I held my peace
"I have never repented."

54. Abbâ Anthony said, "The cell of a monk is the furnace
"of Babylon wherein the Three Children found the Son of
"God, and it is also the pillar of cloud wherefrom God spake
"with Moses."

55. On one occasion the Fathers in Scete were gathered
together, and because certain folk were wishing to see Abbâ
Moses, they treated him with contumely, saying, "Why doth
"this Ethiopian come and go in our midst?" But Moses
hearing this held his peace. And when the congregation was
dismissed, they said unto him, "Abbâ Moses, wast thou not
"afraid?" And he said unto them, "Although I was afraid I
"uttered not a word."

56. On one occasion certain brethren came unto John the
Less to tempt him, for they had heard that he never permitted
his mind to think about any of the affairs of this world, and
that he never spoke about them. And they said unto him,
"Father, we thank God because He hath brought down this

"year rain in abundance, and the palms are thriving and are
"flourishing beautifully, and work for the hands of the bre-
"thren is abundant." The old man John saith unto them,
"Even thus is it with the Holy Spirit of God, for when It
"descendeth upon the hearts of holy men they blossom and
"bring forth the fruit of the fear of God."

57. A certain brother came to take some baskets from John
the Less, and when he had knocked at the door, the old man
came out to him, and said unto him, "What seekest thou?"
And the brother said unto him, "Father, I want baskets." And
John the Less went in to bring them out to him, but he forgot to do so, and sat down, and went on plaiting. And the
brother knocked at the door again, and when Abbâ John went
forth to answer him, he said unto him, "Wilt thou bring out
"the baskets to me, Father?" And again John went in, and
sat down, and went on plaiting, and when the brother knocked
again, John went forth and said unto him, "Brother, what
"seekest thou?" And he said unto John, "Baskets, Father";
and John took his hand and led him inside, saying, "If thou
"wishest for baskets take them and get thee gone, for I am
"not able [to bring them to you]."

58. Some time ago Abbâ Evagrius went to Scete to a certain father and said unto him, "Speak some word whereby I
"may be able to save myself." The old man saith unto him,
"If thou wishest to be saved, when thou goest unto any man
"speak not before he asketh thee a question." Now Evagrius
was sorry about this sentence, and shewed regret because he
had asked the question, saying, "Verily I have read many
"books, and I cannot accept instruction of this kind"; and
having profited greatly he went forth from him.

59. On one occasion there was a congregation in the Cells
concerning a certain matter, and Abbâ Evagrius spoke. And
a certain elder said unto him, "We know, Abbâ, that hadst
"thou been in thine own country where thou art a bishop and
"the governor of many, [thou wouldst have been right in
"speaking]; but in this place thou sittest [as] a stranger."
Now Evagrius was sorry, but he was not offended, and he
shook his head, and bent his gaze downwards, and he wrote
with his finger and said unto them, "Verily, it is even as thou
"sayest, O my fathers; I have spoken once, but I will not do
"it a second time."

60. Abbâ John, who was in prison, said that there was a
man sitting in his cell who always made mention of God, and
in this was fulfilled that which is written, "I was in prison,
"and ye came unto Me" (St. Matthew xxv, 36).

61. They used to say about Abbâ Agathon that for a period

of three years he placed a stone in his mouth [and kept it there], until he had learned thoroughly how to hold his peace.

62. A certain brother went to Abbâ Moses in Scete, and asked him to speak a word; and the old man said unto him, " Get thee gone, and sit in thy cell, and thy cell shall teach " thee everything."

Chapter ij. Of Fasting and Abstinence and of other [similar] Labours

63. THEY used to say about Abbâ Paphnutius that he would not readily drink wine, and that on one occasion he came by chance upon a band of thieves, and found them drinking; and the captain of the thieves recognized him, and knew that he never drank wine; and he looked closely at him [and saw that] he was a man of great ascetic works. And the captain filled a cup with wine and, taking a sword in his hand, he said unto the old man, "If thou wilt not drink I will slay " thee"; and the old man knew that the grace of God wished to work on the captain of the thieves through him, and sought to do good to him, so he took [the cup] and drank [the wine]. Then the captain made excuse to him and said, " Forgive me, " father, for having distressed thee"; and the old man said unto him, " I believe, by God, that through this cup God will " forgive thee thy sins." And the captain of thieves said unto him, "I believe, by God; from this time forth I will never vex " any man." Thus, because for God's sake Paphnutius gave up his own wish, he was able to do good to all that band of thieves.

64. A certain old man came unto one of the holy men who was a companion of his, and who cooked a few lentiles; and one of the two said unto his fellow, "Shall we sing a part of " the service?" And he sang the whole of the Psalms of David, and his companion repeated two books of the Great Prophets, and when it was morning the old man departed to his own place, and they forgot all about the food. And the old man went another evening and found the food which had been cooked, and he was sorry and said, "Oh! how was it that we " came to forget that little mess of lentiles, and did not eat it?"

65. On one occasion a brother came to Abbâ Isaiah, who threw a handful of lentiles into a saucepan to boil, but when they had just begun to boil he took them off the fire; and the brother said unto him, "Are they not yet cooked, O father?" And the old man said unto him, "Is it not sufficient for thee " to have seen the fire? For this [alone] is great refreshing."

66. A certain old man became very seriously ill, for he suffered from some disease of the stomach, and much blood came

16

away from him; and one of the brethren had some dried prunes, and because of the severe illness of the old man he cooked a little food, and put some of the prunes in it, and brought it to him, and entreated him, saying, "Father, do [me] an act of "grace, and take a little of this stew, for perhaps it will do "thee good." And the old man lifted up his eyes and looked at him, and said, "In which of the Scriptures hast thou found "this thing? Verily I have wished that God would leave me " in this illness for the last thirty years, for when I am weak "then am I strong"; and the old man, although he was grievously sick, would not take even a little of the food, and when the brother saw [this] he took it and went back to his cell.

67. They used to say concerning Abbâ Macarius, the Egyptian, that if it happened that he ate with the brethren, he would make an agreement with himself that if there was wine [on the table] and he drank one cup of it, he would drink no water for a whole day; now the brethren, wishing him to be refreshed (*or* pleased), used to give him wine, and the old man took it joyfully so that he might torment his body. And when his disciple saw this thing, he said unto the brethren, "I entreat you, for " our Lord's sake, not to give him wine to drink, for if he "drinketh it he will go to his cell and afflict himself because "thereof"; and when the brethren knew this they did not give him any more wine to drink.

68. There was a certain old man who made a vow not to drink any water during the Fast of Forty Days; and when he became thirsty (*literally*, hot) he would wash a potter's vessel, and fill it with water, and hang it up in front of him. Then the brethren asked him why and wherefore he acted thus, and he said, "That " I may labour the more, and receive a reward from God"; now he said this that he might incite them to great labours.

69. A brother asked an old man questions about comforts [*or* pleasures], and the old man said unto him, "Eat grass, wear " grass, and sleep on grass, and then thy heart will become like " iron."

70. A certain brother was hungry one morning, and he fought against his inclination and determined not to eat until the third hour; and when the third hour had passed, he dipped his bread in water, and sat down to eat, but he forced himself to wait until the sixth hour arrived, when he said within himself, " Let us wait till the ninth hour." And when the ninth hour had come, he prayed, and saw the working of Satan rising up before him like smoke, and he suppressed his desire [to eat], and his hunger passed away from him.

71. A certain brother from the Cells brought some new bread, and he invited all the old men who were under vows at

Scete to partake of a meal; and when each of them had eaten two bread-cakes, they ceased eating. Then the brother, who knew their labours of abstinence, and that they did not usually eat, and never satisfied themselves, made excuses to them, saying, "Eat ye this day, for our Lord's sake, until ye are "satisfied"; and hearing this each ate ten cakes more. All this [sheweth] how much they afflicted themselves in not satisfying themselves with any kind of food.

72. On one occasion two old men were going up from Scete to Egypt, and because of the fatigue of the way they sat down on the bank of the river to eat some food, and one of them took his bread-cake in his hand and dipped it in the water; and he answered and said unto his companion, "Wilt thou not dip "thy cake in water, O father?" And his companion answered and said unto him, "It is written, When a possession increaseth "set not thy heart upon it" (Psalm lxii, 10).

73. They used to say about Abbâ Isaac, the priest of the Cells, that he ate the ashes of the censer which was before the altar with his bread.

74. On one occasion there was an offering [made] in the mountain of Abbâ Anthony, and a skin of wine was there, and one of the monks took some of it in a small vessel, and with a cup in his hand he went and carried it to Abbâ Sisoes. And he mixed him a cupful, and he drank it, and he mixed him a second cupful, and he took it and drank it, but when he mixed him a third cupful Abbâ Sisoes refused to drink it, saying, "Stay thy hand, brother, knowest thou not that [the third cup] "is of Satan?"

75. Abbâ John said, "If a king wishes to subdue a city be-"longing to enemies, he first of all keepeth them without "bread and water, and the enemy being in this wise harassed "by hunger becometh subject unto him; and thus it is in respect "of the hostile passions, for if a man endureth fasting and "hunger regularly, his enemies become stricken with weak-"ness in the soul."

76. They used to say about Abbâ Dioscurus that his bread was made of barley and lentiles, and that at the beginning of each year he would set himself some [new] task of ascetic excellence, saying, "This year I will not hold converse with (or "visit) any man," or, "I will not speak at all," or, "I will not "eat food which hath been boiled," or, "I will not eat fruit," or, "I will not eat vegetables." He began each year with resolutions of this kind and carried them out, and each year he set himself some new task.

77. On one occasion when certain brethren went to the church during the Easter Festival, they gave a brother a cup

of wine, and when they urged him to drink it, he said to them,
" Forgive me, O my fathers, but ye did the same thing to me
"last year, and I drank a cup of wine, and I was greatly
" troubled thereby for a long time."

78. The monks were celebrating a festival in Scete, and they
gave a certain old man a cup of wine, and he handed it back,
saying, " Take this death away from me"; and when the others
who were eating with him saw him [do this] they also would
not take the wine.

79. And again on another occasion certain first-fruits of wine
were sent that it might be given to the brethren cup by cup,
(i.e., a cup each). And one of the brethren went up to a roof,
that he might escape from drinking, and it parted asunder beneath him, and he fell through it; and when the sound came
[to the brethren] they went and found him lying [on the ground],
and they began to think about him, and said, "O lover of vain-
"glory, this hath befallen thee rightly." And an old man laid
him out, saying unto them, " Forgive ye my son, for he hath
" done a good work. And, as the Lord liveth, this breach shall
" not be built up in my days, for all the world shall know that
" because of a cup of wine a schism hath taken place in Scete."

80. It was reported to Abbâ Poemen about a certain brother
that he would not drink wine, and the old man Poemen said,
" The nature of wine is not such as to make it useful to the
" dwellers in monasteries."

81. They used to say about Abbâ Sisoes the Theban that he
never ate bread. During the Easter Festival the brethren came
to him, and having made excuses they entreated him to eat
with them; and he answered and said, " I will do one [of two]
" things; I will either eat bread and bread alone, or I will eat
" of the meats which ye have boiled." And they said unto him,
" Then eat bread only."

82. A certain old man said, " Reduce thy knowledge of the
"things of man, and thy belly also, and thou shalt find all
" [manner of] delights."

83. Abbâ Poemen used to say, " The Spirit of God never
" entereth into the house wherein there are delights and
" pleasures."

84. A brother asked Abbâ Sisoes, "What [good do] I do
"in going to church, for often [the devils] recognize me and
" seize me?" The old man saith unto him, "There is work in
" the matter."

85. Abraham his disciple thereupon said unto him, "Father,
if there happen to be a congregation on the Sabbath, or on
Sunday, and a brother drink three cups of wine, is that too
"much?" The old man saith unto him, "If Satan did not

"exist three cups would not be too much to drink, but since
"he doth exist three cups are too much."

86. On one occasion some early grapes were sent to Abbâ
Macarius because he longed for them, and to give a proof of
his abstinence, he sent them to another brother who was sick,
and who craved for grapes; and having received them, he rejoiced over them greatly, and then he despised his desire, and
sent them on to another brother, as one who had no wish for
food of any kind, and who held his self-denial in contempt.
Now when the brother had received the grapes, although he
desired greatly to eat them, he did the same as the other
brother had done, and no man wished to eat them. And after
they had gone about among many of the brethren, the last one
who received them sent them to the blessed Macarius as a gift of
great honour; and when the blessed Macarius saw the grapes
he marvelled at the extent of the self-denial of the brethren,
and gave thanks unto God, and he did not eat them.

87. On one occasion certain monks went down from Egypt
to visit the Fathers, and when they saw that they were eating
—now it was after prolonged hunger and very much fasting,
and continual abstinence,—they were greatly offended; and
when the elder of the coenobium learned [about this] he came
to quiet their minds. And he proclaimed in the church of the
congregation, saying, "Ye shall fast in your customary man-
"ner, and honour your ascetic rule of life, so that your vol-
"untary abstinence may not be held in contempt." Now the
Egyptian strangers wished to depart, but the monks shut them
in cells. And when they had fasted the whole of the first day
they began to feel faint, but notwithstanding this the monks
made them to fast two days at a time; now the monks who
were in Scete used to fast for a week at a time. And when the
day of the Sabbath came, the Egyptians sat down to eat with
the old men, and when one of the Egyptians began to eat
hurriedly and voraciously, one of the old men caught hold of
his hands, saying, "Eat moderately, (*or* according to rule)
"like the monks." Then one of the others clutched at the old
man's hand, saying, "Let me eat so that I may not die, for
"behold, I have not eaten a piece of boiled food for a whole
"week." And the old man said unto him, "If now ye have be-
"come so very weak after having fasted but one night only,
"why were ye offended at the brethren who live a life of self-
"denial for long periods of time, and who fulfil their seasons
"with voluntary abstinence?" And straightway those Egyptians
made excuses to the old men, and they were edified by their
patient endurance, and departed rejoicing.

88. Once Abbâ Agathon had two disciples, and they sepa-

rated from him, and each of them dwelt in a place by himself.
One day he asked one of them, and said, "How dost thou live
in thy cell?" And the disciple answered and said, "I fast until
"evening, and then I eat two bread-cakes"; and Abbâ Agathon said unto him, "It is a beautiful way of living, but it is
"very laborious." Then Abbâ Agathon said unto the other
disciple, "And how dost thou live?" And the disciple answered
and said unto him, "I fast two days at a time, and after each
"fast I eat two bread-cakes." Then the old man said unto him,
"Thou toilest greatly, and maintainest a twofold strife. For
"one man eateth every day and filleth not his belly, and an-
"other fasteth two days at a time and taketh whatsoever he
"needeth; but thou, though thou dost fast two days at a time,
"dost not fill thy belly."

89. Abbâ Abraham went to Abbâ Areus, and as they were
sitting down, another brother came to Abbâ, and asked him,
saying, "Tell me what I shall do to live?" And he said unto
him, "Go and pass the whole week in plaiting palm leaves and
"twisting ropes thereof, and eat bread and salt once each day
"in the evening, and then come again to me, and I will tell
"thee [what else to do]." And the brother went away and did
as he had told him to do, and when Abbâ Abraham heard this
he wondered. Now when the week was ended that brother came
again to the old man Areus, with whom there happened to be
also Abbâ Abraham. And the old man said unto the brother,
"Get thee gone, and pass thou the whole week in fasting
"two days at a time." And when that brother had gone,
Abbâ Abraham said unto Abbâ Areus, "Why dost thou com-
"mand all the other brethren to bear a light burden, but
"layest a heavy load upon the brother who was here?" Then the
old man said unto him, "The other brethren as they come, ask,
"and according as they ask they receive and depart; but this
"brother cometh for God's sake, that he may hear the word of
"profit, for he is a worker, and whatsoever I say unto him he
"performeth with care and diligence."

90. Abbâ Theodotus used to say, "Abstinence from bread
"quieteth the body of the monk."

91. A certain old man used to say, "I knew Abbâ Pater-
"muthis in the cells, and he did not drink wine, but when they
"took some wine and mixed it with water, and urged him
"to drink [it], he said, 'Believe me, O my brethren, I hold it to
"'be a most beautiful thing.' And he blamed himself and con-
"demned himself because of the mixing, and at the same time
"he gave thanks unto God and accepted His gracious gift."

92. They used to say about Abbâ Paphnutius that he did
not drink wine readily, even though he was sick.

93. Abbâ Poemen said, "The soul can be humbled by no-"thing except thou enfeeble it by the eating of [little] bread."

94. They used to say about Abbâ Sarnâôs that he laboured exceedingly hard, and that he only ate two bread-cakes each day. And when he came to Abbâ Job, who was a man that was perfect in the laborious work of active excellence, and who was also a man that practised strict self-denial and abstinence, he said unto him, "As long as I live in my cell I can observe "my rule of life, but if I go outside my cell I make openly "submission because of the brethren." Then Abbâ Sarnâôs said unto him, "To be able to keep hold upon thy rule of life "only so long as thou art in thy cell is no great act of spiritual "excellence, but it would be if thou couldst do so when thou "didst go forth outside thy cell."

95. Abbâ Poemen used to say, "As smoke driveth away bees, "and men take the sweetness of their labour, even so also "doth ease of the body drive away the fear of God from the "heart, and it carrieth away all the good [effect] of its labour."

96. On one occasion Abbâ Sylvanus and Zechariah his disciple were going to a monastery, and they prepared a little food to eat before they set out on their journey. And when they had gone forth his disciple found water on the way, and he wished to drink, but the old man said unto him, "Zechariah, to-day is "a fast day," but the disciple said, "Nay, O father, for behold "we have eaten." Then Abbâ Sylvanus said unto him, "The "food which we ate was obligatory, but let us keep the fast, "O my son."

97. Abbâ Poemen said, "Every corporeal pleasure is con-"temptible before the Lord."

98. The disciple of Abbâ Sisoes had to say unto him several times, "Rise up and let us eat." And he used to say unto him, "My son, have we not eaten?" And the disciple would say unto him, "Nay, father." Then the old man would say unto him, "If we have not eaten, bring the food and let us eat."

99. Abbâ Daniel used to say, "In proportion as the body "groweth, the soul becometh enfeebled; and the more the "body becometh emaciated, the more the soul groweth."

100. Abbâ Benjamin, the priest of the Cells, said, "On one "occasion we went to a certain old man in Scete, and we "wanted to give him a little oil; and he said unto us, 'Be-"'hold, that little vessel of oil which ye brought to me three "'years ago is still lying in the place where ye put it, and it "'hath remained in the same state as that wherein ye brought "'it.' And when we heard [this] we marvelled at the old man's "manner of life."

101. Abbâ Benjamin also said, "We went to another old

"man, and he took some food which we were going to eat,
"and threw into it a little oil of radishes. And we said unto
"him, 'Father, throw into our food a little sweet oil,' but
"when he heard these words, he made the sign of the Cross
"over himself, and said, 'If there be any other oil besides this
"'I know not of it.'"

102. Abbâ Joseph asked Abbâ Poemen what was the proper
way in which to fast, and Abbâ Poemen said unto him, "I
"prefer the man who eateth every day a very small quantity
"of food, and who doth not satisfy his cravings for food."
And Abbâ Joseph said unto him, "When thou wast a young
"man didst thou not fast two days at a time, O father?" Then
the old man said unto him, "Yea, I did, and three days at a
"time, and four days at a time, and even a week at a time;
"and the old men, like men of might, have tried all these by
"experience, but they have found that it is beneficial for a man
"to eat an exceedingly small quantity of food each day, and
"because of this they have delivered unto us an easy way to
"the kingdom."

103. One of the fathers said, "I knew a brother in the Cells
"who used to fast the whole of the Great Sabbath, and when
"the brethren were assembled in the evening he used to flee
"to his cell in order that he might eat nothing in the church;
"and he would eat a few plantains with salt, and without
"bread, that he might conceal his abstinence."

104. They used to tell about a certain monk who, having
gone forth from the world, and lived in the coenobium for a
number of years, was gracious unto every man in his humility,
and all the brethren marvelled at his abstinence from meats;
then he went to the barren desert, and lived there for many years,
eating for food wild herbs. And afterwards he entreated God
to inform him what reward He would give him, and it was
said unto him by an angel, "Go forth from this desert and
"get thee along the road, and behold a certain shepherd shall
"meet thee, and according to [what he saith] so shalt thou
"receive." Now when he had made ready to depart, the shepherd of whom he had been told by the angel met him, and
saluted him, and having sat down to hold converse with each
other, the monk saw in the shepherd's bag some green herbs,
and he asked him, saying, "What is this? And the shepherd
said unto him, "It is my food." And the monk said unto him,
"How long hast thou been feeding thyself on these green
"herbs?" And the shepherd said unto him, "Behold, for the
"last thirty years, more or less, and I have never tasted any-
"thing else except these herbs which I have eaten once a day,
"and I drink as much water as my food requireth; and the

"wages which are given to me by the owner of the sheep
"I give unto the poor." Now when the monk heard these
things he fell down at the feet of the shepherd, and said, "I
"imagined that I had laid hold upon abstinence, but thou
"through thy well-ordered life art worthy of a greater reward
"than I, because I have eaten every kind of green thing im-
"mediately it came in my way." Then the shepherd said unto
him, "It is not right that rational men should make them-
"selves like unto the beasts, but they should eat whatsoever is
"prepared for them at the seasons which are duly ordered and
"appointed for them, and afterwards they should fast from every-
"thing until an appointed time." And the monk profited by
these words, and he added to his labour and became perfect,
and he praised God, and marvelled how many were the saints
in the world who were not known to the children of men.

Chapter iij. Of the Reading of the Scriptures, and of watching by Night, and of the Service of the Psalms, and of constant Prayers

THEY used to say about Abbâ Arsenius that no man was
able to attain to the manner of life in his abode. And they
also said about him that on the night of the Sabbath
105. which would end in the dawn of Sunday, he would
leave the sun behind him, and would stretch out his hands towards heaven, and would pray [in this position] until the sun
rose in his face, when he would satisfy his eyes with a little
slumber.

106. A certain old man was complete in all perfection, and
he could see what was happening from a very long way off;
and he said, "I once saw in a monastery a certain brother who
"was meditating on the study of God in his cell, and behold,
"a devil came and stood outside, and he wanted to go in, but
"he could not do so, so long as the brother was meditating.
"Finally, however, when the monk ceased his contemplation
"the devil was able to enter his cell, for his power is not able
"to vanquish those whose converse is with God."

107. An old man said, "Whensoever a man readeth the
"Divine Books, the devils are afraid."

108. They used to say about Abbâ Pachomius that he spent
much time in striving with devils like a true athlete, and after
the manner of Saint Anthony. And because many devils came
against him in the night season, he asked God to keep away
sleep from him both by day and by night, so that he might
not sleep at all, and might be able to bring low the might of
the Enemy, even according to that which is written, "I will
"not turn back until I have made an end of them"; for they

are powerless against the faith which is in the Lord. Now this gift was given unto him, even as he had asked, for a certain time, and because he was pure, his heart used to see God, Who is invisible, as in a mirror.

109. They used to say about Abbâ Pachomius and Abbâ John that they lived together in the same religious house (now John was larger in stature than Pachomius), but both had adopted a life of poverty voluntarily, and they possessed nothing whatsoever except the fear of God. Whatsoever they gained by the work of their hands they gave to those who were in need, and they kept for themselves only what was sufficient for their bare necessities; in respect of clothes they were well-nigh destitute, and they had so few of them that they were obliged to wash those which they wore [and put them on again]. Now Abbâ Pachomius always wore a garment made of hair, because of the toil of his body. And whensoever they wished to refresh their bodies by a little sleep after their vigil and prayer, each of them would sit down in the middle of the cell, and, without leaning against a wall, would go to sleep. And they continued to do this for fifteen years, and many of the fathers heard of them, and saw them living thus, and they also strove in like manner to humble their bodies for the redemption of their souls.

110. They used to say about Abbâ Joseph that when he was about to die, and the old men were sitting about him, he looked at the window and saw Satan sitting there; and he cried out to his disciple and said, " Bring me a stick here, for " this devil thinketh that I have become old, and that I am " no longer able to stand up against him," and as soon as he grasped the stick in his hand, Satan, in the form of a dog, threw himself from the window, and the old man saw him taking to flight.

111. They used to relate concerning Abbâ Sisoes that if he did not bring down his hands swiftly when he was standing up in prayer, his mind would be carried off on high; but whensoever it chanced that one of the brethren was with him he would bring his hands down hurriedly lest peradventure his mind should be carried off, and he should be left alone.

112. Abbâ Isaiah, the elder of the church, rebuked the brethren when they were eating that which had been prepared for them because they began to talk with each other, and he said to them, " Hold ye your peace, O my brethren. I know " a brother who eateth with us and drinketh with us full (?) " cups even as we do, and yet his prayer ascendeth up before " God like fire."

113. One day Abbâ Arsenius called Abbâ Alexander and

Abbâ Zôtlâ, and said unto them, "Because the devils are
"striving with me, and because I do not know but that they
"may carry me off during [my] sleep, toil ye here with me
"this night, and keep vigil, and watch me and see if I sleep
"during [my] vigil." So they sat down, one on his right hand,
and the other on his left, from the evening even until the
morning. And they said, "We slept and we woke up, and we
"did not observe that he slept at all; but when it began to be
"light there came unto us three times the sound of breathing
"in his nostrils, but whether he did this purposely so that we
"might think he slept or whether slumber had really fallen
"upon him we know not." And he stood up and said unto us,
" ' Have I been asleep? " And we answered and said unto him,
"We do not know, O father, for we ourselves went to sleep."

114. A brother asked Abbâ Poemen, saying, "How, and in
"what manner is it right for a man to walk in the path of
"righteousness?" Abbâ Poemen said unto him, "We have
"seen Daniel, and also that his enemies were unable to bring
"any accusation whatsoever against him except in respect
"of his service of God."

115. On one occasion Abbâ Sisoes was sitting in his cell, and
when his disciple knocked at the door [meaning to] go in, the
old man cried out, saying, "Flee, Abraham, and do not come
"in now, for this place is not empty."

116. They say concerning Abbâ Sisoes of Babylon that, wishing to vanquish sleep, he stood upright upon a mountain crag,
and that the angel of the Lord came and rescued him from that
place, and commanded him never to do such a thing again, and
not even to hand on this tradition to another.

117. An old man said, "I knew a brother who used to sit
"with the brethren at the meal which is made for the coming
"of the brethren, and although the brethren ate and drank, he
"never made himself to be remote from converse with God in
"his prayer, and he did not drink even a cup of wine. Now
"this man's manner of life was marvellous, and a certain man
"used to say about him, 'I once wished to count the prayers
"which he made, and I saw that he did not cease to pray
"'either by day or by night.'"

118. On one occasion a Bishop was sent secretly to Abbâ
Epiphanius by the head of a certain monastery in Palestine, saying, "We have not treated lightly thy services of prayer since
"thy departure from us, but we perform most carefully the
"services for the third, and sixth, and ninth hours, and also
"vespers." Then Abbâ Epiphanius blamed those who sent him,
and wrote a message, which he sent to them, saying, "Ye must
"know that ye are indeed neglectful of the services and prayers

" which belong to the other eight hours which are in the day,
" for it is right for the monk who hath made himself to be re-
" mote from the world to be occupied with prayers to God un-
" ceasingly, and he should pray either in his heart, or in a care-
" fully defined service, or in that service which he performeth
" with his will and with understanding. For the Calumniator
" addeth greatly to any small failing which he may find in a
" monk, and by being with him continually he enlargeth greatly
" the breach which he hath made, and by his habit of persist-
" ency he acquireth his natural power, and more particularly
" is this so in the case of those who are careless and lazy."

119. Abbâ Epiphanius also said, "Whatsoever food thou
" wishest to eat with gratification, that give not to thy body,
" especially when thou art in good health, and that which thou
" lustest after, eat not; and when thou feedest upon the things
" which are sent unto thee by God, give thanks unto Him at
" all seasons, and receive His gracious gift, the delights and
" the pleasures which we have received through the name of
" monk, [although] we do not do the works of monks. And [if]
" it be that thou art a monk, wilt thou then not make thyself
" strong, lest peradventure thou art arrayed in apparel which
" is strange to thee? Tell me, O brother, dost thou possess the
" seal of the service, that is to say, humility? For the holy man
" who seeth another man sin weepeth bitterly, saying, 'It is
" 'this man who sinneth now, but some time subsequently it
" 'may be myself.' However much then a man may sin before
" thee, condemn him not, but esteem thyself a sinner far greater
" than he is, even though he may be a child of this world, and
" besides there is the fact that he may have sinned greatly
" against God."

120. And he said also, "Know thyself, and thou shalt never
" fall. Give thy soul work, that is to say, constant prayer, and
" love of God, before another can give it evil [and filthy] thoughts;
" and pray ye that the spirit of error may be remote from you."

121. And he also said, "Whatsoever ye do successfully, and
" what ye boast of, destroy, for it is not right for a monk to
" boast of his fair deeds, and if he boasteth he will fall."

122. [And he also said], "When thou prayest speak unto
" God in a quiet voice and say, 'How can I possess Thee, O
" 'Lord? Thou knowest full well that I am a beast, and that I
" 'know nothing. Thou hast brought me to the prime of this
" 'life, deliver me then for Thy mercy's sake; I am Thy ser-
" 'vant, and the son of Thine handmaiden, O Lord, by Thy
" 'will, vivify Thou me.' The old man is falsehood, and the new
" man is truth; the truth is the root of good works, and false-
" hood is death. If the liar, and the thief, and the calumniator

" knew that they would finally be made known unto all and
" [their works] revealed, they would never offend. And thus
" also was it with the adulterous sons of Eli, Hophni and
" Phinehas, for they were not priests of the Lord, and they feared
" not God, and they perished, together with all their house.
" And the man who taketh hold of, and bindeth to himself, and
" shutteth within himself the memory of evil things is like unto
" the man who hideth fire in straw. If thou speakest to a man
" concerning life, and if thou sayest a word unto him let it be
" with feeling, and penitence, and with tears; and say thy word
" to the man who will hearken and will do it, but if not, speak
" not, lest thou die, and thou depart from this world without
" any profit from the words whereby thou didst wish to give
" life unto others. For unto the sinner God saith, 'What hast
" 'thou to do with the Books of My Commandments? For
" 'thou hast taken My covenant in thy mouth [only]'" (Psalm
l, 16).

123. Abbâ Epiphanius said, "Whensoever a thought cometh
" and filleth thy bosom, that is to say, thy heart, with vain-
" glory or with pride, say thou unto thyself, 'Old man, behold
" 'thy fornication.'"

124. And he also said, "If we do evil things God will be un-
" mindful of His longsuffering; but if we do good things, it
" will not help us greatly because we increase the advantage
" of freedom, and the merchandise is not plundered thereby,
" for the will rejoiceth in the striving."

125. Certain brethren entreated Abbâ Epiphanius on one
occasion, saying, "Father, speak unto us some word of life,
" even though when thou speakest we may not grasp the seed
" of thy word, because the soil is salt." Then the old man answered and said unto them, "Whosoever receiveth not all the
" brethren, but maketh distinctions between them, cannot be-
" come a perfect man. If a man revile thee, bless him, whether
" it be good for both of you, or whether it be not; it will be he
" who will receive a reward of blessing. This is the right way
" for a monk to live, and in this way lived Abbâ Arsenius, who
" took care each day to stand up before God without sin,
" and he drew nigh unto Him with tears like the sinful woman.
" In this manner pray to the Lord God—as if He were standing
" before thee, for He is nigh unto thee and He looketh upon
" thee. It is right that the man who wisheth to dwell in the
" desert should be [as] a teacher in his knowledge, and he must
" not be in need of instruction lest he be swept away by the
" devils; and he must look into his mind most minutely,
" both in respect of the things which are above, and those
" which are below, lest he become a laughing-stock unto them

"by some means or other. It is right that the manner of life
"of the man who loveth God should be blameless."

126. A certain man made answer to the brethren against evil
thoughts, saying, "I entreat you, O my brethren, let us cease
"from ascetic works, and let us give up also anxious thoughts.
"For what are we? A voice which cometh out of the dust, or
"a cry which riseth from the mud? When Joseph of Ramah
"had asked to be allowed to take the body of Jesus, he took
"it, and wrapped it round in a sheet of clean linen, and then
"he laid it in a new sepulchre of the new man" (St. Matthew
xxvii, 59).

127. On one occasion a certain monk saw a devil who was
calling to his fellow to come with him, so that the two together
might wake up a monk for service, and might lead him into
error thereby, [and cause him to think] that angels had appeared unto him. And the monk heard the voice of the other
devil, who made answer to his fellow, saying, "I cannot do
"this. For once I woke him up, and he stood up and broke
"me with a terrible breaking, and [all the time he was doing
"it] he sang psalms and prayed."

128. A brother asked an old man and said, "Why is it that
"when I go forth to labour I feel wearied and disgusted in my
"soul, and my mind is wholly empty of spiritual thoughts?"
And the old man said unto him, "Because thou dost not de-
"sire to fulfil that which is written, 'I will bless the Lord al-
"'ways, and His praises shall be ever in my mouth' (Psalm
"xxxiv, 1). Therefore, whether thou art inside or outside, and
"whithersoever thou goest thou must not cease from blessing
"God; not only in actions, but with word and mind thou shalt
"bless thy Maker. For God doth not dwell in any place which
"hath bounds and limits, but He is everywhere, and by His
"Divine Power He sustaineth all things, and is capable of all
"things."

129. A brother asked Abbâ Poemen concerning the thoughts
which invaded his mind, and he said unto him, "This matter
"is like unto that of a man who hath a fire on his left hand,
"and a tank of water on his right hand; if he wisheth to ex-
"tinguish the fire, he taketh the water from the tank and doeth
"it, and it is right for a man to act thus every hour. Now the
"fire is the evil thought, which cometh from enemies, and the
"water is the pouring out of the soul before the Lord which a
"man should do."

130. There was a certain monk who did not do any work
whatsoever with his hands, but he prayed without ceasing; and
at eventide he would go into his cell and find his bread laid
there [for him], and he would eat it. Now another monk came

to him, who had upon him [materials] for the labour of his hands, and wheresoever he entered in he worked, and he made the old man, into whose cell he had entered, to work with him. And when the evening had come, he wished according to his custom, to eat, but he found nothing, and he therefore lay down in sorrow; and it was revealed unto him, saying, "Whilst "thou wast occupied in converse with Me, I fed thee, but now "thou hast begun to work, thou must demand thy food from "the labour of thy hands."

131. They tell the story that on one occasion, whilst the blessed Anthony was dwelling in the desert, thoughts of dejection and despair rose up in his mind, and he was in deep gloom of thought, and said unto God, "Lord, I wish to live, "but my thoughts will not permit me to do so. What shall I "do in my tribulations to be saved?" And he came a little nearer [to the town] from the place where he was, and he saw a man who was like unto himself, and was in his own form, and he was sitting down and twisting palm leaves into ropes; and this man rose up from his work, and prayed, and afterwards he sat down again and continued his work, and then he stood up once more, and prayed. Now the man was an angel who had been sent from God to correct and to admonish the blessed Anthony, who afterwards heard him say unto him, "O "Anthony, do thou also do this and live"; and when Anthony heard this, the blessed man had great joy, and afterwards he did as the angel had done, and lived.

132. They said concerning Abbâ John the Less that, on one occasion, he steeped the palm leaves for two baskets in water, and sewed one basket to the other without perceiving it until he came to the side of it, for his mind was led captive by the sight of God.

133. And Abbâ Daniel used to say concerning Abbâ Arsenius that he would pass the whole night in vigil, and when, for the sake of nature, he wished for the approach of the morning so that he might have some relief, he would struggle against sleep, and say, "Get thee gone, O wicked handmaiden"; then he would snatch a very little slumber and stand up straightway.

134. Abbâ Arsenius used to say, "One hour's sleep is suffi- "cient for a monk, provided that he be strenuous.

135. They used to say about a certain monk who lived in a monastery of the brotherhood, that although he kept frequent vigil and prayed he was neglectful about praying with the congregation. And one night there appeared unto him a glorious pillar of brilliant light from the place where the brethren were congregated, and it reached up into the heavens;

and he saw a small spark which [flew] about the pillar, and
sometimes it shone brightly, and sometimes it was extinguished. And whilst he was wondering at the vision, it was explained
to him by God, Who said, "The pillar which thou seest is
"the prayers of the many [brethren] which are gathered to-
"gether and go up to God and gratify Him; and the spark is
"the prayers of those who dwell among the congregation,
"and who despise the appointed services of the brotherhood.
"And now, if thou wouldst live, perform that which it is cus-
"tomary to perform with the brethren, and then, if thou
"wishest to do so, and art able to pray separately, do so."
And the monk related all these things before the brotherhood,
and they glorified God.

Chapter iv. Of how it is meet for us to Weep for our Sins and to Mourn for them always

A BROTHER asked Abbâ Ammon, and said unto him,
"Tell me some word whereby I may live"; and Abbâ
Ammon said unto him, "Go and make thy mind like
136. "unto the minds of those evil-doers who are in the prison
"house, and who ask those who go to them, saying, 'Where
"'is the governor? When will he come here?' And their minds
"tremble in fearful expectation. Thus also is a monk bound to
"wait in expectation always, and he must admonish himself,
"saying, 'Woe is me! For how can I stand before the throne
"'of Christ? And how shall I be able to make answer unto
"'Him?' If thou art able to think thus always thou wilt be
"able to live."

137. Abbâ Poemen was once passing through Egypt, and
he saw a woman sitting in the cemetery and weeping, and he
said, "If every kind of instrument of sweet music in the world
"were to come [here] they would not be able to change the
"grief of this woman's soul [into gladness]; even thus it is
"meet for a monk to have pain (or grief) within himself."

138. Three old men once came to Abbâ Sisoes because they
had heard that he was a great man. And the first one said
unto him, "Father, how can I escape from the river of fire?"
And Abbâ Sisoes answered him never a word. Then the second
old man said unto him, "Father, how can I escape from the
"gnashing of teeth, and from the worm which never dieth?"
And Abbâ Sisoes answered him never a word. Then the third
old man said unto him, "Father, what shall I do? For the re-
"membrance of the outer darkness troubleth me." And Abbâ
Sisoes answered and said unto them, "I never think on any
"of these things, but I believe that God is Merciful, and that
"He will shew mercy unto me"; then the old men went away

31

grieved at the answer which Abbâ Sisoes had spoken unto them. Now because he did not wish to send them away sorrowful, he brought them back, and said unto them, "Blessed "are ye, O my brethren, for I have been jealous of you"; and they said unto him, "In what matter hast thou been jealous "of us?" And he said, "The first one of you spake about a "river of fire; and the second spake about the gnashing of "teeth and the worm which dieth not; and the third spake "about the outer darkness; if remembrances of this kind "have dominion over your minds it is impossible for you to "commit sin. What can I do who am stubborn of heart? For "hardness of heart will not allow me to perceive even that "there a punishment for men existeth, and because of this "I sin every hour." And when the old men had heard these words, they made excuses to him, and said, "In very truth "according to what we have heard, even so have we seen."

139. A certain father said that on one occasion when the brethren were eating the food of grace, one of them laughed at table; and Abbâ Sînû saw him, and burst into tears, and said, "What can there be in the heart of this brother who "hath laughed? It is meet that he should weep because he is "eating the food of grace."

140. They say that when Abbâ Sisoes was sick the old men who were sitting with him saw that he was talking [to some one], and they said unto him, "What seest thou, O father?" And he said unto them, "Some people came to take me away, "and I entreated them to leave me [here] a little longer that "I might repent." Then one of the old men said unto him, "What power hast thou in thee now for repentance?" Abbâ Sisoes said unto them, "If I can do nothing else I can sigh "and lament a little over my soul, and this will be sufficient "for me."

141. Certain brethren went to an old man and, making apologies to him, they said, "Father, what shall we do, for Satan "is hunting after us?" And he said unto them, "It is right "for you to be watchful and to weep continually. My own "thoughts are always fixed upon the place where our Lord "was crucified, and I sigh and lament and weep about it "always;" and thus having received a good example of repentance the brethren departed and became chosen vessels.

142. A brother asked Abbâ Muthues, saying, "Speak a word "to me"; and the old man replied, "Cut off from thee con- "tention concerning every matter whatsoever, and weep, and "mourn, for the time hath come."

143. Abbâ Ammon said that he saw a young man who laughed, and he said unto him, "Laugh not, O brother, for if

" thou dost, thou wilt drive the fear of God out of thy
" soul."

144. Abbâ Paule used to say, "I had sunk in the mire up to
" my neck, and I wept and spake before God, saying, 'Have
" 'mercy on me.'"

145. They used to say that Abbâ Theodore and Abbâ 'Ôr
put on the skins of lambs for clothing; and they said to each
other, "If God were to visit us now what should we do?"
and they left [the skins], and departed to their cells weeping.

146. A blessed Archbishop, when he was about to depart
from this world, said, "Blessed art thou, O Arsenius, because
" thou hast remembered this hour."

147. An old man said, "God dwelleth in the man into whom
" nothing alien entereth."

148. A brother asked a certain old man, and said unto him,
" My soul desireth tears, even as I have heard that the old
" men [desire] them, but they will not come to me, and my soul
" is vexed." And the old man said unto him, "The children of
" Israel entered into the land of promise [after] forty years;
" now tears are the land of promise, and since thou wouldst
" enter therein thou must not henceforward be afraid of fight-
" ing. For God wisheth to bring tribulation upon the soul in
" this manner in order that it may at all times be wishful to
" enter into that land [of promise]."

149. A brother asked Abbâ Poemen a question and said unto
him, "What shall I do? for my thoughts disturb me, and they
" say unto me, 'Thy sins have been forgiven thee,' and they
" make me to pry into the shortcomings of the brethren."
Then Abbâ Poemen spake to him about Abbâ Isidore, who
dwelt in a cell and wept over his soul, and his disciple used to
dwell in another cell; and the disciple came to the old man,
and finding him weeping, said unto him, "My father, why
" weepest thou?" And the old man said unto him, "I am
" weeping for my sins." Then the disciple said unto him,
" And hast thou any sins, father?" And the old man said unto
" him, " Indeed I have, my son, and if I were permitted to
" see my sins, not three or even four men would suffice to
" weep with me for them." Then Abbâ Poemen said, " Thus
" it is with the man who knoweth himself."

150. I have heard that the old men who lived in Nitria sent
to Macarius the Great, who was living in Scete, and entreated
him, saying, " In order that all the people may not be vexed,
" we beseech thee, O our father, to come to us so that we may
see thee before [thou departest] to our Lord. And having gone
[to them] they all gathered together to him, and the old men
begged and entreated him to speak unto the brethren one

word of profit; and the holy old man wept, and said unto them,
"Let us weep, O my brethren, and let us make our eyes to
"overflow with tears before we go to the place where the tears
"of our eyeballs will burn up our bodies." And they all wept,
and they fell upon their faces, saying, "Father, pray for us."

151. When the blessed Arsenius was about to deliver up his
spirit the brethren saw him weeping, and they said unto him,
"Art thou also afraid, O father?" And he said unto them,
"The dread of this hour hath been with me in very truth from
"the time when I became a monk, and was afraid." And so
he died.

152. And when Abbâ Poemen heard that he was dead, that
is to say, that Abbâ Arsenius had gone to his rest, he said,
"Blessed art thou, O Abbâ Arsenius, for thou didst weep
"over thyself in this world. For he who weepeth not for him-
"self in this world must weep for ever in the next. He may
"weep here voluntarily, or there because of the punishments
"[which he will receive], but it is impossible for a man to
"escape weeping either here or there."

153. A brother asked Abbâ Poemen and said unto him,
"What shall I do in the matter of my sins?" And the old man
said unto him, "When Abraham went into the Land of Pro-
"mise he bought himself a grave, and through the grave he
"inherited the land." And the brother said unto him, "What
"is a grave?" Then the old man said unto him, "Weeping
"and mourning are a grave and a place [of burial]."

154. One of the brethren asked Abbâ Poemen, saying,
"Father, what shall I do in the matter of my sins?" The old
man said unto him, "Whosoever wisheth to blot out his offences
"can do so by weeping, and he who wisheth to acquire good
"works can do so by means of weeping; for weeping is the
"path which the Scriptures have taught us, and the fathers
"have also wept continually, and there is no other path except
"that of tears."

155. And the same old man (i.e., Poemen) said, "There are
"two things [to remember]: We must fear our Lord, and do
"good unto our neighbour."

156. Abbâ Noah asked Abbâ Macarius, and said unto him,
"Speak to me a word"; and the old man said, "Flee from the
"children of men." Noah said unto him, "Father, what doth
"it mean to flee from the children of men?" The old man said
unto him, "Thou shalt sit in thy cell and weep for thy sins."

157. A brother asked an old man, and said unto him, "What
"shall I do, father?" The old man said unto him, "It is right
"that we should sigh and lament always." Now it happened
that one of the old men fell asleep, and that after a long inter-

val he came to himself again, and the brethren asked him, saying, "What didst thou see there, O father?" and he said unto us with many tears, "I heard there the sound of the weeping "of many, who were crying out and wailing incessantly, and "saying, 'Woe is me! Woe is me!' And it is meet that we "should always be saying the same thing."

Chapter v. Of Voluntary Poverty

158. ABBÂ ARSENIUS once fell sick at Scete, and he was in need of a bowl of pottage; and since this was not to be found there, he took the remains of the Eucharist (or food of grace), and said, "I give thanks unto Thee, "O Christ, that, because of Thy name, I am able to receive the "food of grace."

159. There was a certain holy man whose name was Philagrius, who lived in Jerusalem, and he worked with his hands and toiled [to earn] the food which he needed; and the old man rose up to see the work of his hands, and he found a purse containing one thousand darics which had dropped from some one [on the road], and he remained in the place where he was, saying, "The man who lost this will come back seeking for "it." And behold the man did come back, and he was weeping, and the old man took him aside and gave him the darics; and their owner laid hold upon him, and wished to give him some small sum of money, but the old man refused to accept anything. Then the owner of the darics began to cry out and say, "Come ye and see what the man of God hath done"; but the old man fled secretly and departed from the city, lest what he had done should become known, and men should pay him honour because of it.

160. They say that Abbâ Serapion the Bishop went on one occasion to one of the brethren, and found [in his cell] a hollow in the wall which was filled with books; and the brother said unto him, "Speak to me one word whereby I may live." And the Bishop said unto him, "What have I to say to thee? "For thou hast taken that which belongeth to the orphans and "widows and laid it up in a hole in the wall."

161. Abbâ Theodore of Parmê possessed some beautiful books, and he went to Abbâ Macarius and said unto him, "Father, I have three books, and I gain profit from them, "and the brethren borrow them from me, and they also have "profit from them; tell me, now, what shall I do with them?" And the old man answered and said, "Ascetic labours are "beautiful, but the greatest of them all is voluntary poverty." And when Abbâ Theodore heard these words he went and sold the books and gave the price of them to the poor.

162. They say about a certain monk that when his food came to him he was in the habit of taking so much of it as he needed, [but that if it happened that another man was brought to him he would not accept any of it], saying, "It is sufficient "for me; behold my Lord hath fed me."

163. A certain monk used to live in a cave in the desert, and a message was sent unto him by his kinsfolk, saying, "Thy "father is grievously sick, and is nigh to die, therefore come, "and inherit his possessions"; and he made answer unto them, saying, "I died to the world long before he will die, and a "dead man cannot be the heir of a living one."

164. An old man was asked by a brother the question, "How shall I live?" Then the old man took off his garment, and girded up his loins therewith, and lifted up his hands and said, "It is meet for a monk to be as naked in respect of this "world's goods as I am of clothing. And in his striving "against his thoughts he must stand as upright as a vigorous "athlete, and when the athlete contendeth he also standeth "up naked, and when he is anointed with oil he is quite naked, "and hath nothing upon him; and he learneth from him that "traineth him how to contend, and when the enemy cometh "against him he throweth dust upon him, which is a matter "of this world, that he may be able to grasp him easily. In "thyself, then, O monk, thou must see the athlete, and he "who sheweth thee how to contend is God, for it is He Who "giveth the victory, and Who conquereth for us; and those "who contend are ourselves, and the striving is [our] op-"ponent, and the dust is the affairs of the world. And since "thou hast seen the cunning of the Adversary, stand thou up "and oppose him in thy nakedness, being free from any care "which belongeth to this world, and thou shalt overcome "[him]. For when the mind is weighted down with the care of "the world it cannot receive the holy word of God."

165. They say concerning Abbâ Arsenius that as, when he lived in the world, his apparel was finer than that of anyone else, so, when he lived in Scete, he wore raiment which was inferior to that of every one else. And when, at long intervals, he came to church, he used to sit behind a pillar so that no one might see his face, and he might not see the faces of others; now his face was like that of an angel, and his hair was as white as snow, and as abundant as [that of] Jacob. His body was dry by reason of his labours, and his beard descended to his belly, but his eyelashes were destroyed by weeping; he was tall in stature, but somewhat bowed by old age and he ended his days when he was ninety-five years old. He lived n the world, in the palace, for forty years, in the days of

Theodosius, the great king, who became the father of the Emperors Honorius and Arcadius, and he lived in Scete forty years, and he lived for ten years in the Troja of Babylon which is opposite the Memphis which is in Egypt, and he dwelt for three years in Canopus of Alexandria, and during the two remaining years he came to Troja again, where he died. And he finished his career in peace and in the fear of God.

166. On one occasion a certain Bishop came to the Fathers in Scete, and a brother went forth to meet him, and having met him, he took him and brought him into his cell; and having set before him bread and salt, he said, "Forgive me, O my "father, for I have nothing else to set before thee." And the Bishop said unto him, "I wish that when I come another year "I may not find even bread and salt in thy cell."

167. One of the old men said, "If thou sittest in a place and "seest people with abundant provisions, look not at them ; "but if there be a man who is destitute, look at him as one "who hath no bread, and thou shalt find relief."

168. Abbâ Isaac, the priest of the Cells, used to say that Abbâ Pambô said, "The manner of the apparel which a monk "ought to wear should be such that if it were cast outside the "cell for three days no one would carry it away."

169. A certain brother asked one of the old men a question, and said unto him, "Dost thou wish me to keep two darics as "provision for the needs of the feebleness of the body?" And the old man, perceiving his mind and also that he wished to keep them, said unto him, "Yea." Now when the brother had gone to his cell, he became troubled in his mind, and he debated in his thoughts, saying, "Did the old man speak truth-"fully or not?" Then he rose up, and went back to the old man, and made excuses to him, and said, "For our Lord's sake, "tell me the truth, because my thoughts are troubling me "about these two darics." The old man said unto him, "I spake "to thee as I did because I saw that thy mind was to keep "them, but it is not necessary for thee to keep the two darics, "except only for the need of thy body. But why is thy hope "set upon two darics? If by chance they were lost would not "God take care of thee? Let us then cast [our] care upon "Him, for it belongeth to Him to take care of us continually."

170. Some of the old men used to tell a story about a gardener who used to work and to give away whatsoever he gained thereby in alms, but subsequently his thoughts said to him, "Gather "together a few oboli, lest when thou hast grown old thou fall "into want"; so he gathered together some money, and filled a large vessel therewith. And it fell out that he became sick, and the disease seized upon his foot, and he spent the whole of the money in the vessel on the physicians, and was not in the least benefited thereby. At length another physician came unto him and said, "If thou dost not cut off thy foot all thy "body will putrefy," and he came to consider the cutting off of his foot. And in the night he came to himself, and he groaned, and wept, and said, "Remember, O Lord, my former deeds," and straightway a man appeared behind him, and said unto him, "Where are thy oboli?" and the gardener said immediately, "I have sinned, forgive me"; and straightway the man approached his leg, and it was made whole forthwith, and he rose up, and went to the garden to work. And in the morning the physician came to cut off his foot as he had said, and [the servants] told him, "He went to this work in the night"; and straightway [the gardener] glorified God.

171. Abbâ Agathon saw Abbâ Nastîr wearing two shoulder wrappers, and he said unto him, "If a poor man were to come, "and ask thee for a garment, which of them wouldst thou "give him?" And Abbâ Nastîr replied, "I would give him the "better of them"; and Abba Agathon said unto him, "And if "another poor man came, what wouldst thou give him?" Abbâ Nastîr saith unto him, "I would give him the half of "that which remained." And Abbâ Agathon said unto him, "Supposing yet another beggar came, what wouldst thou "give unto him?" And Nastîr said unto him, "I would cut the "half which remained into two pieces, and give one to him, "and with the other I would cover my body." And Abbâ Agathon said unto him, "And supposing yet another beggar "were to come?" and Nastîr said, "I would give him what "was left. For though I do not wish to receive anything from "any man, yet I would go and sit down in some place until "God sent me wherewith to cover myself."

172. The blessed woman Eugenia said, "It is right for us to "beg, but only we must be with Christ. He who is with Christ "becometh rich, but he who honoureth the things of the body "more than the things of the spirit shall fall both from the "things which are first and the things which are last."

173. One of the old men said, "How can a man teach unto "his neighbour that which he himself doth not observe?"

174. They say that Abbâ Theodore excelled in the three following things more than any other man, and that he attained in their performance a degree which was greater than that of many, namely, voluntary poverty, self-abnegation, and flight from the children of men.

175. Abbâ Poemen used to say, "He who laboureth and "keepeth [the result of] his work for himself is a twofold "grief."

Of Voluntary Poverty

176. Abbâ Isaac used to say to the brethren, "Our fathers "and Abbâ Panbô used to wear old garments which were much "mended and were patched with rags, but at this present ye "wear very costly apparel; get ye gone from this place, for ye "have laid the country waste, and I will not give you com- "mandments, for ye will not keep them."

177. On one occasion a brother came to the church of the Cells wearing a small head-cloth which came down to his shoulders, and when Abbâ Isaac saw him he followed him, and said, "Monks dwell here, but thou art a man in the world, "and thou canst not live here."

178. A certain man, having made himself remote from the world, and divided his possessions among those who were in need, left to himself the remainder of his riches. And when the blessed Anthony heard [this] he said unto him, "Dost thou "wish to become a monk? If thou dost, get thee to such and "such a village, and take some meat, and lay it upon thy body, "and come hither alone"; and having done this the dogs, and the hawks and other birds of prey rent and tore his body. And when he returned to the blessed man, Saint Anthony asked him whether he had done as he had commanded him, and when the man had shewn him his body which was rent and torn, the blessed Anthony said unto him, "Even thus are those who "wish to go out from the world, and who nevertheless leave "themselves certain possessions, wherefrom arise for their "owners war and strife."

179. A brother asked Abbâ Poemen the question, saying, "An inheritance hath been bequeathed to me; what shall I do "with it?" Abbâ Poemen said unto him, "Go, and after three "days come unto me, and I will give thee counsel." And the bro- ther came, and Abbâ Poemen said unto him, "What counsel "shall I give thee, O brother? If I tell thee to give it to the "church, they will make feasts with it; and again, if I tell thee "to give it to thy kinsmen, thou wilt have no reward; but if I "tell thee to give it to the poor, thou wilt have no [further] "care. Therefore go and do with thine inheritance what thou "pleasest, for I am not able to advise thee rightly."

180. A certain man entreated an old man to accept from him a gift of grace for his wants, but he refused to do so because the labour of his hands was sufficient for him; and when he who asked him to accept it persisted, saying, "If thou wilt not "accept it for thine own needs, at least do so for the wants of "others," the old man answered and said unto him, "It would "be a twofold disgrace [unto me]. First, because I should ac- "cept something which I do not want, and secondly, because I "should be giving away with boasting the charity of another."

181. An old man used to say, "It is not right for a man to "have any care whatsoever except the fear of God, for," said he, "although I am forced to take care for the needs of the "body, no thought whatsoever concerning anything riseth in "my mind before the time when I shall require to make use "of it."

182. The same old man used to say, "When thou risest up, "in the morning, say, 'O body, work that thou mayest be "'fed; O soul, rouse up that thou mayest inherit life.'"

Chapter vj. Of Patient Endurance

ON one occasion certain brethren went to Abbâ Agathon, because they had heard that he took the greatest possible care that his mind should not be disturbed by anything, 183. and they sought to try him, and to see if his mind would rise [to any matter]; and they said unto him, "Art thou indeed "Agathon? We have heard that thou art a whoremonger and a "boastful man." And Agathon said unto them, "Yea, I am." And again they said unto him, "Agathon, thou art a garrulous and talkative old man"; and he said unto them, "Indeed I am." And again they said unto him, "Agathon, thou art a heretic"; and he said unto them, "I am not a heretic." Then they said unto him, "Tell us now why in answer to all these things "which we have said to thee thou hast replied, 'Yea,' and that "thou hast endured them all with the exception of the accu- "sation of being a heretic." Abbâ Agathon said unto them, "The earlier things I accounted as profitable to my soul, but "heresy meaneth separation from God, and I do not wish to "be separated from God." And when the brethren heard [these words] they marvelled at his solicitude, and went away rejoicing.

184. A certain father used to tell the story of a father who had a book wherein were the New Testament and the Old Testament, and the price thereof was more than eighteen darics, and he laid up the book in a hole in the wall; and there came a certain stranger and stayed there, and he coveted the book greatly, and stole it, and departed, but the old man did not go after him, although he knew that he had taken it. And the brother went to a neighbouring village and wished to sell the book, and he asked as its price sixteen darics, and the man who wanted to buy it said unto him, "Give it to me, that I may "shew it [to a friend]," and he took it and carried it to the old man who had lost it. Then the old man said unto him, "How "much doth he ask for it?" And when he heard how much he said to him, "It is well" (or "it is a good price"). Then the man went and said unto the brother who wished to sell the

book, "Behold, I have shewn it to Father So-and-so, and he "hath told me that thy price is dear." And the brother answered and said unto him, "I did not tell thee anything to the "contrary," and the would-be buyer said, "No, thou didst "not." Said the brother, "I will not then sell thee the book," and straightway he repented, and came to the old man and made excuses to him, and offered him the book, but the old man refused to accept it. And the brother entreated him, saying, "Allow me [to restore it to thee], O father, for if thou dost not "accept it I cannot obtain life"; so the old man was entreated, and he took it, and that brother remained with him until his death, and through the patient endurance of the old man he gained life.

185. On one occasion certain philosophers came to the desert to try the monks. And there was living there a man who led a life of fair works, and they said unto him, "Come "thou hither," and his anger rose and he reviled them. Now there passed by a certain great monk who was a Libyan, and they said unto him, "O thou monk who hast grown grey-"headed in iniquity, come hither"; and he went to them readily, and they smote him on one cheek, whereupon he turned the other to them. And when they saw this they rose up straightway and worshipped him, and they said, "Verily this is a "monk"; then they set him in their midst, and asked him, saying, "What things do ye who are living in the desert do "more than we? Ye fast, and we also fast; ye lead pure lives, "and we also lead pure lives; whatsoever ye do we also do; "what do ye who live in the desert do more than we?" The Libyan said unto them, "We keep watch over our minds"; and the philosophers said unto him, "We are unable to keep "watch over our minds."

186. They say that Abbâ Macarius the Egyptian on one occasion went up from Scete to the Nitrian mountain, and as he drew nigh unto a certain place, he said unto his disciple, "Pass "on a little in front of me"; and when he had done so there met him a certain heathen priest, who was running along and carrying some wood about the time of noon. And that brother cried out to him and said, "O minister unto devils, whither "runnest thou?" And the priest turned round and smote him with many severe blows, and he left him with but very little breath remaining in him, and he took up his wood and went on his way; and when he had gone on a little further the blessed Macarius met him on his journey, and said unto him, "Mayest "thou be helped, O man of labours?" And the priest was astonished, and came to him and said, "What fair thing hast "thou seen in me that thou shouldst salute me [in this gracious

"fashion]?" And the old man said unto him, "I see that thou
"toilest, and that thou dost not know that thou art toiling for
"naught"; then he said unto the old man, "At thy salutation
"I also was very sorry, and I learned that thou didst belong
"to the Great God. But a wicked monk met me just before
"thou didst, and he cursed me, and I smote him even unto
"death." And the old man knew that it was his disciple [of
whom he spake], and the priest laid hold upon the feet of Macarius, and said unto him, "I will not let thee [go] until thou
"makest me a monk"; and they came to the place where the
brother was lying, and they carried him and brought him to
the church of the mountain. Now when the fathers saw the
heathen priest with him, they marvelled that he had been con-
verted from the error which he had held; and Macarius took
him and made him a monk, and through him many of the
heathen became Christians. And Abbâ Macarius said, "'An evil
"'word maketh wicked even those who are good, and a good
"'word maketh good even those who are wicked,' as it is
"written."

187. On one occasion thieves came to the cell of an old man,
and said unto him, "We have come to take away everything
"which thou hast in thy cell"; and he said unto them, "My
"sons, take whatsoever ye please"; and they took everything
which they saw in his cell and departed. Now they forgot [to
take] a wallet which was hanging there, and the old man took
it and ran after them, and entreated them, saying, "My sons,
"take this wallet which ye have left behind in your cell." And
when the thieves saw this they marvelled at the good disposition of the old man, and they gave back everything which they
had taken from his cell, and they repented, and said to each
other, "Verily, this man is a man of God."

188. Abbâ Macarius the monk loved money so little that, on
one occasion when thieves came to his cell by night, and took
out whatsoever they could find in it, as soon as he perceived
what they were doing, he helped them in their work and also
to carry [their plunder] out of the desert.

189. They say that once when Abbâ Macarius was absent a
thief entered his cell, and that when he returned and found a
thief therein loading upon a camel everything which he had in
his cell, he also went in and took some of the things and laid
them on the camel; and when the thief had loaded the camel,
he began to beat it in order to make it rise up, but it would
not move. Now when Abbâ Macarius saw that the beast would
not stand up, he took a basket which was remaining, and
brought it out and laid it on the camel, and said, "The camel
"wisheth to carry off this also, O brother, and because of this

"it would not stand up." Then the old man cried out to the camel, "Stand up," and straightway, because of the old man's words, it stood up; but when it had gone forward for a little it lay down again, and it would not rise up until the thief had emptied the whole of its load.

190. And another of the fathers when he was being plundered said unto the thieves, "Make haste, and be quick, before "the brethren come."

191. On one occasion when some men of iniquity, and doers of wickedness, and thieves, rose up against him on the eve of the day of the congregation, an old man said unto the brethren, " Let them do their work, and let us do ours."

192. And when certain evil-doers rose up against one of the brethren in his cell, he brought forth a basin and entreated them to wash their feet, and the thieves were ashamed and repented.

193. And another brother who was travelling on a journey, and did not know the road, asked a man to shew him the way and to direct him; now the man whom he had asked was an evil-doer, and he led the brother out of his road into a waste place, and he made him to arrive at the river Nile, which he commanded the brother to cross over. And when he began to cross over, behold a crocodile was swiftly pursuing the man who was a thief, but the servant of God, not being unmindful of him, cried out to him, and made known to him concerning the fierce attack which the animal was about to make. Then, the thief having been delivered from death, gave thanks to that brother, and marvelled at his affection, and protected him.

194. The blessed Pîôr was on one occasion working for a man in the fields in the summer time, and he was weary, and reminded the lord of his hire about his wages, and when he delayed [in paying him] Abbâ Pîôr returned to his monastery. And on another occasion, when the time of harvest had arrived, Abbâ Pîôr went to the same man, and reaped his crops with a good will, and he returned to his monastery, the man having given him nothing. And again in the third year Abbâ Pîôr came and helped him to harvest his crops, and when he had made an end of the work of harvest according to custom, and yet received nothing, he departed again to his monastery. Meanwhile the man, who was worthy of blessing, laboured according to his custom in the life and works of spiritual excellence, and rejoiced that he had been defrauded of his hire. And Christ worked upon the lord of his hire in his house, and he took the wages of the blessed man, and went round about among the monasteries seeking for him, and when, after the greatest difficulty, he had found him, he fell at his feet and

entreated him to receive his hire. But when the holy man refused the wages and said, "Perhaps thou hast need of them, "and as for me God will give me my hire," the man increased his supplications unto him, and finally the holy man permitted him to give the money to the church.

195. An old man used to say, "We do not advance because "we do not know our capacity, and we have not sufficient "patience in the work which we begin, and we wish to pos-"sess spiritual excellences without working for them, and we "go from place to place, and expect to find some spot where "Satan is not, and when we see the temptation of Satan in "that place whereunto we have been called, he who knoweth "what the war is will remain in God. For the kingdom of "heaven is within you."

196. An old man used to say, "If it should happen that a "sickness of the body overtake thee, let it not be grievous "unto thee, for if thy Lord wisheth thee to be sick in the body, "who art thou that thou shouldst be in despair? Doth He not "take care for thee in everything? Couldst thou live without "Him? Be patient, and entreat thou Him to give thee such "things as are helpful, and which are according to His will; "and besides this eat thou His food of grace with long-suffer-"ing."

197. Abbâ Poemen used to say, "The certain sign that "a monk is a monk is made known by trials (or temp-"tations)."

198. A certain brother was estranged from a fellow monk, and he came to Abbâ Sisoes the Theban, and said unto him, "I am estranged from a fellow monk, and I wish to take ven-"geance for myself"; and the old man said, "Let us pray." And whilst he was praying, he said in his prayer, "O God, "henceforward we have no need of Thee to take care of us, "for we will take vengeance for ourselves"; and when the brother heard these words he fell down at the feet of the old man straightway, and said unto him, "Henceforward I will "not enter into judgement with that brother. Forgive me, "O Father." And thus Abbâ Sisoes healed that brother.

199. They say that Abbâ John the Less, the Theban, the disciple of Abbâ Ammon, ministered unto the Abbâ in his sickness for twelve years, and he sat by him when the old man was in a state of exhaustion, and he persevered and endured so patiently, even whilst he was performing great labours, that the old man never once said unto him, "Rest, my son; rest, my "son!" And when the old man was about to die, and the other old men were sitting before him, Abbâ Ammon took his hand, and said unto him, "Live, my son, live!" Then he committed

him to the old men and said unto them, "This is an angel, and
"not a man."

200. Abbâ Paulê and Tîmâth his brother dwelt in Scete, and
there was contention between them frequently; and Abbâ Paulê
said, "How long are we to remain thus?" Abbâ Tîmâth said
unto him, "When I come upon thee bear with me; and when
"thou comest upon me I will bear with thee." And from that
time they were at peace.

201. Certain brethren asked Abbâ Sisoes a question, and
said unto him, "If we are going along a road, and he who is
"conducting us forgetteth the way, is it necessary for us to
"tell him?" And Abbâ Sisoes said unto them, "No." Then
a brother said unto him, "Are we then to let him lead us
"astray?" And the old man said unto him, "What then?
"Thou hast a stick, canst thou not take it and smite him?
"Now I knew twelve brethren who were travelling along the
"road, and in the night time he who was leading them lost the
"way, and all the brethren knew that he had done so; and
"every one of them struggled with his thoughts, [and de-
"cided] not to tell him. And when the day had come he who
"had been leading them learned that he had wandered off the
"road, and he made excuses and said unto them, 'Forgive me
"'because I lost the way'; and they all said, 'We all of us
"'knew it, brother, but we held our peace.' And when he heard
"this he marvelled, saying, 'The brethren would endure even
"'unto death and would utter never a word'; and he glorified
"God. Now the distance which they had wandered from the
"road was twelve miles."

202. Certain brethren came unto Abbâ Anthony, and said
unto him, "Speak unto us a word whereby we may live"; and
the old man said unto them, "Behold, ye have heard the
"Scriptures, and they are sufficient for you," and the brethren
said, "We wish to hear [a word] from thee also, O father."
Abbâ Anthony said unto them, "It is said in the Gospel, 'If a
"'man smite thee on the [one] cheek, turn to him the other
"'also'" (St. Luke vi, 29); and they said unto him, "We can-
"not do this." Abbâ Anthony said unto them, "If ye cannot turn
"the other cheek, continue [to be smitten] on the one cheek";
and they said to him, "And this we cannot do." The old man
said unto them, "If ye cannot do even this, do not pay back
"blows in return for the smiting which ye have received"; and
they said, "We cannot even do this." Then the old man said
unto his disciples, "Make then for the brethren a little boiled
"food, for they are ill"; and he said to them, "If ye cannot do
"this, and ye are unable to do the other things, prayers are
"necessary forthwith."

203. They used to say that Mother Sarâ, who dwelt above the river and was sixty years old, had never looked out [from her abode] and seen the river.

204. A certain old man dwelt in the desert at a distance of ten miles from the monastery, wherefrom he had always to draw water, and on one occasion the matter became very wearisome to him, and he said, "What is the necessity for "me to labour so much? I will come and will take up my "abode by the side of this stream." And having said this, he turned behind him and he saw a man coming after him, and he was counting his footsteps, and he asked him, saying, "Who art thou?" And he answered and said unto him, "I am "an angel of the Lord, and I have been sent to count thy foot-"steps, and to give thee thy reward"; and having heard this the old man was consoled greatly, and he went five miles further from the place wherein he was, and took up his abode there.

205. They say that three thieves went into the cell of Abbâ Theodore, and that two of them laid hold upon him whilst the third carried off the things which he had in his cell; and having taken out even the books which he had there, they were going to carry away his cloak, when he said unto them, "Leave me "this"; and as they refused to do so, he moved his arms and hands and hurled the two men who were holding him from him, and when they saw this they were afraid. Then the old man said unto them, "Fear ye not, but divide what ye have taken "into four parts, and take three of them, and leave me one."

206. They used to say that the cave in Patârâ which belonged to Abbâ Chaeremon who was in Scete, was forty miles distant from the church, and twelve miles further from a spring of water. And he used to bring to the church, with the labour of his hands, two pitchers of water, one for each day, and when he was tired he would set one down by the roadside and go back afterwards and fetch it.

207. They used to say that the cell of the blessed Arsenius also was two and thirty miles from the church, but he never went anywhere and others brought him whatsoever he required.

208. The blessed Arsenius never changed the water [wherein he soaked] the leaves which he twisted into ropes except once a year, but he used to add frequently to it, for he twisted palm leaves and sewed them together until the sixth hour [daily]. And the fathers entreated him, saying, " Tell us why thou dost "not change the water of the leaves, for it is very foul"; then the old man answered, and said, " It is right that I should en-"dure this foul smell in return for the odours of the sweet "scents, and oils, and delightful odours, which I enjoyed when "I was in the world."

209. It is related of a certain old man that if he heard a brother speak evilly to him he would labour very hard to make something which would please the brother who had spoken to him, and that if that brother did not live with him, the old man would send whatsoever he had made to the place where he was.

210. A certain old man used to say, " It is a disgrace for a " monk to enter into judgement with the man who hath done " him an injury."

211. A brother asked a certain old man, saying, " Tell me " one thing, whereby, if I keep it, I shall live." The old man said unto him, " If thou canst endure being reviled and cursed, " this command is the greatest of all the commandments."

212. A brother asked Abbâ Poemen, saying, " What shall I " do to my heart which flaggeth and is frightened if a little " toil, and tribulation overtake me, or if temptation come upon " me?" The old man said unto him, "Therefore we should " wonder and admire the righteous man Joseph who, being " only a very young man—that is to say, seventeen years " of age—was sold into slavery into the land of Egypt, the " land of the worshippers of idols, and he endured tempta- " tions, and God made him glorious to the end."

213. And he said also, " We may consider also the blessed " Job, who never became slothful, for he persevered in his trust " in his God, and his enemies were not able to shake him from " his hope."

214. On one occasion the brethren who were in Scete were cleaning and dressing palm leaves, and there was among them a man who had become ill through his excessive spiritual labours, and he was coughing, and bringing up clots of phlegm and spittle; and as he spat, involuntarily, some of the spittle fell upon a certain brother. Then the mind of that brother on whom the spittle had fallen said unto him, " Tell that brother " not to spit upon thee"; but straightway he licked up the spittle, and he turned and said to his mind, " Thou hast not " licked up the spittle, therefore do not tell him not to spit upon " thee."

215. Abbâ Poemen used to say that John Colob, who made entreaty unto God, and [his] passions were removed from him, and he was set free from anxious care, went and said unto a famous old man, " I perceive that my soul is at rest, and that " it hath neither war nor strife [to trouble it]." Then the old man said unto him, " Go and entreat God to let war and strife " come unto thee again, for it is through war and strife that " the soul advanceth in spiritual excellence." And afterwards, whensoever war stood up before him, he did not pray, "O Lord, " remove striving from me," but he made supplication unto

God, saying, "O Lord, give me patience to endure the "strife."

216. There was a certain man who had within himself love and affection for the brotherhood, and who never had in his mind any evil thought whatsoever; and a certain brother stole some things and brought [them] and deposited them with him, and the man did not consider or perceive by what means the brother had obtained them. Now some days later the matter was discovered, and it was pointed out to the owner of the things that they had been deposited with the old man, who made excuses to them, saying, "Forgive ye me, for I repent." And after a few days the brother who had stolen the things came to him, and he began to demand [them from] the old man, and said unto him, "Thou thyself didst take the things"; and the old man made excuses to him, saying, "Forgive me"; and the old man brought out all the work of his hands, and gave it to him, and the brother took it and departed. Now the disposition of the old man was such that, if one of the brethren committed a fault, and denied it, he would make excuses for him, saying, "It was I who did this thing"; thus meek and humble was the holy man, and he never wronged any man even by the least word.

217. A certain brother lived by himself, and he was disturbed in his mind, and went and revealed the matter to Abbâ Theodore of Parmê. And the old man said unto him, "Go and "humble thy mind, and submit thyself to live with the breth-"ren"; and he went and did as the old man had told him, and took up his abode with other men. And he went back to the the old man, and said unto him, "Father, I am not content to "dwell with other men"; then the old man said unto him, "If "thou art not content to live either by thyself or with others, "why didst thou come out to be a monk? Is it not necessary "for thee to endure trials? Tell me, how long hast thou lived "this life?" And the brother said unto him, "Eight years." The old man said unto him, "Verily I have led the life I lead "now for seventy years, and not one pleasure hath come in "my way [the whole time], and yet thou wishest to find plea-"sure (*or* rest) in eight years!"

218. A certain brother, who had vanquished Satan in everything, subsequently had his eyes blinded by Satan so that he could not see, yet this blessed man did not pray for himself, and that he might be able to see, but he only prayed that he might be able to endure patiently his trial; and through his constancy his eyes were opened.

219. A monk was smitten by a man on the leg and was severely injured, but the holy man was neither angry nor wroth with him that had smitten him, [but he nursed the place wherein he had been wounded, and made excuses to the man who had struck him].

220. Abbâ Arsenius used to say, "When an unbaked [or "moist] brick is laid in the foundations of a building by the "river-side, it will not support it, but if it be burnt in the fur-"nace it will support the building like a stone. And thus it is "with the man who possesseth a carnal mind, and who doth "not become hot and burn with heat, even as did Joseph with "the word of God, for when he cometh to have dominion "he will be found to be wanting. For very many of those "upon whom trials have come have straightway been swept "away and have fallen. It is therefore a good thing for a man "to know the gravity of dominion, and to be required to bear "trials, which are like the onset of many mighty waters, so "that he may remain firm and unmoved." And of this holy man Joseph—if a man wisheth to have the story told—Arsenius used to say that "He was not a being of earth at all—so much was "he tempted. And [consider] the country [of Egypt] wherein "formerly there was not even a trace of the fear of God! But "the God of his fathers was with him, and He delivered him "out of all his tribulations, and Joseph is now with his fathers "in the kingdom of heaven; and let us also make supplication "with all our might that we too may in the same manner be "able to flee from and escape from the righteous judgement of "God."

221. They say that there was with Abbâ Isidore, the priest of Scete, a certain brother who was infirm in his mind, and he was a man who used abusive language and possessed very little intelligence, and Abbâ Isidore wished to turn him out from his abode; and when that brother came to the door of the monastery, the old man said once again, "Bring him to me," and he rebuked him, saying, "Brother, be silent, lest through thy little "intelligence and thine impatience thou provoke our Lord to "anger"; and thus by his longsuffering Abbâ Isidore quieted that brother.

222. A lover of ascetic labours saw a man carrying a dead person on a bier, and he said unto him, "Dost thou carry a "dead man? Go and carry the living."

223. They say that there was a certain monk who, whenever he found a man reviling and cursing him, used to run towards him with all his power, saying, "These [words] are the causes "of spiritual excellence in those who are strenuous, for those "who ascribe blessing to a man disturb the soul, as it is "written, ' Those who ascribe blessing to you lead astray "'your soul.' "

224. Certain old men came unto an old man who dwelt in the desert that they might reveal unto him their thoughts, and might profit by his knowledge, and they found some young men outside his cell who were pasturing sheep, and they were saying unto one another words which were unseemly. And the old men said unto the old man, " Father, how is it that thou "dost not command these young men not to curse?" And the old man said unto them, " My brethren, believe me, I have " many times wished to command them [not to do so], but I " have rebuked myself, saying, 'If thou canst not endure this " 'little thing, how couldst thou bear some severe trial if it " ' were to come upon thee?' I have therefore never said any-" thing to them, so that the matter might be a cause of remem-" bering that I have to endure the things which are to come."

225. A certain brother ministered unto one of the fathers who was sick, now his disease was decline of the body, and he used to bring up foetid pus; and the mind of the brother said unto him, "Flee from him, for thou canst not endure this foe-" tid smell." Then the brother took an earthen vessel and put into it some of the water in which the old man had washed, and when he was thirsty he used to drink some of it ; and his mind began to say unto him, " Flee not, but drink not of this " filthy water." But that brother laboured on greatly in respect of the water in which the sick man had washed, and although his soul shrank from that filthiness, he persevered in drinking it; and God saw his labour and tribulation, and He changed the filthy washing water which was in the earthen vessel into clean water, and He healed that old man.

226. One of the monks wished to go out from his monastery and to wander about so that he might have a little relaxation and enjoyment, and when they saw him, an old man said unto him, "Seek not gratification in this world, O my son, but " work rather and persevere therein in the invincible power of " the Holy Trinity."

227. Abbâ Moses used to say, "Secret withdrawal [from " work] maketh dark the mind, but for a man to endure and " to persevere in his works maketh light the mind in our Lord, " and it strengtheneth and fortifieth the soul."

228. And he used to say also, "Bear disgrace and affliction " in the Name of Jesus with humility and a troubled heart; " and shew before Him thy feebleness, and He will become " unto thee might."

229. Certain people praised one of the brethren before the blessed Anthony, and when that brother came to the blessed man the old man put him to the test, and he found that he could not bear contempt and contumely. And the old man said unto

him, "Thou art like unto a palace the front of which is deco-
"rated and beautiful, but the back whereof hath been broken
"into by thieves and plundered."

230. A brother asked an old man a question, saying, "What
"shall I do?" And the old man said unto him, "Go and learn
"to love putting restraint upon thyself in everything."

231. One of the old men said concerning Lazarus, the poor
man, "We cannot find that Lazarus ever did one excellent
"thing except that he never murmured against the rich man
"as being one who had never shewn him an act of mercy; but
"he bore his infirmity with the giving of thanks, and because
"of this God took him to Himself."

232. Abbâ Macarius used to say, "If contumely be accounted
"by thee as an honour, and blame as praise, and poverty as
"wealth, thou wilt not die."

233. A certain brother asked Abbâ Poemen, saying, "What
"mean the words, 'If a man be angry with his brother with-
"'out a cause?'" (St. Matthew v, 22.) The old man said unto
him, "If thy brother make use of oppression, and wrong, and
"fraud in respeĉt of thee, and thou art angry with him [be-
"cause of them], thou art angry with him without a cause.
"And if he tear out thy right eye, or cut off thy right hand,
"and thou art angry with him, thou art angry with him with-
"out a cause; but if a man wisheth to separate thee or to put
"thee away from God, then to be angry and wroth with him
"is a good thing."

234. There were two men in the desert who were brethren
in the flesh, and a devil came to separate them from each other;
and one day the younger brother lit a lamp and set it upon a
candlestick, but, by the agency of the Evil One, he overturned
the candlestick and extinguished the lamp. Then the elder
brother was angry and smote him, and the younger brother
made excuses to him, saying, "Have a little patience with me,
"and I will light the lamp again." Now when God saw his
patient endurance, He punished that devil until the morning,
and the devil came and told the prince of devils what had
happened; and there was with the prince of devils a certain
priest of idols, and straightway this man left everything, and
he went and became a monk. And at the very beginning he
laid hold upon humility, saying, "Humility is able to bring to
"naught all the power of the Adversary, even as I have heard
"from the devils, who said, 'Whensoever we stir up the
"'monks, they turn to humility, and they make excuses one
"'to the other, and thus they do away all our power.'"

235. Abbâ Poemen said, "Abbâ Isidore, the priest of the
"church, on one occasion spake to the people, saying, My

" brethren, when ye are working in a certain place it is not
" strength to depart therefrom because of the labour; and as
" for myself, I wrap myself up in my cloak and I go to the
" place where labour is, and labour becometh unto me a
" pleasure."

236. Paesius, the brother of Abbâ Poemen, had an affection
for the people who were outside his monastery, and Abbâ
Poemen did not wish this to be, and he rose up and fled to
Abbâ Ammon, and said unto him, "My brother Paesius hath
" made a promise of love to certain folk, and I am not pleased
" thereat." Abbâ Ammon said unto him, " Poemen, thou art
" still alive. Go, and sit in thy cell, and meditate in thy
" mind, saying, 'Behold, there is a year for thee in the
" ' grave.'"

237. There were two monks who lived in one place, and an
old man came to them, and wishing to put them to the test,
he took a stick, and began to beat to pieces the garden herbs
of one of them; and when one monk saw him doing this, he
hid himself. And when only one root was left, the other brother
said unto him, "Father, if it please thee, leave me this root
" that I may boil it and we may eat together." Then the old
man made excuses to that brother, and said unto him, "The
" Spirit of God hath rested upon thee, O my brother."

Chapter vij. Of Obedience towards God, and towards our Fathers and Brethren

THEY say that Abbâ John, the disciple of Abbâ Paulê,
possessed great obedience. Now in the place where
they used to live there was a sepulchre, wherein dwelt
238. a savage panther, and Abbâ Paulê saw in it a few little
heaps of goods, and he said unto John, "Go to the sepulchre
" and bring me some of the things from there"; and John said
unto him, "My father, what shall I do with the panther?"
And the old man laughed and said unto him, "If he cometh
" against thee, tie him up and bring him here"; so John went
there at eventide, and the panther came against him, and when
he went to lay hold of him the animal fled from him. Then
John pursued him, saying, "My father told me to fetter thee,"
and he seized him, and bound him with cords. Meanwhile the
old man was very much troubled about John, and he was sitting
waiting for him anxiously; and behold, he came dragging along
the panther which was tied with ropes, and the old man saw
and marvelled. Then the brother said unto him, "Father, be-
" hold, I have taken prisoner the panther according as thou
" didst command, and I have brought him here"; and the old
man, wishing to remove from him the occasion for boasting,

smote him, and said, "Thou hast brought a wandering dog!" and he untied the animal and let him depart.

239. Abbâ Joseph used to say, "There are three things "which are held in honour before God: first, when a man is "sick, and he addeth to his toil, and receiveth it with thanks-"giving; secondly, when a man maketh all his works to be "pure before God, and when he hath in them no human con-"sideration; thirdly, when a man submitteth himself to autho-"rity, and obeyeth his father, and setteth aside his own will. "Such a man hath one crown the more, but I personally would "choose the sickness."

240. They used to say that Abbâ Sylvanus had in Scete a disciple whose name was Mark, and that he possessed to a great degree the faculty of obedience; he was a scribe, and the old man loved him greatly for his obedience. Now Sylvanus had eleven other disciples, and they were vexed because they saw that the old man loved Mark more than them, and when the old men who were in Scete heard [of this] they were afflicted about it. And one day when they came to him to reprove him about this, Sylvanus took them, and went forth, and passing by the cells of the brethren, he knocked at the door of each cell, and said, "O brother, come forth, for I have need of "thee"; and he passed by all their cells, and not one of them obeyed him quickly. But when they went to the cell of Mark, he knocked at the door and said, "Brother Mark," and as soon as Mark heard the voice of the old man, he jumped up straight-way, and came out, and Sylvanus sent him off on some busi-ness. Then Sylvanus said unto the old men, "My fathers, "where are the other brethren?" And they went into Mark's cell, and looked at the quire of the book which he was writing, and they saw that he had begun to write [one side of] the Greek letter o (or ω), and that as soon as he heard the voice of his master, [he ran out] and did not stay to complete the other side of the letter. Now when the old men perceived these things, they answered and said unto Sylvanus, "Verily, O old "man, we also love the brother whom thou lovest, for God "also loveth him."

241. On another occasion the mother of Mark came to see him, and she had with her an abundant company of members of her household; and an old man went forth to her, and she said unto him, "Abbâ, tell my son to come forth and see me"; and the old man went in, and said to him, "Go forth and see "thy mother." Then Mark wrapped himself up in rags, and blackened his face by standing up in the sooty chimney, and he went forth thus fulfilling the behest of his master, and shutting his eyes, he said unto those [who were with his

mother], "Live ye! Live ye!" but he did not look at them.
Now his mother did not recognize him, and she sent in again
to the old man a message, saying, "Send me my son, O father,
"so that I may see him." Then the old man said unto Mark,
"Did I not tell thee to go out and see thy mother?" And he
said unto him, "Father, I went forth according to thy word,
"but I beseech thee do not tell me to go forth again, lest per-
"adventure I feel myself compelled to disobey thee"; and [the
old man] spake with her, and quieted her, and sent her away
in peace.

242. And they used to tell about two brethren who lived in
a monastery, and who both had arrived at a high grade in the
ascetic life; the one devoted himself to an austere life of self-
denial and poverty, and the other was obedient and humble.
And being angry with each other they wished to know which
of the two [kinds of] service was the greater, and they went
down to the river where there were many crocodiles, and that
brother who possessed the faculty of obedience went in, and
stood up among them, and they all worshipped him. Then he
cried out to his fellow who was a mourner, and said unto him,
"Forgive me, O my brother, I have not yet attained to such
"a high degree of faith as thou hast"; and when they returned
to the monastery, the head of the monastery heard a voice,
saying, "The man who obeyeth is better than the man who
"leadeth a life of voluntary poverty."

243. Abbâ Daniel used to say, "On one occasion Abbâ
"Arsenius called me and said unto me, 'Make thy father to
"'be gratified, so that when he goeth to our Lord, he may
"'make entreaties to Him on behalf of thee, and good shall
"'be unto thee.'"

244. A certain brother was engaged in a war against Satan,
and he told the matter to Abbâ Herakles; and wishing to
strengthen and confirm him the old man told him the following
story:—There was a certain old man who had a disciple, and
he had been very obedient unto him for many years, and when
the war came upon him, he made a request to his master,
saying, "I beseech thee to make me a monk." And his master
said unto him, "Seek out a place for thyself, and we will build
"a cell for thee, and thou shalt become a monk." So the disciple went and found a place, which was distant from his
master about one hundred paces, and he made himself a cell.
Then the old man said unto that brother, "Whatsoever I say
"unto thee, that do. When thou art hungry, eat; and when
"thou art thirsty, drink; and sleep, but thou must not go out
"from thy cell until the Sabbath Day, when thou shalt come
"to me." Then the old man went back to his cell. And the

brother did according as the old man told him for two days,
but on the third day he became dejeƈted, and wearied, and
said, "What hath the old man done for me, seeing that he
"hath not commanded me to make prayers?" Then he rose up
and sang more Psalms than usual, and after the sun had set
he ate his food, and he rose up, and went, and lay down upon
his mat; and he saw, as it were, an Ethiopian who stood up
and gnashed his teeth at him, and the monk, by reason of his
great fear, ran quickly to his master, and he knocked hastily
at his door, saying, "Father, have mercy upon me, and open
"to me immediately." Now because the old man knew that
he had not kept his commandment he refused to open the door
to him until the morning, and when he opened the door in the
morning, he found him [there], and as the brother entreated
him to be allowed to enter, the old man had compassion upon
him and brought him in. Then he began to say unto the old
man, "I beseech thee, O father, [to believe me]. When I went
"to lie down to go to sleep, I saw a black Ethiopian on my
"bed." The old man said unto him, "This [happened] be-
"cause thou didst not keep my words." Then he laid down a
rule for him which was suitable to his strength and to the
monastic life, and dismissed him, and little by little he became
an excellent monk.

245. A man who wanted to be a monk came to Abbâ Sisoes
the Theban, and the old man asked him, if he had any possession whatsoever in the world, and he said, "I have one
"son"; and the old man, wishing to find out if he possessed
the faculty of obedience, said unto him, "Go, and throw him
"in the river, and then come, and thou shalt be a monk," and
because the man was obedient he went straightway to do it.
Now when he had departed the old man sent another brother
to prevent him from doing this thing, and when the man had
taken up his son to throw him into the river, the brother said
unto him, "Thou shalt not cast him in." Then the man said
unto him, "My father told me that I was to cast him in," and
the brother replied, "He told me that thou wast not to cast
"him in," so the man left him, and came [unto the old man],
and through his obedience he became a chosen monk.

246. The Abbâ who was in Îlîû used to say, "Obedience
"cometh into existence because of obedience; for if a man
"obeyeth God, God also will obey him."

247. On one occasion four brethren came to Abbâ Pambô
from Scete, and they were wearing skins, and each one of
them, whilst his neighbour was absent, recounted [to him]
his works, [saying], the first one fasteth very often, and the
second leadeth a life of poverty, and the third possesseth great

love, and concerning the fourth the other three said, "He hath "been in subjection to the old men for twenty-two years." Then Abbâ Pambô said unto them, "I say unto you that the "spiritual excellence of this man is great. Each of you hath "chosen the ascetic virtue which he possesseth according to "his own wish, but this man hath cut off his own desire, and "hath performed the will of others; and those who are thus "will, if they keep these things to the end, become confessors."

Chapter viij. Of Scrupulous Watchfulness in our Thoughts and Words and Deeds

ABBÂ POEMEN used to say, "Satan hath three kinds "of power which precede all sin. The first is error, and "the second is neglect (or laxity), and the third is lust. 248. "When error hath come it produceth neglect, and from "neglect springeth lust, and by lust man fell; if we watch "against error neglect will not come, and if we be not negligent, "lust will not appear, and if a man worketh not lust, he will, "through the help of Christ, never fall."

249. They used to say that there was a certain father who was [occupied] in great works, and that [on one occasion], when he was singing the Psalms and praying, one of the holy men came unto him, and he heard him striving with his thoughts, and saying, "How long for the sake of one thought wilt thou go "through all this?" Then the man who had come thought that the father was striving with another man, and he knocked at the door before going in to make peace between them; but when he had gone inside he saw no other man there. And because he possessed some authority over the father, he said unto him, "Father, with whom wast thou striving?" And he said, "With my thoughts. For I can repeat fourteen Books, but if "I hear one little word outside it will make useless my service "to me, and [the repetition] of all these Books will be in vain. "And this word only cometh and standeth before me at the "season of prayer, and it is because of this that I strive." And when the holy man heard [these things], he marvelled at the spiritual excellence and purity of the old man, and how openly he had told him about his war.

250. One of the old men used to say, "The Prophets com- "piled the Scriptures, and the Fathers have copied them, and "the men who came after them learned to repeat them by "heart; then hath come this generation and [its children] have "placed them in cupboards as useless things."

251. A disciple of Abbâ Ammon told the following story: "On one occasion when we were singing the service, my mind "became confused, and I forgot the verse in the Psalm; and

"when we had ended the service Ammon answered and said
"unto me, 'Whilst I was standing up during the service it
"'seemed that I was standing on fire and was being consumed,
"'and my mind was unable to make me turn aside either to the
"'right hand or to the left. And as for thee, where was thy mind
"'when we were singing the service? for thou didst omit a
"'verse from the Psalm. Didst thou not know that thou wast
"'standing in the presence of God, and that thou wast
"'speaking unto Him?'"

252. A certain brother came to dwell in a cell with one of the
fathers, and he told him of a thought whereby he was afflicted;
and the old man said unto him, "Thou hast left upon the earth
"the excellent service of the fear of God, and thou hast taken
"and hast laid hold upon a staff made of a reed, that is to say,
"evil thoughts. Take unto thyself the fear of God, which is the
"fire, and as soon as they come nigh unto thee they shall be
"burned like reeds." Now this man was, according to what his
disciple related about him, a great old man, and for twenty
years he never lay upon either of his sides, but slept upon the
seat whereon he sat to work. Sometimes he ate once in two
days, and at other times once in four days, and at others once
in five days, and in this manner he passed twenty years. Now
I said unto him, "What is this which thou doest, O father?"
And he said unto me, "Because I set the judgement of God
"before my eyes I cannot be negligent, for I keep in remem-
"brance [the fact that] my sins are many.

253. Whilst Abbâ Arsenius was dwelling in Canopus of
Alexandria a certain noble lady came to him; she was a virgin,
and was exceedingly rich, and she feared the Lord, and she was
from Rome and had come to see Abbâ Arsenius. Now Theophilus, Archbishop of Alexandria, received her, and she begged
him to entreat the old man to receive her. Then Theophilus
went to Abbâ Arsenius and entreated him, saying, "Such and
"such a noble lady hath come from Rome, and she wisheth to
"see thee, and to be blessed by thee"; but the old man refused
to receive her. And when Theophilus informed her that the old
man refused to receive her, she commanded them to make
ready the beasts [for travelling], and she said, "By God, I
"believe that I shall see him. I did not come to see men, for
"there are men in my own city, but I came to see a prophet."
And when she came outside the cell of the old man, he happened, through the working of God, to be there, and she saw
him, and fell down at his feet; then he lifted her up eagerly,
and looking at her, said, "If thou wishest to look upon my
"face, behold, look"; but she by reason of her bashfulness,
was not able to look upon his face. Then the old man said unto

her, "Hast thou not heard about my works, and that I am a "sinner? For it is these which it is necessary for thee to see. "How didst thou dare to travel hither by ship? Didst thou not "know that thou wast a woman, and that it was incumbent "upon thee not to go forth anywhere? Wouldst thou go back "to Rome and make a boast to the women [there] that thou "hast seen Arsenius, and dost thou wish to make the sea into "a road whereby women shall come unto me?" And the lady said unto him, "Please God I will not let any woman come "unto thee; but pray for me that God may have me in remem-"brance always." Then Abbâ Arsenius said unto her, "I will "pray to God that He may blot out the memory of thee from my "heart"; and when she heard these words she went forth, being afraid. Now as soon as she had come to the city a fever began to come upon her because of her grief of mind, and the people told the Bishop, saying, "That noble lady is ill"; and he came to her, and entreated her that he might learn the cause of her sickness. Then she said unto him, "Would that I never had journeyed "thither! For I said unto the old man Arsenius, 'Make mention "'of me in prayer,' and he said unto me, 'I will pray unto God "'that He may blot out the remembrance of thee from my heart,' "and behold I shall die of grief." And the Archbishop said unto her, "Dost thou not know that thou art a woman, and that "the Enemy doeth battle with the holy men by means of wo-"men? It was for this reason that the old man spake as he "did; for thy soul, however, he will pray always." And the noble lady remembered [these things] in her mind, and she rose up, and went to her country with gladness.

254. They say that Abbâ Hôr (or Ôr) of the Cells dwelt for twenty years in the church, and that he never once lifted his eyes and saw the roof thereof.

255. Abbâ Ammon asked Abbâ Poemen about the unclean thoughts which a man begetteth, and about vain lusts; Abbâ Poemen said unto him, "Peradventure shall an axe boast itself "without him that heweth therewith? (Isaiah x, 15.) Do not "henceforward aid these thoughts and they will come to an "end."

256. They say concerning Abbâ Paphnutius, the disciple of Abbâ Macarius, that when he was a youth he used to look after the oxen with others of his companions; and they went to take some cucumbers to the animals, and as they were going along one of the cucumbers fell, and Abbâ Paphnutius took it up and ate it, and whensoever he remembered this thing, he used to sit down and weep over it with great feeling.

257. One of the fathers went to Abbâ Akîlâ and saw that he was throwing up blood from his mouth, and he asked him,

saying, "What is this, O father?" and the old man said unto
him, "It is a word. I was vexed with a certain brother, and
"I was engaged in a strife of which I knew nothing, and I
"made supplication to God that it might be taken from me;
"and straightway that word became blood in my mouth, but
"when I spat it up I was relieved, and I forgot my vexation."

258. One of the old men used to say: "We were going [on
"one occasion] to the mountain of the blessed Anthony to visit
"Abbâ Sisoes, and when he sat down to eat there came up to
"us a young man who begged for alms; and when we were
"beginning to eat, the old man said, 'Ask that young man if he
" 'wisheth to come in and eat with us.' Now when one had
"said this to him, the young man refused [to do so], and the
"old man said, 'Let whatsoever is left over by us be given to
" 'him to eat outside.' Then the old man brought out a jar of
"wine which he kept for the Offering, and he mixed for each
"one of us a cup, but he gave to the young man two cups,
"whereat I smiled, and said unto him, 'I also will go outside,
" 'and thou shalt give me two cups of wine also.' Abbâ Sisoes
"said, 'If he had eaten with us he would have drunk the same
" 'quantity as ourselves, and he would have have been con-
" 'vinced that we did not drink more than he did; but now he
" 'will say in his mind, These monks enjoy themselves more
" 'than I do. It is good therefore that our conscience should
" 'not hold us in contempt.' "

259. One of the old men came to another old man who was
his companion, and as they were talking together one of them
said, "I have died to the world"; and his companion said,
"Have no confidence in thyself that this is so until thou goest
"forth from the world, for although thou sayest, 'I have died,'
"Satan is not dead."

260. A brother asked Abbâ Sisoes, saying, "Tell me a word
"[whereby I may live]." The old man saith unto him, "Why
"dost thou urge me, O brother, to speak a useless word? What-
"soever thou seest me do, that do thyself."

261. A brother asked Abbâ Poemen, saying, "Is it possible
"for a man to keep hold upon all thoughts, and not to give
"any of them to the Enemy?" The old man said unto him,
"There are some of them who give ten and keep one, and
"there are some who give one and keep ten." And the brother
told this saying to Abbâ Sisoes, who said, "There are some
"who do not give even one [thought] to the Enemy."

262. Abbâ Joseph asked Abbâ Sisoes, saying, "How many
"times is it right for a man to cut off his passions?" The old
said unto him, "Dost thou wish to learn when thou must cut
"them off?" and Joseph said unto him, "Yes." Abbâ Sisoes

said unto him, "Whensoever passion cometh cut it off im-
"mediately."

263. Abbâ Nastîr and a certain brother were walking together in the desert, and they saw a serpent, and both took to
flight; and the brother said to Nastîr, "Father, art thou also
"afraid?" The old man said unto him, "My son, I am not
"afraid, but it was a beneficial thing for me to flee, for other-
"wise I should not have been able to escape from the thought
"of the love of approbation."

264. Certain men who lived in the world came to see Abbâ
Sisoes, and though they spoke much he held his peace and answered them never a word; at length one of them said to his
companions, "My brethren, why do ye trouble the old man?
"He eateth not, and for this reason he is not able to talk."
And when the old man heard this, he made answer unto them
straightway, and said, "My sons, I eat whensoever I feel the
"need of eating."

265. On one occasion a certain judge of the district wished to
see Abbâ Poemen, but the old man refused [to see him]. And,
like a crafty man, the judge made an excuse, and seized Abbâ's
nephew, and threw him into prison, saying, "Unless Abbâ
"cometh and maketh entreaty on his behalf he shall not go
"out." Then Abbâ's sister came and stood by the door of his
cell and wept for her son, but although she importuned him
greatly, he did not give her an answer; now when the woman
saw this she began to revile him, saying, "O thou who pos-
"sessest mercy of brass, have mercy upon me, for my son is
"the only [child] I have." And Abbâ Poemen sent her a message, saying, "Poemen hath no sons," and thus she departed.
And when the judge heard [these things] he answered and said,
"If Abbâ will only give the order I will release him"; and after
this the old man sent him a message, saying, "Examine and
"consider his case according to the Law, and if he be worthy
"of death, let him die; and if he be not do whatsoever thou
"pleasest with him."

266. They say that in the mountain of Abbâ Anthony seven
brethren dwelt, each of whom used to watch in the date season and drive away the birds; and among them was an old
man who, when it was his day for watching [the dates], used
to cry out, saying, "Depart, O ye evil thoughts, from within,
"and depart, O ye birds, from without."

267. On one occasion the Arabs came and plundered Abbâ
Sisoes and the brother who was with him of everything they
had, and being hungry, the brethren went out into the desert
to find something to eat. And when they were some distance
from each other, Abbâ Sisoes found some camel dung, and he

broke it, and found inside two grains of barley; and he ate one grain and placed the other in his hand; and when the brother came, and found that he was eating, he said unto him, " Is " this love ? Thou hast found food, and thou eatest it by thy- " self and hast not called me [to share it with thee]." Abbâ Sisoes saith unto him, " I have not defrauded thee, O brother, " for behold, I have kept thy share in my hands."

268. Mother Sarah used to say, " Whensoever I put my foot " on the ladder to go up, before I ascend it I set my death be- "fore mine eyes."

269. A certain brother came to Abbâ Theodore and entreated him to shew him how he twisted palm leaves, and he sent him away, saying, "Go away, and come here to-morrow morning." Then the old man rose up straightway, and put some leaves to soak in water, and made ready, and when the brother came in the morning he shewed him [how to make] one or two plaits, and he said to him, " Work thus"; and the old man left him and went to his cell. And at the proper season the old man took him food and made him eat, and he rose up and went away; and when he came [back again] in the morning, the old man said unto him, " Why didst thou not take some palm " leaves with thee? Take some now, and get thee gone, for " thou hast made me fall into the temptation of caring about " things," and he did not allow him to come inside [his cell] again.

270. On one occasion Abbâ Muthues went from Re'îth to Mount Gebêl, and he had with him his brother 'Awsâbh, and Kântîrsâ, the Bishop, took the old man and made him a priest. And when they were eating together the Bishop said unto him, " Forgive me, Abbâ, for I know that thou didst not wish for " this thing, but I ventured to do this thing that I might be " blessed by thee." Then the old man said unto him with a meek spirit, and with a sorrowful mind, "I will labour in this work, " though I must be separated from this my brother who is with " me, for I cannot endure the making of all the prayers." The Bishop said unto him, " If thou knewest that he is worthy I " will make him a priest also"; and Abbâ Muthues said unto him, " Whether he be worthy [or not] I do not know, but one " thing I know, and that is, that he is better than I am," so the Bishop laid his hands upon him and made him a priest al- so. And they ended their lives together, but one of them never approached the altar for the purpose of offering up the Offer- ing, for the old man used to say, " By God, I hope that ordi- " nation doth not make it obligatory on me to do so, because " I cannot offer up the Offering, for ordination belongeth un- " to those who are pure [only]."

271. A certain brother in Scete called one of his companions to come to him in his cell to wash his feet, and he did not go; and twice and thrice he said, " Come to [my] cell, and wash " thy feet," and he went not. And at length the brother went to him, and made excuses to him, and entreated him to go with him, and he rose up and went ; and the brother said unto him, " How is it that thou didst not come when I entreated thee so " often to do so? " And he answered and said unto him, " Whilst thou wast speaking my will would not consent to my " coming, but when I saw that thou wast doing the work of " monks, that is to say, repenting, then I rejoiced and came."

272. On one occasion when the old man Zeno was walking in Palestine, he became weary, and he sat down by the side of a cucumber bed to eat; and his thought said to him, " Take " a cucumber and eat, for of what value is one cucumber?" And he answered and said to his thought, " Those who steal " go to torment; try thy soul, then, and see if it be able to en- " dure the torment." And he crucified himself in the heat for five days, and having tortured himself he said unto his thought, " I cannot endure that torment; how then can the man who " cannot do this steal and eat?"

273. They say that on one occasion, when it was time for Abbâ Poemen to go to the congregation for the service, he sat down for about one hour examining and passing judgement upon his thoughts, and that at the end of this time he went forth.

274. They say that a certain old man dwelt by himself in silence, and that a son of the world used to minister unto him continually; and it happened that the son of that son of the world fell sick, and his father entreated the old man to go with him to his house and to pray over him, and, when he had entreated him to do so often, the old man went forth and departed with him. And the man went before him and entered the village, and he said unto the people thereof, "Come forth " to meet the monk"; now when the old man saw the people from afar off, and perceived that they had come forth to meet him carrying lanterns, straightway he stripped off his garments, and dipped them in the river, and he began to wash them, being naked. And when the man who ministered unto him saw [this], he was ashamed, and he entreated the people of the village, saying, " Get ye back, for the old man hath cer- " tainly gone mad"; then he approached the old man, and said unto him, " Father, what is this which thou hast done? For " all the people are saying that the old man hath a devil." And the old man said, " This is what I wished to hear."

275. Paesius on one occasion had strife with the brother who

was with him whilst Abbâ Poemen was sitting by, and they
fought with each other until the blood ran down from both
their heads; and although the old man saw [them] he uttered
no word whatsoever. Then Abbâ Job came and found them
fighting, and he said to Poemen, "Why hast thou let these
"brethren fight, and hast said nothing to them whilst they
"have been fighting?" Abbâ Poemen said unto him, "They are
"brethren, and will become reconciled again." Abbâ Job said,
"What is this that thou hast said? Thou seest that they con-
"tinue to fight, and yet thou sayest that they will be reconciled
"again." Abbâ Poemen said unto him, "Thou must think in
"thy heart that I am not here."

276. Mother Sarah sent a message to Abbâ Paphnutius,
saying, "Dost thou think that thou art doing God's work in
"allowing thy brother to be reviled?" Abbâ Paphnutius saith,
"Paphnutius is here doing the work of God, and I have no
"concern whatsoever about man."

277. The old man Poemen used to say, "Thou shalt have no
"dealings whatsoever with a child of the world, and thou shalt
"hold no converse with women"; and he also said, "Thou
"shalt possess no knowledge of the judge (or governor), lest,
"when thou hearest his words, thou perform his work."

278. One of the old men used to say, "I have never taken
"one step forwards without first of all learning where I was
"about to set my foot, and I have neither crossed my boun-
"dary to walk on a height, nor have I descended into a deep
"place, and been troubled by so doing; for my only care hath
"been to beseech God until He brought me forth from the
"old man."

279. On one occasion the brethren were gathered together
in Scete that they might enquire into the history of Melchisedek,
and they forgot to invite Abbâ Copres to be with them; finally,
however, they did call him, and they enquired of him concerning the matter. And he smote three times on his mouth, and
said, "Woe be to thee! Woe be to thee, O Copres, for thou
"hast left undone what God commanded thee to do, and thou
"art enquired of concerning the things which God hath not
"demanded of thee"; and they all left the place and fled to
their cells.

280. An old man used to say, "Freedom of speech (or bold-
"ness) is a wind which parcheth, and it smiteth the fruit at
"the harvest."

281. An old man used to say, "The act of despising oneself
"is a strong fence for a man."

282. The old man said, "The withdrawal in secret [from
"works] maketh dark the understanding, but the persisting

"in endurance with vigilance illuminateth and strengtheneth
"the soul of a man."

283. An old man used to say, "Laughter and familiar talk-
"ing are like unto the fire which kindleth among the reeds."

284. Certain heretics came on one occasion to Abbâ Poemen,
and they began to calumniate the Archbishop of Alexandria,
and to speak evil things concerning him, and they sought to
prove that as they had received consecration from the priests,
they were consecrated like [other] priests; and the old man
held his peace. Then he called his brother, and said unto him,
"Make ready a table and make them eat," and he dismissed
them that they might depart in peace.

285. Some of the old men asked Abbâ Poemen, saying, "If
"we see one of the brethren committing sin, wouldst thou
"have us rebuke him?" And the old man said unto them,
"If I had some business which made me pass by him, and in
"passing by him I saw him committing sin, I should pass him
"by and not see him."

286. And the old man also said, "It is written, 'Whatsoever
"'thine eyes have seen, that declare.' But I say unto you, that
"unless ye have not first touched with your hands, ye shall not
"testify. For on one occasion the devil led astray a brother in
"a matter of this kind. This brother saw a brother committing
"sin with a woman, and the war being strong against him, he
"went to them, thinking that what he saw was really a man
"and a woman, and he kicked them with his foot, and said,
"'Enough, enough, how long [will ye act thus]?' And sud-
"denly he discovered that the things were sacks of wheat.
"For this reason I say unto you that unless ye have felt with
"your hands ye should not offer rebuke."

287. One of the fathers related a story, saying:—On one occasion in Scete when the clergy were offering up the Offering,
something which was like unto an eagle descended upon the
Offering, and no man saw the appearance except the clergy;
and one day a brother questioned the deacon about the matter,
and the deacon said unto him, "I am not at leisure now [to
"discuss it]." And afterwards when the time arrived for the
Offering, and the clergy went in as usual to offer It up, the
form of the eagle did not appear as it did before; and the priest
said unto the deacon, "What is this? The eagle hath not come
"as usual, and the fault of this lieth either upon me or thee.
"But get thee gone from me, and if the eagle then appeareth
"and descendeth, it will be evident that it did not come down
"now because of thee, and if it doth not descend thou wilt know
"that the fault is mine." Now as soon as the deacon had departed, the eagle appeared as usual, and after the Office had

been said, and the service was ended, the priest said unto the deacon, "Tell me what thou hast done." And the deacon, wishing to shew him everything, made excuses, saying, "I "am not conscious in my soul of having committed any sin, "except when a brother came to me, and asked me a question "on the matter, and I made answer to him, saying, 'I am not at "'leisure [to talk] with thee.'" Then the priest said, "It was "because of thee that the eagle came not down, for the brother "was offended at thee"; and straightway the deacon went to the brother, and expressed his contrition, and entreated him [to forgive] him his offence.

288. They used to speak about a certain father, who for seven years asked God to give him a certain gift, and [at length] it was given unto him; and he went to a great old man and told him about the gift, and when the old man heard thereof, he was grieved, and said, "What great labour!" Then he said unto the father, "Go and spend seven years more in entreat-"ing God that the gift may be taken away from thee, for it will "do thee no good"; and the old man went, and did as he had told him until the gift was taken away from him.

289. A certain brother dwelt in a cell outside his village, and he had passed many years without going into the vil-lage; and he said unto the brethren who were with him, "Be-"hold, how many years have I lived here without going into "the village, whilst ye are always going therein." Now Abbâ Poemen was told about this man, and that he used to say words of this kind to the brethren, and he said, "If I were "[that man] I would go up and walk round about in the vil-"lage during the night, so that my thoughts might not be "able to boast themselves that I had not gone into it."

290. One of the fathers said, "God beareth with the sins of "those who live in the world, but He will not endure the sins "of those who live in the desert."

291. Abbâ Job used to say, "Since the time when I was "[first] called by the Name of Christ, falsehood hath never "gone forth from my mouth."

292. Abbâ Poemen used to say, "If a man dwelleth with a "youth, however much he may guard his thoughts he maketh "a means for sin."

293. A certain brother asked an old man, saying, "What "shall I do because of my negligence?" The old man said unto him, "If thou wilt root out this small plant, which is negli-"gence, a great forest will come into being."

294. Abbâ Poemen used to say, "Do not dwell in a place "wherein thou seest that there are those who have envy "against thee, for if thou dost thou wilt never advance."

295. Abbâ Chronius used to say, "The man who dwelleth
" with a youth will, unless he be mighty, go downwards, and if
" he be mighty, even though he doth not go downwards tempo-
" rarily, yet he will never advance in spiritual excellence."

296. Abbâ Anthony used to say, "There are some monks
" who vex their bodies with the labours of abstinence and self-
" denial, and who, because they have not found understanding,
" are remote from the path of God."

297. Abbâ Poemen used to say, "Teach thy heart to keep
" that which thy tongue teacheth."

298. Abbâ Poemen used to say, "One man is thought to be
"silent, yet his heart condemneth others, and he who is thus
" speaketh everything; and another speaketh from morn until
" evening, and yet keepeth silence, but such a man speaketh
" not without profit."

299. I have heard that there were two old men who dwelt
together for many years, and who never quarrelled, and that
one said to the other, "Let us also pick a quarrel with each
" other, even as other men do." Then his companion answered
and said unto him, "I know not how a quarrel cometh," and
the other old man answered and said unto him, "Behold, I
" will set a brick in the midst, and will say, 'This is mine,'
" and do thou say, 'It is not thine, but mine'; and from this
" quarrelling will ensue." And they placed a brick in the midst,
and one of them said, "This is mine," and his companion answered and said after him, "This is not so, for it is mine";
and straightway the other replied and said unto him, "If it
" be so, and the brick be thine, take it and go." Thus they
were not able to make a quarrel.

300. There was a certain brother who lived a life of very
strict seclusion, and the devils, wishing to lead him astray,
[used to appear] to him, when he was sleeping at night, in the
form of angels, and wake him up to sing the Psalms and pray,
and they would shew him a light. And he went to an old man,
and said unto him, "Father, the devils come to me with a light
" and wake me up to sing and pray"; and the old man said
unto him, "Hearken not unto them, O my son, for they are
" devils, but, if they come to wake thee up, say unto them,
" 'When I wish to rise up I will do so, but unto you I will not
" 'hearken.'" And when they came to wake him he said unto
them what the old man had told him, and they said unto him
forthwith, "That wicked old man is a liar, and he hath led
" thee astray. For a certain brother came to him and wished
" to borrow some oboli on a pledge, and although he had
" money to lend, he lied and said, 'I have none,' and he gave
" him none, and learn from this thing that he is a liar." Then

the brother rose up early in the morning and went to the old
man and related unto him everything which he had heard, and
the old man said unto him, "The matter is thus. I had some
"oboli, and a brother came and asked me for some money,
"and I would not give him any because I saw that if I did so
"we should arrive at the loss of [our] soul[s]. And I made up
"my mind that I would treat with contempt one of the com-
"mandments, and not ten, and [therefore] we came to en-
"mity [with each other]. But do thou hearken not unto the
"devils who wish to lead thee astray." And when he had been
greatly confirmed by the old man, that monk departed to his
cell.

301. Abbâ Isaac, the priest of the Cells, said, "I saw a cer-
"tain brother reaping the harvest in the field, and he wanted
"to eat one ear of wheat; and he said to the owner of the field,
"'Dost thou wish me to take one ear of wheat to eat?' And
"the owner of the field wondered (now he profited greatly
"therefrom), and said unto him, 'My son, the field is thine,
"'and dost thou ask [my] permission to eat?' To this extent
"did that brother shew scrupulous care."

302. A brother asked an old man, and said unto him, "What
"shall I do? For the thoughts which make war with me are
"many, and I know not how to contend against them." The
old man said unto him, "Do not strive against them all, but
"against one, for all devilish thoughts have only one head,
"and it is necessary for a man to understand and to make war
"upon this head only, for afterwards all the rest will perforce
"be brought low. Just as in war, if on one side a very mighty
"man appear, the men on the other side use every means in
"their power to set up in opposition to him a mighty man who
"is stronger than he is, because, if he be able to hurl down
"that chief, all the rest will take to flight and be van-
"quished. In this same manner there is one head to all the
"thoughts which come from devils, whether it be fornica-
"tion, or riotous living, or love of money, or wandering about
"from place to place, for if thou wilt first of all recognize it
"and wilt drive it out, it will not lead thee astray in respect
"of other things." And [when] that chief thought came, and
stood up and fought against him, he recognized which it was,
and contended against it only.

303. Abbâ Lôt went to Abbâ Joseph, and said unto him,
"Father, according to my strength I sing a few Psalms, and
"I pray a little, and my fasting is little, and my prayers and
"silent meditations [are few], and as far as lieth in my power
"I cleanse my thoughts, what more can I do?" Then the old
man stood up, and spread out his hands towards heaven, and

his fingers were like unto ten lamps of fire, and he said unto him, "If thou wishest, let the whole of thee be like unto fire."

304. A certain brother entreated one of the old men to interpret to him some words which he had asked him, saying, "If I see a man doing something, and I tell others about it, I "mean not by way of passing judgement upon him, but merely "for the sake of conversation, would this be considered as "evil talk of the thoughts?" The old man said unto him, "If "there be any motion of passion the repetition is wicked, but "if it be free from passion the repetition is not wicked, but "speak in such a way that evil increase not." And another brother made answer to the old man, and said, "If I come to one "of the old men and ask him, saying, 'I wish to dwell with such "'and such a man, [may I do so?]' and I know at the same "time that it will not be profitable for me, what answer must "he make me? If he saith, 'Thou shalt not go,' hath he not "condemned that man in his mind?" Then the old man answered and said unto him, "This refinement [of thought] is "not [given] to many, and I do not regard it as a sure mat-"ter. If there be any passion in the motion of the soul I "should say that he would injure himself; but in words there "is no power [to do so]. And as to 'What is he bound to "'say?' I say that I do not know, if his soul be [not] free "[from passion]; but if it be free from passions he will not "condemn any man, and he will condemn himself, and say, "'I am a changeable person,' now perhaps [this] will not help "thee, but if he be a man of understanding he will not go." Now the old man did not speak concerning wickedness, but only that wickedness might not be multiplied.

305. Abbâ Arsenius said unto Abbâ Alexander, "When thou "hast finished the work of thy hands, come to me and we will "eat; but if strangers come, eat with them, and do not come "to me." Now Alexander continued at his work late, and when the time for the meal had arrived, and palm leaves were still standing before him, although he was anxious to keep the word of the old man, he also wanted to finish up the leaves, and then to go to him. Now when the old man saw that Abbâ Alexander delayed [in coming] to eat, he thought that it was because strangers had come to him. And when Abbâ Alexander had finished his work he went to the old man, who said unto him, "Did "strangers come to thee?" And Alexander said unto him, "No, "father." Then the old man said unto him, "Why hast thou "delayed [in coming]?" And Alexander answered and said unto him, "Because thou didst say unto me, 'When thou hast "'finished thy leaves come to me'; and paying heed to thy "word, and having finished [my work], behold, I have come."

And the old man marvelled at this scrupulous obedience, and
said unto him, "Make haste and perform thy service of praise
"and prayer, and bring it to an end, and drink some water,
"for if thou dost not do it quickly thy body will become sick."

306. Abbâ Poemen used to say often, "We need nothing
"except a watchful and strenuous heart."

307. A brother asked Abbâ Poemen, saying, "How is it
"right for me to live in the place wherein I am?" The old
man saith unto him, "Acquire the thought of sojourning in
"the place where thou livest, and desire not to cast thy word
"among the multitude, or to be the first to speak, and thou
"wilt find rest."

308. Abbâ Agathon said concerning Abbâ Mûaîn that, on
one occasion, he made fifty bushels of wheat into bread for
the needs of the community, and then laid it out in the sun,
but before it became dry and hard he saw something in the
place which was not helpful to him, and he said to the brethren
who were with him, "Arise, let us go hence"; and they were
greatly grieved. And when he saw that they were grieved, he
said unto them, "Are ye troubled about the bread? Verily I
"have seen men take to flight and forsake their cells, although
"they were well whitewashed and contained cupboards which
"were filled with books of the Holy Scriptures and service
"books, and they did not even shut the cupboard doors, but
"departed leaving them wide open."

309. Abbâ Copres used to say, "Blessed is the man who
"beareth temptation with thanksgiving."

310. Abbâ Poemen used to say, "The mighty ones have
"been many, and those who never felt envy have been many,
"and they have neither been jealous in an evil way, nor have
"they stirred up their own passions."

311. Abbâ Sisoes used to say, "Seek the Lord, and search
"[Him] out, but not only in the place where [thou] dwellest."

312. An old man used to say, "Eat not before thou art
"hungry; lie not down to sleep before thou art sleepy; and
"speak not before thou art asked a question."

313. An old man used to say, "Prepare not a table before
"the time when thou art alone, and speak not before thou art
"asked a question, and if thou art asked a question, speak
"that which is fair and helpful, and not that which is evil and
"destructive."

314. Abbâ Euprepius said, "If thou art not certain in thy-
"self that God is faithful and mighty, believe in Him, and
"associate thyself with those who are His, but if thou art
"doubtful thou canst not believe. For we all believe and con-
"fess that God is mighty, and we are certain that all things

"are easy for Him [to do]; do thou then also shew thy belief
"in Him by thy works, for in thee also He worketh miracles,
"and doeth wonders, and sheweth forth marvels."

315. Abbâ Theodore used to say, "If thou hast affection
"for a man, and it happeneth that he fall into temptation,
"stretch out thy hand to him, and lift him up therefrom, but
"if he fall into heresy, and will not be persuaded by thee to
"return, cut him off from thee immediately, lest, if thou tarry
"long with him, thou be drawn unto him, and thou sink down
"into the uttermost depths."

316. One of the fathers used to tell the story of Abbâ John,
the Persian, who by reason of the abundance of his spiritual
excellence arrived at goodness; now this man used to dwell
in the Arabia of Egypt. And on one occasion he borrowed one
dînâr from a brother, and bought some flax to weave, and a
brother came and entreated him, saying, " Give me a little flax
"that I may make a tunic for myself "; and he gave it to him
with joy; and then another [brother] entreated him, saying,
"Give me a little flax that I may make myself a turban,"
and he gave unto him also, and the man departed. And many
other brethren borrowed from him, and he gave them [the flax]
with rejoicing; but finally the owner of the dînâr came, and
wanted to take it back. Then the old man said unto him, " I
"will go and bring it to thee," but as he had no place wherefrom he could give it to him, he rose up and went to Abbâ
Jacob, so that he might persuade him to give him a dînâr
wherewith to repay the brother; and as he was going he found
a dînâr lying on the ground, but he was not disposed to offer
it to him, so he prayed and returned to his cell. And the brother
came again and pressed him to let him have what was his own,
and the old man said unto him, " Have patience with me this
"time only, and I will bring it to you." And he again rose up and
went to that place where he had found the daric, and, having
made a prayer, he took it. And he came to the old man Jacob,
and said unto him, " As I was coming to you, O father, I found
"this dînâr on the road. Do now, O father, an act which is
"worthy of love, and make a proclamation throughout these bor-
"ders, for perhaps some one hath lost the dînâr, and if its owner
"be found, give it unto him." Then the old man went, and made
a proclamation for three days, and he could not find the man
who had lost the dînâr. Then the old man said unto Abbâ Jacob,
" If no man hath lost the dînâr give it unto that brother to
"whom I owe one, for I was coming to obtain one from thee
"for the Lord's sake, when I found it." And the old man Jacob
marvelled at him, because, although he owed a dînâr, and had
found one, he did not immediately take it and pay his debt.

Of Watchfulness

Now this habit also was found with that old man who owed
the dînâr: if any man came and wanted to borrow something
from him, he did not give it unto him with his own hands, but
he said unto him, "Take for thyself whatsoever thou wish-
"est"; and when the man brought back that which he had
taken, the old man would say unto him, "Place it where thou
"didst take it from," and if he did not bring it back he would
say to him nothing at all.

317. Abbâ Daniel used to say that on one occasion certain
fathers came from Alexandria to see Abbâ Arsenius, and one
of them was the brother of Timothy, Patriarch of Alexandria,
and they were taking his nephew also. Now the old man was
ill at that season, and he did not wish to spend much time
with them, lest, peradventure, they should come to visit him
another time and trouble him; and he was then living in Patârâ
of Estôrîs, and the fathers went back sorrowfully. And it happened on one occasion that the barbarians invaded the country,
and then Abbâ Arsenius came and dwelt in the lower countries;
and when those same fathers heard [of his coming] they went
to see him, and he received them with gladness. Then the
brother who belonged to them said unto him, "Father, know-
"est thou not that when [these fathers] came to thee on the
"first occasion at Estôrîs thou didst not protract thy conversa-
"tion with us?" The old man said unto him, "My son, ye ate
"bread, and ye drank water, in very truth, but I refused to eat
"bread and drink water, and I would not sit upon my legs
"through torturing myself, until the time when I knew from ex-
"perience that ye must have arrived at your homes, for I knew
"that for my sake ye had given yourselves trouble." Thus they
were pleased and gratified in their minds and they departed
rejoicing.

318. Abbâ Daniel used to say: Abbâ Alexander dwelt with
Abbâ Agathon, and the old man loved Abbâ Alexander because
he was a man of labour, and he was gentle and gracious. And
it happened that all the brethren were washing their linen
armcloths in the river, and Alexander was quietly washing his
with them ; but the brethren said unto Abbâ Agathon, "Bro-
"ther Alexander doeth nothing," and the old man, wishing to
quiet his disciples, said unto him, "Wash well, O brother, for
"the armcloth is [made] of linen." Now when Alexander
heard [this] he was grieved, and afterwards the old man entreated him, saying, "What then? Do I not know that thou
"canst wash well? But I spake as I did to thee before them
"so that I might rebuke their minds by thine obedience."

319. They used to say that one day when Abbâ John came
to the church which was in Scete he heard the brethren quar-

relling with each other, and that he went back to his cell, and
went round it three times, and then entered it; now the brethren saw him, and they expressed their contrition to him,
saying, "Tell us why thou didst go round thy cell three times."
And he said unto them, "Because the sound of the quarrel
"was still in my ears, and I said, 'I will first of all drive it
"'out from them, and then I will go into the cell.'"

320. They used to say about Abbâ 'Ôr that whilst other
monks would give a pledge for the palm leaves when they
wished to buy, he would never give any pledge whatsoever,
but whensoever he required leaves he would send the price of
them, and take them. Now his disciple went on one occasion
to buy leaves, and the gardener said unto him, "A man gave
"me a deposit, but he hath not taken away his leaves, and
"therefore thou mayest take them"; and having brought them
he came to the old man and related unto him the matter as
it had happened. And when the old man heard it, he wrung his
hands, and said, "'Ôr will not work this year," and he did
not cease [to importune] his disciple until he had returned the
palm leaves to their [proper] place.

321. They used to tell the story of a certain brother who
never ate bread, but only unleavened cakes soaked in water;
and whenever he visited the monks when they sat down to eat
he would set before himself unleavened cakes and eat [them].
And it happened that one day he went to a certain great Sage,
and there also visited him at the same time other strangers,
and the old man boiled a few lentiles for them; and when they
sat down to eat that brother also brought out his soaked
cakes, and set them before himself, and ate them. Now when
the old man saw this, he held his peace and did not rebuke
him before the brethren who happened to be there, but when
they rose up from the table, he took him aside privately, and
said unto him, "O brother, if thou goest to visit a man do not
"reveal thy rule of life, but eat with the brethren that thou
"mayest not think within thyself that thou art better than
"they, and so condemn them. But if thou wishest to keep hold
"upon thy self-denial, sit in thy cell and do not go out of it."
Then the brother was persuaded by the old man, and he ate
with the brethren what they ate so as to deceive them, according to what the old man had said.

322. A certain father whose name was Eulogius, having led
a life of great austerity and labour in Constantinople, obtained
great fame and reputation; and he came to Egypt in order that
he might see something more excellent, and when he heard
about Abbâ Joseph he came to him, expecting to see a very
much more laborious form of life than his own. And the old

man received him with gladness, and said unto his disciple,
"Make some distinction in the food which ye have to prepare,
"and let it be suitable for strangers." Now when they had sat
down to eat, those who were with Abbâ Eulogius said, "Bring
"a little salt, for the father will not eat this"; but Abbâ
Joseph ate, and drank, and held his peace. And Eulogius
passed three days with him, but he never heard them singing
the Psalms, and he never saw them praying, for every act of
worship which they performed was in secret; and he went
forth from them having profited in no wise. And by the Providence of God it happened that they lost their way, and they
returned the same day, and they came and stood at the door
of the old man's cell; and before they could knock at the door,
Eulogius heard them singing the Psalms inside, and having
waited for a long time, they knocked, and immediately those
of the company of Joseph who were singing inside stopped.
Now when Eulogius and those who were with him had gone
inside the old man received them again with gladness, and because of the heat which they had endured, Abbâ Joseph's
monks gave Eulogius [some] water to drink; and this water
was a mixture, part being sea water and part being river water,
and when Eulogius had tasted it he was unable to drink it.
Then he repented within himself, and he went in to Abbâ
Joseph and fell down at his feet, and entreated him to be allowed to learn his rule, for he wished so to do, and he said,
"What doth this mean? When we were with you ye sang no
"Psalms, but as soon as we have left you ye perform services
"overmuch. And when I want to drink water I find it to be
"salt." The old man said unto him, "It was brother Sylvanus
"who did this, and he mixed the water without knowing";
and Eulogius entreated him [to tell him about it], for he wished
to learn the truth. Thereupon Abbâ Joseph said unto him,
"That mixture of wine which we drink we drink for the sake
"of the love of Christ, but the brethren always drink this
"water." And Abbâ Joseph taught him the difference [be-
tween their rules of life], and that he toiled in secret and not
before the children of men; and he ate a meal at the same table
with them, and he partook of whatsoever was set thereupon;
and Eulogius learned that, even as the old man had said,
Abbâ Joseph performed his ascetic labours in secret, and having profited greatly he departed with gladness, giving thanks
unto God.

323. On one occasion there was a feast, and the brethren
were eating in the church; and there was among them a brother who said unto him that ministered at the tables, "I do
"not eat boiled food, but bread and salt," and the servant

cried out to certain other brethren before the whole assembly,
saying, "Such and such a brother doth not eat boiled food,
"therefore bring him salt." Then one of the old men came to
that brother, and said unto him, "It would have been better
"for thee this day to have eaten flesh in thy cell than that this
"word should have been heard before the whole assembly."

324. On one occasion Ammon came to the brethren, and the
brethren expressed contrition, saying, "Tell us a word [where-
"by we may live]." The old man said unto them, "It is this:
"we must travel along the path of God with due order."

325. They used to say that the face of Abbâ Panbô never
smiled or laughed. Now one day when the devils wished to
make him laugh, they hung a feather on a piece of wood, and
they carried it along and danced about therewith in great haste,
and they cried out, "Hâilâw, Hâilâw." Now when Abbâ
Panbô saw them, he laughed, and the devils began to run
and jump about, saying, "Wâwâ, Abbâ Panbô hath laughed."
Then Abbâ Panbô answered and said unto them, "I did not
"laugh [for myself], but I laughed at your weakness, and be-
"cause it needeth so many of you to carry a feather."

326. On one occasion a certain brother committed an offence
in the coenobium, and in the places which were therein a certain old man had his abode; now he had not gone out of his
cell for many years. And when the Abbâ of the coenobium came
to the old man he told concerning the folly (*or* offence) of that
brother, and about his transgression. Then the old man answered and said, "Drive him out from you"; and when that
brother was driven out, he departed and went into a reedy
jungle, and as some brethren happened to pass by to go to
Abbâ Poemen they heard the voice of the brother weeping; and
they went in and found him in great labour, and they entreated
him to let them take him with them to Abbâ Poemen, but he
would not be persuaded [to go], and said, "I will die here."
And when they came to Abbâ Poemen they told him about him,
and he entreated them, saying, "Go to that brother, and say
"ye unto him, Abbâ Poemen calleth thee"; now when the
brother learned that Abbâ Poemen had sent the brethren to
him, he rose up and went. And when Abbâ Poemen saw that
he was sorrow-stricken, he rose up and gave him the salutation
of peace, and smiling with him, gave him [food] to eat. Then he
sent his brother to the old man, saying, "For many years past
"I have greatly longed to see thee, because I have heard
"about thee, but through negligence both of us have been pre-
"vented from seeing each other. Now therefore that God
"wisheth it, and the opportunity calleth, I beg thee to trouble
"thyself [to come] hither, and we will each welcome the other."

Now, as I have already said, the old man had up to that time never gone out of his cell. And when the old man heard the message, he said, "If God had not worked in him he would "not have sent for me"; and he rose up and came to him; and having saluted each other, they sat down with gladness. And Abbâ Poemen said unto him, "There were two men living in "one place, and both of them had dead, and one of them left "weeping for his own dead and went and wept over that of his "neighbour"; and when the old man heard these words he repented, and he remembered what he had done, and said, "Abbâ "Poemen is above in heaven, but I am down, down, on the "earth."

327. An old man used to say, "It is right for a man to keep "his work in all diligence so that he may lose nothing thereof; "for if a man worketh even a very little, and keepeth it, his "work remaineth and abideth." And the old man used to narrate the following matter: An inheritance was left unto a certain brother, and whilst he was wishing to make therefrom a memorial to him that had died, a certain brother who was a stranger came to him, and he roused him up in the night saying, "Arise, and help me to sing the service." Then the stranger entreated him, saying, "Leave me, O my brother, for "I am away from labour, and I cannot [get up]"; and the brother who had welcomed him said, "If thou wilt not come, "get up and depart from this place"; and the stranger rose up and departed. And at the turn of the night he saw in his dream him who had driven him out giving wheat to the baker, and that the baker did not give him [back] even one loaf of bread; and he rose up and went to an old man and related unto him the whole matter even as it had taken place, and the old man said unto him, "Thou hast performed a beautiful action, but "the Enemy hath not allowed thee to receive the reward "[thereof]." And after these things the old man said that [this] story was a proof according to which it is right for a man to be watchful and to guard his work with great care.

328. An old man said, "The Calumniator is the Enemy, and "the Enemy will never cease to cast into thy house, if he "possibly can, impurity of every kind, and it is thy duty "neither to refuse nor to neglect to take that which is cast in "and to throw it out; for if thou art negligent thy house will "become filled with impurity, and thou wilt be unable to enter "therein. Therefore whatsoever the Enemy casteth in little by "little do thou throw out little by little, and thy house shall "remain pure by the Grace of Christ."

329. On one occasion Abbâ Poemen entreated Abbâ Macarius with frequent supplication, saying, "Tell me a word [whereby

"I may live]"; and the old man anwered and said unto him,
"The matter which thou seekest hath this day passed from
"the monks."

330. Abbâ Nicetas used to tell about two brethren who had met
together, and who wished to dwell together; and one of them
thought, saying, "Whatsoever my brother wisheth that will I
do," and similarly the other meditated, saying, "Whatsoever
"will gratify my brother that will I do." Now when the Enemy
saw this, he went to them and wished to separate each from the
other, and as he was standing before the door, he appeared unto
one of them in the form of a dove, and to the other in the form
of a raven. Then one of them said unto his companion, "Seest
"thou this dove?" and the other replied, "It is a raven." And
they began to quarrel with each other, neither of them yielding
to his companion, and they stood up and fought with each other,
even unto blood, and at length, to the joy of the Calumniator,
they separated. And after three days they came to themselves
and were sorry for what had happened, and they went back
and lived together in peace as they did formerly, and each expressed his sorrow unto the other. And each of them devoted
himself to performing the will of his companion, and they lived
together until the end.

331. One of the old men used to say, "If thou seest a man
"who hath fallen into the water, and thou canst help him,
"stretch out thy staff to him, and draw him out, lest, if thou
"stretch out thy hand to him, and thou art not able to bring
"him up, he drag thee down and both of you perish." Now he
spake this for the sake of those who thrust themselves forward
to help other people who are being tempted, and who, through
wishing to help [others] beyond their power, [themselves] fall.
It is right for a man to help his brother according to the power
that he hath, for God demandeth not from a man that which
is beyond his strength.

332. A brother asked an old man, and said unto him,
"Supposing that I find sufficient for my daily wants in any
"place, dost thou wish me not to take care for the work of
"my hands?" The old man said unto him, "However much
"thou mayest have, do not neglect the work of thy hands;
"work as much as thou canst, only do not work with an
"agitated mind."

333. An old man used to say, "When the soldier goeth into
"battle he careth for himself only, and so also doth the watch-
"man; let us then imitate these men, for riches, and family,
"and wisdom, without a correct life and works, are dung."

334. An old man used to say "I await death evening, and
"morning, and every day."

335. The same old man used to say also, "As he who is a
" stranger is not able to take another stranger into the house
" of one by whom he hath not been entreated to enter, so also
" is it in the case of the Enemy, for he will not enter in where
" he is not welcomed."

336. Abbâ Epiphanius said, "He who revealeth and dis-
" covereth his good work is like unto the man who soweth
" [seed] on the surface of the ground, and doth not cover it
" up, and the fowl of the heavens cometh and devoureth it;
" but he who hideth his good works is like unto the man who
" soweth his seed in the furrows of the earth, and he shall
" reap the same at harvest."

337. Abbâ Epiphanius used to say, "Whensoever a thought
" cometh and filleth thy breast, that is to say, thy heart, with
" vainglory or pride, say thou unto it, 'Old man, behold thy
" fornication.'"

338. And he also said, "O monk, take thou the greatest
" possible care that thou sin not, lest thou disgrace God Who
" dwelleth in thee, and thou drive Him out of thy soul."

339. The old men said, "Let no monk do anything whatso-
" ever without first of all trying his heart [to see] that what
" he is about to do will be [done] for God's sake."

340. One of the fathers asked a youthful brother, saying,
" Tell us, O brother, is it good to hold one's peace or to
" speak?" then that young brother spake unto him, saying,
" If the words [to be said] be useless, leave them [unsaid], but
" if they be good, give place to good things, and speak [them].
" Yet, even though the words be good, prolong not thy speech,
" but cut it short, for silence is best of all."

341. Rabbâ Paul the Great, the Galatian, used to say, "The
" monk who living in his cell hath some small need, and who
"goeth out to provide therefor, is laughed at by the devils."

342. The blessed woman Eugenia said, "It is helpful to us
" to go about begging, only we must be with Jesus, for he
" who is with Jesus is rich, even though we be poor in the
" flesh. For he who holdeth the things of earth in greater
" honour than the things of the Spirit falleth away both from
" the things which are first and the things which are last. For
" he who coveteth heavenly things must, of necessity, receive
" the good things which are on the earth. Therefore it be-
" longeth unto the wise to await not the things which now
" exist [here], but the things which are about to be, and the
" happiness which is indescribable, and in this short and trouble-
" some life they should prepare themselves therefor."

343. On one occasion when Abbâ Arsenius was living in the
lower lands, and was troubled, he determined to leave his cell

without taking anything from it, and he departed to his disciples in the body, that is to say, to Alexander and Zoilus. Then he said to Alexander, "Arise, and go back to the place "where I was living"; and Alexander did so; and he said to Zoilus, "Arise; and come with me to the river, and seek out "for me a ship which is going to Alexandria, and then come "back, and go to thy brother." Now Zoilus marvelled at this speech, but he held his peace; and thus they parted from each other, and the old man Arsenius then went down to the country of Alexandria, where he fell ill of a serious sickness. And his disciples went back and came to the place where they had been formerly, and they said to each other, "Perhaps one of us "hath offended the old man, and it is for this reason that he "hath separated from us"; but they could not find in themselves anything with which they had ever offended him. Now the old man became well again, and he said, "I will arise and "go to the fathers," and he journeyed on and came to Patârâ where his disciples were. Now when the old man was nigh unto the river-side a young Ethiopian woman saw him, and she came behind him, and drew near him, and plucked his raiment; and the old man rebuked her. Then the maiden said unto him, "If thou art a monk, depart to the mountain." Now the old man being somewhat sad at this remark, said within himself, "Arsenius, if thou art a monk, depart to the moun-"tain"; and afterwards his disciples Alexander and Zoilus met him, and they fell down at his feet, and the old man threw himself down [on the ground] also, and he wept himself, and his disciples wept before him. And the old man said unto them, "Did ye not hear that I have been sick?" And they said unto him, "Yes." And the old man said, "Why did ye not seek to "come and see me?" And Abbâ Alexander said, "Because "the way in which thou didst leave us was not right, and be-"cause of it many were offended, and they said, 'If they had "'not wearied (or pressed) the old man in some way he would "'never have separated from them.'" The old man saith unto them, "I know that myself, but men will also say, 'The dove "'could not find rest for the sole of her foot, and she returned "'to Noah in the ark'"; thus the disciples were healed, and they took up their abode with him again.

344. Abbâ Daniel used to tell concerning Arsenius that he never wished to speak about any investigation into the Scriptures, although he was well able to speak [on the subject] if he had been so disposed, but he could not write even a letter quickly.

345. A certain old man used to say, "Vaunt not thyself over "thy brother in thy mind, saying, 'I possess a greater measure

" "of self-denial than he doth, and I can endure more than he,'
" but be subject unto the Grace of Christ, with a humble spirit,
" and love which is not hypocritical, lest through thy haughty
" spirit thou destroy thy labours. For it is written, 'Let him
" 'that thinketh he standeth take heed lest he fall' (1 Corin-
" thians x, 12); and, 'A man must be seasoned with Christ as
" 'with salt.'"

346. An old man used to say, "Let there be not unto thee
" free converse with the governor or with the judge, and be
" not with either of them continually; for from such freedom
" of speech (*or* boldness) thou wilt acquire [the habit of think-
" ing], and from merely thinking thou wilt covet."

347. Abbâ Agathon used to say, "I have never lain down
" to sleep and kept anger in my heart, or even a thought of
" enmity against any man; and I have never allowed any man
" to lie down to sleep keeping any anger against me."

348. The old man Hyparchus used to say, "Do not abuse
" thy neighbour, and drive not away a man who turneth to-
" wards thee, so that thou mayest be able to say to our Lord,
" 'Forgive us our sins, even as we also forgive those who
" 'trespass against us.'"

349. One of the fathers used to say, "If a man ask thee for
" anything, and thou givest it to him grudgingly, thou wilt not
" receive a reward for that which thou hast given, as it is
" written, 'If a man ask thee to go with him a mile, go with
" 'him two'; and the meaning of this is, 'If a man asketh
" 'anything of thee give [it] unto him with all thy soul and
" 'spirit.'"

350. One of the fathers related that there were three things
which were especially honoured in monks: that is to say, with
fear and trembling, and spiritual gladness they thought it meet
to draw nigh, I mean to the participation in the Holy Mysteries,
and the table of the brethren, and the washing of one another,
according to the example which their true Rabbâ Christ shewed
unto them, before the great day of His Resurrection was fulfilled. And the old man himself produced an illustration [of this],
saying, "There was a certain great old man who was a seer
" of visions, and he happened to be sitting at meat with the
" brethren, and whilst they were eating, the old man saw in
" the Spirit as he was sitting at the table that some of the
" brethren were eating honey, whilst others were eating bread,
" and others dung; and he wondered at these within himself.
" And he made supplication and entreaty unto God, saying,
" 'O Lord, reveal unto me this mystery, and tell me why
" 'when the food is all the same, and when the various
" 'things which are laid upon the table are only different forms

" 'thereof, the brethren appear to be eating different kinds of
" 'food, for some seem to be eating honey, and others bread,
" 'and others dung.' Then a voice came unto him from above,
" saying, 'Those who are eating honey are those who eat with
" 'fear, and with trembling, and with spiritual love when they
" 'sit at the table, and who pray without ceasing, and whose
" 'praise goeth up to God like sweet incense; for this reason
" 'they eat honey. And those who eat bread are those who con-
" 'fess and receive the Grace of God, which is given unto them
" 'by Him for these things. And those who eat dung are those
" 'who complain, and say, This is sweet and pleasant, and
" 'that is not seemly and prospereth not.' Now it is not right
" to think about these at all, but we should glorify and
" praise God the more, and receive (or welcome) His abundant
" provisions which come to us without labour, so that there
" may be fulfilled in us that which was said by the blessed
" Apostle, 'Whether ye eat, or whether ye drink, or whether
" 'ye do anything else, do all things unto the glory of God'"
(1 Corinthians x, 31).

351. They say that Abbâ 'Ôr never told a lie, and never swore,
and never cursed a man, and never spoke unless it was abso-
lutely necessary.

352. One of the old men said, "That which thou observest
" not thyself, how canst thou teach to another?"

353. And it was he who said unto his disciple, "Take heed
" that thou never bringest an alien word into this cell."

354. An old man used to say, "As far as I have been able to
" overtake my soul when it hath transgressed, I have never
" slipped (or committed an offence) a second time."

355. An old man used to say, "Strive with all thy might so
" that thou mayest never in any way do evil to any man, and
" make thine heart to be pure with every man."

356. Abbâ Agathon used to say to himself, whensoever he
saw any act or anything which his thought wished to judge
or condemn, "Do not commit the thing thyself," and in this
manner he quieted his mind, and held his peace.

357. The old men used to say, "For a man to be so bold as
" to condemn his neighbour resembleth the sweeping of the
" lawgiver, or the judge, from off his seat, and the wishing to
" pass judgement in his place, and it is as if a man were to bring
" an accusation against the weakness of the judge and to con-
" demn him, and such an act will be found to be the rebellion
" of the slave against his Lord, and against the Judge of the
" living and the dead."

358. An old man used to say, "From the greatest to the least
" of the things which I perform, I carefully consider the fruit

"which will be produced from it, whether it be in thoughts, or
"in words, or in deeds."

359. They used to tell the story about Abbâ Pachomius and
say that on many occasions he heard the devils repeating many
evil things of various kinds, some of which were to come upon
the brethren. First of all he heard one of them saying, "I have
"[strife] with a man who constantly [defieth] me, for whenso-
"ever I approach to sow thoughts in his mind, immediately
"he turneth to prayer, and I depart from him being consumed
"with fire." And another devil said, "I have [strife]with a man
"who is easy to persuade, and he doeth whatsoever I counsel
"him to do, and I love him dearly." It is right then, O my
brethren, that we should keep ourselves awake always, and that,
making ourselves mighty men in the Name of the Lord, we
should strive against the devils, and then they will never be
able to overcome us.

360. One of the holy men used to say, "Through holding
"small wickednesses in contempt we fall into great ones;
"consider then attentively the following story which is told
"even as it took place. A certain man laughed in an empty
"manner, and his companion rebuked and condemned him;
"[another brother] happened to be there, and he thought lightly
"of the matter, saying, 'This is nothing; for what is it for a man
"'to laugh?' [And the brother replied, 'From laughter] plea-
"'sure is produced, and next empty words, and filthy actions,
"'and iniquity, and so from the things which are thought
"'to be small that wicked devil bringeth in great wicked-
"'nesses. And from great wickednesses a man cometh to
"'despair, for this cruel and wicked evil hath the Evil One
"'discovered (*or* invented) through the malignity of his crafti-
"'ness, for a man to commit sin is not so destructive as for
"'a man to cut off hope from his soul. For he who repenteth
"'in a fitting manner, and according to what is right blotteth
"'out his offences; but he who cutteth off hope from his soul
"'perisheth because he will not offer unto it the binding up of
"'repentance. Therefore let not a man hold in contempt small
"'wickednesses. For this is the seed which the Calumniator
"'soweth, for if he made war openly it would not be difficult to
"'fight, and victory would be easy; and even now, if we be
"'watchful and strenuous, it will be easy for us to conquer,
"'for it is God Who hath armed us, and He teacheth us and
"'entreateth us not to hold even the smallest wickednesses in
"'contempt. Hearken thou unto Him as He admonisheth [us],
"'saying, (St. Matthew v, 22) "Whosoever shalt say unto his
"""brother 'Râkâ,' shall be guilty of the fire of Gehenna"; and,
"""He who looketh upon a woman to desire her hath already

" "committed adultery with her in his heart" (St. Matt. v, 28).
" 'And in another place He rebuked and admonished those who
" 'laugh, and concerning the idle word also He said, "Its
" "answer is given"; and on account of this the blessed Job,
" 'because of the thoughts which were in the hearts of his sons,
" 'offered up an offering. Now therefore, since we know all these
" 'things, let us take good heed to ourselves [and avoid] the
" 'beginning of the movement of our thoughts, and then we
" 'shall never fall.'"

361. A brother said unto an old man, "Dost thou not see
" that I have not even one war in my heart?" The old man
said unto him, "Thou hast an opening in thee at each of the
" four points of the compass, and whatsoever wisheth can go
" in and come out without thy perceiving it. But if thou wilt
" set up a door, and wilt shut it, and wilt not allow evil
" thoughts to enter, thou wilt then see them standing outside;
" for if our minds be watchful and strenuous in loving God,
" the Enemy who is the counsellor of wickednesses will not
" approach [us]."

362. A certain Mother of noble rank said, "As the stamped
" silver coin which is current loseth its weight and becometh
" less, so doth the spiritual excellence which is apparent and
" is made manifest become destroyed; and as wax melteth be-
" fore the fire, so also doth the soul become lax and confused,
" and strenuousness departeth from it."

363. One of the old men used to say, "The man who doeth
" many good deeds doth Satan cast down by means of small
" matters into pits, so that he may destroy the wages of all
" the good things which he hath performed."

364. A brother asked Abbâ Poemen, saying, "For what
" purpose were spoken the words, 'Take no thought for the
" 'morrow?'" The old man said unto him, "For the man who
" is under temptation, and is in affliction; for it is not meet
" that such a man should take thought for the morrow, or
" should say, 'How long shall I have to endure this tempta-
" 'tion?' but he should think upon patient endurance, saying,
" 'It is to-day, and the temptation will not remain thus for a
" 'long time.'" And the old man said, "It is good that a man
" should be remote from temptation of the body, for he who
" is nigh unto the temptation of the body is like unto him
" that standeth upon the mouth of a deep pit, and whom, when-
" soever his enemy wisheth, he can easily cast therein. But if
" he be remote from the temptation of the body, he is like unto
" a man who is far away from the pit, and even though his
" enemy may wish to cast him into it, he is not able to do so
" because the pit is far away from him, and whilst he is either

"urging him or dragging him thereto, God, the Merciful One,
"sendeth him a helper."

365. And a brother said unto Abbâ Poemen, "My body is
"weak, and I am not able to perform ascetic labours; speak
"to me a word whereby I may live"; and the old man said
unto him, "Art thou able to rule thy thought and not to per-
"mit it to go to thy neighbour in guile?"

366. And a brother also asked him, "What shall I do? For
"I am troubled when I am sitting in my cell." The old man
said unto him, "Think lightly of no man; think no evil in thy
"heart; condemn no man and curse no man; then shall God
"give thee rest, and thy habitation shall be without trouble."

367. And the same old man used to say, "The keeping of
"the commandments, and the taking heed to oneself in every-
"thing, and the acquisition of oblations, are the guides of the
"soul."

368. Abbâ Poemen said, "A brother asked Abbâ Moses,
"saying, 'In what manner is a man to keep himself from his
"'neighbour?' The old man said unto him, 'Except a man
"'layeth it up in his heart that he hath been already three
"'years in the grave, he will not be sufficiently strong [to
"'keep] this saying.'"

369. Abbâ Poemen said, "If thou seest visions and hearest
"rumours, repeat them not to thy neighbour, for this is vic-
"tory of the war."

370. The same old man also said, "The chief of all wicked-
"nesses is the wandering of the thoughts."

371. Abbâ Poemen said, "If a man perform the desire, and
"pleasure, and custom of these, they will cast him down."

372. A brother asked Abbâ Poemen, saying, "If a brother
"owe me a few oboli, shall I remind him of it?" The old man
saith, "Remind him once." And the brother said unto him,
"And if I have reminded him and he hath given me nothing,
"[what am I to do then?]" The old man saith unto him, "Let
"the thought perish, only do not harass the man."

373. A brother asked Abbâ Joseph, saying, "What shall I
"do? For I cannot be disgraced, and I cannot work, and I
"have nothing [wherefrom] to give alms." The old man said
unto him, "If thou canst not do these things, keep thy con-
"science from thy neighbour, and guard thyself carefully
"against evil of every kind, and thou shalt live; for God de-
"sireth that the soul shall be without sin."

374. A brother asked Abbâ Sisoes of Shĕkîpâ about his life
and works, and the old man said unto him that which Daniel
spake, "The bread of desire I have not eaten," that is to say,
"A man should not fulfil the lust of his desire."

375. On one occasion Abraham said unto Abbâ Sisoes, "Abbâ, "thou hast grown old, let us draw nigh unto the habitations "of the children of men for a little"; and Abbâ Sisoes said unto him, "Let us go where there is no woman"; then his disciple said unto him, "And what place is there without a "woman except the desert?" The old man said unto him, "Then let us go to the desert."

376. On one occasion certain brethren came to Abbâ Pambô, and one of them asked him, saying, "Father, I fast two days "at a time, and then I eat two bread-cakes; shall I gain life, "O father, or am I making a mistake?" And another asked him and said, "I perform work with my hands [each] day to "the value of two kîrâts (i.e., carats), and I keep a few oboli "by me for my food, and the remainder I spend upon the relief "of the poor; shall I be redeemed, O father, or am I making "a mistake?" And the other brethren asked of him many things, but he answered them never a word. Now after four days they were wishing to depart, and the clergy entreated them, saying, "O brethren, trouble not ye yourselves, for God "will give you a reward. The custom of the old man is not to "speak immediately, for he doth not speak until God giveth "him permission to do so." Then the brethren went to the old man and said unto him, "Father, pray for us"; and he said unto them, "Do ye wish to depart?" And they said unto him, "Yes." Then he took their actions into his consideration, and he put himself in the position of one who was writing on the ground, and said, "Pambô, one fasteth two days at a time, "and then eateth two bread-cakes; shall he become a monk "by such things as these? No! Pambô, [another] worketh for "two carats a day, and giveth to those who are in need, shall "he become a monk by such things as these? No!" And he said, "[Thy] actions are good, and if thou preservest thy con-"science with thy [good actions] thou shalt live"; and being consoled by these words, the brethren departed rejoicing.

377. Certain of the old men used to say, "If temptation "cometh upon thee in the place where thou dwellest, forsake "not the place in the time of temptation, lest peradventure "thou findest wherever thou goest that from which thou "fleest; but endure until the period of temptation be overpast, "and thy departure can be [effected] without offence and with-"out affliction, for thou wilt have departed in a time of peace. "Now if thou departest during a period of temptation, many "will be afflicted because of thee, and will say that thou didst "depart because of the temptation, and this will be unto them "a source of grief."

378. On one occasion when Abbâ Sisoes was sitting down

with a certain brother, he sighed unknowingly, and he did not perceive that the brother was with him, because his mind was carried away by the noonday [prayer]; and he made apologies to that brother, and said unto him, "Forgive me, O my "brother, that I heaved a sigh before thee [proves] that I have "not yet become a monk."

379. An old man used to say, "Whensoever I bring down "the bar of the loom, and before I raise it up again, I always "set my death before mine eyes."

380. Another old man used to say, "When I am plaiting "(or sewing) a basket, with every stitch which I put into it I "set my death before my eyes before I take another stitch."

381. Abbâ Daniel used to say, "On one occasion we went "to Abbâ Poemen, and having eaten together, he said unto "us subsequently, 'Go ye and rest yourselves a little, O my "'brethren'; and when the brethren had gone to rest them-"selves I remained that 1 might be able to talk to the old man "privately. And I rose up and came to his cell, and I saw that "he was sitting outside on a mat, and seeing me he lay down; "now he did not know that I had seen him seated, and he "pretended to be asleep. And this was the custom of the old "man, for everything which he did was done by him in secret."

382. One of the fathers asked Abbâ Sisoes, saying, "If I am "living in the desert and the barbarians come against me to "kill me, supposing that I have strength may I kill one of "them?" The old man said unto him, "No. Commit thyself "unto God, and leave [it to Him]. For with every trial which "cometh upon a man he should say, ' It hath come because of "'my sins'; but if something good happeneth to him, let him "say, 'It is of the Providence of God.'"

383. One of the old men used to say, "When the eyes of the "ox are covered over then he is subjugated by the yoke bar, but "if they do not cover [his] eyes he cannot be made to bow "beneath the yoke; and thus is it with Satan, for if he can "cover over the eyes of a man he can bring him low with every "kind of sin, but if his eyes be able to see (or shine), he is able "to flee from him."

384. Abbâ Anthony said, "It is not seemly for us to re-"member the time which hath passed, but let a man be each "day as one who beginneth his toil, so that the excessive "weariness [which we shall feel] may be to our advantage. "And let him say, as Paul said, 'That which is behind me I "forget, and I reach out to that which is before me'" (Phi-"lippians iii, 13). And let him also remember the word of Eli-"jah, who said, 'As the Lord liveth, before Whom I stand "this day'" (1 Kings xvii, 1).

385. And the same old man said also, "Let us not consider "the time which is past, but let a man be even as he who be-"ginneth, and let him take care in such wise that he shall "make himself stand before God."

386. Abbâ Paphnutius said: "A monk is bound to keep not "only his body pure, but his soul free from unclean thoughts. "Now we find that the body is consoled by thoughts, and "unless the thoughts withdraw themselves they will sink the "body; and the manner in which the thoughts work is as fol-"lows: they feed all lusts of the flesh, which is ruled by them, "and in welcoming the lusts they stir up the body also in re-"volt, and they cast it down, like a pilot who is caught in a "storm, and they make the ship to sink. And is it fitting that "we should know that if one man loveth another he will say "nothing evil about him? for if he doth speak against him he "is not his friend; similarly he who loveth lust will not speak "anything evil against it, and if he doeth so he is not its "friend. But if a man [speak] against that which he knoweth "not, (or against that which causeth him no affliction), or "against that which causeth him no pain, [he may speak "evil], but against that which he hath suffered, and that "wherewith he hath been tried by the Enemy, he will speak "evil, and he will not talk about him as a friend, but as an "enemy. Thus whosoever speaketh evil of and who despiseth "lust is not a friend of lusts.

387. And he also said, "As judges (or governors) slay the "wicked, even so do labours slay evil lusts; and as wicked "slaves fly from their lords even so do lusts fly from the ex-"haustion [caused by] ascetic labours. But good slaves hold "their masters in honour as sons hold in honour their fathers. "For the exhaustion [caused by ascetic labours] produceth "good works, and from it the virtues spring up, even as the "passions are produced from dainty meats. Exhaustion then "begetteth good works, when a man hath wearied himself "with [all] his soul, and it bringeth forth virtues and de-"stroyeth vices, even as a righteous judge [destroyeth the "wicked]."

388. A brother asked Abbâ Poemen, saying, "Since I suffer "loss in spirit when I am with my Abbâ, dost thou wish me "to continue to live with him any longer?" Now that old man knew that the brother was suffering loss through living with his Abbâ, and the old man marvelled how the brother could ask him the question, "Dost thou wish me to dwell with "him any longer." And the old man said unto him, "If thou "wishest, dwell [with him]," and the brother went and did so, but he came again to the old man and said, "I am suffering "loss in spirit"; and the old man said unto him nothing. And, when for the third time the brother came and said unto him, "Indeed, I cannot henceforth dwell with him," Abbâ Poemen said unto him, "Now thou knowest how to live; depart, "and dwell with him no longer."

389. Therefore the old man said, "If there existeth a man "who knoweth how to suffer loss in his spirit, and who still "[feeleth] the need to ask a question about [his] secret thoughts, "it is a good thing that he should ask; and it belongeth unto "the old men to search into and investigate a matter of this "kind, for concerning open sins a man doth not feel it neces- "sary to enquire, but he cutteth them off immediately."

390. A brother asked one of the fathers, saying, "Tell me "a word whereby I may live"; and the old man answered and "said, 'We must be careful to work a little, and we must be "' neither negligent nor contemptuous, and then we may be able "'to live.'" And an old man told him the following story, saying, "There was a certain prosperous husbandman who was ex- "ceedingly rich, and wishing to teach his sons husbandry he "said unto them, 'My sons, behold, see how I have become "'rich, and if ye will be persuaded by me, [and will do as I "'have done], ye will become rich also.' Then they said unto "him, 'Father, we will be persuaded [by thee], tell us how "'[to become rich].' Now although the husbandman knew well "that he who laboureth always becometh rich, yet because he "thought that they might be negligent, and despise [work], he "made use of cunning in his words, and said unto them: "'There is one day in the year whereon if a man worketh he "'will become rich, but because of my exceedingly great old "'age I have forgotten which it is; therefore, ye must work con- "'tinually, and ye must not be idle even one day, and ye must "'by every possible means in your power go forwards. But if "' ye are neglectful and disinclined to work, even for one day, "' take good heed to yourselves lest the day whereon ye do "' not work be that very day, and that lucky day pass you by, "' and your labour for all the rest of the year be in vain.'" Thus also, O my brethren, if we labour and work each day, and we do not make use of sloth and negligence and contempt we shall find the way of life.

391. Abbâ Agathon asked Abbâ Alônîs, saying, "I wish "to hold my tongue that it may not speak falsehood, [what "shall I do?]" Abbâ Alônîs said unto him, "If thou dost not "lie, thou art about to commit many sins." Agathon said, "How?" And the old man said unto him, "Behold, two brethren "are going to commit a murder, and one of them will flee to "thee. And it will happen that the judge will come and search

" for him, and he will ask thee, saying, 'Did this murder take
" 'place in thy presence?' And if thou dost not wish to tell a
" lie thou wilt deliver up to death the other man, whom it would
" be right for thee to let go free, so that he might be reserved
" for the judgement hall of God, Who knoweth all things."

392. A certain brother was travelling on a road, and his aged
mother was with him, and they came to a river which the old
woman was not able to cross; and her son took his shoulder cloth
and wound it round his hands so that they might not touch his
mother's body, and in this manner he carried her across the
river. Then his mother said unto him, " My son, why didst
" thou first wrap round thy hands with the cloth, and then take
" me across?" and he said, "The body of a woman is fire, and
" through thy body there would have come to me the memory
" of [the body of] another woman, and it was for this reason
" that I acted as I did."

Chapter ix. Of Love, and Charity, and of the Welcoming of Strangers

A CERTAIN old man used to dwell with a brother in a
cell in a friendly manner, and he was a man of compassionate disposition; now a famine broke out, and
393. the people began to be hungry, and they came to him
that they might receive charity, and he gave bread unto them
all. And when the brother saw that he was giving away large
quantities of bread, he said unto the old man, "Give me my
" portion of the bread"; and the old man said unto him,
" Take [it]," and he divided [what there was] and gave him
[his share], and the brother took it from him for himself. And
the old man was compassionate, and gave away bread from
his portion, and many folk heard [that he was doing this] and
came unto him, and when God saw the generosity of the old
man He blessed his bread; but the brother took all his portion
and ate it up, and when he saw that his bread was finished,
and that the portion of the old man was still lasting, he made
entreaty unto him, saying, "My portion hath come to an end,
" and this [bread of thine is all] that I have; receive me as a
" partner [therein]." And the old man said unto him, "Good,"
and he associated him with himself again. And when there was
abundance [again], the people came to take [bread] from him,
and he gave it unto them again. Now it came to pass that
they lacked bread, and the brother went and found that
bread was wanting, and a poor man came for some, and the
old man said unto the brother, "Go in and give him some,"
and the brother said, "There is none"; for he was filled with
bread. The old man said, "Go in and search [for some]," and

having gone in he found that the place wherein they used to set [the bread] was filled with loaves to the very top, and he took [some] and gave to the poor man, and he was afraid. Thus that brother knew the excellence and the faith of the old man, and he gave thanks unto God, and glorified Him.

394. Two brethren went to the market to sell their wares, and whilst one of them had gone to perform the service, he who was left by himself fell into fornication; and the other brother came and said unto him, "My brother, let us go to the cell," but he said unto him, "I cannot go, for I have fallen "into fornication." Now whilst he was seeking to do better, the brother began to swear to him, saying, "I also, when I "was away from thee, fell in the same manner, nevertheless, "come, and let us repent together, and it may happen that "God will pardon us." And when they came to their cells they informed the old men about the temptation which had come to them, and whatsoever the old men told them to do the two brothers did, and the one brother repented with the other, just as if he had sinned with him. Now God saw the labour of his love, and in a few days He sent a revelation unto one of the old men concerning the matter, saying, "For the sake of the love of "that brother who did not sin, forgive thou him that did com-"mit sin." This is what is meant by the words, "A man should "lay down his soul for his friend."

395. And they also say that there was a certain self-denying and ascetic brother who wished to go to the city to sell his handiwork, and to buy the things which he needed; and he called a brother, and said unto him, "Come with me, and let "us go and return together." And when they had gone as far as the gate of the city, the man of abstinence said unto his companion, "Sit down here, O my brother, and wait for me "while I go in and perform my business; and I will return "speedily." And having gone into the city, and wandered round about in the streets, a certain rich woman tried her blandishments upon him, and he stripped off his monk's garb and took her to wife. Then he sent a message to his companion, saying, "Arise, get thee to thy cell, for I can never see thee "again"; now the man who had been sent to him with this message related unto him the whole matter, even as it had happened, and he said to the messenger, "God forbid that such "things should be spoken about my holy brethren, and God forbid "that I should depart from this place until my brother cometh, "according to his word to me." And having tarried there a long time, and ceasing not from weeping and praying either by night or by day, the report of him was heard throughout the city, and the clergy, and the monks, and the governors of the

city entreated him to depart to his monastery, but he would not hearken unto their supplication, and he said, "I cannot "transgress my brother's command, and I cannot leave this "place until we go back together to the monastery." So he stayed there for seven years, being burned by heat in the summer, and dried up by the cold and ice in the winter, and with hunger, and thirst, and weeping and watching, he made supplication on behalf of his brother. Then at length one day his former companion himself came unto him, dressed in costly garments, and said unto him, "O So-and-so, I am he "who was with thee the monk So-and-so, arise, get thee gone "to thy monastery"; and the brother looked at him and said, "Thou art not, for he was a monk, and thou art a man in the "world." Then God looked upon the trouble of that brother, and at the end of the seven years the woman died, and the brother who [had married her] repented, and again put on the garb of the monk, and went out to his companion; and when he saw him, he rose up, and embraced him and kissed him, and he took him with gladness, and they went forth to the monastery. Then that brother renewed his former ascetic works, and he was worthy of the highest grade of perfection. Thus by the patience of one man the other lived, and the saying, "A "brother is helped by his brother, even as a city is helped by its "fortress," was fulfilled.

396. On one occasion two old men came to an old man, whose custom was not to eat every day; and when he saw them he rejoiced, and said, "Fasting hath its reward, and he who eateth for the sake of love fulfilleth two commandments, for he "setteth aside his own desire and he fulfilleth the command- "ment, and refresheth the brethren."

397. They used to tell the story of a certain brother who fell into sin, and he came unto Abbâ Lôt, and he was perplexed and confused, and was going in and coming out, and was unable to rest. And Abbâ Lôt said unto him, "What is the "matter with thee, O my brother?" and he said, "I have com- "mitted a great sin, and I am unable to confess it before the "fathers." The old man said unto him, "Confess it unto "me, and I will bear it"; and then the brother said unto him, "I have fallen into fornication, and I thought thou hadst dis- "covered the matter." And the old man said unto him, "Be "of good courage, for there remaineth repentance; get thee "gone and sit in thy habitation, and fast for two weeks, and "I will bear with thee one half of thy sin"; and at the end of three weeks it was revealed unto the old man that God had accepted the repentance of that brother, and he remained with the old man, and was subject unto him until the day of his death.

©f %ove, Cbarity, anb Ibospitality

398. Certain of the fathers came to Joseph to ask him a question about welcoming the strangers who came to them, that is to say, whether it was fitting for a man to forsake his work, and to be with them in the ordinary way or not; and before they asked him, he said unto his disciple, "Lay to heart "that which I am about to do this day, and wait." Then the old man placed two pillows, one on his right hand, and the other on his left, and he said unto the fathers, "Sit ye down"; and he went into his cell, and put on the apparel of beggars, and went forth to them; and again, he took this off, and put on the beautiful apparel of the monks, and he went forth again, and passed among them; and he went in again and took this off, and having put on his own clothes, he sat down in their midst, and they marvelled at the doings of the old man. Then he said unto them, "Have ye understood what I did?" and they said unto him, "Yes." He said unto them, "What is it?" And they said unto him, "Thou didst put on first of all the apparel of "beggars"; he said unto them, "Peradventure I have been "changed by that disgraceful apparel?" and they said unto him, "No." The old man said unto them, "Since I have not "myself been changed by all these changes of raiment, for "the first change brought no loss upon me and the second "did not change me, so are we in duty bound to welcome the "brethren, according to the command of the Gospel, which "saith, 'Give to Caesar the things of Caesar, and to God the "things of God' (St Matthew xxii, 21). Therefore, whenso- "ever strange brethren arrive we must welcome them gladly, "for it is when we are alone that it is necessary for us to "suffer." Now when the fathers heard [these words] they marvelled that he had spoken unto them that which was in their hearts before they asked him, and they glorified God, and departed with rejoicing; and they received his word as if it had [come] from God, and they accepted what he had said, and did it.

399. They used to speak about an old man, who was from Syria, and who used to dwell on the road of the desert of Egypt, and whose work was as follows:—At whatever time a monk came to him he would welcome him. And it came to pass that on one occasion a man came from the desert and asked him to allow him to rest, but he would not permit him to do so, and said unto him, "I am fasting." Then the blessed man was grieved and said unto him, "Is this thy labour, that thou "wilt not perform thy brother's desire? I beseech thee to come, "and let us pray, and let us follow after him with whom this "tree, which is here with us, shall bow." Then the man from the desert knelt down, and nothing happened, but when he who received strangers knelt down, that tree inclined its head at the same time, and seeing this he profited, and they glorified God.

400. On one occasion Abbâ Ammon came to a certain place to eat with the brethren, and there was there a brother concerning whom evil reports were abroad, for it had happened that a woman had come and entered his cell. And when all the people who were living in that place heard [of this], they were troubled, and they gathered together to expel that brother from his cell, and learning that the blessed Bishop Ammon was there, they came and entreated him to go with them. Now when the brother knew [this], he took the woman and hid her under an earthenware vessel. And much people having assembled, and Abbâ Ammon, understanding what that brother had done, for the sake of God hid the matter. And he went in and sat upon the earthenware vessel, and commanded that the cell of the brother should be searched, but although they examined the place they found no one there. Then Abbâ Ammon answered and said, "What is this that ye have done? May God forgive "you"; and he prayed and said, "Let all the people go forth," and finally he took the brother by the hand, and said unto him, "Take heed to thy soul, O my brother," and having said this he departed, and he refused to make public the matter of the brother.

401. There were two brethren who lived in the wilderness, and they were neighbours, and one of them used to hide whatsoever he gained from his work, whether it was bread or whether it was oboli, and place it with his companion's goods; now the other brother did not know this, but he wondered how it was that his goods increased so much. One day, however, he suddenly caught him doing this, and he strove with him, saying, "By means of thy corporeal things thou hast robbed me "of my spiritual goods"; and he demanded that he should make a covenant with him never to act in this manner again, and then he left him.

402. On one occasion Abbâ Macarius went to visit a certain monk, and he found him to be ill, and he asked him if he wanted anything to eat, for he had nothing whatsoever in his cell, and the monk said unto him, "I want some honeycakes"; and when the wonderful old man heard [this] he set out for Alexandria, and he did not regard this journey as a trouble, although [the city] was sixty miles away from them, and he brought the honeycakes to give to the sick monk. And this he did himself, and did not tell anyone else to bring them, and the old man thus made manifest the solicitude which he felt for the monks.

403. They used to tell the story of an old man who lived in Scete; now he had fallen sick, and wished to eat a little fine

bread. And when a certain brother heard [this], he took his
cloak and placed in it some dry bread, and he went to Egypt
and changed it [for fine bread] and brought [it] to the old man,
and the old man looked upon him and wondered. But the old
man refused to eat it, saying, "This is the bread of blood, O my
"brother," and the old men entreated him to eat lest the offering of the brother should be in vain, and having pressed him
the old man was persuaded and he ate the bread.

404. The blessed Anthony never deemed it right to do that
which was convenient for himself to the same extent as that
which was profitable for his neighbour.

405. An old man used to say, "I have never desired any
" work which doeth good to myself and harm to my neighbour,
"and I have the hope that what is of benefit to my brother will
"be labour that is beneficial to me, and that it will be a thing
" that will invite a reward for me."

406. A certain brother from the Great Monastery was accused
of fornication, and he rose up and came to Father Anthony; and
there came brethren after him from that monastery to inform
him about the matter and to take him away, and they began
to accuse him, saying, "Thus and thus hast thou done," and
the brother made excuses, and said, "I never acted in this
"manner." Now Abbâ Paphnutius happened to be there, and
he spake a word unto them, saying, "I saw a man in the river
"with the mud up to his knees, and some men came to give
"him help and to drag him out, and they made him to sink up
"to his neck." And when Abbâ Anthony heard [him say this],
he spake concerning Abbâ Paphnutius, saying, "Behold, in-
" deed, a man who is able to make quiet and to redeem souls!"
And the eyes of those brethren were opened, by the word of
the old men, and they took that brother, and he departed with
them to their monastery.

407. They used to say about Abbâ Theodore that when he
was a young man he dwelt in the desert, and that he went to
make his bread in the same place as the monks made theirs;
and he found a certain brother who wished to make bread, but
he had no one to do the work for him, and he was unable to do
it for himself. Then Abbâ Theodore left his own bread and
made that of the brother, and a second brother came and he
made his also, and a third brother came, and he did likewise;
and finally when he had satisfied them, he made bread for himself.

408. A brother asked an old man, saying, "There were two
" brethren, and one of them led a life of silent contemplation
"in his cell, and used to fast six days at a time, and to devote
" himself to great labour, and his companion used to minister

" to the sick; which of them will receive the [greater reward for]
" his service?" The old man saith, " If he who fasted were to
" raise himself up upon the works which are profitable, he
" would not find himself equal before God with him that visited
" the sick."

409. There was a certain head of a monastery in a house of
monks in the desert, and it happened that the brother who
ministered unto him had a desire to leave the monastery, and he
departed and dwelt in another monastery; now the old man was
unwilling to let him go, and on this account he was always going
to him to visit him, and he entreated him to return to his monastery, and the brother refused to do so. And for three whole years
the old man used to go to the brother and entreat him to return, and
finally he was constrained, and he departed with him. One day
the old man told him to go out and bring in some fuel for the
fire, and whilst he was gathering the firewood, by the agency
of Satan, a stick stuck in his eye and it was put out; and when
the old man heard of this he was greatly grieved, and being
full of sorrow he began to speak to him words of good cheer.
And the brother answered, and said, " Be not afflicted, O father,
" for I was the cause of this myself, for this hath happened to
" me through all the toil and labour which I brought upon thee
" when thou usedst to go and come to me." And after a little
time, when the brother had recovered from the sickness caused
by the injury to his eye, the old man said unto him, "Go out
" and bring in some palm leaves from the ground," for this
was the work which the monks who dwelt there had to do; and
whilst the brother was cutting them, once again, as it were by
the agency of Satan, a stick sprang up in the air, and smote the
man in the other eye, and it was put out, and he came to the
monastery in grief, and he was perforce idle and useless because he was unable to do any work. Thus the old man was
deprived [of a servant], and he had no one with him, because
each of the brethren dwelt in his own cell. And after a short
time the day of his departure, which he had known beforehand,
drew nigh, and he sent and called all the brethren and said unto
them, "The day of my departure hath drawn nigh. Watch ye
" yourselves, and take good heed to the service of your lives
" (or life's work), and treat not lightly your ascetic labours."
And each one of them began to say to him sorrowfully, "Father,
" why art thou leaving us?" and the old man held his peace.
Then he sent and brought the blind man, and revealed to him
concerning his departure, and the blind man wept and said
unto him, "Wherefore leavest thou me, the blind man?" The
old man saith unto him, "Pray that I may have openness of
" face with God, and that I may find mercy before Him, and

"I have hope through His help, that on the First Day of the "Week thou wilt be able to perform the service with thy com-"panions"; and straightway the old man died. And, according to his word, a few days later he appeared unto that brother, and his eyes were opened, and he became an Abbâ and a head of monks. Now these things were related unto us by those who were acquainted with the period wherein the old man lived.

410. A certain man of abstinence saw a man who had a devil, and who was unable to fast, and he was exceedingly sorry for him; and by reason of the love for Christ with which he was filled, and because he not only took care for himself, but for his companion also, he prayed and entreated God that the devil might come to him, and that the man might be released from him. Now God looked upon his prayer and upon his good will, and saw that the holy man was carrying a great load on behalf of that demoniac, and since that brother began to prolong his fasting and prayer, and to practise continually self-denial, in a few days that evil spirit departed.

411. They used to say concerning Abbâ Poemen that when he was pressed by any man to go with him to eat at an unusual time, he would go, with the tears streaming from his eyes, so that he might not resist the wish of that brother and cause him annoyance; for he would forgo his own will, and he would humble himself and go.

412. There was an old man in the Cells whose name was Apollo, and when one of the brethren came to call him to work, he would go joyfully, saying, " I go to-day with the King " Christ to work on my own behalf, for this is the reward of " this labour."

413. On one occasion Abraham, the disciple of Abbâ Sisoes, was tempted by Satan, and the old man saw him fall down, and straightway he spread out his hands towards heaven, and said to God, " My Lord, I will not let Thee go until Thou hast " healed him," and straightway Abraham was healed.

414. A certain monk was sitting by the monastery, and whilst he was occupied in great labours, it happened that strangers came to the monastery, and they forced him to eat with them contrary to his usual custom, and afterwards the brethren said unto him, " Father, wast thou not just now af-"flicted?" And he said unto them, " My affliction is to break " my will."

415. On one occasion three old men went to Abbâ Akîlâ, and on one of them [rested] some small suspicion of evil; and one of them said unto him, " Father, make me a net," and he replied, " I will not make thee a net." Then another said unto him, " Do [us] an act of grace, and make us a net, so that we

"may be able to keep thee in remembrance in our monastery";
and Akîlâ said again, " I am not at leisure [to do so]." Then
the third brother, on whom [rested] the suspicion of evil, also
said unto him, "Father, make me a net which I can possess
" [direct] from thy hands "; and Akîlâ answered straightway,
and said unto this man, " I will make one for thee." And afterwards the [other] two brethren said unto him privately, "[Con-
" sider] how much we entreated thee, and yet thou wouldst not
" be persuaded to make [a net] for us, and thou didst say to
"this man, 'I will make thee one immediately!'" The old
man said unto them, " I told you that I would not make one,
" and ye were not grieved, because I had not the leisure; but
" if I had not made one for this man, he would have said, 'It
" 'was because the old man had heard about my sins that he
" 'was unwilling to make a net for me.'"

416. On one occasion three brethren went to harvest, and
the three of them undertook to reap the harvest [in certain
fields] together for a certain sum of money; but one of them
fell sick on the first day, and was unable to work, and he went
back and lay down in his cell. Then one of the two brethren
who remained said unto his companion, "Behold, O my
" brother, thou seest that our brother hath fallen sick, let us
" exert ourselves a little, thou and I, and let us believe that by
" his prayers we shall be sufficiently strong to do his share of the
" work of harvest for him." Then when the harvest was ended, and
they came to receive their hire, they called the [sick] brother,
and said unto him, "Come, brother, and take also the hire of
" thy harvesting "; and he said, " What hire can there be for
" me since I have not been harvesting?" And they said unto
him, "Through thy prayers the harvest hath been reaped;
" come now, and take [thy] hire." Then the contention between
them waxed strong, for the [sick] brother contended that he
ought not to receive [any wages], and they said, " We will not
" leave thee until thou dost." So they went, that they might be
heard by a certain great old man, and that brother answered
and said, " O father, three of us went to harvest, but I fell sick
" on the first day, and went and lay down in my cell, and al-
" though I did not work even one day these brethren urge me,
" saying, 'Come and take the hire for which thou didst not
" 'work.'" Then the two brethren said, " Three of us went to
" the harvest, and we took certain fields [to reap] together,
" and if we had been thirty we should have succeeded in reap-
" ing them with great labour; but through the prayers of this
" our brother the two of us reaped them quickly, and we
" said to him, 'Come, take thy hire, because, through thy
" 'prayers, God helped us, and we reaped quickly,' but he

"would not take [it]." Then the old man said unto the brethren who were with him, "Beat the board, and let all the "brethren be gathered together," and when they were assembled he said unto them, "Come, O ye brethren, and hear "this day a righteous judgement," and he related before them the whole matter, and they decided that the brother was to receive his hire, and that he might do whatsoever he wished [therewith]. And the brother went away weeping and distressed.

417. On one occasion a certain demoniac came to Scete, and having passed a long time there without being healed, he complained about the matter to one of the old men, who made the sign of the Cross over him, and healed him. But the devil was angry, and said unto the old man, "Now that thou hast cast "me out I will come upon thee"; and the old man said unto him, "Come gladly, and I shall rejoice." And the old man passed twelve years with the devil inside him, vexing him, now he used to eat twelve dates each day, and after these years that devil leaped out of him, and departed from him. Now when the old man saw that he was taking to flight, he said unto him, "To whom dost thou flee? Continue [with me] longer"; and the devil answered and said unto him, "By Jupiter, God hath "made thee useless, O old man; God alone is equal to thy "strength."

418. The old man Theodore asked Abbâ Pambô, saying, "Tell me a word"; and with much labour he said unto him, "Theodore, get thee gone, and let thy mercy be poured out on "every man, for [thy] lovingkindness hath found freedom of "speech (or boldness) before God."

419. A certain brother went to buy some linen from a widow, and as she was selling it to him, she sighed; the brother said unto her, "What aileth thee?" and the widow said unto him, "God hath sent thee this day that my orphans may be fed." Now when that brother heard [these words] he was distressed, and he took secretly from the linen which was his, and threw it on to the widow's side of the scales until he fulfilled an act of charity towards her.

420. A certain brother came to Abbâ 'Ôr, and said unto him, "Come with me to the village, and buy me a little wheat of "which I am in need"; now the old man was greatly troubled at this, because he was not accustomed to go to the village, nevertheless, being afraid [of transgressing] the commandment, he rose up and went with him. And when they arrived at the village the old man saw a man passing by, and he called him and said unto him, "Do an act of kindness, and "take this brother and satisfy his need," and in this way he was able to flee to the mountain.

421. On one occasion Adlêp, Bishop of Neapolis, went to visit Abbâ Sisoes, and when he wished to depart the old man made him and the brethren who were with him to eat in the morning; now the days were the first days of the fast. And when they had made ready the table to eat, behold, certain men from the plough knocked at the door, and the old man said unto his disciple, "Open to them, and put some of the "boiled food in a dish, and set it before them to eat, for they "have just come from labour." The Bishop said, "Let it "alone, or perhaps they will say that Abbâ Sisoes eateth at "this time." And the old man looked at the youth and said unto him, "Go, and give them the food"; and when the strangers saw the boiled food they said unto him, "Have ye "strangers with you? Peradventure Abbâ is also eating with "them?" And the disciple said unto them, "Yes." Then they cried out and spake words of condemnation to the company, saying, "May God forgive you, for ye have made the old man "to eat at this time of the day. Perhaps ye are unaware that "ye are causing him much vexation thereat?" And when the Bishop heard these things he expressed contrition, and said unto him, "Forgive me, I have behaved after the manner of a "man, but thou hast acted like God."

422. They used to say that, [on one occasion] when Abbâ Agathon came to the city to sell his handiwork, he found a stranger lying sick in the market, and he had no man to care for him, and the old man stayed with him; and he hired a room in the town and remained therein working with his hands, now [what he received therefor] he spent on the rent of the room and on the needs of the sick man, for a period of four months, and when the sick man was made whole the old man departed to his own cell.

423. And an old man used to say, "It is a defect in a man "if, when he is reviled by his brother, or when any evil cometh "to him from him, he cannot strengthen his love before he "meeteth him."

424. A brother was, on one occasion, sent from Scete by his Abbâ on a camel to Egypt to fetch palm leaves for [making] baskets, and having gone down and brought the camel, another brother met him and said unto him, "Had I known "that thou wast coming up I should have begged thee to bring "a camel for me also"; and when the brother came and told his Abbâ what had been said unto him by his companion, his Abbâ said unto him, "Take the camel and lead it to that "brother, and say unto him, 'We have taken counsel, and we "'have given up the intention of bringing up palm leaves at "'present, but do thou take [the camel] and bring some up

" 'for thyself.' " Now the brother did not wish to accept the
camel, but [his companion] entreated him [to do so], saying,
" If thou dost not take him we shall waste what we have paid
" in hire for him." So the brother took the camel and brought
up his palm leaves. And after he had gone up to Egypt that
brother took the camel a second time, and he came back that
he himself might go up; and the brother said unto him, "Where
" takest thou the camel?" and he said unto him, "To Scete,
" so that we also may bring up our palm leaves"; and that
brother repented and was very sorry, and he expressed contrition and said, " Forgive me, my brethren, for your great
" charity hath taken away my hire."

425. One of the brethren said, "Whilst we were sitting and
" talking about love, Abbâ Joseph said, 'Do we know what
" 'love is?' And he said that Abbâ Agathon had a little knife,
" and that a certain brother came to him and said, 'Father,
" 'the little knife which thou hast is pretty'; and Abbâ Agathon
" did not let him depart until he had taken it."

426. Abbâ Agathon used to say, "If I could find an Arian to
" whom I could give my body and take his in its place, I would
" do so, because this would be perfect love."

427. A brother asked Abbâ Muthues, saying, "What shall I
" do if a brother come unto me, and it be a time of fast or the
" morning, and I am in tribulation?" The old man said unto
him, " If thou art afflicted, and dost eat with the brother thou
" doest well; but if thou dost not look at the man, and dost
" eat, this is a matter of thy will only."

428. Mother Sarah used to say, "It is a good thing for a
" man to give alms, even though he do so for the approbation
" of the children of men, for from this he will come to do it for
" God's sake."

429. A brother asked Abbâ Poemen, saying, "If I find a
" place wherein there is pleasure for the brethren, dost thou
" wish me to dwell there?" The old man said unto him, "Where
" thou wilt not do harm to thy brother, there dwell."

430. Abbâ Poemen used to say that whenever Isidore, the
priest of Scete, used to address the brethren in the church, he
spake the following words only: "My brethren, it is written,
" Forgive thy brother that thou also mayest be accounted
" worthy of forgiveness" (St. Luke vi, 37; St. Matthew vi, 14).

431. They used to say that at the beginning Abbâ Zeno refused to take anything from any man, and that those who
brought him things used to go away sorrowfully because he
would not be persuaded to accept them from them. And other
men used to come and ask him to give them gifts as of a great
old man, and they also went away sorrowfully because he re-

fused to do so. Then the old man said within himself, "Those
"who bring go away in sorrow, and those who beg also go
"away grieving because they have received nothing; I will,
"therefore, act as follows: If any man bringeth me anything
"I will take it, and if any man asketh me for anything I will
"give it"; and he did so, and pleased every one.

432. The disciple of Abbâ Theodore said, "A certain man on
"one occasion came to sell onions, and he filled a basin with
"some of them and gave them to us; and the old man said
"to me, 'Fill [the basin] with wheat and give it to him.' Now
"there were two baskets of wheat there, one full of clean
"wheat, and the other was full of wheat which was dirty, and
"I filled the basin with the dirty wheat and gave it to him.
"Then the old man looked at me in wrath and anger, and in
"my fear I fell down, and broke the basin; and the old man
"said unto me, 'Arise, thou art not akin to me, but I know
"'well what I said unto thee.' And the old man went in and
"filled his garment with clean wheat, and gave it to the man
"with the onions, together with his onions."

433. A certain monk used to dwell by the side of a coenobium,
and he was occupied in great ascetic labours, and led a life of
hard work, and strangers came to the coenobium, and forced
him to eat before his time; and afterwards the brethren said
unto him, "Art thou not now afflicted, father?" He said
unto them, "Although I am afflicted I have cut off my
"desire."

434. A certain old man used to say, "It is right for a man
"to take up the burden for those who are akin (*or* near) to
"him, whatsoever it may be, and, so to speak, to put his own
"soul in the place of that of his neighbour, and to become, if
"it were possible, a double man; and he must suffer, and
"weep, and mourn with him, and finally the matter must be
"accounted by him as if he himself had put on the actual body
"of his neighbour, and as if he had acquired his countenance
"and soul, and he must suffer for him as he would for him-
"self. For thus is it written:—'We are all one body,' and this
"[passage] also affordeth information concerning the holy and
"mysterious kiss."

435. An old man said that the father had a custom of going
to the cells of the new brethren, who wished to live by themselves, to visit them, lest one of them might be tempted and
injured in his mind by the devils, and if they found any man
who had been harmed they would bring him to the church,
and would place a wash-basin full of water [in the midst], and
when prayer had been made on behalf of him that had been
brought there, all the brethren would wash themselves and

then pour some of the water upon him, and immediately that brother was cleansed.

436. A brother asked an old man, saying, "If I find a "brother concerning whom I have heard [that he hath com-"mitted] some offence, I never rest until I have brought him "into my cell; but if I see a man who leadeth a good life I "bring him unto myself gladly." The old man said unto him, "Do that which is good twice over unto the former man, for "he is sick, and he needeth help."

437. An old man used to say, "Defeat cometh to a man if, "when he is reviled and treated with contempt by his brother, "he doth not shew him evenness of heart before he repenteth "and asketh him to forgive him."

438. There was a monk, and away on the mountain, which was about ten miles distant from him, was another monk; and the first monk had some bread in his cell, and he meditated in his mind and determined to invite the other monk to come and partake of his bread. And again he thought in his mind, say-ing, "Since the bread is with me I shall give my brother the "labour [of walking] ten miles [if I invite him to come here], "but it will be more helpful [to him] if I take one half of the "bread which I possess, and carry it to him"; so he took the bread to carry it to the cell of the other brother. Now as he was journeying along, he tripped up, and fell, and injured one of his fingers, and as the blood was running down he began to cry because of the pain; and there appeared unto him sud-denly an angel who said unto him, "Why weepest thou?" And the monk said unto him, "I have hurt my finger, and it "paineth me"; and the angel said unto him, "Dost thou weep "because of this? Weep not, for the number of every step "which thou takest for our Lord's sake is written down, and "is estimated at a great reward (*or* hire) before Him, and the "report of the labour of such things goeth up to Him. And "that thou mayest be certain that such is the case, behold, in "thy presence I will take some of this blood and carry [it] to "our Lord"; and immediately the monk was healed, and with rejoicing and thanksgiving to God he set out again on his journey to go to his companion. And having come to him and given him the bread, he related unto him concerning the love for man which is found in the good Lord, the Creator of the universe, and then went back to his cell. Now after one day he took the other half of the bread and went to carry it to another monk. And it happened that he also was found to be burning with anxiety to emulate works of this kind, and he wanted to do even as the other monk had done; and having set out to go and carry the bread of the first monk, they happened to meet each other on the way. Then the first monk who had done good to the other monk began to say unto him, "I possessed a certain treasure, and thou wishest to rob me "[of it]"; and the other monk said unto him, "Where is it "written that the strait and narrow door is sufficient for thy- "self alone? Let us, even us, go in with thee." Then straight- way, whilst they were holding converse, the angel of the Lord appeared, and said unto them, "Your contending hath as- "cended unto the Lord even as a sweet smell."

439. On one occasion, a certain excellent man, who feared God in his life and works, and who was living in the world, went to Abbâ Poemen, and some of the brethren, who were also with the old man, were asking him questions [wishing] to hear a word from him. Then Abbâ Poemen said to the man who was in the world, "Speak a word to the brethren"; but he entreated him, saying, "Forgive me, father, but I came to "learn." And the old man pressed him [to speak], and, as the force of his urging increased, he said, "I am a man living in "the world, and I sell vegetables, and because I do not know "how to speak from a book, listen ye to a parable. There was "a certain man who had three friends, and he said to the first, "'Since I desire to see the Emperor come with me'; and the "friend said unto him, 'I will come with thee half the way.' "And the man said to the second friend, 'Come, go with me "'to the Emperor's presence'; and the friend said unto him, "'I will come with thee as far as his palace, but I cannot go "'with thee inside'; and the man said the same unto his third "friend, who answered and said, 'I will come with thee, and "'I will go inside the palace with thee, and I will even stand "'up before the Emperor and speak on thy behalf.'" Then the brethren questioned him, wishing to learn from him the strength of the riddle (or dark saying), and he answered and said unto them, "The first friend is abstinence, which leadeth as far as "one half of the way; and the second friend is purity and "holiness, which lead to heaven; and the third friend is loving- "kindness, which stablisheth a man before God, and speaketh "on his behalf with great boldness."

440. A brother went to visit a certain monk, and when he went forth from him, he said unto him, "Forgive me, father, "for having made thee to desist from thy rule"; and the monk said unto him, "My rule is to refresh thee, and to send thee "away in peace."

441. On one occasion a command was given to the brethren who were in Scete, and it was said unto them, "Fast ye this "week, and celebrate the Passover." And it happened that some brethren came from Egypt to Abbâ Moses, and whilst

he was boiling for them a little food, his neighbours saw the smoke [of his fire] rising up, and they said to the clergy, "Be-"hold, Moses hath broken the command, and hath boiled "some food in his cell"; and they said unto them, "Hold ye "your peace, and when he cometh to us we will speak to him." Now when the Sabbath arrived, the clergy, having regard to his great ascetic labours, said unto him before the whole assembly, "O Abbâ Moses, though thou dost break the com-"mand of men, thou stablishest [that of God]."

442. They used to tell the story of a certain brother who, when he was throwing away the handles of his baskets, heard his neighbour say, "What shall I do? For the festival draweth "nigh, and I have no handles to put on my baskets"; and the brother went straightway and picked up the handles of his baskets, and brought them to his companion, saying, "Be-"hold I have these, of which I have no need, take them and "put them on thy baskets"; and he left his own work and completed that of his companion.

443. Certain of the old men went to Abbâ Poemen, and said unto him, "Dost thou wish us if we see brethren sleeping "in the congregation, to smite them so that they may wake "up?" And he said unto them, "If I see my brother sleeping, "I place his head upon my knees, and I give him a place to "rest upon"; then an old man said unto him, "And what dost "thou say unto God?" Abbâ Poemen said unto him, "I say "unto Him thus: Thou Thyself hast said, 'First of all pluck "'the beam out of thine own eye, and then thou wilt be able "'to see to take the mote out of the eye of thy brother'" (St. Matthew vii, 3).

Chapter x. Of Humility and of how a Man should think lightly of himself, and should esteem himself the Inferior of every Man

444. ABBÂ ISAAC, the priest of the Cells, used to say: When I was a young man I used to dwell with Abbâ Chronius, and he never at any time told me to do any work; now he was an old man and he trembled, but he would stand up and give water with his hands to me, and to all of us alike. And with Abbâ Theodore of Parmê it was the same, for he never told me to do any work whatsoever, but he would make ready the table with his own hands, and would say, "Brother, come [and] eat." And I said unto him, "Father, I "came that I might assist thee, and how is that thou dost not "tell me to do something?" But the old man in all this held his peace. And I went up and informed the old men, and they came to him, and said unto him, "Father, this brother came

" unto thy holiness that he might be assisted [by thee], and
" why dost thou not tell him to do something?" Then the old
man said unto them, " Am I the head of a monastery that I
" should give him a command? I shall say unto him nothing ex-
" cept that [I] wish him to do that which he seeth me do." And
from that time I was always before him in doing that which
the old man was going to do; now whatsoever he did, he did
in silence, and in this manner he made me to know and taught
me to work in silence also.

445. There was a certain Egyptian monk in Constantinople
under the reign of Theodosius the Less, and he used to dwell
in a little cell, and when the Emperor went forth [on one occa-
sion] to take his pleasure, he came by himself to the monk;
now the following of men who were with him waited for him
at a distance. And the Emperor took off his crown from his
head, and hid it, and he knocked at the door of the monk, and
when he opened to him he knew that it was the Emperor, but
he [feigned] forgetfulness and would not recognize him, and he
welcomed him as one of his own rank in life, and he prayed
and sat down. Then the Emperor began to question him, saying, " How are the fathers who are in Egypt?" And the monk
said unto him, " They all pray for thy health." And the Emperor examined his cell, and saw nothing there except a small
basket wherein was bread, and the monk said to him, " Eat,"
and he dipped the bread in water, and poured oil on it, and
salt, and he gave it to the Emperor, who ate it; and he gave
him some water, and he drank. Then the Emperor said unto
him, " Knowest thou who I am?" And the monk said unto
him, " God knoweth who thou art." And the Emperor said
unto him, " I am Theodosius, the Emperor," and straightway
the monk paid homage unto him. Then the Emperor said unto
him, " Blessed art thou in that thou hast none of the cares of
" this world; verily I was born to kingship and before this day
" I have never been satisfied with bread and water, and they
" have pleased me greatly "; and the Emperor began to pay
honour to him. And straightway that monk fled to Egypt with
all the speed that was possible.

446. A certain brother came to Abbâ Macarius, the Egyptian,
and said unto him, " Father, speak to me a word whereby I
" may live." Abbâ Macarius saith unto him, " Get thee to the
" cemetery and revile the dead"; and he went and reviled them,
and stoned them with stones, and he came and informed the
old man [that he had done so]. And the old man said unto
him, " Did they say nothing unto thee?" and the brother said
unto him, " No." And again the old man said unto him, " Go
" to-morrow and praise them, and call them, ' Apostles,

" 'Saints, and Righteous Men'"; and he came to the old man,
and said, " I have praised them." And the old man said unto
him, " And did they return thee no answer?" and he said
" No." And the old man said unto him, " Thou seest how
" thou hast praised them, and that they said nothing to thee,
" and that although thou didst revile them they returned thee no
" answer. And thus let it be with thyself. If thou wishest to
" live, become dead, so that thou mayest care neither for the
" reviling of men nor for [their] praise, for the dead care for
" nothing; in this wise thou wilt be able to live."

447. One of the fathers used to relate that he had an old
man in a cell, who performed many ascetic labours, and who
clothed himself in a palm-leaf mat; and this old man went to
Abbâ Ammon, who, seeing that he wore a palm-leaf mat only,
said unto him, " This will profit thee nothing." And the old
man asked him, saying, " Three thoughts vex me. Shall I go
" to the desert, or shall I go forth into exile, or shall I shut
" myself up in a cell, and receive no man, and eat once every two
" days?" Abbâ Ammon said unto him, " Thou art not able to
" do any one of these things, but go, sit in thy cell, and eat a
" very little food each day, and let there be in thine heart al-
" ways the word[s] of the publican, ' God be merciful to me
" 'a sinner,' and thus thou shalt be able to live" (St. Luke
xviii, 13).

448. Abbâ Daniel used to relate a story, saying:—There was
with us in Babylon of Egypt the daughter of a man who was
the captain of a company of soldiers, and she was possessed of
a devil, and her father took her to many places, but she could
not find healing. Now her father had a friend who was a
monk, and he said unto him, " No man is able to cure her ex-
" cept those monks of whom I spake unto thee, but even if we
" entreat them to do this they will not agree to it, because they
" flee from the love of the approbation [of men]. Nevertheless,
" when they come to sell [their] baskets, ye shall pretend that
" ye wish to buy some, and when they come to sell and to take
" the price of the baskets from thy house, we will say unto
" them, ' Put up a prayer, and this maiden shall be healed' "; and
the man did so. And they came as it were to buy baskets, and they
found the disciple of these holy men sitting down and selling
[them], and they took him and the baskets, and carried him to their
houses, and then they set another man in his place, and commanded him when the monks came to bring them to them. Now when
their disciple entered the house, the maiden who was possessed
of a devil went forth and smote him on the cheek, but that
brother fulfilled the commandment and turned to her the other
cheek, and straightway that devil, who was unable to bear the

blow of the commandment of Christ which was fulfilled, cried out with a loud voice, and departed. And when the monks came [the people in the house] related unto them the reason for what had happened, and they glorified God, and said, " It " is customary for the boasting of the Evil One to fall before " the humility of the commandments of Christ. "

449. On one occasion Abbâ Ammon went to Abbâ Anthony, and he lost the way, and sat down for a little and fell asleep; and he rose up from his slumber, and prayed unto God, and said, "I beseech Thee, O Lord God, not to destroy that which " Thou hast fashioned." Then he lifted up his eyes, and, behold, there was the form of a man's hand above him in the heavens, and it shewed him the way until he came and stood above the cave of Abbâ Anthony; and when he had gone into the cave to the old man, Abbâ Anthony prophesied unto him, saying, "Thou shalt increase in the fear of God." Then he took him outside the cave, and showing him a stone, said, "Curse " this stone, and smite it," and he did so, and Abbâ Anthony said unto him, " It is thus that thou shalt arrive at this state, " for thou shalt bear heaviness, and great abuse"; and this actually happened to Abbâ Ammon. Now, through his abundant goodness Abbâ Ammon knew not wickedness. And after he had become a Bishop, through his spiritual excellence they brought unto him a virgin who had conceived, and they said unto him, "So-and-so hath done this deed; let them receive " correction"; but he made the sign of the Cross over her belly, and ordered them to give her six pair of linen cloths, and he said, "Peradventure when she bringeth forth either she or the " child will die, [and if either dieth] let them be buried." Then those who were with him said unto him, "What is this that " thou hast done? Give the command that they receive correc- " tion." And he said unto them, "See, O my brethren, she is " nigh unto death, and what can I do?" Then he dismissed her. And the old man never ventured to judge anyone, for he was full of lovingkindness and endless goodness to all the children of men.

450. They used to say that [on one occasion] when Abbâ Arsenius the Great fell ill in Scete, a priest went and brought him to the church, and he spread a palm-leaf mat for him, and [placed] a small pillow under his head; and one of the old men came to visit him and saw that he was lying upon a mat and that he had a pillow under his head, and he was offended and said, "And this is Arsenius lying upon such things!" Then the priest took the old man aside privately, and said unto him, "What labour didst thou do in thy village?" and the old man said unto him, "I was a shepherd." And the priest said unto

him, "What manner of life didst thou lead in the world?" and
he said unto him, "A life of toil, and sore want." And when
the old man had described all the tribulation which he had endured in the world, the priest said unto him, "And here what
" manner of life dost thou lead?" And the old man said unto
him, "In my cell I have everything comfortable, and I have
" more than I want"; and the priest said unto him, "Consider
" [the position of] Abbâ Arsenius when he was in the world!
" He was the father of kings, and a thousand slaves, girt
" about with gold-embroidered vests, and with chains and or-
" naments round their necks, and clothed in silk, stood before
" him; and he had the most costly couches and cushions [to
" lie upon]. But thou wast a shepherd, and the comforts which
" thou didst never enjoy in the world thou hast here; but this
" man Arsenius hath not here the comforts which he enjoyed
" in the world, and now thou art at thine ease whilst he is
" troubled." Then the mind of the old man was opened, and
he expressed contrition and said, "Father, forgive me; I have
" sinned. Verily this is the way of truth. He hath come to a
" state of humility, whilst I have attained to ease." And the
old man having profited went his way.

451. They used to say that on one occasion Abbâ Macarius
was passing along the road when Satan met him, and the
Devil wished to cut him down with the scythe which he held
in his hand, but he was unable to do so, and he said unto him,
" Macarius, I am dragged along by thee with great force, but
" I cannot overcome thee. Now, behold, everything which
" thou doest I can do also. Thou fastest, and I never eat at
" all. Thou watchest, and I never go to sleep, and there is one
" thing only wherein thou dost conquer me." Then Macarius
said unto him, "And what is that?" And Satan said, "It is
" thy humility, for it is because of this that I cannot vanquish
" thee"; then Macarius spread out his hands in prayer, and
the Devil was no more seen.

452. On one occasion a devil took a knife and stood over
Abbâ Macarius wishing to cut off his leg, and when he was
unable to do so on account of the humility [of the old man],
he answered and said unto him, "Everything which ye pos-
" sess we possess also, and it is only in humility that ye are
" superior to us, and [it is only by means of it] that ye con-
" quer us."

453. Abbâ Anthony said, "I saw all the snares of the Enemy
laid out upon the ground, and I groaned and said, 'Who can
" 'escape from these?'" And the devils said unto me, 'Humility
" 'maketh a man to escape from these, for we cannot attain
" 'unto it.'"

454. An old man said, "Whensoever a man is praised it is
" meet for him to think upon his sins, and he should consider,
" saying, 'I am unworthy of the things which are said about me.'"

455. The blessed Macarius behaved towards all the brethren
without any wicked suspicion, and certain people said unto
him, "Why dost thou act in this manner?" And he said, "Be-
"hold, for twelve years I have been supplicating my Lord to
" give me this gift, and would you advise me to relinquish it?
" If it happen that one of the brethren commit a sin before
" the eyes of him who possesseth no wickedness, and he know
" that it is an evil thing, it is not right that he should bear
" some of the pain of him that hath fallen."

456. Abbâ Poemen used to say, "No monk should condemn
" any man in anything, and no monk should reward a man
" with [evil for] evil, and no monk should be a man of anger."

457. An old man asked Abbâ Poemen, saying, "Some breth-
" ren dwell with me; dost thou wish me to give them command-
" ments?" And he said unto him, "No, but thou thyself must
" first do work, and if they wish to live, they will observe [it]
" and do [it]." The old man said unto him, "Ought they also
" to wish me to govern them?" And Abbâ Poemen said unto
him, "No, be unto them an example, and not a lawgiver."

458. Abbâ Poemen said, "If a brother come unto thee, and
" thou be not benefited by his coming in [to thee], enquire in
" thine heart, and learn what thought thou hadst [in thy mind]
" before the entrance of that brother, and then thou wilt learn
" whence cometh the source of injury; if thou wilt do this with
" humility and knowledge, behold, thou wilt live without
" blame with thy brother, and thou wilt bear thine own short-
" comings. If a man maketh his habitation with knowledge
" it will not fall, for God is before it, and, as it appeareth to
" me, from this habitation a man may acquire the fear of God."

459. A brother asked an old man, saying, "By what means
" may a man go forward? and the old man said unto him,
" The greatness of a man consisteth of humility, for in pro-
" portion as a man descendeth to humility, he becometh exalted
" to greatness."

460. Abbâ John used to say, "We relinquish a light burden
" when we condemn ourselves, but we take upon ourselves a
" heavy burden when we [attempt to] make ourselves righteous."

461. On one occasion Abbâ Theophilus went to the Nitrian
Mountain to visit the fathers, and the priest of the Mountain
came to him; and Abbâ Theophilus said to him, now he was
Theophilus the Bishop of Alexandria, "What thing of excel-
"lence hast thou found on this road?" And the old man said
unto him, "I make accusations against myself, and I blame

"myself at all times"; and Abbâ Theophilus said unto him,
"Verily this is the way of truth."

A variant reads: "On one occasion the Archbishop Theo-
"philus went to the mountain of Nitria, and a certain Abbâ of
"the monks who was in the mountain came unto him; Abbâ
"Theophilus said unto him, "What more do the monks find
"in this way [than in any other]?" The old man said unto him,
"They condemn themselves continually, and they do not judge
"their neighbours"; and Abbâ Theophilus said, "There is no
"way but this."

462. On one occasion they brought a man possessed of a
devil to one of the old men of Thebes, and entreated him to
cast the devil out, but the old man was unwilling [to do so];
but since they urged him strongly he was persuaded, and he
had mercy on the man, and he said to the devil, "Get thee out
"from that which God hath fashioned." Then the devil answered and said, "I am going out, but I would ask thee to
"tell me one thing: What is the meaning of that which is
"written in the Gospel, Who are the goats and who are the
"sheep?" The old man answered and said, "I myself am [one
"of] the goats, but God knoweth who the sheep are"; and
when the devil heard this, he cried out with a loud voice,
saying, "Behold, I go forth because of thy humility," and
straightway he left the man and departed.

463. They used to say that on one occasion a few early, white
figs came to Scete, but because they were nothing [of im-
portance] they did not send any to Abbâ Arsenius, not wishing
to insult him; and when the old man heard of this he did not
come to the congregation, saying, "Ye separated me from the
"blessed gift which God sent to the brethren because I was
"unworthy to partake of it." And when the old man heard
[this] they profited [greatly] by his humility, and the priest went
and carried some of the figs to him, and brought him to the
congregation with great joy.

464. A certain Abbâ asked Abbâ Muthues, saying, "If I go to
"a place to dwell, how wouldst thou have me conduct myself?"
The old man said unto him, "If thou wishest to dwell in a cer-
"tain place, [do so,] but do not let go forth concerning thyself
"any fame for praiseworthy acts, [or say,] 'I do not eat,' or,
"'I do not drink,' for such things only produce empty fame;
"and thou wilt find at length that thou wilt profit from many,
"for men will go where they can find qualities of this kind."
Then the brother said unto him, "What shall I do?" and the
old man said unto him, "Wheresoever thou dwellest conduct
"thyself in a simple manner like every one else, and what thou
"seest those who fear God do, [I mean] those in whom thou

" hast confidence, that do also, and thou shalt be at ease. For
" to be as all other men are is true humility, and the men who
" see that thou art like unto all other men will regard thee as
" they regard every one else, and thou wilt not be troubled."

465. A certain brother went on one occasion from Egypt to
Syria to visit Abbâ Zeno, and the Egyptians began to make
accusations against his thoughts before the old man. And
when Abbâ Zeno heard this, he marvelled and said, "The
" Egyptians always hide the spiritual excellences which they
" possess, but they describe the shortcomings which they do not
" possess; on the other hand, the Syrians and the Greeks declare
" that they possess the virtues which they have not, and they
" hide the shortcomings which they do possess."

466. They used to talk about a certain old man who fasted
for seventy weeks, and who only ate each Saturday; and he
asked God that a word from the Book might be given unto him,
but it was not given. Then he said within himself, "Behold, I
" have laboured in all these things, and I have omitted nothing;
" I will arise and go to my brother and question him [about
" it]." And when he had shut the door to depart, the angel of
the Lord appeared, and said unto him, "The seventy weeks
" wherein thou didst fast have not come nigh unto God, but,
" inasmuch as thou hast humbled thyself to go to thy brother,
" I have been sent to make known unto thee a word, and to
" give thee rest"; thereupon he made the word known unto
him, and gave him rest, and departed.

467. A brother asked an old man, saying, "What shall I do?
" For the love of praise is killing me." The old man said unto
him, "Thou doest well, for behold, thou hast made the heavens
" and the earth." Then the brother was sorry because of what
the old man had said unto him, and he expressed contrition,
and said, "Father, forgive me, but I have done nothing of the
" kind"; the old man said unto him, "If now He Who did
" make them came into this world in humility, why dost thou
" who art mud boast thyself?"

468. One of the old men said, "Be not humble in thy words
" only, but also in thy deeds."

469. On one occasion a certain governor came to see Abbâ
Sîmôn, and when the old man heard of his coming from those
who came to make it known to him beforehand, he straightway
girded up his loins, and went up a palm tree to clean it. And
when those who came cried out to him, saying, "Old man, tell
" us where the monk is," he said unto them, "He is not here";
so they departed from that place.

470. One of the fathers from Parmê told a story of how, on
one occasion when he had returned to Abbâ Theodore, he found

him wearing a ragged shirt, and his breast was naked and bare,
and his outer garment was dragged round in front of him. And,
behold, a certain Count came to see him, and when his followers knocked at the door, and called the old man, he went out
to meet him quite carelessly; and I took a small piece of coarse
cloth and threw it over his shoulders that his breast might be
covered, but the old man took it in his hand and waved it, and
threw it away. And when the Count went I said to him,
" Father, what is this that thou hast done? For a nobleman
" came unto thee to be helped, and to gain profit, and behold,
" he hath perhaps gone away offended." And the old man said
unto me, "Get thee gone, Abbâ. We are still subject unto men.
" We have done the deed, and he is gone; but whether he
" wisheth to be benefited, or whether he wisheth to be offended
" is his affair. As for me, as far as I am able I shall always
" meet men of this kind in this way." And he commanded his
disciple, saying, "If any man cometh and wisheth to see me,
" say not to him anything after the manner of men, but if I
" am eating, tell him that I am eating, and if I am asleep, tell
" him that I am asleep."

471. A certain woman who was afflicted in her lungs with
the disease called cancer, heard concerning Longinus and
wished to see him; now he used to dwell in [the monastery of]
Hantôn in Alexandria. And whilst the woman was seeking
and wishing for him, it happened that the blessed man was
gathering sticks on the sea-shore, and when the woman found
him, she said unto him, "Father, where dwelleth the man of
" God, Abbâ Longinus?" Now she did not know that he himself was Longinus. And he said unto her, "What dost thou
" want with that lying hypocrite? Do not go to him, for he is
" a liar. What is it that causeth thee pain?" Then the woman
shewed him the place, and the old man made the sign of the
Cross over it, and he dismissed her, saying, "Go, and may our
" Lord heal thee, for Longinus is unable to do thee any good
" whatsoever." And the woman went away believing in the
word, and she was healed straightway; and afterwards when
she was telling folks the story, she said, "I have learned by
" the marks which were on the old man that he himself was
" Abbâ Longinus."

472. On one occasion a certain governor arranged to see
Abbâ Sîmôn, and the clergy told him beforehand, saying,
" Father, make thyself ready, for a certain governor hath heard
" of thy life and works, and he wisheth to come and be blessed
" by thee"; and the old man said unto them, "I am ready."
Then the old man went in and took in his hand some bread
and cheese, and went out to the door and sat down there, and

he changed about from place to place eating; and when the governor came with his company, and saw him sitting and eating, they despised him, saying, "So this is the monk of whom "I have heard!" And they left him and departed.

473. An old man was asked, "How is it that there are men "who say, 'We have seen a vision of angels?'" and the old man said, "Blessed is he who seeth his sins continually."

474. They used to say that when any man came to Abbâ Poemen he used to send him to Abbâ Job, his brother, saying to him, "He is older than I am"; and Job used to say to those who came, "Go unto my brother Poemen, for he possesseth "the grace of these gifts." Now if Abbâ Joseph was sitting with him Abbâ Poemen would not speak before him.

475. When a certain brother went to the festival he asked Abbâ Poemen, "What wouldst thou have me to do?" The old man said unto him, "Be thou a friend unto him that lead- "eth thee away by force, and sell thy work graciously."

476. A brother asked an old man, "What is the work of "exile?" And the old man said unto him, "I knew a brother "who went forth into exile, and he went in to lodge in a church, "and it happened that the brethren were about to eat some of "the sacramental bread; and when they sat down this man "sat down with them. Now when some of the other monks "saw him, they said, 'Who hath brought this man in [to eat] "with us?' And one of them said [unto him], 'Arise, and get "'thee outside,' and straightway he rose up and went forth "as the brother had told him; but the others being sorry about "this matter went out and brought him in. And after these "things a certain man asked him, 'What was in thy mind "'when thou didst go out and come in again?' He said unto "them, 'I thought in my mind that I was like a dog which "'when he is driven out goeth out, and when he is called "'cometh in.'"

477. They used to say that when Abbâ Moses was one of the clergy he wore a long outer garment, and that the Bishop said unto him, "Behold, thou art wholly white, O Abbâ "Moses." The old man said unto him, "Is the Pâpâ within "or without?" And again, wishing to try him, the Bishop said unto the clergy, "When Abbâ Moses goeth into the "sacrarium drive him out, and go after him and hear what he "saith." Now when he went into the sacrarium they rebuked him and drove him out, saying, "Get outside, O Ethiopian"; and having gone forth he began to say to himself, "They have "treated thee rightly, O thou whose skin is dark and black; "thou shalt not go back as if thou wert a [white] man."

478. An old man used to say, "Do not despise or think

"lightly of him that standeth before thee, for thou knowest
"not whether the Spirit of God is in thee or in him, though
"thou callest him who standeth before thee him that minis-
"tereth unto thee."

479. Abbâ John the Less used to say, "Humility and the
"fear of God are more excellent than all the [other] virtues."

480. They used to say that a certain old man, who had
young men living with him, told them on one occasion to do
something, and when they did it not he said nothing further
to them about it, but rose up himself in their sight and did
what he had told them to do without anger, and without
labour.

481. Another old man used to say, "Humility is not with-
"out salt, but it is salted with salt."

482. An old man used to say, "I would rather learn than
"teach."

483. And he also used to say, "Do not learn before the
"time, so that thou mayest not have little admonition all thy
"time."

484. Abbâ Agathon said, "If a man of wrath were to raise
"the dead, he would not be accepted by any man."

485. A brother asked Abbâ Timothy, saying, "I myself can
"see that my memorial is ever before God"; and the old man
said unto him, "It would not be any great thing for thy thought
"(*or* mind) to be with God, but it would be a great thing for a
"man to see his soul beneath all creation."

486. Abbâ Theodore used to say, "There is no spiritual
"excellence greater than that of a man who despiseth not his
"companion."

487. An old man was asked, "By what means doth the soul
"receive humility?" And he said, "By searching into it, and
"by remembering the evil things which have been done by it."

488. One of the old men said, "I asked Abbâ Sisoes, saying,
"'Tell me a word,' and he said, 'It is right for a monk to
"'humble himself lower than the idols'; and I went to my cell,
"and took counsel with myself, and meditated for an hour,
"saying, 'What do the words "lower than the idols" mean?'
"Then I returned and went to the old man, and said unto
"him, 'What do the words "lower than the idols" mean?' And
"he said unto me, 'It is written concerning the idols, "They
"'"have a mouth and speak not, and they have eyes and see
"'"not, and they have ears and hear not"; even thus is it right
"'for a monk to be.' And because idols are an abomination, a
"man must hold himself to be abominable in his own sight."

489. A brother asked Abbâ Sisoes of Thebaïs, saying, "Speak
"a word to me," and Sisoes said unto him, "What have I to

" say unto thee? I read the New Testament, and I reflect on
" the Old Testament."

490. That same brother went to Abbâ Sisoes of Pâtârâ, and
told him the word which Abbâ Sisoes of the Thebaïd had
spoken, and Abbâ Sisoes said unto him, "I lie down to sleep
" in my sins, and I rise up in my sins."

491. There was a certain monk who lost himself in the desert,
and he said to himself, "I have kept myself rightly, and I pos-
" sess all the virtues," and he prayed to God and said, "If I
" be lacking in anything, shew Thou me how I may perform
" it." And God, wishing to humble his mind, said unto him,
" Go to such and such a head of a monastery, and whatsoever
" he telleth thee to do that do." And God sent a revelation to
the head of the monastery, and said unto him, "Behold, such
" and such a monk will come unto thee, and say thou unto him,
" 'Take a whip in thy hands, and go forth and pasture swine.'"
And the monk went forth immediately, even as the head of the
monastery told him, and pastured swine, and when those who
had known him formerly, and those who had heard about him,
saw him pasturing swine, they said, "Ye see the great monk
" about whom we have heard, behold, his heart hath gone mad,
" and a devil hath seized him, and he is [now] pasturing swine."
Then God, when He saw his humility, and that he was hearing and bearing the reproach of men, set him free so that he
might go back where he had been formerly.

492. An old man used to say, "If a man hath laid some work
" upon a brother to do, he must perform that command in the
" fear of God and in humility; for he who for God's sake layeth
" [some work] upon a brother maketh the brother to submit
" himself thereto, and [the one brother] must do what [the other
" brother] hath laid upon him. But if a man wisheth to give
" commands to a brother, not in the fear of God, but on his own
" authority, wishing to be unto him a master and a governor,
" God, Who seeth the hidden things of his heart, will not allow
" him to be obedient unto him and to do [that] work, for the
" work that is for God's sake is evident, and that which is of the
" man's own authority is well known. For that which is for God's
" sake cometh with humility and entreaty, whilst the works
" which are of man's own authority are with wrath and trouble,
" and they come from the Evil One."

493. A brother asked Abbâ Isidore, "Why is it that the
" devils fear thee so greatly? The old man said, "Because
" from the time that I became a monk I have laboured hard
" not to allow anger to enter into my throat; that is why they
" fear me."

494. An old man used to say, "On one occasion I went to

" the fair to sell with [other] brethren a few things, and I saw
" anger drawing nigh unto me, and I left the things and fled
" straightway."

495. Abbâ John the Less used to say, "On one occasion
" when I was going up on the Scete road with some palm leaves
" I heard a camel speaking words to me, and he was about to
" make me angry, but I straightway left the palm leaves and fled."

496. The same old man when he was in the harvest [field]
heard a brother speaking to his companion in anger, saying,
" Come hither," and straightway he left the harvest and fled.

497. A brother asked an old man, " Why is it, when I am
" performing my little services of prayer and praise, that I some-
" times see in myself that there is nothing lacking in my heart,
" and that I do not wish it?" The old man said unto him,
" How then can a man appear to love God?"

498. Abbâ John the Less said unto the brethren who were
with him, " Although we be little folk in the eyes of men, let
" us consider how we may be held in honour before God."

499. They used to say that Abbâ Patrâ and Abbâ Ampîkôs
were close and affectionate friends, and that when the old men
were eating in the church, and they were urging them to come
to the table of the fathers, it was only with hard work that Abbâ
Patrâ would go by himself; and after he had eaten, Abbâ
Ampîkôs said unto him, "How didst thou dare to go to the
" table of the old men?" Abbâ Patrâ said unto him, "If I had
" sat with you the brethren would have honoured me as an old
" man, and they would have required it of me to be the first to
" say the blessing, and I might have thought in my mind that
" I was greater than you all. But since I went to the fathers I
" am the least of you all, and I am abased, and I think in my
" thoughts that I am nothing."

500. On one occasion a brother committed sin in the church,
and the priest drove him out therefrom, and there was there a
man of discretion whose name was Bessarion, and he also arose
and went out of the church, and said, " If ye have judged that
" this man who hath committed only one offence is not fit to
" worship God, how very much less fit am I, who have com-
" mitted many sins, to do so?" And the old man said, "'Woe
" 'be unto him that is without more than unto him that is with-
" 'in,' that is to say, 'Woe be unto him that is [within him that
" 'is without!'] Now this is what I would say, When a man in
" the world findeth a cause [of complaint] against a man who
" liveth a life of silent contemplation, or who hath departed
" from the world, this is a [cause of] judgement and of a fall
" unto him who giveth him reason [for complaint]. Take the
" greatest possible care then, O monk, not to commit sin, lest

" thou disgrace God, Who dwelleth in thee, and drive Him out
" from thy soul."

501. Abbâ Pîôr worked hard to be able to overcome the disposition to say "Thou" to any of the brethren.

502. The disciple of Abbâ Arsenius used to say, "When
" the old man was about to die, he commanded us, saying,
" 'Do not let it be a care unto you to make a commemoration
" 'for me, but offer up the Offering only; for, he used to say,
" 'if during my life-time I have done anything which is worthy
" 'of commemoration, I shall most certainly find [a memorial
" 'of it].'"

503. Abbâ Ammon said, "A man may pass one hundred
" years in his cell, and not know rightly how a monk should
" live in his cell, or even how to live secluded for one day."
And he used to say, "The proper way and manner for a monk
" to live is to condemn himself continually."

504. Abbâ Poemen used to say, "If a man will only condemn
" himself he will be able to endure and continue wheresoever
" he dwelleth."

505. Abbâ Poemen used to say, "We live in the troubles and
" trials which come upon us because we do not take to our-
" selves the humble names which the Scriptures have given us;
" and because we do not consider how our Lord Jesus relieved
" the Canaanitish woman (St. Matthew xv, 22) who took to her-
" self abominable names, moreover, we do not consider how,
" when Abigail said unto David, 'On me be the sin' (1 Samuel
" xxv, 24), he was entreated by her and loved her. Abigail must
" be taken as [representing] the person of the soul, and David
" as the Godhead; if then, the soul will condemn itself before
" God, He will love it, and will give it the delight of rest."

506. An old man used to say, "In all thy trials blame no man;
" blame thyself only, saying, 'These things have happened to
" 'me because of my sins.'"

507. On one occasion Abbâ John was called to the church,
and the brethren surrounded him and asked him questions
about their thoughts; and one of the old men said unto him,
" John is like unto a whore who adorneth herself that she may
" multiply lovers for herself; thus art thou." And Abbâ John
sighed and said, "Father, thou hast spoken the truth." Afterwards a certain man told him that he loved him, [and said],
" Art thou not disturbed within?" He said unto him, "No.
" But as I am without, even so am I within."

508. One of the old men used to say about Abbâ John, that he
lived in such a way that, through the humility which he possessed, he held all Scete suspended on his finger.

509. Abbâ John of the Thebaïd used to say that, before all else, it was right for a monk to acquire humility, for this was the first commandment of our blessed Redeemer, Who said, "Blessed are the poor in spirit, for theirs is the kingdom of "God" (St. Matthew v, 3).

510. John Kolob used to say, "Humility is the door which "leadeth into the kingdom, and our fathers, through many "revilings, have gone into the city of God rejoicing."

511. An old man used to say, "It is good for a man to say, "'Forgive me,' and then to make an offering of something; "for this suiteth the monkish garb."

512. The same old man also said, "A dog is better than I "am, for he hath love, and he cometh not to judgement."

513. Abbâ Eupraxius used to say, "The tree of life which "riseth in the heights is humility." He also said, "Make thy-"self like unto the publican; and be not made guilty with the "Pharisee; choose for thyself the meekness of Moses, so that "thine heart, which is as hard as steel, thou mayest change into "a fountain of water.

514. One of the old men said, "I would rather have defeat "with humility than conquest with boasting."

515. An old man said, "When the thought of pride goeth "up in thee, and thou becomest arrogant, examine thy con-"science [and see] if thou hast kept all the commandments, "and if thou lovest thine enemies, and if thou lovest the ap-"probation of thine enemy, and if thou art grieved when he "is afflicted, and if thou art considered by thyself to be an "unprofitable servant, and a sinner greater than any other "man. And even if thou hast performed rightly all the de-"mands of ascetic excellence, thou shalt not be proud, for "thou must know that the thought of pride abrogateth and "maketh unprofitable all the virtues."

516. An old man used to say, "He who is held in greater "honour or is more praised than he deserveth suffereth great "loss; but the man who receiveth neither honour nor praise "from men shall be praised above all."

517. A brother asked an old man, saying, "Is it a good thing "for us to repent many times?" The old man said unto him, "We see that when Joshua, the son of Nun, lay upon his face "the Lord spake with him" (Joshua v, 14).

518. An old man was asked, "Why do the devils fight "against us in the way they do?" And he said, "Because we "throw away from us our armour, that is to say, obedience, "humility, and abstinence."

519. The old men used to say, "Whensoever we have no "war to wage then especially it is meet that we should abase "ourselves, for God, because He knoweth our feebleness,

" giveth us His protection for nothing, but if we boast ourselves,
" He removeth it from us and we perish."

520. A brother asked an old man, saying, "What is the per-
" fection of a monk?" The old man saith unto him, " Humility,
" for when once a man hath arrived at humility, he can reach
" forward to the goal."

521. The old man said, " If a man can say unto his brother,
" ' Forgive me,' and can humble himself, this belongeth to the
" perfection of the monk."

522. One of the old men said, " When a man saith unto his
" companion, ' Forgive me,' and at the same time humbleth
" himself, the devils are consumed."

523. A certain brother was offended at his brother, and when
the latter heard thereof he went to him to express his contrition, but he would not open the door; then he who had offended
his brother went to another old man and related the matter
unto him, and the old man answered and said, " Observe lest
" in thine own mind thou art justifying thyself, and art con-
" demning thy brother, as if he were the offender, for it may
" be that because of this he would not be persuaded to open
" unto thee. Nevertheless, do thou what I am going to tell thee.
" For although he hath offended thee, go thou, and hold firmly
" [to the belief] that thou hast offended against him, and may
" God put it into thy brother's mind to be reconciled to thee."

524. And the old man related unto him a story which
explained the matter, saying, " There were two men who
" were living in the world, and were fearers of God, and
" they were both of the same mind, and they went forth
" and became monks; and when they heard in a plain man-
" ner the word of the Gospel which saith, ' There are eu-
" ' nuchs who have made themselves eunuchs for the sake
" ' of the kingdom of heaven' (St. Matthew xix, 12), they
" arrived at the hottest point of their love, and they made them-
" selves eunuchs for the sake of the kingdom of heaven. Now
" when the Bishop heard [of this] he set them aside and excommu-
" nicated them. Then those men, wishing to show that they
" had done what was good, said unto one another, ' We have
" ' made ourselves eunuchs for the sake of the kingdom of heaven,
" ' and this Bishop driveth us out! Let us go and make a com-
" ' plaint against him to the head of our monasteries, that is,
" ' to the Bishop of Jerusalem '; and when they had gone to
" him they related unto him the whole matter. Then the Bishop
" said unto them, ' And I also set you aside and excommu-
" ' nicate you'; and being greatly grieved at this remark also
" they went to the Bishop of Antioch, and related the matter
" unto him, and he also drove them away with the same words.

" Then the two brethren said unto each other, ' Let us go to
" ' the Patriarch of Rome, and he will avenge us and will take
" ' vengeance on all these [Bishops].' And having gone to the
" great Patriarch and Bishop of Rome, and made him to know
" their matter, and what the Bishop and Patriarch [of Antioch]
" had said unto them, they said at length, ' We have come
" ' unto thee because thou art the head of them all.' Then the
" Bishop of Rome also said unto them, ' I also excommunicate
" ' you and excommunicate ye shall be.' Then, not knowing what
" to do, they said to each other, ' All these men accept the
" ' persons each of the other, and each honoureth the other,
" ' because they are accustomed to assemble together at the
" ' Synods, but let us go to the holy man of God, Epiphanius,
" ' Bishop of Cyprus, because he is indeed a Bishop, and he
" ' doth not accept the person of any man.' Now when they
" drew nigh unto the city, it was revealed unto Epiphanius
" concerning them, and he sent [a man] to meet them, and to
" say unto them, ' Ye shall not come into the city.' And when
" they came to themselves they repented, and said, ' In very
" ' truth we have sinned; with what can we justify ourselves?
" ' For, even supposing that the Bishop and the Patriarchs
" ' have excommunicated us in an unseemly manner, perad-
" ' venture this man is a prophet besides, for behold, God hath
" ' revealed unto him concerning us beforehand; let us then
" ' condemn ourselves in respect of everything which we have
" ' done.' Then when God, Who knoweth that which is in the
" hearts [of men] saw that they had in very truth condemned
" themselves, He worked upon the mind of Epiphanius so that,
" of his own accord, he sent and brought them, and associated
" them in communion with him. And he also wrote concerning
" them to the Bishop of Jerusalem, saying, ' Receive thy sons,
" ' for they have repented in truth.' "

And the old man said, " This is the healing of a man,
" and God desireth that a man should lay the offence of his
" companion upon himself." And when that brother heard [this
story] he acted according to the word[s] of the old man, and
he went and knocked at the door of that brother, who, immediately he perceived and knew from inside [that it was he], expressed his contrition to him whilst he was as yet inside, and
then straightway opened the door; and they made friends together, each with each, with all their souls, and the two of them
were in great peace.

525. Abbâ Poemen used to say, "As the earth falleth not,
" because it is fixed from below, even so he who abaseth him-
" self shall never fall."

526. Abbâ Sisoes asked Abbâ 'Ôr, and said unto him, "Tell

" me a word of excellence"; and he said unto him, "Dost thou
" think me true, and dost thou believe my promise?" And Abbâ
Sisoes said unto him, "Yes." Abbâ 'Ôr said unto him, "Go,
" and whatsoever ye have seen me do, that also do thyself";
and Abbâ Sisoes said unto him, "What do I see in thee, O my
" father?" And Abbâ 'Or answered and said unto him, "My mind
" is more abased than that of the least of all the children of men."

527. On one occasion seven brethren came to Abbâ Arsenius and they entreated him, saying, "What is the work of
" monks?" And the old man answered and said, "When I
" came to dwell in this place I went to two old men, and I
" asked them this same question. And they answered and
" said unto me, 'Dost thou believe in us?' and I said, 'Yes.'
" Then they said unto me, 'Go, and whatsoever thou hast seen
" 'us do, that also do thyself.'" And the brethren asked him
subsequently, saying, "Tell us, father, what was their work?"
Then the old man said unto them, "The one acquired great
" humility, and the other obedience." And they said unto him
next, "Tell us what is thy work?" and the old man said unto
them, "According to my will, and according to my mind; it is
" a great thing for a man not to bind himself with any matter";
and having profited they departed in gladness, giving praise
unto God.

528. A brother asked Abbâ Poemen, saying, "What shall I
" do with the weight of weariness which holdeth me?" And
the old man said unto him, "Both large and small boats are
" provided with thick ropes for towing, and if there be blowing
" a wind which is not favourable to the course of the ship,
" they throw them round their breasts and pull them along
" [from] dry land; and quietly and little by little they let the
" ship go on her way until God sendeth a wind which is suit-
" able for bearing her along whithersoever they wish her to
" go. But if they learn that a storm hath begun to rise, they
" make haste and drive a stake in the ground, and tie up the
" ship lest she should drift away. Now the stake is that a man
" should condemn himself."

529. A brother asked Abbâ Poemen, "How is it possible for
" a man to avoid speaking evilly to his neighbour?" The old
" man answered and said unto him, "We and our brethren
" possess two images. Whensoever then a man condemneth him-
" self, his brother appeareth unto him beautiful and excellent;
" but whensoever a man appeareth beautiful to himself, his
" brother will be found to be, in his sight, hateful and
" abominable."

530. Another old man said also, "Humility is not insipidity,
" but it is seasoned, as it were, with salt."

531. He also used to say, " For a man to despise himself is " a strong wall."

532. He also used to say, " Him who hath become despised "for our Lord's sake, will our Lord make wise."

533. An old man used to say, "Take heed, with all thy " might, that thou doest nothing which meriteth blame, and " desire not to adorn thyself."

534. An old man used to say, "If humility descendeth to " Sheol it is exalted unto the heavens; and although pride " goeth up to the heavens it shall be brought down to Sheol."

535. There were two brethren in Scete, and he who was younger than his fellow was the older in the monastic garb, and one of the fathers having come to visit them, they brought out a vessel of water and wanted to wash him. And the man who was the younger in respect of years drew nigh to wash the old man, but the old man laid hold upon his hands, and prevented him, and then he drew near him that was the elder [in respect of years] to wash him. And the brethren who were standing near him said unto him, "The younger brother, O " father, is the older in respect of the monastic garb"; then the old man said unto them, "I take the priority in the monastic " garb of the younger man and place it upon him that is the elder."

536. There was a certain brother in a monastery, and he used to take the whole weight of the brethren upon himself, and seeking to be held in contempt in the sight of every man, he used to make accusations against himself, even to the committing of fornication, and he used to say, "I have committed " it." Now the brethren who did not understand his life and works used to murmur against him, saying, "How very many " are the wickednesses which this man doeth here, and because " of them he doth not even work." Then their Abbâ, because he knew his works, and because he knew also that he was taking the affairs of every man upon himself, and that he did not do these things, spake unto the brethren, saying, "I will " undertake that he will make one mat in a week, in humility, " [which is more than all] your work [which is done] with " boasting, and if ye wish to know whether the matter be so " [or not], bring hither all your work, and bring hither also the " mat of that brother, and light a fire and throw therein all your " work"; [and when they had done so] everything was consumed except the mat of that brother. Now when the brethren saw this, they feared, and expressed their contrition, and from that time they held him to be an Abbâ.

537. They used to say that Abbâ Poemen never gave his mind to the Lord, and that his knowledge was superior to that of [any] one of the old men.

538. Abbâ Ammon asked Abbâ Poemen concerning the impure thoughts that were born of a man, and [concerning] vain lusts; and Abbâ Poemen said unto him, "Shall the axe boast "itself against him that wieldeth it?"

539. Abbâ Betimius asked Abbâ Poemen, saying, "If a man "be angry with me, and I express my contrition, and he will "not accept it, what am I to do?" the old man said unto him, "Take with thee two of thy friends, and express thy contrition "[in their presence]." And the old man Betimius said unto him, "And if he will not be persuaded [to accept it] then? And Abbâ Poemen answered and said, "Take with thee five others"; and Abbâ Betimius answered and said, "And if he will not "be persuaded by these?" Abbâ Poemen saith, "Then take "with thee a priest"; and Abbâ Betimius said, "And if he will "not be persuaded [then]?" Abbâ Poemen said unto him, "Without anger and without excitement pray unto God that "He may put into his mind [the desire for peace], and straight-"way thou shalt have no further care."

540. An old man used to say, "Tell me, brother, if thou "hast acquired the seal of work, which is humility?" A holy man who saw another sinning wept bitterly, saying, "This "man may sin to-day, but how many times shall I sin to-mor-"row? In whatsoever way a man may sin before thee, do not "condemn him, but think in thy mind that thou art a greater "sinner than he, even though he be a man in the world, and [re-"member] besides that he is sinning greatly against God."

541. Certain brethren went to visit Abbâ Poemen, and whilst they were sitting with him, they praised a certain brother, saying, "He hateth evil things." Abbâ Poemen said unto him that spake unto him, "What is the hatred of evil things?" Now the brother was astonished, and he found nothing to say; and he rose up and threw himself before the old man, saying: "Do thou tell me what is the hatred of evil things." And the old man said unto him, "The hatred of evil things is for a man "to hate his own sins, and to justify those of his neighbour."

542. A certain brother committed an offence in Scete, the camp of the monks, and when a congregation was assembled on this matter, they sent after Abbâ Moses, but he refused to come; then they sent the priest of the church to him, saying, "Come, for all the people are expecting thee," and he rose up and came. And he took a basket with a hole in it and filled it with sand, and carried it upon his shoulders, and those who went out to meet him said unto him, "What meaneth this, O "father?" And he said unto them, "[The sands are] my sins "which are running down behind me and I cannot see them, "and I, even I, have come this day to judge shortcomings

" which are not mine." And when they heard [this] they set
" free that brother and said nothing [further] to him.

543. Abbâ Moses entreated Abbâ Zechariah, saying,
" Speak a word of consolation unto the brethren," and Zech-
" ariah took his cloak, and laid it beneath his feet, saying,
" Except a man let himself be trodden upon thus he cannot
" be a monk."

544. A brother asked Abbâ Alônîs, saying, "What is the
" meaning of a man despising himself?" The old man said unto
him, " It meaneth that thou must set thyself below all the
" beasts, for thou must remember that they will not be judged."

545. And the same old man said also, "If a man accustom
" himself to be a teacher, this act belongeth to labour."

546. A brother asked Abbâ Poemen, saying, " What is the
" right manner for me to live in my cell?" Abbâ Poemen said
unto him, "How a man should live in his cell is known to
" men, that is to say, he must work with his hands, and eat
" once [daily], and hold his peace always, and meditate on the
" Holy Scriptures; but for a man to gain profit inwardly (*or*
" secretly), he must bear the condemnation of himself whither-
" soever he goeth, and he must not neglect the times of ser-
" vice and of secret labour. And if it happen that thou hast
" made the time unprofitable, when thou goest into the con-
" gregation of service complete thy service without troubling
" thyself; by the fulfilment of these things, grasp to thyself
" an upright congregation, so that thou mayest draw nigh
" thereto, but keep thyself remote from the assemblies of evil
" things."

547. On one occasion when Abbâ Arsenius was in his cell
the devils rose up against him and vexed him; and those who
used to minister to him came to him, and as they stood outside his cell they heard him crying out to God, saying, "O
" God, forsake me not. I have never done before Thee anything
" which is good, but grant, O Lord, according to Thy grace,
" that I may begin in the way."

548. Now, when he was about to die Alexander and Zoilus, his brethren and disciples, were greatly disturbed, and
he said unto them, "Why are ye troubled? The hour hath
" not yet come." They said unto him, " We are not troubled
" about thee, father." And he said unto them, "When the
" hour hath come I will tell you, for it will be for me to rise up
" against you before the throne of Christ if ye give my bones
" to any man." Then they said unto him, " What shall we do
" then? For we do not know how to bury [thee]." The old man
said unto them, "Do ye not know how to throw a cord round
" my legs and to carry me outside the mountain?"

549. And his word at all times was this, "Arsenius, because "thou didst go forth"; and he used to repeat this saying, "That I have spoken I have many times repented; that I held "my peace I have never repented."

550. On one occasion the governor of the country seized one of the inhabitants of his village, and the people entreated the old man to go and bring out him that had been seized; and the old man said unto them, "Leave me for three days, and after- "wards I will go." Then Abbâ Poemen prayed to the Lord, and said, "Lord, if thou dost not grant me this act of grace the "people will not allow me to live in this place"; and the old man went to entreat the governor, and the governor said unto him, "Yea, father, thou makest entreaty for a thief." And the old man rejoiced that he did not receive from Him this act of grace.

551. On one occasion certain old men went to visit Abbâ Anthony, and Abbâ Joseph was with them, and the old man wishing to try them spake a word from the Book, and began to question the youngest of them, saying, "What is the mean- "ing of this word?" And each of them said, "I have never "yet understood it," and last of all Abbâ Anthony said unto Abbâ Joseph, "And what dost thou say that this word meaneth?" Abbâ Joseph saith, "I do not know." And Abbâ Anthony said unto him, "In truth, Abbâ Joseph, thou hast found the way to say, 'I do not know.'"

552. Abbâ Muthues said, "In proportion as a man draweth "nigh unto God, it is meet that he should regard himself as a "sinner, for the Prophet Isaiah (chap. vi, 5), who saw the "Lord, calleth himself wretched and unclean."

553. The old man used to say, "Who sold Joseph?" They said unto him, "His brethren," and the old man said unto them, "No, it was humility that sold him. For he never said, "'I am your brother,' and he never answered them, but held "his peace. He sold himself by his humility, and this humility "made him governor over the land of Egypt."

554. A brother came to Abbâ Muthues, and said unto him, "How is it that those who are in Scete do more than that "which is written in the Book, for they love their enemies "more than themselves?" Muthues said unto them, "I do "not yet love even the man who loveth me more than I love "myself."

555. There was a certain old man in Egypt before those who belonged to the company of Abbâ Poemen came there, and he possessed knowledge and great honour; and when those of the following of Abbâ Poemen went up from Scete, every man left [that old man] and came to Abbâ Poemen and those who

were with him, and the old man was filled with envy, and he
cursed the followers of Abbâ Poemen because of this. Now
Abbâ Poemen heard of it, and he was vexed about it, and he
said unto the brethren who were with him, "What shall we
"do for this old man? For the men who have forsaken him
"have cast us into vexation, and they have left that holy old
"man and turned their looks upon us, who are nothing. How
"then can we satisfy this old man?" Then he said unto the
brethren who were with him, "Make ye some bread and boil
"a little food, and we will go to him, and will take with us
"also a vessel of wine, and we will eat with him, and perhaps
"by these means we shall be able to pacify him"; and they
took the food and went to him. And when they had knocked
at the door his disciple looked out and asked them, "Who
"are ye?" And they said unto him, "Tell the Abbâ that it is
"Poemen, and he wisheth to be blessed by him"; and when
his disciple had told him this, the old man said, "Send them
"away," and he said, "I have not leisure [to receive them]."
Then the disciple told them these things, but they stayed there
lovingly, saying, "We will not go away unless we are held to
"be worthy of the blessing of the old man." Now, when the
old man saw their humility and patient persistence, he repented, and opened the door to them, and when they were
eating together, he said unto them, "Verily, the things which
"I have heard were in you are not in you, but indeed what I
"see in you is a hundredfold [greater than what I expected]";
and he became unto them a friend from that day.

556. On a certain occasion when Abbâ John was sitting before the church, the brethren surrounded him, and asked him
about their thoughts, and when one of the old men saw him,
he said unto him, "Thy repentance is full of sorceries." Abbâ
John said unto him, "It is even so, and this thou sayest hav-
"ing only seen what is without, but if thou couldst see what
"is within what wouldst thou say?"

557. Muthues repeated the following:—"When I was a
"young man I used to say to myself, 'Perhaps thou wilt do
"'something good'; but now that I am an old man I see that
"I have not done even one good work."

558. He used to say concerning Abbâ Macarius that, if the
brethren drew nigh unto him in fear, as to a great and holy old
man, he would not answer them a word, but if one of the brethren treated him with familiar contempt, [saying], "Father, if thou
"wert a camel wouldst thou not steal the natron and sell it,
"and would not the driver beat thee?" he would answer him.
And if any man spake unto him in anger, or with words similar
to these, he would answer any question which was put to him.

Chapter rj. Of Fornication

559. A CERTAIN monk was engaged, on one occasion, in a war against fornication, and he had in his heart, as it were, a burning fire by day and by night; but he bore this agony, and did not bring low his mind, and after a long time the war passed away from him, but he was unable to vanquish it in any way except by patient endurance, and straightway light rose on his mind.

560. And another brother also was engaged in a war against fornication, and he rose up by night, and came to one of the old men and told him his mind, and the old man persuaded him [to endure], and he was helped, and went [back] to his cell. And again he came unto the old man, and again he helped him, and the brother went [back] to his cell; and the war came upon him the third time, and again he went back by night to the old man, and the old man did not cause him pain but spake with him for his benefit, and said unto him, "Give it no op-"portunity, but come hither whensoever the devil vexeth thee, "and thou wilt expose him, and when he hath been exposed he "will take to flight. For nothing vexeth the devil of fornica-"tion so much as that a man should hide his thoughts and "not reveal them." Now that brother came to the old man eleven times and made accusations against his thoughts, for he wished to be helped; and when the old man spake unto him that devil took to flight, but when he came [back] to his cell the war came upon him. At length the brother said unto the old man, "Do an act of grace, father, and tell me a word "[whereby I may live]." The old man said unto him, "Be of "good courage, my son, and if God permitteth my thought it "shall come to thee, and thou shalt bear it no longer, but "thou shalt depart being innocent." He said this, and God did away the war of that brother.

561. And another brother was engaged in a war against for-nication, and he bore it with very great self-restraint for four-teen years, and he guarded his mind against being subservient to lust, and at length he came to the church, and made known the matter unto all the people; and when they heard [it] they were pained, and they prayed for a whole week to God on his behalf, and afterwards He did away the war that was in him.

562. On one occasion Abbâ Moses of Pâtârâ was engaged in a war against fornication, and he could not endure being in his cell, and he went and informed Abbâ Isidore of it; and the old man entreated him to return to his cell, but he would not agree [to this]. And having said, "Father, I cannot bear it," the old man took him up to the roof of his cell, and said unto him, "Look to the west," and when he looked he saw multitudes of devils with troubled and terrified aspects, and they shewed themselves in the forms of phantoms which were in fighting attitudes. Abbâ Isidore saith unto him, "Look to the "east," and when he looked he saw innumerable holy angels standing [there], and they were in a state of great glory. Then Abbâ Isidore said unto him, "Behold, those who are in the " west are those who are fighting with the holy ones, and those " whom thou hast seen in the east are they who are sent by " God to the help of the saints, for those who are with us are "many." And having seen [these] Abbâ Moses took courage and returned to his cell without fear.

563. One of the old men said concerning the lustful thoughts which come into the heart of a man, and which are not carried into effect, that they are like unto a man who seeth a vineyard, and who desireth to eat the grapes thereof, but is afraid to go in lest he be caught and suffer death. If he be caught outside the hedge he will not die, because he hath neither gone into the vineyard nor hath eaten the grapes, but hath only desired; now he shall be beaten with few stripes, because he hath coveted, but he shall not die.

564. There was a certain old man, who lived in a cell, and his thoughts said unto him, "Go, take to thyself a woman"; then he rose up straightway and kneaded together some mud, and made the figure of a woman, and he said to himself, "Be- "hold thy wife! It is necessary for thee to labour with all thy " might that thou mayest be able to feed her." And he laboured with his hands and twisted many ropes. Then after a few days, he rose up and made a figure of a woman, and said unto his thoughts, "Behold, thy wife hath brought forth, it is ne- " cessary for thee to work harder to keep thy wife and to clothe "thy daughter"; and thus doing he vexed his body sorely. And he said unto his thought, "I cannot bear [all] this work, " and since I am unable to bear the work, a wife is unneces- " sary for me"; and God saw his labour, and did away his thoughts [of fornication], and he had peace.

565. Abbâ Poemen used to say, "As the sword-bearer stand- " eth before the king, being always ready [to smite], so is it " meet for the soul which is prepared to stand [ready] to re- " sist the devil of fornication."

566. They used to say that Mother Sarah contended against the devil of fornication for seven years on the roof [of her house], before she vanquished him.

567. One of the old men said, "It is written concerning " Solomon that he loved women, but every male loveth the fe-

"males, and we must restrain and draw onwards our nature
"by main force to purity."

568. A brother asked Abbâ Daniel, and said unto him, "De-
"liver to me a commandment"; [and he said unto him], "Never
"place thy hand in a dish and eat with a woman, and thou wilt
"be able to flee from the devil of fornication."

569. They used to say that the great old man Abraham arrived at a monastery, and that he also saw there a youth, and
that he refused to pass the night there; and the brethren who
were with him said unto him, "Art thou also afraid, O father?"
The old man said unto them, "Indeed, my sons, I am not afraid,
"but of what use is a vain war to me?"

570. A brother asked an old man, saying, "What shall I do?
"For my thoughts are [fixed] always upon fornication, and they
"will not give me peace even for a moment; and thus is my
"soul vexed." And the old man answered and said unto him,
"When these thoughts spring up in thee speak not with them,
"for it belongeth to them to rise up with continual anxiety,
"and not to be sluggish, but they have no power to force thee,
"for it belongeth to thee either to accept them or not. Hast
"thou not seen what the Midianites did, how they adorned their
"women and set them up, but they forced no man to take
"them? those who wished to do so fell into them, and those
"who did not became wroth, and made a slaughter in their
"wrath. Even so is it with the thoughts." Then that brother
said unto him, "What then shall I do? For I am weak, and
"passion overcometh me." The old man said unto him, "Con-
"sider thy thoughts well, and when they begin to speak to
"thee, answer them never a word, but rise up and pray, and
"meditate upon holy words." And the brother said unto him,
"Behold, father, I do meditate [on holy words], and the passion
"riseth not in my heart, but I do not know the power of the
"words"; then the old man answered and said unto him,
"Thou canst only [continue] to meditate, but I have heard
"Abbâ Poemen and many fathers say this word: 'The en-
"'chanter knoweth not the power of the words which he
"'uttereth, but when the animal heareth them, it knoweth
"'their power, and he becometh subservient, and submitteth
"'itself [to him].' Even so is it with us, for although we do not
"know the power of the words whereon we meditate, the devils
"know their power as soon as they hear them."

571. The old men in Scete were asked concerning fornication,
"When doth a man see a face in the passion stirred up in him?"
And they said, "This matter is like unto a table which is loaded
"with meats of all kinds, and a man who seeketh and desireth
"to eat of them; but if a man putteth not forth his hand and

" taketh not of the meats he becometh a stranger unto
" them."

572. They used to say that Abbâ Isaac went out and found
the footprint of a woman on the road, and he thought about it
in his mind and destroyed it, saying, " If a brother seeth it he
" may fall."

573. A brother asked Abbâ Agathon concerning fornication,
and he said unto him, "Go, cast thy feebleness before God,
" and thou shalt find relief."

574. A brother asked a father, and said unto him, "There is
" a war of fornication against me," and the old man said unto
him, "If it be a good thing, why goest thou away from it, but
" if it be a bad thing why dost not thou command it [to de-
" part]?"

575. A certain brother, being vexed by the spirit of fornication, went to a great old man, and entreated him, saying,
" Do an act of grace, and pray for me, for I am disturbed by
" fornication," and the old man made supplication unto God
and entreated Him. And the brother came to him a second
time, and said the same words as before, and the old man also
was not neglectful in beseeching God on his behalf. Now when
the brother had come to the old man, and troubled him in this
way many times because he was disturbed by fornication, the
old man afterwards entreated God, and said, "O Lord, reveal
" unto me the manner in which this brother liveth, and whence
" cometh the reason why I have entreated Thee so often on his
" behalf, and he hath not found relief." Then God revealed unto
him the affair of that brother, and he saw him dwelling with the
spirit of fornication by him, and that brother lusting for it, and
an angel was standing by [ready] to help him; and he was
angry with that brother because he did not cast himself upon
God, but was involving his mind therein. And straightway the
old man knew that the cause lay with the brother himself, and
he made him to undertand this, and he roused him up, and
afterwards he took heed to himself.

576. A brother asked Abbâ Poemen, saying, "The body is
" feeble, but my passions are not weak"; the old man said unto
him, "The passions make thorns to grow and burst into flower."

577. A brother asked Abbâ Poemen concerning the passions
of the body, and the old man said unto him, "They are like
" unto those who sang praises to the image of Nebuchad-
" nezzar, for if those who sang had not burned men [people]
" would never have worshipped the image; and in this wise the
" Enemy also singeth to the soul by means of the passions, so
" that he may perchance be able to make it commit sin through
" the passion of the body."

578. An old man used to say, "Salt is produced by water, but " if it falleth into water it becometh dissolved and is lost; " similarly monks are born of women, but if they fall into wo- " men they are dissolved and perish from God."

579. A certain father when he went out to become a monk was a virgin, and he did not even know that a whore existed among the children of men. And when he was dwelling in his cell the devils began to stir up in him the passion of fornication, and lifting up his eyes he saw the devils going round about him in the forms of Ethiopians, and they incited him to yield to the passion; then he rose up straightway and prayed, and said, " O Lord, help me," and when he had said these things immediately a stone fell from the roof, and he heard, as it were, a sweet voice, and he seemed to enjoy a short respite from the thoughts of fornication. And he rose up and came to one of the old men and related the matter to him, and the old man answered and said, "I know not what this meaneth"; and he sent him on to Abbâ Poemen, and that brother related the matter unto him also. Then the old man said unto him, "The stone which thou " didst see fall is the Calumniator, and that voice which thou " didst hear is lust. Take heed unto thy soul, and make suppli- " cation unto God, and behold, thou shalt be freed from this " war"; and Abbâ Poemen taught him how to contend against devils, and having prayed, he dismissed him, and that brother came to his cell. And he made entreaty and supplication unto God, and God granted him to attain to such a gift [of excellence] that, when that brother died, He was pleased that there should be revealed unto him whether it was well with his soul or not.

Now in another manuscript instead of the words, "He " rose up and prayed," it is thus written:—He saw the devils surrounding him in the forms of Ethiopians and they were inciting him to yield to the passion. And he said, "This natural " member which stablisheth man is like unto a spout in a tank " which letteth out water, and it is also like a conduit which " carrieth the water off a roof; similarly this member carrieth " off water from a man." And having said these words straightway the stone fell, &c.

580. On one occasion a certain man went out to Scete to become a monk, and he took with him his son as soon as he had been weaned; and when the boy was grown up and had become a young man, the war of fornication attacked him, and he said unto his father, " I will go into the world, father, for I cannot " endure this striving against fornication." Then his father entreated him to persevere, but at length the boy said to his father, " Father, I cannot bear it any longer, let me go"; and his father said unto him, " My son, hearken to me for this time only.

" Take thee seven pairs of cakes of bread, and a few palm
" leaves, sufficient for forty days, [and get thee into the desert],
" and may God's will be done." And his son hearkened unto
him, and he took [the bread and palm leaves] and departed,
and he remained [in the desert] working, and twisting dry
palm leaves into ropes, and plaiting mats, and eating dry
bread, and he lived a life of seclusion for twenty days. And he
looked, and behold, the work of fornication came and drew
nigh unto him, and it stood up before him in the form of an
Ethiopian woman whose smell was exceedingly foul; but he
was unable to endure her smell, and he drove her away from
his presence. Then she said unto him, " In the hearts of men
" I am a sweet smell, and a pleasant one, but because of thine
" obedience and labour God hath not permitted me to lead thee
" astray; but I have, nevertheless, made thee acquainted with
" my smell." And the young man rose up, and came to his father, and said unto him, " I no longer wish to go into the
" world, for I have seen the matter of fornication, and I have
" smelled its foul odour"; now the father knew of a certainty that
the young man had been satisfied in his mind on the subject,
and he said to his son, " Hadst thou remained [in the desert]
" forty days and kept my commandment, thou wouldst most
" certainly have seen a vision which was far more excellent."

581. On one occasion a brother came to Abbâ Poemen, and
said unto him, " What shall I do, father, for I am vexed by
" fornication? And behold, I came unto Nebatîôn [Anicetus],
" and he said unto me, ' It is not right that those thoughts
" ' should stay with thee so long.'" Abbâ Poemen saith unto
him, " The labour of Abbâ Anicetus is high and exalted, and his
" thoughts are above with the angels, and he hath forgotten
" that I and thou are whoremongers; but if thou wishest,
" hearken unto me, and I also will speak to thee: If a monk
" can hold fast his belly, and his tongue, and his love for going
" about as a stranger, thou mayest be sure that he is able to
" become a monk in very truth, and that he will not die."

582. A brother asked an old man, and said unto him, "What
" shall I do? For fornication is killing me." The old man said
unto him, " When a mother is about to wean her son she
" smeareth aloes over her breasts, and when the child cometh
" to suck as usual, he shrinketh away and taketh to flight. Do
" thou also then put bitter aloes in thy heart, and straightway
" the wicked devils will fly therefrom." And the brother said
unto him, " What kind of bitter aloes is it right for me to place
" therein." The old man saith unto him, " The remembrance
" of the death and punishment which are laid up in the world
" which is to come."

583. A brother asked an old man, "Whence come the "temptations of fornication which attack me?" The old man said, "They come because thou eatest and drinkest largely, "and because thou sleepest until thou art satisfied."

584. Abbâ John used to say, "Whosoever talketh as much "as he can with a woman, hath already committed adultery "with her in his mind."

585. On one occasion a certain brother came to Abbâ Muthues and asked him, saying, "Is calumny worse than fornication?" And the old man said, "Fornication is worse." The brother said unto him, "How can this be?" And the old man said unto him, "Calumny is a wicked thing, but it receiveth healing "quickly, and the calumniator repenteth, saying, 'I have "'spoken evilly many times'; but fornication in the body is "death in [its] nature."

586. There was in Scete a certain monk who strove hard [against sin], and the Enemy sowed in him the remembrance of a certain woman with a beautiful face, and he troubled him greatly through her. And by the Providence of God a certain brother who came down from Egypt went to visit him, and it came to pass that whilst they were conversing together the brother who had gone to visit him said, "Such and such a "woman is dead"; now she was the very woman the remembrance of whom was being stirred up in the monk. And when the other brother heard this, he rose up, and took his headcloth, and went up by night to Egypt, and opened her grave, and he smeared himself with the filthy and putrefying matter of the dead body of the woman, and then went back to his cell. And he set that thing of filth before his mind at all times, and he did battle with his thought, saying, "Behold thy lust, and "that which thou didst require! Behold, I have brought it unto "thee; take thy fill thereof." And he used to torture himself with [the remembrance of] that filthy thing until the war which was in him was quieted.

587. One of the brethren asked Abbâ Zeno, now he had great freedom of speech with him, saying, "Behold, thou hast "grown old, how is the matter of fornication?" The old man said unto him, "It knocketh, but it passeth on." Then one of the brethren asked him, "What is the meaning of 'It knock-"'eth, but it passeth on?'" The old man said unto him, "Imagine now that one brought to thy mind the remembrance "of a certain woman, and that thou didst say, 'Oh,' but that "thou didst not allow it to go up in thy mind; [that is what 'It "'knocketh, but passeth on' meaneth]; now young men are "excited by it."

588. A brother asked Abbâ Theodore of Scete, saying, "The

" thought of fornication cometh, and it troubleth and disturb-
" eth the mind, but it is not able to commit the deed; and it
" certainly cannot help, but it can hinder the course towards
" spiritual excellence "; and the old man said unto him, " The
" man who is wakeful and strenuous struggleth and casteth
" it from him and standeth up to prayer."

589. And again a certain old man from Parmîs [spake]
against this thought, saying, " If we do not possess thoughts
" we become the prey of the Enemy, for he, even like an
" ordinary enemy, demandeth that which is his; therefore
" let us, in the same manner, do what is ours to do. Let us
" stand up in prayer, and straightway he will flee; be constant
" in the service of God, and thou shalt conquer; strive, and
" thou shalt be crowned."

590. Against this thought of fornication a brother asked an
old man, saying, " What shall I do about the mind of fornica-
" tion which vexeth me?" And Abbâ Copres the Alexandrian
answered and said, " If thou hast no minds (*or* thoughts) thou
" wilt have no hope, so then their work is with thee; for he
" who performeth their work hath no thoughts. Peradventure
" thou hast the custom of talking with a woman?" And the
brother said unto him, "No, I have not, but they are thoughts of
" former times and of recent times which trouble me." The old
man said unto him, " Thou shalt not be afraid of the dead, but
" fear the things which are living, and cast thyself down in
" prayer before God. For if we have no thoughts we are mere
" animals. As the enemy worketh for that which is his, even
" so let us do for that which is ours. Let us stand up in prayer,
" and let us have a care for doctrine, and let us endure, for
" patient endurance is victory. Unless a man striveth he will
" never be crowned. For there are in the world athletes who
" though wounded conquer nevertheless, and however many
" times one man may be wounded by two [others], if he can
" endure the blows he will be able to conquer those who smote
" him. Observe then what a degree of endurance is possessed
" by such men for the sake of the merchandise of this world!
" Do thou then endure, and God shall strive with thine enemies
" on thy behalf whilst thou mayest remain quiet."

591. Against the thought [of fornication] another old man
who dwelt in the desert used to say, "Thou wishest to live
" whilst thou art asleep! Go, and labour. Go, and work. Go,
" seek, and ye shall find. Awake and stand up. Knock, and it
" shall be opened unto thee. For there are in the world athletes
" who are called 'pugilists,' who smite each other, and who
" are held to be worthy of the victory because they fight per-
" sistently and endure; these men do not withdraw defeated

" when they are wounded, for however many times one [of
" them] may be smitten by two [others], and however [many
" may be] the blows which he will suffer from them, he con-
" tinueth to fight, and he conquereth and is crowned."

592. Against the thought [of fornication] another old man
said, "Such things will happen unto thee through negligence.
" For if it be certain to us that God dwelleth in us, we can never
" become a habitation for others, and we can never give our
" souls over to become vessels for the service of aliens. For
" our Lord Who dwelleth in us, and is found in us, is able to
" watch over our lives; and it is not right for us to neglect or
" to hold lightly Him for Whose sake we have put Him on,
" and Whom we see. But let us make ourselves pure even as
" He is pure. Stand up then upon a rock, and if the river be
" violently disturbed thou shalt not fear, and behold, thy
" building shall not shake; and sing with might, saying,
" 'Those who put their hope in the Lord shall be like Mount
" 'Zion (Psalm cxxv, 1), and he who dwelleth in Jerusalem
" 'shall never be moved.' The Enemy said unto our Redeemer,
" 'I will send these who belong to me against those who be-
" 'long to Thee that they may drive them back; and if they
" 'do evil to Thy chosen ones I cannot [help it], and I will
" 'trip them up, even though I can only do so in dreams of
" 'the night.' Then our Redeemer said unto him, 'If an abor-
" 'tion can inherit his father['s possessions] this also shall be
" 'accounted as sin to My chosen ones.'"

593. Against the thought [of fornication] another old man
spake, saying, "Be thou like unto a man who passeth through
" a street of tavern-keepers, and who smelleth the odour of
" boiling meats, or the whiff of something which is being
" roasted; he who wisheth entereth into [one of them] and
" eateth, and he who doth not wish [to do so] smelleth the
" meats as he passeth by and then goeth on. Drive away then
" from thee the fetid smell of evil thoughts, and stand up and
" pray, saying, 'O Son of God, help me.' The same thing is
" also to be said about other thoughts, for we are not the roots
" of the thoughts, but are those who strive against them."

Excellent Counsels concerning Fornication by one of the holy old Men

NOW on thy account, O son of man, Christ was born,
and the Son of God came that He might make thee to
live. He became a Child. He became a man, being also
594. God. He Who was the Lawgiver became a reader [of the
Law], and He took the Book in the congregation, and He read,
saying, " The Spirit of God is upon me, and for this reason He

"hath anointed me, and hath sent me to preach the Gospel unto
"the poor." Like a servant He made a whip of rope, and He
drove forth from the temple all those who sold oxen, and cattle,
and doves, and other things. Like a servant He girded a napkin
about His loins, and washed the feet of His disciples, and He
commanded them to wash the feet of their brethren. Like an
elder He sat among the elders, and taught the people. Like a
Bishop He took bread, and blessed [it], and brake, and gave
to His disciples; and He was beaten for thy sake, that is to
say, for thy sake He was crucified, and for thy sake He died.
Yet thou for His sake wilt not even endure insult! He rose as
God. He was exalted as God. All these things for our sake,
all these things by Divine Providence, all these things properly
and in due order did He do that He might redeem us. Let us
then be watchful, and strenuous, and constant in prayer, and
let us do everything which will please Him, and will gratify His
friends, so that we may be redeemed and live. Was not Joseph
sold into Egypt, and did he not live in an alien land? And the
three simple young men in Babylon, had they not men who
opposed them? Yet, because they were fearing God, He helped
them, and made them glorious.

595. An old man who had delivered himself unto God used
to say, "The monk must have no will of his own, but he whose
"will is of God continueth to minister to Him unwearyingly;
"for if thou doest thine own will, thou becomest weary, and
"thou labourest, and God hearkeneth not to thee." And the
old man also said, "He who liveth in God liveth with Him,
"for He saith, I will dwell in them, and I will walk in them,
"and they shall be to Me a people, and I will be to them a
"God" (Exodus vi, 7).

596. And the old man also said, "God saith unto thee thus:—
"If thou lovest Me, O monk, do that which I ask, and do
"not that which I do not desire. For monks should lead lives
"wherein they act not in iniquity, and a man should not look
"upon evil things with his eyes, nor hear with his ears things
"which are alien to the fear of God, nor utter calumnies with
"his mouth, nor plunder with his hands; but he should give
"especially to the poor, and he should not be [unduly] exalted
"in his mind, and he should not think evil thoughts, neither
"should he fill his belly. Let him do then all these things with
"discretion, for by them is a monk known." The old man also
said, "These things [form] the life of a monk: Good works,
"and obedience, and training. A man should not lay blame
"on his neighbour, and he should not utter calumnies, and he
"should not complain, for it is written, The lovers of the Lord
"hate wickedness."

597. A brother on several occasions troubled an old man, and said unto him, "What shall I do with the impure and " wicked thoughts of divers kinds which force their way into " me by various means?" The old man answered and said unto him, "Thou art like unto a cistern which hath been dug out, " and which is sometimes full, but which, when a man cometh " to draw water thereat, is found [to be dry]. Why dost thou " not make thyself more like a fountain of water which is never " without [water]? Persistence is victory, and victory is con- " stancy, and constancy is life, and life is kingdom, and king- " dom is God."

Here end the Questions concerning the Thoughts of Fornication, and the Answers thereto, and the Counsels of the Holy Old Men

Chapter xij. Of the Acceptance of Repentance, and of how it is right for us to Repent in Truth

TWO brethren were in restraint to the lust of fornication, and they went and took to themselves wives. At length, however, they repented, and said to each other,
598. "What have we gained by leaving the labour of angels, " and coming to this [state of] impurity, since after the present " life we shall be delivered over to fire and everlasting torture? " Let us return to the desert and repent." And they went forth straightway, and came to the desert to the fathers, and they entreated them to offer up supplications on their behalf; now the outward appearance of both was the same, and they shut themselves up for one year, and they made supplications to God, and entreated Him to pardon them, and to each of the two brethren a like quantity of bread and water was given. Now after their period of repentance was fulfilled, they went forth from their seclusion; and the old men saw that the countenance of one was changed, and that it was exceedingly sad, whilst that of the other brother was cheerful and glad, and the fathers marvelled why, seeing that the two men had been partaking of the same amount of food, and had endured the same restraint, the face of one was so different from that of the other. And they asked him of the sad face, saying, "What didst thou think about in thy cell?" And he said, "On the evil things which I have committed, and I think " about the torture which is to come, and by reason of my fear " my flesh cleaveth to my bones." And they asked him whose appearance was cheerful, saying, "Do thou also tell us what thou " didst think about in thy cell." And he said, "I gave thanks " unto God, Who hath delivered me from the impurity of this " world, and from everlasting punishment, and Who hath

On the Acceptance of Repentance

" brought me to this labour of angels, and with such things I
" remembered God and rejoiced." Then the old men said,
" The repentance of each is equal before God."

599. An old man was asked by one who toiled, " Is the re-
" pentance of sinners accepted by God?" And the old man,
after he had taught him with many words, said unto him,
" Tell me, O my beloved one: if thy cloak were to be torn in
" rags, wouldst thou throw it away?" And he said unto him,
" No, but I would sew up the rents, and then I could use it
" again." And the old man said unto him, " If thou wouldst
" shew pity upon thy garment which hath no feeling, shall not
" God shew pity on that which He hath fashioned, and which
" is His work?"

600. A certain brother fell into temptation, and through
tribulation relinquished the garb of monkhood; and he wished
to begin to renew his ascetic life, but he saw the great difficulty of the matter, and he drew back, and said, " When shall
" I ever find myself in the same condition as I was formerly?"
And through fear he did not begin his work, and he went and
made the matter known to an old man, and the old man said,
" The matter is thus: There was a certain man who possessed
" an estate, and he held it to be of no account and did not
" cultivate it, and it became full of tangled undergrowth and
" thorns. Now one day he remembered it, and he sent his
" son, and said unto him, 'Go, clean the estate.' And when he
" had gone and seen the abundance of the undergrowth he
" was afraid, and said to himself, ' When shall I be able to
" ' clean away all this undergrowth?' And he threw himself
" upon a bed, and lay down, and went to sleep, and thus he
" did every day. Then his father went forth and found that he
" was asleep, and that he had done nothing; and he said unto
" him, ' How is it, my son, that no work whatsoever hath
" 'been done by thee?' And he said to his father, ' When I
" ' came to work and saw the abundance of the undergrowth,
" ' I was afraid and said, When shall I be able to clean all
" ' this away?' And his father said unto him, ' My son, work
" ' according to the measure of thy sleep each day, and it shall
" ' be sufficient for thee'; and when he heard [this] the young
" man plucked up courage, and did thus, and in a short time
" he cleansed the estate. Thus also thou shalt not be afraid,
" but begin the work of thy rules, and God, by His Grace, will
" establish thee [among those in] the first rank." Now when
the brother had done thus he was helped.

601. A brother asked one of the old men, and said, " If a
" monk stumble and fall into sin, are many labours necessary
" for him, and if he doeth them will he be able to stand in the

"grade wherein he was formerly? He who goeth forth from
"the world, and beginneth the cultivation of spiritual excel-
"lence, will find it easy to advance, for he who is occupied in
"labours, if it be that he is reduced from the grade wherein
"he stood by his stumbling, will be afflicted and grieved in his
"mind." Then the old man answered and said unto him, "A
"monk is like unto a house which hath fallen down, and if he
"be awake in his mind (or thought), and if he be zealous and
"anxious to build that which was fallen down, he will find
"ample material which will be of use in his building among
"the remains of that which fell down before [he began to
"build]; for he will find the foundation stones, and the old
"stones from the walls, and other things, which were em-
"ployed in the old building, and out of these, if he be so
"disposed, he will be able to make his building to rear itself
"up better than the man who hath not yet dug the places for
"the foundations and laid the foundation stones, and who doth
"not possess the materials which are to be employed in the
"building, and who only beginneth to build with the hope
"that he will be able to finish. And thus is it with him that
"falleth from the practice of rules and works of the monkish
"life into temptation, for if he turn back, and repent, he will
"possess ample material from [his] former works of the ascetic
"life which he possesseth [to begin his building afresh], I
"mean to say, the training and the service of the work of the
"hands, which is the foundation [thereof]. Whosoever then
"hath gone forth from the world, and beginneth the cultiva-
"tion of ascetic excellence, when he hath done these things
"he will still be found standing in the front rank of the soli-
"tary (or monkish) life."

602. One of the old men told the following story, saying:—
There was a certain monk who dwelt in the desert, and he
lived a life of strict and severe rule, and he was famous among
men, and he could even cast out devils and heal the sick. And
it came to pass that, through the agency of Satan, the passion of fornication was stirred up against him, and because he
was not sufficiently humble to reveal his war unto the old men
who were before him, in a few days' time he fell into fornication
with a woman who used to come to him continually for assistance. Now having fallen, he despaired about himself, and he
rose up to go to the world, and he was sad and grieved concerning his fall; and he meditated, saying, "I will go into
"the desert which is further away, and I shall not see any
"man, and I shall not be seen of any, and there I will die
"like the wild animals." And when he had gone, and he
was wandering about in the desert and in the mountains,

he used to cry out by night and by day, saying, "Woe is me! woe is me!" And he ceased not to weep and to groan. Now there was in that desert a certain solitary old man who dwelt in a cleft in the rock, and when he heard the sound of the weeping and lamentation, his mercy for him revealed itself, and he went forth and met him, and they saluted each other. And the old man answered and said unto him, "Why weepest thou in this fashion?" And the young man said, "Because I have angered God, and because I have fallen "into fornication." Then was the old man astonished, and he said, "O how greatly did I fear and tremble at thy lugubrious "voice. For I thought that thou hadst been entrusted with the "governorship of the brethren, and that thou hadst governed "unjustly, or that thou hadst squandered in an unseemly "manner the work of the community. For the harlot repented, "and for the unbeliever there is a foundation, and the thief is "a son of the kingdom, but Ananias and Sapphira were slain "because they stole the money of the community of the breth- "ren, and thus is slain the soul of every one who with fraud "or carelessness squanders the possessions of the religious "houses. But be thou of good courage, O brother, and go "back again to thy cell, and make thine entreaty to God as "thou repentest, and He will stablish thee in thy former "grade." Then the monk went back to his place, and he shut himself in, and never again undertook to talk with any man, except him that handed in to him his food through the little window of his cell, and there he remained until the end of his life, and he attained to a most exalted state of perfection.

603. Abbâ Ammon of Rîtheaôn asked Abbâ Poemen about the impure thoughts which are produced in a man, and the vain lusts; and Abbâ Poemen said unto him, "It belongeth to "Satan to sow them, but it is our affair not to welcome them."

604. A brother asked Abbâ Ammon, saying, "Behold, there "were two men, the one was a monk, and the other a son of "the world; now the monk used to determine in the evening "to cast away from him in the morning the garb of the monk, "and the son of the world used to make up his mind that on "the morrow he would take the garb of monkhood. Now it "happened that both men died on the same night; how will "they be regarded, and which determination will be reckoned "to them?" The old man said unto him, "He who was a monk "died a monk, and he who was a child of the world died as "such, for as they were found [to be] so were they taken."

605. A brother asked Abbâ Sisoes, saying, "What shall I "do, father? For I have fallen." The old man said unto him, "Rise up"; and the brother said unto him, "I did rise up, but

"I fell again." The old man said unto him, "Rise up again"; and the brother said unto him, "I did rise up again, many "times, and I fell [again]." The old man said unto him, "Rise "up again"; and the brother said unto him, "Until when?" The old man said unto him, "Until thou advancest, either in "good deeds or in falling; for in the road wherein a man ad- "vanceth he goeth, whether it be to death or to life."

606. It happened on one occasion that a brother in the mona- stery of Abbâ Hatîl (*or* Helît) was tempted, [and he fell,] and having been expelled from that place he went to the mountain, to Abbâ Anthony, and having remained with him for a long time, Abbâ Anthony sent him back to the monastery from which he had gone forth. Now when the sons of the monastery saw him, they cast him out, and he returned to Abbâ Anthony, and said unto him, "Father, they have refused to receive me"; and Abbâ Anthony sent them a message, saying, "A storm "rose up against a ship on the sea, and destroyed the freight "which she carried, but with the greatest difficulty she was "saved [and brought] to land. Now what do ye wish to do? "Do ye wish to drown him that hath been saved?" And when those monks [heard the words of] Abbâ Anthony, they sent to the brother, and welcomed him with gladness.

607. Abbâ Anthony used to say, "There are many who fall "and who rise up to an attitude of rectitude, but there are "some who fall from good deeds to polluted things; better is "he who falleth and riseth up than he who standeth and then "falleth."

608. Abbâ Poemen said, "If a man sinneth, and he saith, "'I have not sinned,' and thou chidest him, thou cuttest off "his will; but if thou sayest unto him, 'Be not sorry about this, "'but guard thyself from sinning again,' by these means thou "wakest his soul to repentance."

609. He also said, "I prefer a man who hath sinned, and "done wickedly, and repented, to the man who hath not sinned "and hath not manifested repentance; for the former possesseth "a humble mind, and the latter esteemeth himself in his "thoughts a just man."

610. Abbâ Sarmâtâ used to say, "I prefer a man who hath "sinned, and who knoweth how to acknowledge his sins, to him "that doeth righteousness, and who saith, 'I do what is fair.'"

611. Abbâ Theodore of Parmê used to say, "The man who "is in [a state of] repentance is not bound by the Law."

612. They used to say that the thoughts of a certain old man used to say unto him, "Let to-day go by, and repent to- "morrow"; but he would say, "Nay, not so, for I will repent "to-day, and to-morrow shall be as God willeth."

Of the Fathers who wrought Wonders

613. There was at one time among the brethren a certain man who at the beginning of his [ascetic] career took good heed unto his soul, but when a short time had elapsed, he began to treat the salvation of his life with contempt; and his Abbâ ordered him to strip off the garb of the monks, and to put on the apparel of men who are in the world, and to depart from among the brethren. Then the man fell down at his feet, and entreated him, saying, "If thou wilt forgive me this once only, thou wilt " gain me henceforward, for I repent of these things which I have " done through negligence." And having multiplied and prolonged his entreaties, and made many promises that he would in the future mend his ways, he was held worthy of forgiveness; and he struggled with all the power of his soul to such purpose as to become a pattern to great and small.

Chapter riij. Of [the Fathers who] wrought Wonderful Works

ABBÂ Sisoes said: When we were in Scete, with Abbâ Macarius, seven of us went up to reap with him, and behold, a certain widow followed after us gleaning, and **614.** she ceased not to weep. And the old man cried to the lord of the estate, and said unto him, "What is the matter with the old woman who weepeth continually?" He said unto him, " Her husband took a deposit of money from a man and he " died suddenly without saying with whom he had placed it, " and the owner of the deposit wisheth to take her and her " children as slaves." The old man said unto him, "Tell her to " come to us at the place where we rest at the season of noon," and it was told to her. And at the season of noon the woman came to them, and the old man said unto her, "Woman, why " dost thou weep continually?" And she said, "My husband is " dead. He had taken a deposit from a certain man, and he died " suddenly without telling us where he had laid it up." The old man said unto her, "Come [and] and show me where ye have " laid him"; and he took the brethren with him, and went with her, and having arrived at the place where the man was laid, the old man said unto her, "Get thee now to thy house." And after [she had departed] and he had made an end of his prayer, the old man cried out to the dead man and said, "O Such-an- " one, where hast thou laid up the deposit which belongeth to " the stranger?" Then the dead man answered straightway, and said, "It is hidden in my house beneath the leg of the bed"; and the old man said unto him, " Sleep now until the Resur- " rection." Now when the brethren saw what had been done, they all fell down at his feet in fear; and the old man said unto them, " This hath not happened because of me, O my brethren,

"nor is the matter a great one, but God hath wrought this thing
"for the sake of the widow and the orphans; but what is great
"is that God desireth a soul which is pure and sinless." And when
they had come they told the widow that the deposit was laid
up in such and such a place, and then the old woman brought it
up, and gave it to its owner, and set free her children from slavery.
And every one who heard [of this] gave thanks unto God.

615. When Abbâ Miles (*or* Manilius) was passing through
a certain place he saw a man holding a monk by force as if
he had committed murder, and the old man drew nigh and
questioned the brother, and when he learned that he was being
wrongfully accused, he said unto those who had seized
him, "Tell me where is the man who hath been murdered";
and they shewed him. Then the old man drew nigh to the
murdered man, and said unto all who were standing [there],
"Let us pray"; and when he had spread out his hands in
prayer before God, the dead man rose up. And the old man
said unto him before every man, "Tell us who it was that slew
"thee"; and he answered and said, "I went into the church and
"gave some money to the elder, and it was he who rose up
"and killed me, and he carried me out and threw me in the
"habitation of this monk. I entreat you that the goods which
"I have given to him may be taken back and given to my
"children."

616. On one occasion a certain man in the world went to
Abbâ Sisoes in the mountain of Abbâ Anthony, and he had
his son with him, and as they were going along the road his
son died; now the man was in no wise disturbed, but he took
him up in faith and brought him to the old man, and he came
with his son, and fell down before him with his son upon his
knees as if he was entreating him to bless them; and the father
of the boy went out and left his son [lying] dead at the feet of
the old man. Now the old man did not know that the boy was
dead, but he thought that he was making supplication and
entreaty to him; and he answered and said unto him, "Arise,
"and go forth," and straightway without any delay whatsoever, the youth rose up and went out to his father, who, when
he saw him, marvelled; and his father took him and went in
and did homage to the old man, and informed him about the
matter. Now when the old man heard this he was troubled,
for he did not wish this thing to happen because of the praise of
men; and his disciple commanded them not to tell the story
before any man until the day of his death.

617. One of the fathers used to relate that Abbâ Paule, who
dwelt in Thebes, would take snakes, and scorpions, and horned
snakes in his hands, and kill them. And the brethren made

apologies to him, and said, "Father, tell us through what "labour thou hast received this gift." And he said unto them, "Forgive me, O my fathers, if ye possess purity of heart, "every living thing will be subject unto you as it was unto "Adam before he transgressed the commandment of God."

618. On one occasion one of the old men of Thebes came to Mount Sinai, and having departed from there, one of the brethren met him on the way, and with a groan he said unto the old man, "We are distressed, O father, through the want of "rain." And the old man said unto him, "Why do ye not pray "and ask God for some?" And the brother said unto him, "We have prayed and made earnest supplication, and the "rain hath not come." The old man said unto them, "Then "ye did not pray with all your hearts; do ye wish to know "that the matter is thus?" And after [this] the old man stood up in prayer, and he spread out his hands to heaven, and straightway, without any delay whatsoever, the rain came; and the brother saw, and feared, and he fell down and did homage to him. Now the old man took to flight, but the brother made known everything which had happened, and when [the brethren] heard [thereof] they all glorified God.

619. They used to say that, when on one occasion, Abbâ Moses of Scete was going into Patârâ, he grew weary through the length of the road, and he was afraid and said, "How can "I bring water for myself into this place?" And a voice was heard by him, saying, "Go on, and fear not." Now one day a large number of the fathers came to him, and he had there only one vessel of water, and having boiled some lentiles the water came to an end; at this the old man was troubled, and went out and in, and prayed to God, and afterwards a great cloud came and poured down upon them much rain, and it filled all the vessels which he had with water. Then afterwards the fathers said unto him, "Abbâ Moses, tell us why "thou didst come in and out"; and he said unto them, "I en-"tered into judgement with God, who brought me hither be-"cause there was want of water, and because I had no water "for His servants to drink; therefore I came in and out."

620. The old man Joseph used to say: "I went on one occa-"sion to Abbâ Poemen and found many old men with him, and "behold, a certain man had brought a youth who was a kins-"man of Abbâ Poemen, and whose face had been turned back-"wards through the operation of the Evil One; and when his "father saw the multitude of the old men who were coming to "Abbâ Poemen, he took him and brought him outside the "door of the monastery, and sat down there and wept. Now "when one of the old men had ended his business, and was

"going forth [from the building], he saw him, and said unto
"him, 'Why weepest thou, O man?' The father of the youth
"said unto him, 'I am of the family of Abbâ Poemen. A
"'trial hath come upon this youth, but we are afraid to
"'take him to him, for he refuseth to see us, and now, if he
"'learneth that I am here, he will send and drive me away;
"'but when I knew that ye were coming here, I ventured to
"'come also.' And he cast the youth down on the ground at
"his feet, and wept, saying, 'If thou wilt, have mercy on me,
"'and take this youth inside, and pray over him'; and the old
"man took him and carried him in with him to Abbâ Poemen.
"Now the old man acted wisely in the matter, and he did not
"take the youth at once to Abbâ Poemen, but beginning with
"the last of the brethren who was there, he brought the youth
"to each and every one of them, saying, 'Make the sign of the
"'Cross upon this youth'; and having brought him alike to
"all the brethren and to all the old men who were there, finally
"he brought him to Abbâ Poemen, but the blessed man refused
"to touch him. Thereupon a contention arose, and they all
"entreated him, saying, 'Father, do thou even as we all have
"'done'; then Abbâ Poemen sighed, and he rose up and prayed,
"and said, 'O God, heal that which Thou hast fashioned so
"'that it may not be destroyed by the Enemy,' and he finished
"his prayer, and made the sign of the Cross over him, and
"straightway the face of the youth was made straight,
"and he was healed. And Abbâ Poemen gave him to his
"father made whole, so he took him and departed with
"rejoicing."

621. They used to say that the face of Abbâ Pambô was like
lightning, even as Moses received the glory of the likeness of
Adam, and that his face shone, and that he was like a king
who sitteth upon his throne; and thus was it also with Abbâ
Silvanus and with Abbâ Sisoes.

622. They used to say about one of the old men that as he
was in the light during the day, so also was he [in the light] in
his cell by night, and that he used to work with his hands and
read in the night time just as he did during the day.

623. One of the old men sent his disciple to draw water, now
the well was a very long way off from their cell, and that
brother forgot to take the rope with him; and being distressed
[thereat] he bowed himself in prayer, and he prayed and cried
out, saying, "O well, my father [saith], 'Fill this vessel for me
"'with water, and without delay'"; and the water came up,
and the brother filled [the vessel], and as soon as he had done
so the water descended to its place.

624. On one occasion Abbâ Moses came to the well to draw

water, and he saw Abbâ Zechariah praying to the stream, and the Spirit of God was resting upon him like a dove.

625. On one occasion one of the brethren went to the cell of Abbâ Arsenius in Scete, and he looked through the window, and saw the old man standing up, and all his body was like fire; now that brother was worthy to see this sight. And having knocked at the door the old man came out to him; and seeing that the brother was marvelling at the sight which he had seen, he said unto him, "Hast thou been knocking a long "time? Peradventure thou hast seen something?" and he said unto him, "No; [I have not]." And Abbâ Arsenius spake with him and dismissed him.

626. They used to say that a certain old man said, "Verily, "as he who worketh gold, and as he who maketh beautiful "work, cleanly and at peace, so thou also by thy beautiful "thoughts must inherit the kingdom of God; but I who have "passed the whole period of my life in the desert have not "been able to overtake thee."

627. They used to say about a certain great old man, who lived in Pûrpîrînê, that when he lifted up his eyes to heaven he could see whatsoever was therein, and that if he gazed into the earth, he could see into the depths, and whatsoever was in them.

628. Abbâ John, who was cast out by the Marcionites, used to say:—On one occasion we went from Syria to Abbâ Poemen, and when we wished him to speak to us about hardness of heart [we found that] the old man did not know Greek, and there was no interpreter with leisure [to interpret there]. And the old man saw that we were troubled at this, and he began to talk to us in the Greek tongue, and at the beginning of his speech he said, "Water is by nature soft, and stone is hard, "nevertheless if thou suspendest a vessel full of water above "a stone, and wilt pour it out upon it drop by drop, it will "wear away the stone. In the same way the Word of God is "soft, and our heart is hard, but if it heareth continually the "Word of God, the heart will be opened, and will turn to the "fear of God."

629. A certain monk lived in the desert, and there was another brother who lived in a cell by his side, and when he visited him from time to time he used to see him praying and entreating our Lord that the wild animals might be at peace with him. And after the prayer a panther which was suckling her young was found by him, and that brother went down upon his knees and sucked with them. And on another occasion the blessed man saw that brother praying and beseeching God to make fire to be at peace with him; and he lit a fire, and knelt

down in the middle of it, and prayed. And that old man used to say, "If thou wishest to become a monk, bring thyself into "subjection that thou mayest be in the congregation of the "community, and mayest enter the monastery; but if thou "canst not cast away from thee care concerning [all kinds of] "occupations and affairs, thou canst never dwell in the con- "gregation. All the power thou hast is over a bottle of water."

630. And there are also wonderful things which the blessed Bessarion performed. He made the waters of the sea sweet, and Saul his disciple drank [of them]; he crossed over the water of the river; he prevented the sun from setting in the heavens; and the rooting up of the temples of the idols was revealed unto him. As they were going to John the Theban his disciple became thirsty, and Bessarion prayed, and water bubbled up, and he gave him to drink; and he healed also the young man who was a paralytic, so that he ran to his father; and he cast out a devil from a young man who was always asleep, and whom his parents besought him to wake up. I have, however, written down all these things in the history of the holy man Bessarion, wherein it is written that he was sitting at the door of the monastery and weeping bitterly.

Chapter xiv. Of the Greatness of the Sublime Rule of the Solitary Life

THERE was a certain old man amongst the fathers who used to see visions, and this man testified, and said, "That power which I have seen existing in baptism, I 631. "have also seen in the apparel of the monks when they "take the garb of the monk."

632. An old man from Thebaïs used to say:—I was the son of a priest of idols, and when I was young I lived in the temple, and I have on many occasions seen my father go into the temple to perform the sacrifices to the idols. Once I went in secretly after him, and I saw Satan sitting [there], with his whole army before him, and, behold, one of his devils came and did homage to him. And Satan answered and said unto him, "Whence comest thou?" And the devil made answer, saying, "I was in such and such a country, and I stirred up "many wars and revolts, and I caused the shedding of blood, "and I have come to tell thee these things." Satan said unto him, "How long did it take thee to do this?" and the devil said "Thirty days." Then Satan commanded him to be beaten, saying unto him, "Is this all that thou hast done in so long a time?" And, behold, another devil came and worshipped him, and to him he said, "Whence comest thou?" And the devil answered and said, "I was in the sea, where I stirred up storms, and

"sank ships, and drowned many men, and I have come that "I may inform thee of these things." Then Satan answered and said unto him, "In how much time hast thou done this?" and the devil answered and said unto him, "In twenty days," and Satan commanded that he also should be beaten, saying unto him, "Why is it that in all these days thou hast only done "[what thou sayest]?" And when he had said this, behold, a third devil came and worshipped Satan, who answered and said unto him also, "And where dost thou come from?" and the devil answered and said unto him, "I have been in such "and such a city wherein there was a marriage feast, and I "stirred up a war there, and caused the shedding of much "blood, and the death of the bridegroom and the bride; and "as soon as I had done this I came to inform thee." And Satan said unto him, "In how many days hast thou done this?" and the devil said, "In ten days"; and Satan commanded that he should be beaten, saying, "In all these days thou hast only "done this." Then afterwards, behold, a fourth devil came and worshipped him, and Satan answered and said unto him, "And whence comest thou also?" And he who was asked answered and said unto him, "I have been in the desert for forty "years striving with a monk, and to-night I have hurled him "into fornication"; and when Satan heard this, he rose up straightway and embraced and kissed that devil, and he took the crown off his head, and placed it upon him, and he made him to sit by his side upon his throne, saying, "And so thou "hast been able to do so great a work as this in so short a "time! For there is nothing which I prize so highly as the fall "of a monk." And the old man went on to say:—When I saw these things I said within myself, "Yea, so great then is the "army of the monks! And by the operation of God, Who de-"sired my redemption, I came forth, and became a monk."

633. In the time when Julian, the rebellious Emperor, was going down to the territory of the Persians, he sent a certain devil to go speedily to the country of the West, and to bring him from thence an account of what he had sent him [to do]. Now when that devil arrived at a certain place wherein dwelt a monk, he stopped and tarried there for a period of fifteen days without being able to move anywhere, and he was unable to travel onwards, because the monk did not cease from praying, either by night or by day; so he returned to the heathen who had sent him without having done anything. Then the wicked Julian said unto him, "Why hast thou tarried so long?" And the devil answered and said unto him, "I delayed in "coming, and I have done nothing; for a monk, who con-"tinued in prayer, came in my way and I tarried with him

"fifteen days, expecting that he would some time cease to
"pray and that I should be able to go on my way; but he
"never ceased from his prayer, and I was prevented from going
"on, and so I delayed in coming, and I have done nothing."
Then was the wicked Julian angry, and he said, "When I
"come back I will take vengeance upon him"; but before a
few days were over, he was slain by Divine Providence. And
straightway one of the eparchs who were with him went and
sold everything which he possessed and gave [the money] to
the poor, and he came to that monk, and himself became a
chosen monk; and he died with a good ending, and with works
which were pleasing unto God.

634. On one occasion Abbâ Pambô was travelling with some
monks in the districts of Egypt; and seeing some worldly folk
sitting down he said unto them, "Rise up, and salute the
"monks so that ye may be blessed, for they are always hold-
"ing converse with God, and their mouths are holy."

635. Abbâ John used to say, "The whole company of the
"holy men is like unto a garden which is full of fruit-bearing
"trees of various kinds, and wherein the trees are planted
"in [one] earth, and all of them drink from one fountain;
"and thus is it with all the holy men, for they have not one
"rule only, but several varieties, and one man laboureth in one
"way, and another man in another, but it is one Spirit which
"operateth and worketh in them."

Book ij.

Chapter j. Questions and Answers on the Rule of Life of the Holy Men which they taught before the Multitude and in their Cells on every kind of Spiritual Excellence

TWO of the fathers entreated God to inform them as to the measure [of spiritual excellence] to which they had arrived, and a voice came to them which said, "In "such and such a village of Egypt there is a certain man in "the world who is called Eucharistos, and his wife Mary, and "ye have not as yet arrived at the same measure as they." Now when the fathers heard [this] they marvelled, and they rose up and came to that village, and they enquired for and found the house and the wife of Eucharistos, and they asked her, saying, "Where is thy husband?" And she answered and said unto them, "He is a shepherd, and he is in the field pas- turing sheep"; and she brought them into her house. And when the evening had come her husband came from the sheep, and seeing the fathers he rejoiced with great joy, and he prepared a table [for them], and brought water that he might wash their feet. Then the fathers answered and said unto him, "We will "eat nothing, but tell us what is thy work"; and Eucharistos said unto them with great humility, "I am a shepherd, and "this is my wife." Now the fathers entreated him to inform them concerning his life and works, but he concealed the mat- ter, and refused to speak. Finally they said unto him, "God "told us to come to thee," and when Eucharistos heard this he was afraid, and he told them, saying, "Behold, we inherited "these sheep from our parents, and whatsoever God provid- "eth as [our] income from them we divide into three portions; "one portion [we devote] to charity, one portion to the love "of strangers, and the remaining part serveth for our own "use. Since the time when I took this woman to wife we have "not defiled ourselves, and she is a virgin, and each of us "sleepeth alone; at night time we wear sackcloth, and in the "daytime we put it off and array ourselves in our [ordinary] "attire, and no man hath known this thing until the present "moment." And when the fathers heard [this] they glorified God.

2. They say concerning Abbâ Anthony that on one occasion, when he was praying in his cell he heard a voice which said unto him, "Anthony, thou hast not yet arrived [at the state of "excellence] of a certain man who is a tailor and who dwell- "eth in Alexandria." Then Anthony rose up in the morning,

and took a palm stick and departed to him, and when the
man saw him, he was disturbed; and the old man said unto
him, "Tell me what thou doest, and how thou livest," and the
tailor said unto him, "I do not myself know that I do any
"good, and I know only that when I rise up in the morning,
"before I sit down to the labour of my hands, I give thanks
"unto God, and praise Him, and that I set my evil deeds be-
"fore mine eyes, saying, 'All the men who are in this city will
"'go into the kingdom of God, because of their alms and good
"'deeds, except myself, and I shall inherit punishment for my
"'sins'; and again in the evening, before I sleep, I do the same
"things." Now when Abbâ Anthony heard these things, he
said, "Verily, as the man who worketh in gold, and who doeth
"beautiful work, cleanly, and in peace, even so art thou;
"through thy beautiful thoughts thou wilt inherit the king-
"dom of God, whilst I, who have passed the whole of my life
"in the desert, separated [from men], have never overtaken
"thee."

3. Abbâ Anthony received a revelation in the desert, saying,
"In such and such a city there is a man who resembleth thee;
"he is a physician, and he worketh and giveth whatsoever he
"earneth to the poor and needy, and each day he, with the
"angels, ascribeth holiness to God three times a day."

4. When Abbâ Macarius was praying in his cell on one occasion he heard a voice which said, "Macarius, thou hast not
"yet arrived [at the state of excellence] of two women who are
"in such and such a city"; and the old man rose up in the
morning, and took in his hand a palm stick, and he began to
set out on the road to that city. Now therefore, when he had
arrived at the city, and learned the place [of the abode of the
women], he knocked at the door, and there went forth one of
the women and brought him into the house. And when he had
been sitting down for a little, the other woman came in, and
he called them to him, and they came nigh and sat down before him. Then the old man said unto them, "On your account
"I have made this long journey, and have performed all this
"labour, and with great difficulty have come from the desert;
"tell me, then, what works do ye do." And they said unto
him, "Believe us, O father; neither of us hath ever been
"absent from, or kept herself back from, her husband's
"couch up to this day; what work, then, wouldst thou see in
"us?" Then the old man made apologies to them, and entreated them to reveal to him and to show him their labour,
and thereupon they said unto him, "According to worldly
"considerations we are strangers one to the other, for we are
"not kinsfolk, but it fell out that the two of us married two

" men who were brethren in the flesh. And behold, up to this
" present we have lived in this house for twelve years, and we
" have never wanted to quarrel with each other, and neither
" of us hath spoken one abominable word of abuse to her com-
" panion. Now we made up our minds together to leave our
" husbands and to join the army of virgins, but, although we
" entreated our husbands earnestly to allow us to do so, they
" would not undertake to send us away. And as we were un-
" able to do that which we wished, we made a promise between
" ourselves and God that, until death, no worldly word should
" go forth from our mouths." Now when Macarius heard
[this] he said, "Verily, virginity by itself is nothing, nor
" marriage, nor life as a monk, nor life in the world; for God
" seeketh the desire [of a man], and giveth the Spirit unto
" every man."

5. They used to tell a story about certain brethren who were
members of the household of Abbâ Poemen. Now whilst these
men were dwelling in Egypt their mother wished to see them,
but was unable to do so, and she watched for them as they
were going to the church, and went out to meet them, but as
soon as they saw her they went back to their cell and shut the
door on themselves, and then their mother took up her stand
by the door, and spake [unto them], and wept and sighed
heavily. And when Abbâ Job heard her, he went in to Abbâ
Poemen and said unto him, "What shall we do in respect of
" this old woman who is weeping by the door?" Then Abbâ
Poemen rose up and drew nigh to the door and pressed himself against it and, hearing her speaking in the deepest sorrow,
he said unto her, "Wilt thou, who art an old woman, cry in
" this fashion?" Now as soon as she heard his voice she wept
the more, and she cried out, saying, "I want to see my sons.
" For what is this that I see in you? Peradventure I did not rear
" you? Peradventure I am not your mother? Peradventure ye
" did not suck at my breasts? Peradventure ye did not go forth
" from my womb? I am prevented by mine old age, but now
" that I have heard thy voice my bowels have been moved."
The old man said unto her, "Dost thou wish to see us here,
" or wouldst thou see us in that country [beyond the grave]?"
She said unto him, "My sons, if I do not see you here I shall
" see you there." And the old man said unto her, "If thou wilt
" compel thyself not to see us here, thou shalt, in very truth,
" see us there." Then the old woman departed, saying, "Yea,
" my son, if I shall see you there I shall not seek to see you
" here."

6. There was a certain old man who lived a life of such strict
self-denial that he never drank wine. And when I arrived at

his cell we sat down to eat, and one brought dates and he ate, and he took water and drank; and I said unto him laughingly, "So thou art angry with absinthe, O father? Since thou hast "eaten dates and hast drunk water, why dost thou not drink "wine?" And he answered and said unto me, "If thou takest "a handful of dust and throwest it on a man will it hurt him?" and I said unto him, "No." And he said unto me, "If thou "takest a handful of water and throwest it over a man, per-"adventure he will feel pain?" and I said unto him, "No." And he said unto me, "And again, if thou takest a handful of "chopped straw and throwest it over a man, peradventure it "will cause him pain? and I said unto him, "No." Then he said unto me, "But if thou bringest [them all] and dost mix "them together, and dost knead them well, and dost dry them, "thou mayest throw and hurl the mass on the skull of a man "and thou wilt not break it"; and I said unto him, "Yea, "father, [that is true]." And he said unto me, "The monks "do not abstain from certain things without good reason, and "thou must not listen to the men who are in the world who "say, 'Why do they not eat this, and why do they not drink "'that?' Is there not sin in them? Such people know not. Now "we abstain from certain things not because the things them-"selves are bad, but because the passions are mighty, and "when they have waxed strong they kill us."

7. On one occasion the priest of Scete went to the Archbishop of Alexandria, and when he had returned to Scete he wanted to send the brethren [to Alexandria], and he said unto them, "I have heard you say that there is a large assembly of people "in Alexandria. Verily, I say unto you that I who went there "did not see the face of any man except the Archbishop." Now when they heard [this] they were disturbed, and said, "Have they sunk into the ground, then?" And he said, "Nay, "not so, but my thoughts did not compel me to look at a man"; and when they heard [this] they marvelled, and they were greatly confirmed by these words [in their desire] to keep themselves from looking upon the vain things of the world.

8. One of the old men used to say: On one occasion the fathers were sitting and conversing together on the subject of ascetic excellence, and there was in their midst one of the old men who was a seer of visions, and he saw angels flying about over [the fathers]; but when they came to another subject of discourse, the angels departed, and he saw pigs rolling about among them and wallowing in the mire. And afterwards when the fathers renewed their conversation on spiritual excellence the angels came back and glorified God.

9. One of the fathers used to say that there were two

brethren who were neighbours of his in the desert, and that one was a stranger and the other a native of the country; now the stranger was a man of little faith, but the native performed many works in the service of God. And it happened that the stranger died, and the old man, who saw divine visions, saw multitudes of angels bearing away in triumph his soul until it arrived in heaven. And an inquiry arose concerning this, and the old man heard a voice from heaven which said, "He was "certainly a negligent man, but because of his being a stranger "they opened unto him." And afterwards the man who was a native of the country died, and his kinsfolk came to him and buried him, and the old man saw that there were no angels with him, and he marvelled, and he fell on his face and entreated God to inform him how it was that the stranger who was a negligent man was worthy of glory, whilst the man who had all those labours [to his credit] was not granted the same thing. And he heard a voice which said, "When the native "with all his works came to die, he opened his eyes and saw "his kinsfolk weeping, and his soul was refreshed; but the "stranger, although he was negligent, saw none of his kins- "folk, and he sighed and wept."

10. One of the fathers told a story, saying: There was a certain monk in the desert of Linopolis, and a man who was in the world ministered unto him; and there was in the city a certain rich and wicked man who died, and he was accompanied to his burial by the whole city, and by the Bishop, with lights and great honour. Now the man who ministered to the monk went forth to give him some bread, but he found him dead and eaten by the panthers; and he fell upon his face before the Lord and said, "My Lord, I will not rise up from "this place until Thou makest me to know why this wicked "man is buried with such great honour, and why this monk "who served Thee by night and by day hath come to such an "end." And an angel came and said unto him, "That wicked "man did one good work, and he was rewarded here so that "he might not find even one pleasure in the world to come; "but this holy man, because he was a man who was adorned "with divine virtues, although inasmuch as he was a man he "possessed certain shortcomings, will receive these things in "the world to come, so that there he may be found perfect "therein." And having heard [this] he returned, and glorified God for His judgements because they are good.

11. A brother asked an old man, saying, "Is it the name "or the work which maketh to live?" The old man said unto him, "I knew a certain brother who was praying on one "occasion, and who thought within himself, saying, 'I wish

" ' to see the soul of a righteous man, and the soul of a sinner
" 'when they are leaving the body'; and because God wished
" neither to make him grieve, nor to deprive him of his desire,
" whilst he was sitting in his cell a wolf went in to him, and
" laid hold of him by his clothes and dragged him outside, and
" then having pulled him along he carried him to the outside
" of a certain city, and then he left him there and departed.

" Now whilst he was sitting outside the city there was a man
" who lived in a monastery, and who had gained renown, and
" and concerning whom a report had gone forth that he was a
" monk of spiritual excellence; and this man was grievously
" sick, and was waiting for the hour of his departure [from
" this world]. And that brother looked on and saw the prepar-
" ations which they were making, and the things which they
" were putting ready for the event, namely, the wax candles,
" and the lamps which they were trimming and preparing, and
" he saw that all the city was weeping for him, and that his
" people were in grief, and saying, ' By his hand God hath
" ' given us meat and drink, and by his hands He hath de-
" ' livered us, and hath kept us and the whole city alive; if
" ' anything happeneth to him we shall die.' And when the time
" for this man to end his life had come that brother looked, and
" saw, and behold, the keeper of Sheol went in having in his
" hand a fork of fire with three prongs, and he heard a voice
" which spake [to the keeper], saying, ' Thou shalt not give
" ' his soul any rest, even for a moment, and thou shalt not
" ' shew any compassion unto him when thou takest away his
" ' soul. Then he who had appeared to that brother went in, and
" he drove that fiery, three-pronged fork which he had in his
" hand into the heart of the dying man, and he tortured him
" for a long time, and then he carried away his soul. And after
" these things, when that brother was going into the city, he
" saw a certain brother who was a stranger, and who was
" lying sick in the market-place, and there was none to care
" for him; and he remained with him for one day, and at the
" time when his soul was departing the brother saw Gabriel and
" Michael come for his soul, and they sat down, one on his
" right hand, and the other on his left, and they stayed there
" entreating his soul and wishing to carry it away. And since
" his soul refused to leave its body, Gabriel said to Michael,
" ' Lift up his soul and take it, so that we may depart'; and
" Michael said unto him, ' We were commanded by our Lord
" ' to bring it out without pain and without suffering, and
" ' therefore we cannot constrain it and do it violence.' Then
" Michael cried out with a loud voice, saying, 'What dost Thou
" ' command concerning this soul which will not be entreated

" ' to come forth, O Lord?' And there came unto him a voice
" which said, ' Behold, I will send David and his harp, and all
" ' those who sing with him, so that when the soul heareth the
" ' sweetness of their voices it shall come forth'; and they came
" down and surrounded the soul, and as they were singing
" psalms and hymns the soul leaped forth, and it was rejoicing
" in the hands of Michael, and was taken up on high with
" gladness."

12. They used to say that a certain old man went on one occasion to a city to sell his handiwork, and it chanced that he
sat down by the door of a house of a rich man who was dying,
and whose death was very near at hand; and as he was sitting
[there] he looked and saw black horses, with their black riders,
who were exceedingly terrible, and they held in their hands
staves of fire. And when they had come to the door of the house,
they set their horses outside, and they went in together, and as
soon as the sick man saw them, he cried out with a mighty
voice, saying, " O Lord, help me." Then those who had been
sent unto him said, "Now that the sun hath set upon thee thou
" hast come to call God to remembrance; why didst thou not
" seek Him while it was yet day? Now thou hast neither a por-
" tion of hope nor consolation left." Then they took away his
soul and departed.

13. There were two brethren who lived in cells, and one of
them was an old man who had persuaded the younger man,
saying, " My brother, let us dwell together," but he said unto
him, " I am a sinner, and I cannot let thee be with me, O fa-
" ther." Then the old man entreated him, saying, " Yes, we
" can [live together]"; now that old man was pure in his
thoughts, and he was not content to hear that there was in the
young man the thought of fornication. And the brother said
unto him, " Father, leave me for one week, and we will speak
" [on the subject] again"; and when the week was ended the
old man came and, wishing to try him, the brother said unto
him, " During the past week, O father, I fell into great temp-
" tation, for I went to a certain village on business, and I met
" a woman." The old man said unto him, "There is repent-
" ance"; and the brother said unto him, " Yea, there is." And
the old man said unto him, " I will bear the half of this sin
" with thee"; then the brother said unto him, " We shall now
" be able to dwell together." So they dwelt together until the
end of their lives.

14. Certain brethren from the great monastery went forth
and departed to the desert, and they came to one of the monks
who received them with gladness; and when he saw that, as
was usual with monks, they had come from labour, he pre-

pared for them a table before the appointed season, and whatsoever he had in his cell he set before them, and refreshed them. Now when the evening was come they sang twelve Psalms, and they did the same thing during the night, but the old man left them to rest, and he departed that he might sing and pray by himself. And whilst he was keeping vigil, he heard the brethren conversing together and saying, "The "monks who live in the desert live more comfortably than do "we who are in the monasteries." And when they were making ready in the morning to go to an old man who was his neighbour, he said unto them, "Salute him for me"; and they said unto him, "Thou shalt not water the green herb," and when he heard [this], he understood the matter. And he kept them until the evening working and fasting, and when the evening had come they sang the great service through, and the brother said unto them, "To-day, because ye have come from toil, we "have shortened the service somewhat," and he also said unto them, "We are not in the habit of eating every day, but be- "cause of you we will eat a little." And he prepared for them dry bread and salt, and he said unto them, "It is fitting that "on your account we should this day make a feast," and he sprinkled a little vinegar in the salt, and they rose up to sing and pray until the morning, and he said unto them, "We are, "on account of you, unable to perform the whole of the ser- "vice as we are wont to do, for ye must rest a little, and ye "are strangers." Now when the morning had come they wished to escape, but he entreated them, saying, "Spend a few days "with us, especially that ye may live according to the custom "of the desert, for we cannot let you go"; and when they saw that he did not want to send them away, they rose up and fled secretly.

15. On one occasion a certain brother came to Mount Sinai to visit Abbâ Sylvanus, and he saw the brethren working with their hands to supply their wants, and he said unto Abbâ Sylvanus, with boasting, "Ye toil for the food which perisheth; "Mary chose a good portion for herself." Then Abbâ Sylvanus said unto Zechariah, his disciple, "Give him a book and "take him to a cell wherein there is nothing." And when the time of the ninth hour had come, the brother looked this way and that way to see if they were going to send for him to come and eat, but no man came to seek him. Then he rose up and came to the old man and said unto him, "Father, have not the "brethren eaten to-day?" and he said unto him, "Yea." And the brother said unto him, "Why have ye not called me?" The old man said unto him, "Thou art a spiritual man and hast "no need of the meat which is for the body, but we are cor-

"poreal beings, and we require to eat, and it is for this reason
"that we work. Thou hast chosen the [good] part; read all
"day, and do not seek after the food of the body." Now when
"that brother heard [this] he expressed his contrition, and
"said, "Father, forgive me"; and the old man said, "Even
"Mary had need of Martha, for through the labour of Martha
"Mary triumphed."

16. It happened on one occasion that a certain heathen priest
came to Scete, and he visited the cell of one of the brethren,
and passed the night there, and he saw the labours of his rule,
and marvelled; and he said unto him, "Do ye labour so greatly
"and yet do not see visions from your God?" and the brother
said unto him, "We do not see [visions]." The priest of idols
said unto him, "When we perform the part of priests to our
"god he hideth nothing from us, and he revealeth unto us his
"mysteries, whilst ye who perform the labours of vigil, and
"abstinence, and silent contemplation, as thou sayest, see
"nothing. There must be in your hearts evil thoughts which
"separate you from your God, and it is for this reason that
"He doth not reveal unto you His mysteries." Then the
brother went and informed the old men of the word[s] of that
priest of idols, and they marvelled and said, "It is thus, for
"the thoughts which are not clean alienate a man from God."

17. One of the brethren said unto one of the great old men,
"If I could find one of the fathers according to my desire, I
"would choose to die with him," and the old man said unto him
with a laugh, "Good, my lord," and the brother said, "Such
"is my desire." Now he did not understand the mind (or
thought) of the old man. And when the old man saw that the
brother was in truth speaking concerning himself that which
he thoroughly believed, he said unto him, "If thou didst find
"an old man according to thy desire, wouldst thou be able to
"dwell with him?" And he said unto him, "Yea." The old man
said unto him, "Well hast thou said, 'If I could find [an old
"'man] according to my desire'"; and afterwards he said unto
him, "Thou dost not wish to be subject to the will of the old
"man, but the old man must be subject unto thee!" Then the
"brother rose up, and made apologies to him, saying, 'For-
"give me, father; I have boasted greatly. I thought that I was
"saying that which was good, but I find that I possess that
"which is of no value."

18. Abbâ Daniel used to say about Abbâ Arsenius that immediately he heard that the fruits were [ripe] on the trees, he
would tell them in his desire to bring him some, and that he
used to eat once a year of every kind of fruit, so that he might
give thanks to God.

19. Abbâ Abraham asked Abbâ Theodore, saying, "Father,
"which is the better thing for me to do, [to give] praise or to
"blame?" The old man said unto him, "I myself prefer to
"perform the works of praise, and not of blame"; and Abbâ
Abraham said unto him, "How is this?" And the old man said
unto him, "If I perform good works, and I be praised there-
"for, I find that I can bring an accusation against my mind
"whilst I flee from the love of approbation, and I can say that
"I do not deserve this praise, but blame belongeth to evil
"works, and how shall I be able to comfort my heart, because
"men are offended at me? It is necessary for us to do good
"works, and to be praised, without receiving upon ourselves
"the love of approbation, and not evil deeds, lest we be
"blamed." And Abbâ Abraham said, "Thou hast said well,
"O father; even so is it."

20. They used to say about one of the fathers who had lived
in the world, that when he was in the desert he was occupied
in fighting [his desire] to return to his wife whom he had
married before [he became a monk], and when he related the
matter to the fathers, they appointed him certain works, so
that he might be kept back from the fight [within him]. Now
because he was an obedient man and one who laboured, he
performed these works in excess, and at length his body became so emaciated that he was unable to rise up from his place.
And, by the operation of God, a certain father who was a
stranger came to the place of Scete, and he passed by the cell
of that monk and found it to be empty; and as he passed by he
said in his mind, "How is it that no man hath come out to
"meet me from this cell? And he went back there, and knocked,
saying, "Perhaps he is sick"; and when he knocked the brother
who was grievously sick went forth, and the father said unto
him, "What is thy sickness, O father?" And the brother told
him of all his suffering, saying, "I belonged to the world, and the
"Enemy made war upon me through my wife, and I told the
"fathers the story, and they imposed upon me severe labours;
"and having performed these my body hath become ill, and
"the war hath waxed stronger against me." Now when the
old man heard these things, he was grieved, and he said unto
him, "The fathers have imposed upon thee great labours as
"if [thou hadst been] a mighty man, but if thou wilt hearken
"to my feeble [voice] thou wilt relinquish those labours, and
"partake of a little food, at the appointed time, and wilt sing
"and pray a little, and wilt cast thy business upon God. For by
"thy pains and sickness thou wilt not be able to conquer this
"matter, because our body is like unto a garment; if thou take
"care of it, it will last, but if thou neglect it, it will come to an

" end." Now the brother having heard these things acted thus,
and in a few days the war passed away from him.

21. One of the fathers asked Abbâ Nastîr, the friend of the
blessed Anthony, saying, "What is the best work for me to
" do?" And he said unto him, "Not all kinds of labour are the
" same. For the book saith that Abraham was a lover of stran-
" gers, and that God was with him; and Elijah was a lover of
" a life of silent contemplation, and God was with him; and
" David was a humble man, and God was with him; therefore
" whatsoever work thy soul wisheth to do, provided that it be
" of God, that do, and keep thy heart from evil things."

And the brother asked him again, saying, "Father, tell me
" other things"; and the old man said, "Abbâ Anbastîon asked
" Abbâ Athrî, saying, 'What shall I do?' And he said unto him,
" 'Go, make thy belly little, and the work of thy hands great,
" 'and be not troubled in thy cell.'"

And again the brother asked him, saying, "If there be a
" persecution, is it better to flee to the desert or to the habi-
" tation of men?" And the old man said unto him, "Go where-
" soever thou hearest that true believers are, and have no
" friendship with a youth, and do not dwell with one; and if
" thou art able so to do, dwell in thy cell, for this is good, and
" cleanse thy garden herbs. This is far better than going to a
" man and asking him questions."

And again the brother asked him, "I wish to dwell in close
" friendship with a brother, and I want to live a life of silent
" contemplation by myself in my cell, and he must give me
" what I want, and I will give him the work of my hands."
The old man said unto him, "The fathers have never sought
" after a thing of this kind; and if thou dost not give bread
" to the poor Satan will not permit thee [so to live]."

22. Abbâ Daniel Parnâyâ, the disciple of Abbâ Arsenius,
used to tell about a man of Scete, and say that he was a man
of great labours but simple in the faith, and in his ignorance
he considered and declared that the bread which we receive is
not in very truth the Body of Christ, but a similitude of His
Body. And two of the fathers heard this word which he spake,
but because they knew of his sublime works and labours, they
imagined that he had spoken it in his innocence and simple-
mindedness; and they came to him and said unto him, "Father,
" we have heard a thing from a man which we do not believe,
" for he saith that this bread which we receive is not in very
" truth the Body of Christ, but a mere similitude." And he said
unto them, "It is I who have said this thing," and they entreated him, saying, "Thou must not say thus, father, but
" according to what the Holy Catholic Church hath handed

"down to us, even so do we believe, that is to say, this bread
"is the Body of Christ in very truth, and is not a mere simili-
"tude. As, in truth, God straightway took dust from the earth,
"and fashioned man in His image, [and no man is able to say
"that he is not the image of God], so also was it the case of the
"bread of which He said, 'This is My Body,' for it is not to be
"regarded as a merely commemorative thing, and we believe
"that it is indeed the Body of Christ." And the old man said,
"Unless I be convinced by the thing itself I will not hearken
"[to this]"; then the fathers said unto him, "Let us pray to
"God for the whole week on this mystery, and we believe that
"He will reveal [it] unto us," and the old man agreed to this
with great joy, and each man went to his cell. Then the old
man prayed unto God, saying, "O Lord, Thou knowest that it
"is not from wickedness that I·do not believe, but in order
"that I may not go astray through ignorance, reveal Thou
"therefore unto me, O Lord Jesus Christ, this mystery"; and
the two other old men prayed unto God and said thus, "O Lord
"Jesus Christ, make Thou this old man to have knowledge
"concerning this mystery, and we believe that he will not
"destroy his labours."

And God heard the entreaty of the two fathers, and when
the week was ended they came to the church, and the three of
them sat down by themselves on one seat, and the old man was
between the other two; and the eyes of their understandings
were opened, and when the time of the Mysteries had arrived,
and the bread was laid upon the holy table, there appeared to
the three of them as it were a child on the table. And when the
priest stretched out his hand to break the bread, behold the angel
of the Lord came down from heaven with a knife in his hand,
and he slew the child and pressed out his blood into the cup;
and when the priest broke off from the bread small members,
the old man drew nigh that he might partake of the Holy
Offering, and a piece of living flesh smeared and dripping with
blood was given to him. Now when he saw [this] he was afraid,
and he cried out with a loud voice, saying, "I believe, O Lord,
"that the bread is Thy Body, and that the cup is Thy Blood";
and straightway the flesh which was in his hand became bread
like unto that of the Mystery, and he took it and gave thanks
unto God. And the old men said unto him, "God knoweth the
"nature of men, and that it is unable to eat living flesh, and
"for this reason He turneth His Body into bread, and His
"Blood into wine, for those who receive Him in faith." Then
they gave thanks unto God for that old man, and because he
had not permitted Satan to destroy him from his labours, and
the three of them went to their cells in gladness.

23. Abbâ Daniel used to say that Abbâ Arsenius told him a story, as if he were speaking of some other man, saying:— Whilst a certain old man was sitting in his cell, there came unto him a voice which said, "Come hither, and I will shew "thee the works of the children of men"; and he rose up and went out. And the voice led him out and shewed him an Ethiopian cutting wood, and he made up a large bundle and wished to carry it away, but he was unable to do so. Then instead of making the bundle smaller, he went and cut down some more wood, and added thereto, and this he did many times. And when he had gone on a little further, the voice shewed him a man who was standing by a pit drawing up water, which he cast in a certain hollowed out place, and when he had thrown the water therein it ran down again into the pit.

And again the voice said unto him, "Come, and I will shew "thee other things." Then he looked, and, behold, there was a temple, and two men, who were riding horses, were carrying a piece of wood as wide as the temple was, and they wanted to go in through the door, but the width of the wood did not permit them to do so, for they would not humble themselves to go in, one after his companion, and to bring it in end-wise, and therefore they remained outside the door. Now these are the men who bear the yoke of righteousness with boasting, and they will not humble themselves to make themselves straight and go in the humble way of Christ, and therefore they remain outside the kingdom of God. And the man who was cutting wood is the man who laboureth in many sins, and who, instead of repenting and diminishing from his sins, addeth other wickednesses thereunto. Now he who was drawing water is the man who doeth good works, and who, because other things are mingled in his good works, destroyeth his works thereby. Now it is meet that a man should be watchful in his labour, lest he toil in vain.

24. On one occasion Abbâ Macarius was going from the wood to his cell, and was carrying [with him] some palm leaves, and Satan met him on the road holding a scythe [in his hand]; and when Macarius sought to wound him, Satan was afraid, and he fell down and did homage to the blessed man. Then the old man fled from that place, and he related to the brethren everything which had happened, and when they heard [it] they glorified God.

25. An old man used to say, "Be like a camel when thou "bearest thy sins, and be thou tied closely to him that know- "eth the way."

26. An old man used to say, "Become not a lawgiver unto "thyself, and judge no man, for thou art not under the Law,

"but under grace; but give thou everything to Him that is
"able to do everything, for thou art unable to do anything.
"Judge then [in] this [way], and do not sin at any time."

27. He also said, "He who wisheth to dwell in the desert
"should become a learner, and he should not practise doctrine
"lest he suffer loss; and his occupation should be with a man
"who loveth God."

28. Unto one of the old men Satan appeared in the form of
an angel of light, and said, "I, even I, am Gabriel who have
"been sent unto thee"; and he said unto him, "Hast thou
"not been sent unto another? for I am a sinner"; and when
Satan heard this he did not again appear. And the old man
said, "If in very truth an angel appeareth unto thee, say, 'As
"'unto whom [hast thou come in coming] to me? I am not
"'worthy.'"

29. When Abbâ Gregory was dying he said these [words]:—
"God demandeth three things from the man who hath been
"baptized, true faith from the soul, and truth from the tongue,
"and chastity from the body."

30. The old man said, "God seeketh nothing from Chris-
"tians except true faith, and [belief] that the things which are
"spoken shall come to pass in deed, and that we should be
"persuaded by the orthodox fathers."

31. An old man was asked, "How can a man find God? By
"fasting? By works? By watching? By mercy?" And he said,
"By means of these certainly when they are mingled with dis-
"cretion, but I say that there are many who have afflicted
"their bodies without discretion, and they have departed vainly,
"having gained nothing. Our mouth becometh foul through
"thirst, and we repeat the Scriptures with our mouth,
"and we go through all the Psalms of David in our service,
"but that which God requireth, and which is necessary we
"have not, that is to say, a good word for each other. For as
"a man cannot see his face in troubled waters, so the soul, un-
"less it be cleansed from alien thoughts, is not able to appear
"before God in prayer."

32. A certain monk was going along the road and he met
some nuns, and he turned aside out of the path, and she who
was leading them said unto him, "Hadst thou been a perfect
"monk thou wouldst never have regarded us as women."

33. Abbâ Anthony used to say, "A man's life or death
"cometh from his neighbour; if we benefit our brother we
"benefit ourselves, and if we offend him we sin against God."

34. A certain brother came to Abbâ Theodore, and he began
to talk and to speak about the things which he had not done;
and the old man said unto him, "So far thou hast not found a

" ship, and thou hast not let down in it thy possessions, and
" before thou hast embarked thou hast gone to the city where-
" to thou wishest to go. First of all do the work, and then
" thou shalt arrive at that concerning which thou art now
" talking."

35. A brother asked Abbâ Anthony, saying, " What [com-
" mandment] shall I keep so that I may please God?" And
he answered and said unto him, " That which I command
" thee observe. Set thou God before thine eyes continually,
" wheresoever thou goest; whatsoever thou doest make to it
" a witness (or testimony) from the Scriptures; and in what-
" soever place thou dwellest be not easily moved therefrom,
" but abide therein persistently. Observe these three things,
" and thou shalt be saved."

36. They used to say about a certain old man that whensoever he sat in his cell toiling in the contest, he saw
the devils face to face, and that he treated them with contempt and despised them through his contest. Now when
Satan saw that he was being overcome by the old man, he appeared unto him in human form, and said unto him, " I am
" Christ." And when the old man saw him, he winked his
eyes and made a mock of him. Then Satan said unto him,
" Why dost thou wink thine eyes? I, even I, am Christ." And
the old man answered and said unto him, " I do not desire to
" see Christ here"; and when Satan heard these things he departed from him and was no more seen.

37. Abbâ John used to say, that he saw in a vision one of
the old men in a state of stupefaction, and behold, three monks
were standing on the shore of a lake, and a voice came to
them from heaven (or from the other shore of the lake), which
said, " Take ye wings of fire and come to me"; and two of
them took wings of fire and flew over to the other side, even
as it was told them. Now the third remained behind, and he
wept abundantly, and cried out, and at length wings were
given to him also, but they were not of fire like those of his
companions, for they were weak and feeble wings, and it was
only with the greatest difficulty, and after dropping down into
the water, and with most painful exertions that he reached
the [opposite] shore. And even so is it with this generation,
for although it taketh to itself wings, they are not the powerful
wings of fire, but it forceth itself to take weak and feeble
wings.

38. An old man used to say, " Every wickedness which is
" not perfect is not wickedness, and every righteousness which
" is not perfect is not righteousness; for the man who hath
" not good and evil thoughts is like unto the land of Sodom,

"which is salted, and which bringeth forth neither green
"herb nor fruit. Now good ground produceth wheat and ex-
"pelleth tares from itself."

39. Certain brethren came and asked Abbâ Anthony a question about the Book of the Levites, and the old man went forth
to the desert, and Abbâ Ammon, who knew his habit, followed
him secretly. And when the old man had gone some distance,
he cried out with a loud voice, and said, "O God, send Moses
"unto me, and let him teach me [the meaning of] this verse";
and straightway a voice was heard holding converse with him.
Now Abbâ Ammon heard this voice, and said, "I heard the
"voice which spake with him, but the force of the verse I
"never learned."

40. On one occasion when Abbâ Poemen was a youth, he
went-to an old man to ask him [concerning] three matters,
and having gone into his presence he forgot one of them, and
he turned to go to his cell; and as he put the key [in the door]
to open [it], he remembered the matter which he had forgotten, and straightway he left the key in the door and returned
to the old man, and the old man said unto him, "Thou hast
"returned quickly, brother." And Abbâ Poemen told him the
story thus:—"When I put the key [in the door] to open [it], I
"remembered the matter which I wanted to know, and I did
"not open the door because I came back hither speedily."
Now the rocky ground which [he had traversed] in the interval was of no inconsiderable length. And the old man said
unto him, "Thy name shall be spoken about throughout all
"Egypt."

41. A brother said unto an old Abbâ, "Behold, I have en-
"treated the old men, and they talk to me about the redemp-
"tion of my soul, but I can lay hold upon nothing in their
"words; what is the use, then, of making them toil when I can
"do nothing [with what they say], for I am wholly in a state
"of uncleanness?" Now there were there two basins, and the
old man said unto him, "Go, bring me one of these basins,
"and pour some oil into it, and rinse the basin round with it,
"and then empty it out"; and he did so twice. Then the old
man said unto him, "Bring now the two [basins] together";
and the brother did as he told him. [And the old man said,
"Look and see which basin is the cleaner," and the brother
said unto him], "That into which the oil hath been poured is
"the cleaner." The old man said unto him, "And thus also is
"it with the soul, for even if it layeth hold of nothing through
"that which it asketh, it is cleaner than if it had never asked
"a question at all."

42. A brother asked Abbâ John, and said unto him, "How is

" it that the soul which hath blemishes in itself is not ashamed
" to speak about its neighbour, and to calumniate it?" And the
old man spake unto him a word concerning calumny, saying,
" There was a certain man who was poor, and he had a wife, and
" he saw another woman who hearkened unto him, and he took
" her to wife also; now the two women were naked. And when
" there was a fair in a certain place the two women persuaded
" him to take them to it, and he took his two wives, and put
" them in a boat, and when he had gone up out of the boat he
" arrived at a certain place. Now when the day had waxed
" hot, and every man was resting, one of the women looked
" out and saw that there was no man outside, and she leaped
" up and went forth to a heap of waste rubbish, and chose
" therefrom some old rags and made a girdle for herself, and
" then walked about boldly. Meanwhile her companion was
" sitting down naked, and she said unto her husband, ' Look
" ' at that harlot going about naked and without shame';
" then her husband, with sadness, said unto her, ' The thing
" ' to be wondered at is that, whilst she hath, at least, covered
" ' her shame, thou art entirely naked, and dost speak these
" ' words without being ashamed.' Now a calumny [uttered]
" against a neighbour is like unto this."

43. They used to say that one of the old men asked God
that he might see the fathers, and he saw them [all], with the
exception of Abbâ Anthony; and he said unto him that shewed
[them] to him, " Where is Abbâ Anthony?" And he said unto
him, " Wheresoever God is there is Anthony."

44. Abbâ Poemen used to say, " This is what is written,
" 'As the hart crieth out for the water-brooks, even so crieth
" 'out my soul unto Thee, O Lord' (Psalm xlii, 1). For the
" harts in the desert swallow many serpents, and when the
" poison of these maketh them hot within, they cry out to
" come to the water-brooks, but as soon as they have drunk
" the burning which cometh from the serpents inside them is
" cooled. And thus is it with the monks who are in the desert,
" for they are burnt up by the envy of evil devils, and they
" wait for the Saturday and Sunday that they may come to
" the fountain of water, that is to say to the body of Christ,
" and they sweeten and purify themselves from the gall of the
" Evil One."

45. On one occasion when the brethren were sitting with
Abbâ Moses, he said unto them, " Behold, this day have the
" barbarians come to Scete; rise up and flee." And they said
unto him, "Wilt thou not flee, father? He said unto them, "I
" have been expecting this day to come for many years past,
" so that might be fulfilled the command of our Redeemer,

" Who said, 'Those who take the sword shall perish by the
" 'sword'" (St. Matthew xxvi, 52). And they said unto him,
" We then will not flee, but will die with thee." He said unto
them, "This is not my affair, but your own desire; let every man
" look after himself in the place where he dwelleth." Now the
brethren were seven in number. And after a little he said
unto them, "Behold, the barbarians have drawn near the
" door"; and the barbarians entered and slew them. Now one
of them had been afraid, and he fled behind the palm leaves,
and he saw seven crowns come down and place themselves on
the heads of those who had been slain.

46. The brethren asked an old man, saying, " How is it that
" God promiseth in the Scriptures good things to the soul,
" and that the soul desireth them not, but turneth aside to im-
" purity?" And he answered and said unto them, " It is my
" opinion that it is because it hath not yet tasted the good
" things which are above, and therefore the good things which
" are here are dear unto it."

47. Abbâ Arsenius used to say, " The monk is a stranger in
" a foreign land; let him not occupy himself with anything
" [therein], and he will find rest."

48. They used to say that on one occasion when Abbâ Macarius the Great went up from Scete, and was carrying
palm leaves, he became weary and sat down; and he prayed
to God, and said, "God, thou knowest that I have no strength,"
and straightway he found that he was by the side of the sea
(or river).

49. There was a certain old man in the mountain of Athlîbâ
(Athribis), and thieves came to attack him, and he cried out;
and when his neighbours heard [his cry] they hunted down the
thieves, and they sent them to the governor, who shut them
up in prison. And the brethren were sorry, and said, " They
" were delivered into our hands"; and they rose up and went
to Abbâ Poemen, and informed him about the matter. Then
he wrote to that old man, and said unto him, " Thou must
" understand whence hath come the first betrayal, and then
" thou wilt perceive how the second betrayal arose; for if thou
" hadst not been betrayed first of all by those that were with-
" in thou wouldst never have effected the second betrayal."
Now when the old man heard the letter of Abbâ Poemen, who
was famous throughout all that country, and who kept himself
strictly secluded in his cell, and never went out, straightway he
rose up and went into the city, and took the thieves out of
prison, and thus the assembly set them free.

50. On one occasion Abbâ Macarius, wishing to rebuke the
brethren, said unto them, " There came here a young man with

"his mother, and he was under the power of a devil, and he
"said unto his mother, ' Rise up, let us depart from here';
"and she said unto him, 'I cannot walk.' Then the young
"man said unto him, 'I will carry thee myself.'" And Abbâ
Macarius marvelled at the wickedness of that devil, and sought
to drive them away.

51. On one occasion five brethren came to visit a great old
man, and he asked the first one, saying, "What kind of work
"doest thou?" And he said unto him, "I twist palm leaves
"into ropes, father"; and the old man said unto him, "God
"shall plait a crown for thee, O my son." Then he said to the
second brother, "And what dost thou do?" And he said unto
him, "I make mats, father"; and the old man said unto him,
"God shall give thee strength, O my son." And he said unto
the third brother, "And what dost thou do?" And he said
unto him, "[I make] sieves, father"; and the old man said unto
him, "God shall preserve thee, O my son." Then he asked the
fourth brother, saying, "What dost thou do?" And he said
unto him, "I can write well." And the old man said unto him,
"Thou knowest." Then he said unto the fifth brother, "And
"what dost thou do?" And he said unto him, "I weave
"linen." Then the old man said, "I am not near," and he said
also, "If the twister of palm-leaf ropes be watchful with God
"He will plait him a crown for him; mat[-making] requireth
"strength because there is labour therein; and God must pro-
"tect him of the sieves because he hath to sell them in the vil-
"lages; as to the scribe, he must be humble in heart, for there
"is in his business exaltation of spirit, as regardeth the linen
"weaver, I am not near (i.e., concerned) to speak, for he is a
"merchant and he tradeth. But if a man seeth a brother afar
"off carrying palm branches, or palm-leaf mats, or sieves, he
"saith, 'This man is a monk, for grass is the work of our
"'hands, and he is avoiding the burning of the fire'; and if he
"seeth a man selling linen, he saith straightway, 'Behold,
"'the merchants have come, for the [selling of] linen is the
"'work of this world, and it doth not benefit many.'"

52. Abbâ Jacob used to say, "It is not only words which
"are required, for in this [life of] time many have abundance
"of words, but it is work which is required, and it is neces-
"sary to have it, and not words wherein there is no work."

53. One of the old men used to say, "That which is hated
"by thee do not unto thy companion; if it be hateful to thee
"for him to calumniate thee, do not thou calumniate any man;
"if it be hateful to thee to be accused, accuse thou no man; if
"it be hateful to thee for a man to revile thee, or to treat thee
"with contempt, or to pluck thee away, or to do any such

" thing unto thee, do not thou do unto any man anything of
" the kind. He who is able to perform this commandment is
" able to redeem his own soul."

54. "On one occasion I went to Abbâ Muthues, and when
" I was about to return, I said unto him, 'I wish to go to the
" ' Cells'; and he said unto me, 'Salute Abbâ John for me.'
" Now when I came to Abbâ John, I said unto him, 'Abbâ
" ' Muthues saluteth thee'; and the old man said unto me,
" ' Behold, Abbâ Muthues is indeed a man of Israel in whom
" ' there is no guile.' And after one year I went to Abbâ
" Muthues, and I told him the greeting of Abbâ John; and the
" old man said unto me, 'I am unworthy of the old man's
" ' words, but know, if ever thou hearest an old man praising
" ' his companion more than himself, that he hath attained
" ' unto a great measure of perfection, for it is indeed obe-
" ' dience for a man to praise his companion more than
" ' himself.' "

55. A brother asked an old man, and said unto him, " My
" brother abuseth me, and I cannot bear him any longer; what
" shall I do? Shall I rebuke him, or shall I speak evil words
" to him?" The old man said unto him, " Both things are bad,
" whether a man rebuke him, or whether a man speak unto
" him evil words"; and the brother said unto him, " And
" what shall I do? For I cannot endure either." The old man
said unto him, " If thou canst not bear both things, speak to
" him, but do not rebuke him; but if thou speakest unto him
" with words of evil, and he listeneth, thou wilt be able to
" quiet him, saying, ' I did not say such and such a thing, and
" ' it will be possible for the matter which is between you to
" ' be healed; but if thou rebuke him to his face, thou wilt
" ' make a sore which will be incurable.' "

56. Certain brethren came to Abbâ Anthony that he might
tell them about the visions which they used to see, whether
they indeed came from devils [or not]; now they had with them
an ass, and he died on the road as they were coming, and
when they had gone into the presence of the old man, he said
unto them straightway, " How was it that your ass died on
" the road?" And they said unto him, " Whence doth the
" Abbâ know that our ass is dead?" And Abbâ Anthony said
unto them, " The devils shewed me [the matter]." Then they
said unto him, " We have come to ask thee questions because
" we have seen phantoms, and also because on several occa-
" sions they have actually become real things, and we want
" to learn whether we have erred or not"; and the old man
shewed them that such phantoms which arise through certain devils cannot be inquired into.

57. They were saying that Abbâ Sylvanus used to sit in secret in a cell with a few chick peas, and he made of them one hundred bundles; and behold, a man came from Egypt leading an ass loaded with bread, and having knocked at the door of his cell, he went in, and set down [the bread], and the old man took these bundles, and loaded them upon the ass, and sent him away.

58. They used to say that when Abbâ Zeno dwelt in a cell in Scete he went forth one night from his cell as if for a purpose, and wandered about; and when he had passed three days and three nights in travelling, being exhausted by toil and hunger, and ready to die, he fell upon the ground. And behold, a youth stood before him carrying some bread and a pitcher of water, and he said unto Abbâ Zeno, "Arise, and eat bread"; and the old man rose up and prayed, thinking that the youth was a phantom. Then the youth answered and said unto him, "Thou hast done well"; and again Abbâ Zeno prayed twice, and three times, and the youth said unto him, "Thou hast "done well"; and the old man took the bread and ate. Then afterwards the youth said unto him, "How is it that thou hast "gone so far from thy cell? But arise and follow me"; and immediately he found himself in his cell. The old man said unto him, "Come, enter into the cell with me, and make thy prayer," and as he was going on in front he was swallowed up from his sight.

59. They used to say that a certain brother had such an attack of blasphemy that he was ashamed to speak, and wherever he heard that there were great old men he used to go to them wishing to tell them [about it]; but whenever he had come to one of them he was ashamed to speak to him. Now having gone to the fathers several times, on one occasion Abbâ Poemen saw him, and he perceived that he was full of thoughts, and he was sorry for him; but when the brother would not reveal the matter to him, and he made as if he would pass him by, as soon as the brother had gone a little way from him, the old man said unto him, "How often hast thou come hither to tell "me the thoughts which thou hast in thy mind! Yet, when "thou comest here, thou findest it hard to tell me. How long "wilt thou go on in this manner and be vexed by such thoughts "in thy mind? Tell me, my son, what is it that aileth thee?" Then that brother answered, and said unto him, "I am fight-"ing against the devil of blasphemy of God, and though I "have often sought [to tell thee] I have been ashamed to do "so." And when he had told him the matter, the face of Abbâ Poemen broke into a smile, and he said unto him, "Be not "vexed, O my son, for when this thought cometh to thee,

" speak thou to it, saying, 'I have nothing to do with this
" 'thought, and my soul desireth it not; let this blasphemy be
" 'upon thee, Satan, for nothing in [my] soul desireth it, for
" 'the time is short.'" And when that brother heard these
things he departed rejoicing.

60. A brother asked an old man, saying, "How is that the
" soul is obstinate, and that it wisheth not to fear God?" The
old man said unto him, "The soul wisheth, O my son, to fear
" God, but there is no time, for the fear of God belongeth to
" perfection."

61. One of the old men used to say, "Be not thou asking
" for one thing after another, but ask concerning the matter
" of the war wherein thou art at the time engaged, and when
" thou hast eradicated that then ask concerning something
" else; but if when there is in thee one passion, thou settest it
" aside and askest about another, the former passion will
" never be eradicated from thee."

62. A brother asked one of the old men, saying, "What
" shall I do? for my thoughts wish to wander and go round
" about by reason of the sight of the fathers." And the old
man answered and said unto him, "If thou seest that thy
" thoughts wish to go forth by reason of the strictness of the
" restraint, or through need, make unto thyself a division in
" thy cell, and thou wilt henceforward seek not to go out; but
" if thou seest that they wish to go out for the benefit of the
" soul, go out."

63. There was a certain brother in the Cells, who, when the
service in the church was ended, used to remain until the last
and to wait for some one to lead him home; one day, however,
when the church was being dismissed, he went out before any
one else and ran to his cell, and the priest saw him and marvelled. And when the brother came on the following day, the
priest said unto him, " Tell me truly why thou, who hadst been
" in the habit of going out last, dost now go forth first of all?"
and he said, "Up to the present I made a distinction by not
" boiling any food [on the First Day of the week], and I waited
" that, peradventure, some one might take me to his cell; on
" that day, however, before I came [to the church] I boiled a
" few lentiles, and therefore I departed quickly." And when
the priest heard this he gave a commandment to the brethren
in the church that before each man came to the service in the
church, he should on the First Day of the week boil some food,
by way of making a distinction.

64. The brethren used to tell about a certain old man who
had a disciple who, when he sat down to eat, used to put his
feet on the table, and although the old man had suffered this

war for many years he did not rebuke him. At length, however, he went to another old man, and told him about the brother, and the old man said unto him, "Complete thy love, and send "him to me." Now when the brother came to that old man, at the appointed time for the meal the old man rose up and made ready the table, and as soon as they had seated themselves the brother straightway put his two feet on the table; and the old man said unto him, "Father, it is not good for "thee to set thy feet on the table"; and he said unto him, "Forgive me, O my son. Thou hast well said, for it is a sin." And the brother returned to his master, and told him about [it], and when the old man had learned this he perceived that this matter had been corrected in his disciple. And from that time the brother did not put his feet on the table.

65. A brother asked Abbâ Muthues, saying, "Speak unto "me a word whereby I may live." He said unto him, "Go, en-"treat God to give thee mourning and meekness of heart, and "consider at all times thy sins, and do not judge other people, "and make thyself lower than every other man, and have no "love for a boy, and no acquaintance with a woman, and no "friendship with heretics, and put aside from thee all free-"dom of speech (or boldness), and restrain both thy tongue "and thy belly, and guard thyself somewhat against wine, "and if a man speak with thee concerning any matter whatso-"ever, do not quarrel with him, but if he saith that a thing is "good, say 'Yes,' and if he say that it is bad, say, 'Thou "'knowest.' This is a meek spirit."

66. A brother came unto Abbâ Poemen and said unto him, "I have very many thoughts, O father, whereby I am vexed"; and the old man took him out into the air, and said unto him, "Spread out thy skirt, and catch the winds," and the brother said unto him, "I cannot do this." The old man said unto him, "Thou canst not do this, neither canst thou prevent thy "thoughts from coming, but it belongeth to thee to stand up "against them."

67. The brethren were on one occasion gathered together to Abbâ Joseph, and as they were sitting and asking him questions about their thoughts he said unto them, by way of [affording] them consolation, "This day am I a king, for I have con-"trolled my passions."

68. A brother asked Abbâ Ammon, saying, "Why is it that "a man laboureth in prayer and maketh petitions, and that "for which he asketh is not given to him?" The old man said unto him, "Hast thou never heard how Jacob wearied himself "for her whom he took to wife, and that he did not obtain her "whom he sought, but her whom he did not seek, and how

"afterwards he worked and toiled more, and finally received
"her whom he loved? Thus is it with the monk also, for he
"shall fast and keep vigil, and yet shall not receive that which
"he asketh; and again, he shall labour with fasting and vigil,
"and shall receive the gift of grace which he asketh."

69. One of the old men asked Abbâ Sisoes, saying, "Did
"Satan persecute the men of olden time as he doth those of
"to-day?" Sisoes said unto them, "He persecuteth the men
"of this age especially, because his time hath come."

70. Abbâ John the Less, who was a young man, and had an
elder brother, used to say, "I wanted to be without any care
"whatsoever, and to be like the angels of God, who do nothing
"except sing and pray to Him." And straightway he cast from
him the garments which he had on, and went forth to the wilderness, and when he had passed one week there, he returned
to his brother; now when he knocked at the door his brother
did not answer it, but asked him, "Who art thou?" And John
said unto him, "I am John," and his brother answered and
said unto him, "John hath become an angel and is no longer
"among men"; and John entreated him, saying, "I indeed am
"John," but his brother left him outside in affliction, and did not
open the door until the morning. And when he came to open the
door he said unto John, "If thou art indeed a man, it is neces-
"sary for thee to work so that thou mayest live."

71. Abbâ Pûrtê said, "If God wisheth me to live, He knoweth
"how to lead me, and to strengthen me, and to provide for
"me; but if He desireth it not unto whom shall I go to live?"
And he would accept nothing from any man, not even when
he was lying upon his bed, "For," he used to say, "if a man
"maketh an offering of any kind to me, and not for the sake
"of God, I myself have nothing whatsoever to give him, and
"he will receive nothing from God, for I am not in the place
"of God, so therefore he who offereth will suffer loss."

72. Abbâ Poemen used to say, "Everything which ariseth
"through passion is sin"; and he used to say also, "Every
"[exercise of] power which is for God's sake, is thanksgiving
"(or confession)."

73. An old man used to say, "Acquire silence, and take no
"care for any earthly thing, and examine closely thy medita-
"tions, and when thou sleepest and when thou risest up, be
"with God, and fear not the attack of the wicked."

74. On one occasion a brother came to a father, and said
unto him, "Abbâ, I sow a field, and I reap the harvest there-
"from, and I give alms also thereof"; and the old man said
unto him, "Be strong, my son, for thou doest well." So the
brother went away rejoicing in this desire. And Abbâ Job said

unto Abbâ Poemen, "Since thou hast spoken unto that brother "in this fashion, [I know that] thou dost not fear God." Then, after two days, Abbâ Poemen sent and called that brother, and said unto him whilst Abbâ Joseph was listening, "What didst "thou say to me when thou camest to me, for my mind was "occupied in another place?" The brother said unto him, "I "sow a field, and I reap the harvest therefrom, and I give alms "also thereof"; and Abbâ Poemen said unto him, "I thought "in my mind that it was thy brother, who is in the world, of "whom thou wast speaking when thou didst tell me that he did "these things; but if it be thou thyself who doest them [I must "say] that it is not the work for monks." And when the brother heard these [words] he was grieved, and he said, "I cannot do "without sowing, for I know not how to do any other work "but this." Now when that brother had departed, Abbâ Job expressed his contrition to Abbâ Poemen, and said unto him, "Forgive me." Then Abbâ Poemen said unto him, "I also "knew that this work was not the works of monks, but, "according to the measure of his desire, I gave him that where-"with I knew he would be edified, and I knew that he would "thus abound in love; but now he hath departed in sorrow."

75. Mother Sarah said, "If I were to pray to God that all "men might be built up through me I should be found express-"ing contrition at the door of each one of them; but I pray to "God especially that my heart may be pure with Him and with "every man."

76. Certain brethren, whilst talking to an old man about the thoughts, said unto him, "Our hearts are hard, and we are "not afraid of God; what shall we do that we may fear God?" The old man said unto them, "I think that if a man have "knowledge in his heart about Him that will rebuke him, it "will bring him to the fear of God." Then the brethren said unto him, "What is the rebuke?" The old man said, "In every "matter a man should rebuke himself, saying, 'Remember that "'thou art about to go forth to meet God.' And he should also "say, 'What do I require from man?' And I think that if a "man remain in these things the fear which is in God will come "to him."

77. Abbâ Poemen used to say, "An evil will is a wall of brass "between a man and God; but if a man would set it aside he "must also say, 'By [the help of] my God I will leap over a "'wall' (Psalm xviii, 29)—God Whose way is without blemish "—but if that which is seemly lendeth help to the thought, a "man is not easily turned aside."

78. They used to say that on one occasion, when Abbâ Alônîs was singing the service, and the old men were sitting [close

by], these old men watched him [performing the] service, and
that they praised him; but when he heard them he answered
them never a word. Then a certain man spake unto him aside
and privately, saying, "Why dost thou not make answer to
"the old men who have praised thee?" Abbâ Alônîs said unto
them, "Because if I made answer to them I should be as one
"who had accepted the praise."

79. An old man used to say, "If a word of the Book goeth
"up in the heart of a brother when he is sitting in his cell, and
"if he pursue that word before it hath arrived at its maturity,
"not being driven by God, the devils will demonstrate the
"word before it [become complete] according to their desire."

80. Abbâ Sarânîs used to say, "I have worked during the
"whole period of my life in reaping, and in twisting ropes,
"and in sewing mats, and notwithstanding these things, if
"the hand of the Lord had not fed me I should not have had
"enough to eat."

81. An old man used to say, "Spread abroad the Name of
"Jesus in humility, and with a meek heart; shew thy feeble-
"ness before Him, and He will become strength unto thee."

82. Abbâ Macarius said unto Abbâ Zechariah, "Tell me,
"what is the work of monks?" He said unto him, "Dost thou
"ask me, father?" The old man said unto him, "I beseech thee,
"my son, Zechariah, for there is something which is right I
"should ask thee." And Abbâ Zechariah said unto him, "Fa-
"ther, I give it as my opinion that the work of monks consisteth
"in a man restraining himself in everything."

83. An old man also said, "He who constraineth himself in
"everything, for God's sake, is a confessor." And again he said,
"He who constraineth himself for the sake of the Son of God
"will not be forgotten by the Son of God." And he also said,
"Him who hath made himself a fool for the sake of God, God
"will make him to be wise."

84. An old man used to say, "If when thou art sitting down,
"or standing up, or when thou art doing anything else, God
"be set before thine eyes continually, no [act] of the Enemy
"can terrify thee; if this thought abide with a man, the power
"of God will abide with him also."

85. An old man also said, "The man who hath his death
"before his eyes continually will overcome littleness of soul."

86. Abbâ Poemen used to say, "Hunger and slumber have
"not allowed me to notice these small matters."

87. Abbâ Theodore said, "Many men in this age are desirous
"of life before God giveth [it] to them."

88. He used to say also, "Be a free man, so that thou mayest
"not be crafty in thy words."

Questions and Answers on the Ascetic Rule

89. Abbâ Poemen used to say, "Keep thyself aloof from "every man who is contentious in speech."

90. An old man said, "In all [thy] trials blame no man ex-"cept thyself, and say, These have happened me for my sins."

91. An old man said, "In the sluggard and the useless man "God hath no pleasure."

92. A brother asked Abbâ Timothy, saying, "I wish to guard "my soul from things that will hurt it"; and the old man said unto him, "How can we guard our soul when the door[s] of "our tongue and belly are open?"

93. They used to say that a certain man asked Abbâ Sisoes about Abbâ Pambô, saying, "Tell us about his life and con-"duct"; the old man made answer to him, saying, "Abbâ "Pambô is great in his works."

94. Abbâ Joseph related that Abbâ Poemen said, "The "meaning of the words which are written in the Gospel, "'Whosoever hath a garment, let him sell it, and buy a "'sword' (St. Luke xxii, 36), is, 'Let him that hath a life of "'ease relinquish it, and lay hold upon [a life of] toil.'"

95. They used to say that [on one occasion] when certain of the old men were sitting with Abbâ Poemen and were discussing some of the fathers, and were [asking each other] if they remembered Abbâ Sisoes, Abbâ Poemen said, "Quit talking "about Abbâ Sisoes, for he hath surpassed the measure (*or* "limit) of all histories."

96. On one occasion a father came to Abbâ Theodore of Perâmê, and said unto him, "Behold, O father, such and such "a brother hath gone back to the world"; and the old man said, "Dost thou wonder thereat? Marvel not at this, but thou "mayest marvel when thou hearest that a man hath been able "to flee completely from the world."

97. An old man related of Moses that when he slew the Egyptian he looked on this side and on that, and saw no man, and explained the meaning of the passage as being that Moses did not see his thoughts. And when he saw himself, and that he was doing no evil thing, and that that which he was about to do was for God's sake, he then slew the Egyptian.

98. An old man also said concerning the verse of the Psalms wherein it is written, "I will place his hand in the sea, and "his right hand in the rivers" (Psalm lxxxix, 25), that it was spoken concerning our Redeemer, Whose left hand is on the sea, that is to say the world, and Whose right hand is in the rivers, that is to say, the Apostles, who water the whole world with faith.

99. A brother asked one of the old men, saying, "What shall "I do? For I am troubled about the works of my hands: I love

"making mats, but I am unable to make [them] here." The
old man said unto him, "Abbâ Sisoes used to say, 'It is not the
"'work which is easy for us that we ought to do, but that
"'which befitteth the place, and a brother should labour
"'according to what it will cost to keep him.'"

100. Abbâ Joseph used to say, "When we were sitting with
"Abbâ Poemen he made mention of Abbâ Agathon, and we
"said to him, 'He was a young man, why dost thou call him
"'Abbâ?' Abbâ Poemen said unto him, 'His mouth made him
"'to be called Abbâ.'"

101. One of the old men used to say, "Wheresoever the bee
"goeth it maketh honey; and thus also it is with the monk,
"for wheresoever he goeth he doeth the work of God."

102. An old man used to say, "Satan is a twister of cords,
"and as long as thou givest him threads he will plait them";
now he spake this concerning the thoughts.

103. Abbâ Sisoes shewed us the cave of Abbâ Anthony, and
said, "Thus in the cave of a lion a fox dwelleth."

104. They used to say of those who were in Scete that no
pride was found among them, because they surpassed each
other in spiritual excellences. They fasted so much that one
would only eat [once] every two days, and another [once] every
four days, and another [once] every seven days; another would
eat no bread, and another would drink no water, and to
speak briefly, they were adorned with every spiritual excellence.

105. They used to relate that a certain old man entreated
God and made supplication unto Him that the devils might
appear to him, and it was revealed to him that "It is not
"necessary for thee to see them"; but the old man made entreaty, saying, "Lord, Thou art able to hide me in Thy grace."
Then God opened his eyes, and he saw them like bees surrounding a man, and they were gnashing their teeth upon him,
and the angels of God were rebuking them and driving them
away from men.

106. A man asked a certain old man from Thebes, and said
unto him, "Tell me how I may be redeemed"; and the old man
said unto him, "Three things [thou must do]. Sit in thy cell
"and keep silence, and consider attentively thy sins, and keep
"thyself wholly from judging any man, and accept no gift
"from any man, and let thine hands be sufficient to find thee thy
"food. And if thou art unable to give alms of thy work at
"least supply all thy needs by thine own hands."

107. They used to say that one day when Abbâ Sisoes was
sitting down he cried out with a loud voice, and said, "O my
"feebleness"; his disciple said unto him, "What aileth thee, O

"father?" And the old man said unto him, "I wish to speak "to a certain man, and I am unable [to do so]."

108. They used to say that when the barbarians came the brethren took to flight, and that Abbâ Daniel, who was in Scete, said, "Unless God taketh care for me, why should I "live?" And he passed through all the barbarians, and they saw him not. Then afterwards he said in himself, "Behold God "hath cared for me, and I am not dead, I also will do as a man "doeth, and I will flee as the [other] fathers have fled."

109. When Abbâ Sisoes was about to die, and the fathers were sitting about him, they saw that his face was shining like the sun; and he said unto them straightway, "Behold, Abbâ Anthony "hath come"; and after a little while he said also, "Behold, the "company of the prophets hath come"; his face shone again, and he said, "Behold the company of apostles hath come"; and again his face shone with twofold brightness, and he became suddenly like unto one who was speaking with some one. Then the old men who was sitting [there] entreated him, and said, "Show us with whom thou art talking, father"; and straightway he said unto them, "Behold, the angels came to take me "away, and I besought them to leave me so that I might tarry "here a little longer, and repent." And the old men said unto him, "Thou hast no need to repent, father"; the old man said unto them, "I do not know in my soul if I have rightly begun "to repent"; and they all learned that the old man was perfect. Then again suddenly his face beamed like the sun, and all who sat there were afraid, and he said unto them straightway, "Look ye, look ye. Behold our Lord hath come, and He "saith, 'Bring ye unto Me the chosen vessel which is in the "'desert'"; and straightway he delivered up his spirit, and he became [like] lightning, and the whole place was filled with a sweet odour.

110. Abbâ Paphnutius, the disciple of Abbâ Macarius, used to say, "I entreated him, saying, 'Father, tell me a word'"; and he said unto me, "Do no harm to any man, and condemn "no man; observe these [words], and thou shalt be redeemed."

111. A brother asked a certain old man, saying, "In what "form doth the fear of God dwell in the soul?" The old man said unto him, "If a man possess humility, and practise absti- "nence, and judge no man, in this manner doth the fear of "God dwell in the soul."

112. Abbâ Hilarion of Syria came to the mountain to Abbâ Anthony, and Abbâ Anthony said unto him, "Hast thou come, "O star of light, who shinest with the morning?" And Abbâ Hilarion said unto him, "Peace be to thee, O pillar of light, "who sustainest creation!"

113. Certain of the fathers used to say, "God bringeth not "young men to monasteries, but Satan, so that he may turn "back the mighty men."

114. A brother said unto Abbâ Anthony, "Pray for me, "father"; the old man said unto him, "I cannot help thee, and "God will not, if thou wilt not abolish thyself and ask Him "thyself [to do so]."

115. They used to tell of a certain old man who had passed fifty years [of his life] without eating bread or drinking water; and he used to say, "I have slain fornication, and the love of "gold, and the love of glory." Now Abbâ Abraham heard [of him], and came to him, and said, "Didst thou say these "things?" and he said, "Yea." Abbâ Abraham said unto him, "If thou wert to go into thy cell, and find a woman on "thy mat, wouldst thou be able to keep from thinking that "she was a woman?" And the old man said unto him, "No, "but I should struggle against my thoughts so as not to touch "her." Abbâ Abraham said unto him, "Behold, then, thou hast "not slain it (i.e., the lust for fornication), but the passion is "still alive, though fettered. Behold, also, if thou wert travel-"ling along a road and thou didst see lying thereon some "potsherds and among them a talent of gold, would thy mind "be able to look upon the money in the same way as the pot-"sherds?" The old man said unto him, "Nay, but I should "contend against my thoughts in such wise as not to take it." Then Abbâ Abraham said unto him, "Behold, the passion [of "love of money] is still alive, though fettered. Behold now, if "thou didst hear of two brethren, one of whom was esteem-"ing thee highly and praising thee, and the other was hating "thee and reviling thee, if these men came to thee wouldst "thou be able to regard each of them with equal friendliness?" And the old man said unto them, "No, but I would strive "against my thoughts in such a way that I would treat him "that cursed me as well as I did him that loved me." Then Abbâ Abraham said unto him, "Behold, then, the passions "are still alive, but they are fettered in the saints."

116. There was a certain old man who was a monk, and who dwelt in the desert far away, and he had a kinswoman who with difficulty discovered after very many years where he was living, and then, by the operation of Satan, she rose up and came to the road to the desert, and she found camels which were going to travel on that road, and she entered [the desert] with them. Now she was [driven to do this] by the devil. And as soon as she had come to the cell of the old man, she began to give him proofs about herself, saying, "I am indeed thy "kinswoman," and she remained with him. Now there was

another monk who lived in the neighbourhood of men, and he
filled a vessel full of water, and set [it] down, and at the season
when he ate, being urged by the operation of God, he meditated within himself, and said, "I will arise and will go into
"the desert, and will learn from that old man what this is."
Now as he was travelling along the way, the night overtook
him, and he went into a house of idols which was on the road,
and passed the night there, and he heard the devils saying to
each other, "This night we have cast down such a monk by
"fornication." Now when he heard this he marvelled, and he
came to the old man, and found him sad, and he said unto him,
" Father, what shall I do? For I filled a vessel with water, but
" when I came to eat my meal I found that it had been spilled."
And the old man said unto him, "Hast thou come to ask me
" about a vessel of water which hath been spilled? What am
" I myself to do? For this night I have fallen into fornication."
The monk said unto him, "I know it also; hold thy peace."
The old man said unto him, "How knowest thou?" And the
monk said unto him, "Last night when I was sleeping in a
" house of idols which is on the road, I heard the devils say
" [so] to each other, and I was distressed [thereat]." And the
old man said unto him, "Henceforth I will go to the world,"
but the monk persuaded him, saying, "Nay, father, but stay
" in thy place, and send the woman away, for this is a temp-
" tation of the Enemy"; and the old man hearkened unto him,
and sent her away, and he himself continued in his ascetic
works, and he mourned, and made supplication unto God with
abundant tears, until at length he arrived at his former state of
ascetic excellence.

117. A brother asked one of the fathers, saying, "What
" shall I do, for I am disturbed in mind when I go up to per-
" form the office of the deacon?" And the old man said unto
him, "It is not good for thee to be disturbed when thou goest
" up to minister, but if thou art, and thou art disturbed in thy
" cell, thou must labour, and give thanks, and receive the hire
" of which thou art worthy." Then that brother said unto him,
" If I can find a man who will minister for me for a gift,
" and I cheat him not, may I [let him] do so?" The old man
said unto him, "If thou canst find a man who is in the world
" who can perform thy ministration, and will take his hire,
" yes, but if he be a monk, no."

118. A brother said unto Abbâ Poemen, " Can a man rely
" upon any one work of spiritual excellence [for salvation]?"
The old man said unto him, "John the Less said, 'I should
" ' wish that a man should take to himself a little of each kind
" ' of spiritual excellence.' "

119. These are the words which Abbâ Moses said to Abbâ Poemen, and the first word which was spoken by the old man was:

120. "It is better for a man to put himself to death rather "than his neighbour, and he should not condemn him in "anything."

121. "It is good for a man to die unto every work which is "evil, and he should not vex a man before his departure from "the body."

122. "If a man doth not put himself in the attitude of a "sinner, his prayer will not be heard before God." A brother said unto him, "What is a sinful soul?" And the old man said, "Every one who beareth his own sins, and considereth not "[those] of his companion."

123. The old man also said unto him, "If works do not cor-"respond to prayer he who prayeth laboureth in vain." And a brother asked him: "What is the equality of works with "prayer?" The old man said unto him, "He who prayeth "that he may receive the remission of sins must not hence-"forth be negligent, for if a man relinquisheth his own will, he "will be accepted by God rightly."

124. A brother asked an old man, saying, "Fasting and "praying which spring from men, what do they effect?" The old man said unto him, "They make the soul to be humble be-"fore God, for it is written, 'Look upon my subjugation, and "'my labour, and forgive me all my sin' (Psalm xxv, 18). "For if the soul be afflicted it will receive mercy from "God."

125. A brother said unto an old man, "What shall a man "do in every temptation which cometh upon him, and during "every thought of the Enemy?" The old man said unto him, "It is right for a man to weep before the grace of God so that "He may help him, and he shall speedily find relief if he make "his supplication with knowledge, for it is written, 'The Lord "'is my Helper, I will not be afraid what man shall do unto "'me'" (Psalm cxviii, 6; Hebrews xiii, 6).

126. The perfection of all spiritual excellences is for a man not to judge his neighbour. For when the hand of the Lord slew the first-born of Egypt, there was no house wherein there was not one dead person. Then a brother said unto the old man, "What is the meaning of these words?" The old man said unto him, "If we allow ourselves to view closely our own sins "we shall not see those of our neighbour. It is folly for a man "to forsake his own dead and to lament over that of his "neighbour."

127. And in respect of the words "A man should put his own

" soul to death rather than [that] of his neighbour," they mean that a man should bear his own sins, and should be remote from the anxiety of all men. And he should not say, "This is "good, and this is bad"; and he should not do harm to any man; and the wickedness of thy neighbour should not be remembered in thy heart; and thou must not hold in contempt the man who hath done wickedness to thy friend; and thou must not deliver thy will over to him that doeth evil to thy neighbour; and thou must not rejoice in that which causeth evil to thy neighbour. This is the meaning of the words that a man "should die rather than [his] neighbour." And thou shalt not speak evilly of a man, but say, " God knoweth every man"; and thou shalt not take pleasure in evil converse, and thou shalt not deliver thy will over to him that revileth thy neighbour. This is the meaning of the words, "Judge not that ye be not "judged." And thou shalt not make enmity against any man, and thou shalt not make any enmity in thy heart, and thou shalt not hate him that worketh enmity against his neighbour, and thou shalt not judge his enmity, and thou shalt not keep wrath against a brother who keepeth wrath against his neighbour. For this is peace.

128. Now the conclusion of all these things is that whatsoever thou hearest thou must speak, but this is not the opinion to which I incline, and I am a sinner; for because of these things God will give thee rest. When thou risest up in the morning each day, lay hold upon a governor who will suit every kind of spiritual excellence, and every command of God with abundant long-suffering, and in humility of soul and of body, and with patience and tribulations, and with thoughts and prayers, and supplications, and with groanings, and with the cleansing of the tongue, and with watching of the eyes, in suffering abuse without being angry and maintaining peace, in not rewarding evil for evil without discretion. And thou must not regard the lapses [of others], and thou must not measure thine own [excellence], but thou must be the lowest thing in creation through alienation from the things of the body and multitudinous affairs, through the agony of the cross, and poverty of spirit, and good desire, and spiritual self-abnegation, and fasting, and repentance, and tears, through the strife of war, and discretion, and purity of soul, through noble patience, and vigil by nights, and hunger, and thirst, and nakedness, and cold, and labours. And thou must keep hold upon thy grave as if thou wert already dead, and as if death were thy neighbour every day, in the mountains, and in the caves, and in the holes of the earth; and take heed that thou dost not become merely a hearer of the Word and not a doer of it. For those who do these things are indeed they who are clothed in the wedding garments, and they it is who have worked with the talents.

129. A brother asked an old man, saying, " Father, what " answer shall I return unto those who abuse us and say that " we do not return to the world because of our laziness, and " that by the work of our hands and the labour of our souls we " do not relieve strangers?" The old man said unto him, " Al- " though we have from the Law and from the commandments " of our Lord many things wherewith we could make answer " concerning the crown of perfection, yet we must make an- " swer, with humility, in this wise: Beloved, when the Nine- " vites were in need of repentance, which of them did these " things for the necessity of the world and the rights thereof? " Did not even the king himself refrain from this thing and take " the same course as the men of olden time, and those of the " later time, and those who were before them? And he kept " silence and was quiet, even according to all the characteris- " tics of the world, and up to the present no [men] have described " the punishment which befitted them. Thus also it is with us, " and because we have sinned against and transgressed the " natural and written law we bring to naught all [the charac- " teristics] of the world until we shall perceive that reconcilia- " tion hath come, and the penalty of the rights of olden time and " of the commandments hath been dissolved. And did not Paul " also teach us this, [when he said], 'He who wageth a strife " 'keepeth his mind [free] from everything else?' (Compare " 1 Corinthians ix, 24, 25.) And a man must not rest until the " Lord blot out seed from Babel."

130. A brother asked an old man, saying, "What shall I do " with my mind which fighteth [against me]? For it is better " and also a greater thing for me to go into the world and " to teach and convert many, and to become like unto the " Apostles." The old man said unto him, "If there be in thy " mind no fear that thou hast fallen short in the matter of any " of the commandments, and if thou hast also felt that thou " hast arrived at the haven of rest, and if thou hast no feeling " about anything in thy mind, then go; but if thou hast not " all these things together in thee, [the desire] is due to the " operation of wickedness which urgeth thee on, so that it may " cast thee down from thine integrity."

131. On one occasion the brethren were eating together in Scete, and John Kolob was with them, and a great priest rose up to give them a pitcher of water, but no man would accept it from him except John Kolob; and they all marvelled and said unto him, "How is it that thou who art the least among " all of us hast been so bold as to take the pitcher from him,

" and drink, whilst none of us dared to do so?" Then Abbâ
John said unto them, "When I stand up I rejoice that every
" man should take [the pitcher] from me and drink, so that
" I may have a reward, and I considered on this occasion also,
" and I took [the pitcher] and drank so that there might be
" a reward to him, and that he might not be grieved because
" no man accepted [water] from him, and that his [good] will
" might not be wronged." And when he had said this the
fathers marvelled at his intelligence, and they all obtained
benefit by his word[s].

132. A brother asked Poemen, saying, "I observe my soul,
" so that wheresoever I go I may find help"; the old man said
unto him, "Even those who bear swords have a God, Who
" hath mercy upon them in this life. If then we were to find
" ourselves in islands of terror God would deal with us accord-
" ing to His mercy."

134. Abbâ Poemen used to say that Abbâ Ammon said, "One
" man spendeth the whole period of his life holding an axe in
" his hand [ready] to cut down a tree, and never findeth the
" opportunity of wielding it; and another man, who knoweth
" well how to fell trees, heweth with three axes, and wieldeth
" them [against trees]. Now," he said, "the axe [in this case]
" is discretion [or discernment]."

135. Abbâ Poemen also said that Abbâ Anthony said concerning Abbâ Pambô, "This man feared God so greatly that
" he made the Spirit of God to dwell in him."

136. Abbâ Poemen used to say, "The fear of God teacheth a
"man all spiritual excellences."

137. A brother asked Abbâ Poemen, saying, " Why do my
" thoughts persuade me to esteem myself and compare myself
" with one whose rule of conduct is more excellent [than mine],
" and to despise that man as much as if he had been my infe-
" rior?" The old man answered and said, "The blessed Apos-
" tle spake concerning this, saying, 'In a large house there
" 'are not only vessels of gold and vessels of silver, but also
" 'vessels of wood and of earthenware. If now a man will
" 'cleanse his soul from all these things, he shall become a
" 'vessel which is suitable and convenient for the honour of
" 'his Lord, and he will be ready for every good work'"
(2 Timothy ii, 20, 21). That brother said unto him, "How are
"these matters to be explained?" And the old man said unto
him, "They are to be explained thus. The house is the world
" and the vessels are the children of men. The vessels of gold
" must be taken as representing the perfect, and those of sil-
" ver are the men who are inferior to them in the measure of
" ascetic deeds, and the other vessels of wood and earthen-

" ware are those who possess a little ascetic excellence. If now
" a man will cleanse his soul from all the things which are out-
" side what is right, he will become a pure vessel of honour
" suitable for the use of his Lord, and be ready for every good
" work."

138. A brother also asked Abbâ Poemen, "Why is it that
" I am not allowed to be free in my thoughts like the other
" old men?" The old man said unto him, "John Kolob used to
" say, 'The Enemy doth not rejoice in anything so much as in
" 'those who do not reveal and lay bare their thoughts to
" 'their fathers.'"

139. Abbâ Poemen used to say, "Men are wont to speak
" great and perfect things, but in their deeds they draw nigh
" unto the things which are little and inferior."

140. An old man used to say, "Neither shame nor fear con-
" firms sin."

141. An old man used to say, "As the company of the monks
" is more excellent than and superior to the children of the
" world, so it is meet that the monk who is a stranger should
" be a mirror to those who are found in a monastery which is
" devoted to the ascetic life."

142. A brother asked an old man, saying, "What shall I
" do?" The old man said unto him, "Go, and love the con-
" straint of thyself in everything."

143. The same old man said unto him, "Reveal and shew
" forth thy gift"; and the brother said unto him, "My thoughts
" will not permit me [to do so]." The old man said, "It is
" written, 'Call upon Me in the day of affliction, and I will
" 'deliver thee, and thou shalt praise Me' (Psalm l, 15); call
" then upon Him, and He shall deliver thee."

144. An old man used to say, "Teach thy heart to keep and
" to take heed unto the things which thy tongue speaketh."

145. An old man used to say, "If a man teacheth and per-
" formeth not he is like unto the large basin which receiveth
" the water for the assembly, which watereth and cleanseth
" many, but cannot itself be cleaned, and is full of dirt and
" impurity."

146. Abbâ Jacob used to say, "As a lamp illumineth a dark
" chamber, so doth the fear of God, if it abide in the heart of
" a man, illumine him, and teach him all the excellences of
" the commandments of God."

147. Abbâ Muthues used to say, "I would rather have the
" man with a little work, which abideth and is constant, than
" him who at the beginning laboureth severely, and soon
" ceaseth altogether."

148. On one occasion Abbâ Theodore went to Abbâ John,

who was an eunuch from his mother's womb, and as they were talking together about spiritual excellences, he said, "When we were in Scete the cultivation of the soul was our "labour, and we worked with our hands only in the ordinary "way, and we only did work of this kind when it came [in "the way]; to-day, however, the cultivation of the soul is "made our ordinary work, which is performed whensoever it "happeneth to come [in the way], and the work of our hands, "which was always regarded as a common matter, hath be-"come unto us a serious matter and an object of earnest "solicitude."

149. A brother asked an old man, saying, "What is the "cultivation of the soul like? And what is the labour of the "hands like?" The old man said unto him, "Whatsoever "happeneth for God's sake is the cultivation (or labour) of the "soul; but whatsoever a man doeth for himself, or whatso-"ever he gathereth together for himself, is the labour of the "hands." That brother said unto him, "Father, teach me a "proof of this matter which I do not understand." The old man said unto him, "It is as if a man were to say, Behold, "thou hearest that I am sick, and thou sayest in thyself, Now "I have a piece of work to do, shall I leave [it], and go and "visit him, or shall I finish it first and then go? And however "many times thou art prevented [from going] for some reason "or cause, and however many times the brother saith unto "thee, Come, take me, and help me, thou sayest within thy-"self, Shall I leave my work and go and help him? But if "thou goest not, behold, thou hast abrogated the command-"ments of God, which are for the cultivation of the soul, be-"cause of the work of the hands. If then a man ask thee, go "with him, since this is a work of God, for He said, 'If a "'man compel thee to go a mile with him, go two'" (St. Matthew v, 41).

150. A brother asked Abbâ Marcianus, saying, "What shall "I do so that I may live?" And the old man answered and said unto him, "He who looketh above seeth not what is "below; he who is occupied closely with the things which are "below hath no knowledge of what is above. And he who "understandeth the things which are above is not concerned "with what is below, for it is written, 'Turn ye, and know "'that I am God'" (Psalm xlvi, 10).

151. Abbâ Poemen said that Abbâ John cultivated all spiritual excellences.

152. A brother asked one of the old men, saying, "If I am "being tempted, and a temptation come upon me, and I have "no one in whom I have confidence to tell about it, what shall

"I do?" The old man said unto him, "I believe in God, and
"that He will send His Grace, and will comfort thee, and give
"thee strength if thou will ask Him in truth and wilt make
"supplication unto Him. For I have heard that a matter like
"unto this took place in Scete, where there was a man whose
"rule and conduct were excellent, and he fell into temptation,
"and he became oppressed in his mind, and because he had no
"man in whom he had confidence to reveal the matter to, and
"none to bid him be of good courage, he made himself ready
"to depart. And behold, the grace of God appeared unto him
"by night in the form of a virgin, and she comforted him,
"saying, 'Depart not, but dwell here with me, for not one of the
"'things of which I have heard shall be performed'; and
"straightway his mind was healed, and he was consoled and
"strengthened."

153. A certain brother used to say, "I knew an old man who
"dwelt in the mountain who would never agree to accept
"anything from any man; now he possessed a little water, and
"with it he used to care for and water a few garden herbs which
"he had. And he lived this life for fifty years, and he never
"went outside the fence of his cell. He was exceedingly
"famous because of the numerous cures which he wrought
"daily upon those who came to him. He died in peace, leaving
"in his place five brethren."

154. There was a certain old man in Scete who toiled in the
works of the body, that is to say, in fasting and in standing up;
and in his thoughts he was a simple man, and he was neither
keen in intellect nor learned. And he went to Abbâ John Kolob
to ask him about his thoughts, and when the old man had
spoken to him he returned and went to his cell, and forgot
what the old man had said to him. And he came a second time
to the old man, who told him what he had already said unto
him, and when he had departed he forgot it again; and
though he did this several times he always forgot what had
been said to him. Then, after these things, he went unto the
blessed man once more, and said unto him, "Thou knowest,
"O father, that I forgot [thy words] again; but I did not come
"to thee because I did not wish to weary thee." Abbâ John said
unto him, "Go, and light a lamp"; and he went and did as he
commanded him. And Abbâ John said unto him, "Bring several
"lamps, and light [them all] from it"; and he lit [them] as he
had told him. And Abba John said to the old man, "Is the
"lamp wherefrom thou hast kindled the many lamps in any
"way the worse?" and he said unto him, "No." And the old
man John said unto him, "If all Scete were to come unto him
"John would not be the worse for it, neither would the gift of

"the grace of Christ be impeded thereby. Whensoever then "thou wishest, and art in doubt, come [to me]." Thus by the patient endurance of both of them he removed and did away error from that brother. For this was the work of those who were dwelling in Scete, and they devoted themselves, and delivered over their wills to compel those who were engaged in [spiritual] war to inherit the good things (*or* virtues) each from each.

155. There was a certain old man who was sick, and as he possessed nothing which he required for his wants, the Abbâ of the coenobium received him [there], and said to the brethren, "Exert yourselves a little to relieve this sick man." Now the man who was sick had a pot full of gold, and he dug a hole below where he was [lying] and buried it; and it happened that he died without confessing and revealing the matter. And after he was buried, the Abbâ who had taken him in said unto the brethren, "Remove this bench from here," and whilst they were rooting it out they found the gold. Then the Abbâ said, "Since he confessed not about this when he was alive, he "cannot reveal the matter when he is dead"—now he knew that the sick man's hope had been in it—"but go ye and bury "it with him." And fire came down from heaven, and it continued above his grave for many days in the sight of every man, and all those who saw it marvelled.

156. A certain brother came on one occasion to the cell of Abbâ John at the time of evening, and he was in a great hurry to depart; and they talked about spiritual excellences [for a long time] without knowing [it], and when he went forth to set him on his way, they tarried talking together until it was the sixth hour of the night. Then Abbâ John made him go back to his cell, and they ate together, and then he sent him away, and he departed.

157. Abbâ Ammon said:—On one occasion I and Abbâ Betimius went to visit Abbâ Akhîlâ, for we had heard that he was meditating upon the passage, "Fear thou not, O Jacob, "to go down to Egypt" (Genesis xlvi, 3), and that he was repeating these words several times; and when we knocked he opened unto us, and he asked us, saying, "Whence are ye?" And being afraid to say, "[We come] from the cells," we made answer that we were from the Mountain of Nitria, and he brought us in, and we found that he was working by night at plaiting palm leaves, and we asked him, saying, "Speak a word "unto us." Then he answered and said, "Between the evening "and the morning I have twisted twenty branches, but in very "truth I have no need for all this, only [I am afraid] lest God "be angry with me, and He chide me, saying, 'Though thou

" ' wast able to work thou hast not done so'; therefore I toil and
" I work with all my might."

158. Certain of the fathers used to tell a story about a holy
man who was indeed a great man, and if people came to ask
him a question he would say unto them with wisdom, "Behold,
" I take upon myself the face (*or* Person) of God, and I sit
" upon the throne of judgement; what now dost thou wish me
" to do for thee? If thou sayest, 'Have mercy upon me,' God
" saith unto thee, 'If thou wishest Me to have mercy upon
" ' thee, thou also must have mercy upon thy brother, and then
" ' I will have mercy upon thee; and if thou wishest Me to for-
" ' give thee, thou also must forgive thy brother, and then I will
" ' forgive thee.' Can any blame rest upon God? God forbid! But
" the cause resteth with us, and if we wish we are able to live."

159. On one occasion a certain brother departed into exile
from the countries and places wherein dwelt Abbâ Poemen,
and he went to a monk who used to live in that country where-
to he was going; now this man was one who possessed love,
and many folk thronged to him—and the brother related unto
that monk stories concerning Abbâ Poemen, and when he heard
about his spiritual excellences he longed to see him. And the
brother came back again to Egypt, and after some time the
monk [unto whom he had gone], who lived in that country,
came to Egypt to him, for the brother had already told him
where he lived, and when the monk saw the brother he rejoiced
greatly. Then the monk said unto the brother, "Do [me an act
" of] love, and take me so that I may go to Abbâ Poemen,"
and he took him to Abbâ Poemen, and the brother told him the
story of the monk who was with him, saying, "He is a great
" man, and is much beloved, and he hath no small honour in
" his own country. I related unto him stories concerning thy holi-
" ness, and he greatly desired to come and see thee"; and Abbâ
Poemen received him with gladness, and having saluted each
other they sat down. Then the stranger began to converse with
Abbâ Poemen from the Scriptures concerning spiritual and
heavenly things, but Abbâ Poemen turned away his face and
returned him no answer whatsoever. And when he saw that
Abbâ Poemen would not speak unto him, he was grieved, and
went outside, and said unto the brother who had brought him,
" In my opinion I have toiled in vain in coming all this long
" journey to see the old man, for behold, he refuseth to speak to
" me." Now when the brother went in to the old man Poemen,
he said unto him, "Father, this great man, who is so greatly
" praised in his own country, came on thy account; why didst
" thou not speak with him?" Poemen said, "He spake about
" the things which are above and concerning heavenly matters,

" but I can only talk about things which are below and about
" the things of earth; had he spoken to me about the pas-
" sions of the soul I would have given him an answer; but since
" he talked about spiritual things, I know nothing about them."
Then that brother went forth to the monk and said unto him,
" The old man is not one of those who wish a man to talk to
" them from the Scriptures, but if thou wilt converse with him
" about the passions of the soul he will return thee answer."
And straightway the monk repented, and he came to the old
man, and said unto him, " Father, what shall I do so that I
" may bring into subjection the passions of the body?" Then
the old man looked upon him gladly, and said unto him,
" Now thou art welcome! Open now thy mouth on such mat-
" ters as these, and I will fill it with good things." And the
monk, having been greatly helped, and having gained benefit,
said, "In very truth this is the way of truth"; and he went back
to his country, giving thanks to God that he had been held
worthy of such converse with the holy man.

160. Abbâ Poemen said concerning Abbâ John that he cultivated spiritual excellences of every kind.

161. Abbâ Muthues used to say that there were three brethren
who were in the habit of coming to Abbâ Anthony, and that
two of them used to ask him questions about the thoughts,
and about life, and redemption, and the discretion (or intelligence) of the soul, whilst the third one held his peace continually. And after a long time Abbâ Anthony said unto him,
" Brother, thou comest here each year, and askest nothing!"
And he answered and said unto the old man, "It is sufficient
" for me to see thee."

162. Abbâ Sisoes asked Abbâ Poemen about filthy thoughts,
and the old man said unto him, "The matter is like unto a box
" of clothes: if a man leaveth the clothes inside it for a long
" time without being turned, they will become eaten up in pro-
" cess of time and destroyed. And thus also is it with the
" thoughts, and if a man doth not drive them out from his body
" they will be destroyed and perish."

163. Abbâ Joseph asked Abbâ Poemen about the wicked and
vain thoughts which a man produceth, and the old man said
unto him, "It is as if a man were to take a snake and a scor-
" pion, and throw them in a vessel (or cloth), and close (or
" wrap) them up tightly for a long time, when they would die
" owing to the period [which they have been shut up]; even so
" do the evil thoughts, which spring up in the mind through
" the workings of devils, decay and become destroyed through
" patient endurance."

164. Abbâ Elijah used to say, "What is sin able to do where

"repentance is found? And what will love profit where there is
"pride?"

165. One of the fathers said, "The early [fathers] did not
"depart from their places except for the three following
"reasons:—First: If one of them was vexed with his neighbour,
"and it was impossible for him to make clean his heart in re-
"spect of him. Secondly: If the abundant approval of the chil-
"dren of men was gathered together to him. Thirdly: If the
"temptation of fornication clung to him. Whensoever they
"saw these three reasons they departed."

166. On one occasion when he saw him pouring some water
over his feet, Abbâ Isaac said unto Abbâ Poemen, as one who
possessed freedom of speech before him, "How is it that,
"whilst the fathers exercised themselves in such stern labours
"and mighty deeds of asceticism that they oppressed their
"bodies, behold, thou art washing [thy feet]?" Abbâ Poemen
said unto him, "We have not learned to be slayers of the body,
"but slayers of the passions."

167. This same Abbâ Isaac heard the voice of a cock, and
he said to Abbâ Poemen, "Are there such things as fowls
"here, father?" And he answered and said unto him, "Isaac,
"why dost thou force me to speak to thee? It is only people
"who are like thyself that hear such sounds as these; he
"who is strenuous concerneth not himself with matters of
"this kind."

168. An old man used to say, "Wisdom and simplicity form
"the perfect order of the Apostles and of those who examine
"closely their rules of life and their conduct, and to this Christ
"urged them, saying, 'Be ye harmless as doves and subtle
"'like serpents' (St. Matthew x, 16). And the Apostle [Paul]
"also admonished the Corinthians to the same effect, saying,
"'My brethren, be not childish in your minds, but be ye as
"'babes in respect of things which are evil, and be ye perfect
"'in your minds' (I Corinthians xiv, 20). Now wisdom without
"simplicity is wicked cunning, and it is the subtlety of the
"philosophers among the pagans of which it is said, 'He
"'catcheth the wise men in their own cunning' (Job v, 13;
"I Corinthians iii, 19), and again, 'The Lord knoweth the
"thoughts of the wise, that they are vain' (Psalm xciv, 11; I
"Corinthians iii, 20). And simplicity without wisdom is the
"foolishness which is prone to error, and concerning this also
"the Apostle spake, and he wrote unto those who possessed it,
"saying, 'I fear lest, even as the serpent led Eve into error by
"'his craftiness, so your minds also may be destroyed in re-
"'spect of your simplicity which is towards Christ' (2 Corin-
"thians xi, 3). For they accepted every word without testing

"it, even as it is said in the [Book of] Proverbs, 'The simple
"'man believeth every word'" (Proverbs xiv, 15).

169. They used to say that one of the old men in Scete had
been a slave, and that he came each year to Alexandria, and
brought with him a gift for his owners from [the results of]
labour, and they received him, and paid him homage. And the
old man [formerly] poured water into a basin, and brought it
so that he might wash the feet of his owners, but they said
unto him, "Nay, father, thou shalt not honour us [thus]."
Then he said unto them, "My lords, I acknowledge that I am
"your slave, and that I have received from you an act of grace
"in that ye have let me become a free man to serve our Lord,
"and if I may not wash your feet accept at least my gift";
but they objected to this, and would not accept [it]. And he
said unto them, "Since ye refuse to accept it I shall dwell here,
"and be subject unto you"; then they allowed him to do what
he wished, and they sent him away with great gifts of various
kinds, so that he might do acts of kindness on their behalf to
the brethren who were in need, and because of this he became
famous in Scete. Now he conducted himself with great humility towards every man.

170. There was a certain man who was a slave and he became a monk, and he persisted in a life of self-abnegation for
five and forty years, and bread, and water, and salt, were
sufficient for his food; now after some time the man who had
been his master repented, and he also made himself to be remote from the world. And when the time came for him to depart from this world, he said unto his slave, who was now his
Rabbâ, "I see the hosts of wickedness surrounding me, but
"through thy prayer they are going back from me." And when
the call came for that slave one stood on his right hand, and
the other on his left, and he heard them saying unto him,
"Dost thou wish to come, O father, or shall we go and leave
"thee?" And he said, "I desire not to remain, take my soul";
and thus he ended [his life].

171. A certain man made himself remote from the world, and
he had a wife and also a daughter, and the latter died before
she had been baptized by the disciples; and her father distri-
buted among the poor the portion which came to her, and also
that of his wife; but he never ceased to make entreaty to God
on behalf of his daughter who had departed from the world
without being baptized. And a voice was heard by him as he
was praying, which said, "I have baptized thy daughter, have
"no sorrow"; but he did not believe. And that voice, which
was hidden, spake again unto him, saying, "Uncover her
"grave, and look [in], and thou wilt not find her"; then he

went to her grave, and dug it up, and he found her not, for she had departed, and had been laid with the believers.

172. The old man Macarius used to say, "These are the three " principal things, and it is right that a man should set them " before him at every season. The remembrance of his death " should be before him at every hour, and he should die to " every man, and he should be constant always in his mind " towards our Lord. For, if a man have not the remembrance " of his death before him at all seasons, he will not be able to " die to every man, and if he die not to every man he will be " unable to be constantly before God."

173. The old man Macarius used to say, "Strive for every " kind of death, for the death of the body, that is to say, if " thou hast not the death which is in the spirit; strive for the " death of the body, and then shall be added unto thee the " death which is in the spirit. And death of this kind will make " thee to die to every man, and henceforward thou wilt acquire " the faculty of being constantly with God in silence."

174. The same old man also said, "If thou hast not the prayer " of the spirit, strive for the prayer of the body, and then shall " be added unto thee the prayer in the spirit. If thou hast not " humility in the spirit, strive for the humility which is in the " body, and then shall be added unto thee the humility which " is in the spirit. For it is written, 'Ask, and ye shall receive'" (St. Matthew vii, 7; xxi, 22).

175. A brother asked an old man, saying, "Why do I keep " my sins in remembrance without being pained about them?" The old man said unto him, "This happeneth unto us through " contempt and negligence. When a man wisheth to boil some " food for his need, and he findeth some small sparks of fire in " his fireplace, he desireth to take care of them, and preserve " them, and to kindle therefrom a large flame; but if he neg- " lecteth them they become black and die out. And thus also " is it with ourselves, for if, according as God hath bestowed " upon us, we remember our sins, and we desire and come " to the life of silence, and we possess persistence in remem- " bering our sins, we shall acquire great grief in our hearts; " but, if we hold them in contempt and do not even remember " them, we shall be rejected.

176. A brother asked Abbâ Poemen, saying, "Who is a " hypocrite?" The old man said unto him, "The hypocrite is " he who teacheth his neighbour to do a certain thing which " he himself hath not performed, and to the doing of which he " hath not attained; for it is written, 'Hypocrite! why dost " 'thou look at the mote which is in the eye of thy brother, and " 'behold there is a beam in thine own eye? And how canst

"'thou say to thy brother, Let me take out the mote from
"'thine eye, seeing that thou hast not first taken the beam
"'out of thine own eye?'" (St. Matthew vii, 5.)

177. A brother asked Abbâ Chronius, saying, "What shall I
"do in respect of the error which leadeth captive my mind?
"For I do not perceive it until it bringeth me to the committal
"of sin." And the old man said unto him, "When the Philis-
"tines took captive the Ark of the Lord because of the evil
"deeds of the children of Israel, they dragged it along and
"carried it until they had brought it into the house of Dagon
"their God, and then Dagon fell down on his face in that
"place" (1 Samuel v, 3). The brother said unto him, "What
"[meaneth] this word?" The old man said unto him, "If the
"unclean devils take captive the mind of a man by their own
"means, they lead it on until they bring it to invisible and un-
"known passion; but if, on the spot, the mind turneth and
"seeketh God, and remembereth fervently the judgement of
"the world which is to come, straightway the passion depart-
"eth, and is destroyed. For it is written, 'When ye repent
"'and groan, ye shall be redeemed, and ye shall know in what
"condition ye are.'"

178. Again a brother asked Abbâ Chronius, saying, "In what
"manner doth a man come to humility?" The old man said
unto him, "In my opinion a man doeth this by restraining and
"withdrawing himself from everything, and by devoting him-
"self to the labour of the body, and as far as he hath the power
"so to do he should remember his departure from the body,
"and the awful judgement of God."

179. Abbâ Anthony used to say, "Behold a time shall come to
"the children of men when they shall become silly, and they shall
"turn aside and depart from the fear of God, and if they see a
"man who is neither as mad nor as silly as they are, they
"shall rise up against him, saying, ' Thou art both mad and
"'silly,' because he is not like unto them."

180. Abbâ Ammon of Nitria went to Abbâ Anthony, and said
unto him, "I see that the labours which I perform are greater
"than thine, how then is it that thy name is more renowned
"among men than mine?" Abbâ Anthony said unto him, "Be-
"cause I also love the Lord more than thou."

181. When Abbâ Poemen heard that Abbâ Nastîr was dwelling in the coenobium he desired greatly to see him, and he
told his Abbâ that he ought to send him to go and visit him,
but he refused to send him by himself, and he would not let
him go. Now a few days afterwards the steward of the coenobium, who had certain thoughts, persuaded Abbâ to send him
to Abbâ Nastîr, and he dismissed him, saying, "Take this

" brother with thee, and send me an old man because of him;
" and because I could not trust myself to send him alone I did
" not send him at all." Now when the steward had come to
the old man Nastîr, he told him his thoughts, and Abbâ Nastîr
healed him. And afterwards the old man asked Abbâ Poemen,
saying, " Whence hast thou gotten such humility that when-
" soever it happeneth that there be trouble in the coenobium
" thou dost not speak, and dost not interfere to put an end to
" contention?" And the old man having pressed the brother,
Abbâ Poemen answered and said unto him, " Forgive me,
" father ! When I first entered the coenobium I said unto my
" mind, I and the ass are one. As the ass is beaten and speak-
" eth not, and is cursed and maketh no answer, so also act
" thou, according to what the blessed David said, ' I was a
" ' beast with Thee ' " (Psalm lxxiii, 22).

182. On one occasion Saint Theophilus, Archbishop of Alexandria, came to Scete, and when the brethren were gathered
together they said unto Abbâ Pambô, " Speak a word to the
" Bishop, so that we may be built in this place"; the old man
said unto them, " If by my silence [we] are not helped, [we]
" shall not be builded by my word."

183. One of the brethren entreated Abbâ Sisoes, saying, " Do
" an act of love, father, and do thou thyself speak to me a
" word"; and he answered and said, " He who holdeth with
" knowledge [the belief] that a man should not esteem himself
" fulfilleth the whole Book."

184. An old man used to say, " This is what is written : Be-
" cause of two, and because of three transactions of Tyre, yea,
" because of four, I will not turn back from them" (Amos i, 9);
" [that is to say,] to be content with wickedness, to fulfil
" a thought, and to utter it; and the fourth is to carry a
" thought into effect. For at such a thing as this [last] the
" wrath of the Lord turneth not back."

185. They used to say concerning a great old man who dwelt
in Scete that, whenever the brethren were building cells in
Scete, he would go out and lay the foundation, and would not
depart until [the building] was completed. Once, however,
when he went forth to build, he was exceedingly sad, and very
sorry, and the brethren said to him, " Why is it that thou art
" thus grieved and sorry?" And he said unto them, "My sons,
" this place shall be laid waste. For I have seen a fire kindled
" in Scete, and have seen that the brethren took palm leaves
" and beat upon it until they extinguished it; and it broke
" out again, and the brethren took palm leaves and ex-
" tinguished it ; but it broke out a third time, and it filled
" all Scete, and the brethren were never again able to ex-

" tinguish it. It is for this reason that I am grieved, and sad,
" and sorry."

186. An old man used to say, " It is written, ' The righteous
" ' man shall blossom like the palm tree ' (Psalm xcii, 12).
" Now these words make known that the soul acquireth height,
" and straightness of stature, and sweetness from beautiful
" deeds. But there is another quality which is found in the
" palm, that is, a single, white heart, which is wholly suitable
" for work (*or* useful for being worked). And this must be
" found in the righteous man, for his heart must be single
" and simple, and it must be accustomed to look towards God
" only. Now the heart of the palm tree is also white by reason
" of that fire which it possesseth naturally, and all the service
" of the righteous man is in his heart; and the hollowness and
" the evenness of the tops of the leaves [typify] the setting up
" of sharpness of the soul of the righteous man against the
" Calumniator."

187. Another of the fathers used to say, " The eyes of the pig
" are so arranged by nature that they look always on the
" ground, and the animal can never look upwards to heaven.
" And thus is it with the soul which hath once been swallowed
" up in the gratification of the lusts, for it is caught hence-
" forward in the filthy mire of the gratification of the passions,
" and it is only with difficulty that it is able to look towards
" God, or to meditate upon any of the things which are worthy
" of praise."

188. The fathers prophesied concerning the later generation,
saying, "What manner of work will they do?" And one of
them, whose conduct was exalted, and whose name was Isô-
khôrôn, said, " We perform the commandments of God"; and
the others answered and said unto him, " And those who will
" come after us, what manner of work will they do?" And he
said, " They will attain to the half of our service." And again
they answered and said, " What manner of work will those
" who come after these do?" And he said, " Those who are in
" that generation will possess no work of any kind, for many
" trials are about to come upon them, and those among them
" who are found to be chosen men will be found to be greater
" than ourselves and our fathers."

189. An old man was [once] asked, " How is it that thou art
" never dejected?" And he said, " Because each day I hope
" to die."

190. A brother asked an old man, " Why is it that, when I
" happen to go out by myself at night, fear attacketh me?"
The old man said, " Because the life of this world is still dear
" to thee."

191. An old man was asked, "What is the work of monks?"
And he said, "To cultivate [all] the virtues, to make them-
" selves strangers to all wickedness, and to be watchful against
" judging and condemning others; prayer, and obedience, and
" the cultivation of the virtues are the mirror of the monk.
" For his soul is a fountain, and if it cast forth from it the
" things which are abominable it shall be made pure; but if he
" dig a pit, God is not wicked that He should lead us out
" from one house of bondage and carry us into another."

192. An old man used to say, "Do nothing without prayer,
" and afterwards thou wilt never be sorry."

193. Abbâ Poemen used to say, "The work of the monastic
" life is poverty, and trouble, and separation; for it is written,
" If there be there these three men, Noah, Daniel, and Job, as
" I live, saith the Lord (Ezekiel xiv, 14). Noah must be taken
" [as representing] the personification of self-abnegation, and
" Job as representing labours, and Daniel as representing
" separation; if then a man possess these three rules of con-
" duct the Lord dwelleth in him."

194. A brother asked Abbâ Poemen, "Which is the better,
" to speak or to keep silence?" The old man said unto him,
" He who speaketh for God's sake is a good man, and he
" doeth well, and he who holdeth his peace for God's sake
" doeth well."

195. A brother asked Abbâ Poemen about pollutions and
impurities of all sorts and kinds, and he said unto him, "If we
" stablish in ourselves a portion [only] of the work of our soul[s],
" a man may seek for impurity or uncleanness and it shall not
" be found."

196. An old man used to say, "We saw in Abbâ Pambô
" three virtues which appertained to the body, namely, fasting
" from one evening to the other, and silence, and abundant
" work of the hands."

197. Abbâ Pambô asked Abbâ Anthony, saying, "What
" shall I do?" The old man said unto him, "Put no confidence
" in thine own righteousness, and regret not nor cogitate upon
" a matter which is past, and be persistent in restraining thy
" tongue and thy belly."

198. An old man was asked, "What is it right for a man to
" do that he may live?" Now the [old man himself] used to
plait palm leaves into mats, and he never lifted up his head
from the work of his hands, but he occupied himself at all
times therewith. And the old man answered and said unto him
that asked him, "Behold, what thou seest."

199. The old men used to say, "There is nothing worse
" than a man passing judgement upon his neighbour."

200. And the old men used to say, "From those who are "beginners in the monastic life God demandeth nothing ex-"cept work, and the vexing of the body, and that a man "should be obedient."

201. An old man used to say that separation was the most excellent of all spiritual virtues.

202. Abbâ Arsenius used to say, "Thou shalt not depart "from a place without great labour, and thou shalt do none "of the things which, evilly, thou desirest, and thou shalt do "nothing without the testimony of the Scriptures."

203. Abbâ Arsenius used to say, "If we seek God He will "be revealed unto us, and if we lay hold upon Him, He will "remain with us."

An old man used to say, "If we seek God He will be re-"vealed unto us, and if we lay hold upon Him, He will re-"main with us."

204. Abbâ Poemen used to say to Abbâ Job, "Turn away "thine eyes from beholding what is vain, the lust for which "destroyeth souls."

205. The old man used to say also, "It is impossible for "him who believeth rightly, and who worketh in the fear of "God, to fall into the impurity of the passions, and into the "error of devils."

206. Abbâ Macarius used to say, "If we remember the wicked-"ness of men we destroy the power of the memory, but if we re-"member how the devils act wickedly we shall remain uninjured."

207. On one occasion Abbâ Macarius went up from Scete to Therenuthum, and at eventide he came upon a certain place wherein he went that he might refresh himself and rest; and there were there some old bones, and bodies of the dead, and he took some of them and placed them under his head that he might lie down and rest a little from the labour of the road. Now when the devils which dwelt there saw his confidence and courage, they were smitten with envy, and wishing to disturb him they cried out and shouted from one to another the name of a woman, saying, "O So-and-so, O So-and-so, "come with us, and let us go to the bath." And another an-swered from out of the bones which were under the head of the blessed man, and said unto him that called him, "There "is a stranger who is lying upon me, and I am unable to "come"; but the blessed man was not moved, neither was he astonished, but with confidence and great courage he knocked upon the bones, saying, "Rise up, and get thee into darkness "backwards." Now when the devils heard this, they cried out with a loud voice, saying, "Thou hast conquered us"; and they fled away ashamed.

208. Abbâ Anthony used to say, "Let us put God before
"our eyes continually; remember death and Christ our Re-
"deemer; hate the world and everything which is therein;
"hate the world and all bodily pleasure; die unto this life, so
"that thou mayest live unto God, for God will require it of
"thee in the day of judgement. Be hungry, and thirsty, and
"naked; weep and mourn; watch and groan in thy heart; ex-
"amine thyself [and see] if thou art worthy of God. Love
"labour and tribulation, so that thou mayest find God, and treat
"with contempt and despise the body, so that thy soul may live."

209. An old man was asked, "What is the straight and nar-
"row way?" And he answered and said, "The straight and
"narrow way is for a man to constrain his thoughts, and to
"restrain his desires for God's sake, and this [is intended to
"be understood when] it is said, 'Behold, we have left every-
"'thing and followed Thee.'"

210. Abbâ Poemen asked Abbâ Joseph, saying, "What am
"I to do when passions rise up against me, wishing to make
"me quake? Shall I stand up against them, and drive them
"away, or shall I allow them to enter?" The old man said
unto him, "Let them shake thee, and do thou strive with
"them." But to another brother who had come from Thebes,
and gone down to Scete, and asked the same old man the same
question, he spake differently; and when he returned from
Scete to Thebes, he said before all the brethren, "I went to
"Abbâ Joseph, and I asked him, saying, 'If passions draw
"'nigh unto me, shall I drive them away so that they may
"'not make me shake, or shall I permit them to enter into
"'me?' And he said unto me, 'Thou shalt not let them draw
"'nigh to thee in any way, but cut them off quickly.'" Now
when Abbâ Poemen, who happened to be there, heard that
Abbâ Joseph had spoken differently to that Theban, he rose
up and went again to Abbâ Joseph, and said unto him, "Abbâ,
"I have believed in thee as in God, and I have revealed unto
"thee my thoughts, and behold, thou hast spoken unto that
"Theban in one way, and to me thou hast declared the oppo-
"site." The old man said unto him, "Dost thou not know
"that I love thee?" And he answered and said unto him,
"Yea, I do." The old man said unto him, "Didst thou not
"say unto me, Tell me as if thou wast telling thyself? If, then,
"thoughts enter into thee, and thou art mingled with them,
"and thou givest and takest, and art not injured, they prove
"thee to be one who is tried and chosen especially. Now I
"spake unto thee as I would unto myself. But there are others
"whom the passions cannot even approach or touch, never-
"theless it helpeth them to cut them off quickly."

211. Abbâ John Kolob used to say, "I am like unto a man
"who is sitting under a great tree, and who seeth multitudes
"of wild beasts and creeping things coming towards him, and
"because he is unable to stand up against them, he runneth and
"goeth up the tree, and is delivered. In like manner I sit in
"my cell, and I see evil thoughts coming against me, and be-
"cause I cannot stand against them I flee and take refuge in
"God by prayer, and I am delivered from the enemies, and I
"live for ever."

212. Abbâ Hilarion was asked, "How can it be right for a
"strenuous brother not to be offended when he seeth other
"monks returning to the world?" The old man said, "It is
"meet that he should consider the hunting dogs which follow
"after hares, for as one of these dogs giveth chase to the hare
"so soon as he seeth it (now the other dogs which are his
"companions look at that dog as he runneth, and although
"they run with him for a certain time, they at length become
"exhausted and turn back, whilst he continueth his running
"by himself, and is not impeded in his headlong course, and he
"striveth to advance, and neither resteth nor ceaseth from run-
"ning because of those who have remained behind, but he
"runneth until he hath overtaken that which he seeth, even as
"I have already said, and he feareth neither the stones which
"come in his way, nor the thorny brambles and briars, and
"passeth on among the thorns, and though often torn and
"lacerated thereby he neither resteth nor ceaseth from his
"course), so also for the brother, who wisheth to follow after
"the love of Christ, is it right to fasten his gaze upon the Cross
"until he overtaketh Him that was crucified, even though he
"see others who have begun to turn back."

213. A brother asked an old man, saying, "What work ought
"the soul to do in order to produce fruits of excellence?" The old
man said unto him, "In my opinion the work of the soul is as
"follows: To live in silence, persistent endurance, self-denial,
"labour, humility of body, and constant prayer. And a man
"should not consider the shortcomings of men, but his own
"lapses; if now a man will persist in these things the soul
"will after no great time make manifest the fruits of spiritual
"excellence."

214. An old man used to say, "Strife delivereth a man over
"to anger, and anger delivereth him over to blindness of the
"mind, and the blindness of the mind maketh him to do every-
"thing which is bad."

215. Abbâ Elijah used to say, "I am afraid of three things:
"When my soul shall be about to go forth from the body; and
"when I am about to go forth to meet Christ; and when the

" sentence of doom shall be about to be sent forth upon
" me."

216. Abbâ John used to say, concerning the soul which wisheth to repent, thus: There was a certain harlot in the city who
had many lovers, and a certain judge came and said unto her,
" Consent to lead a good life, and I will marry thee"; and she
agreed, and he took her and brought her up to his house. Now
when her lovers wanted her, they said, " A judge hath taken
" her up to his house, and if we go to his door, and he learn
" about it he will punish us. But let us come behind the door
" and whistle to her, and she will recognize the whistle and
" will come down to us, and we shall be blameless." And when
the harlot heard the sound of the whistling, she sealed up the
hearing of her ears, and she jumped up and went into the inner
bed-chamber, and shut herself in. Now the harlot is the sinful
soul, and the lovers are the passions, and the judge is Christ,
and the house is the wakeful mind, and those who whistle to the
soul are the wicked devils; but the soul always fleeth to God.

217. They used to tell a story of a certain great old man, and
say that when he was travelling along a road two angels
cleaved to him and journeyed with him, one on his right hand
and the other on his left. And as they were going along they
found lying on the road a dead body which stank, and the old
man closed his nostrils because of the evil smell, and the angels
did the same. Now after they had gone on a little farther, the
old man said unto them, " Do ye also smell as we do?" And
they said unto him, " No, but because of thee we closed our
" nostrils. For it is not for us to smell the rottenness of this
" world, but we do smell the souls which stink of sin, because
" the breath of such is nigh unto us."

218. Abbâ Anthony besought God to inform him why young
children died whilst so many old men lived, and why upright
men were poor whilst the wicked were rich, and why some
were blind and others had their sight, and why the righteous
suffered from illness whilst the wicked were healthy, and a voice
came, which said, "Anthony, take care of thine own self, for
" these matters are the judgements of God."

219. Whilst Abbâ Sylvanus was sitting down and the brethren with him, he dropped into a stupor which was of God, and
he fell upon his face; and after a long time, when he was standing up, he wept, and the brethren entreated him, saying,
" What aileth thee, O father?" But he held his peace, and they
continued to press him to tell them what [ailed him]. Then he
answered and said unto them, " I have just been snatched
" away to the place of the judgement of God, and I have seen many
" who belonged to our order, that is to say, Christians, going

" to punishment, and many men who have lived in the world
" going into the kingdom"; and the old man mourned and refused to come out of his cell. And he covered his face with his
cloak, saying, "Why should I seek to see the light of time
" wherein there is no profit?"

220. On another occasion his disciple Zechariah came to him,
and found him in the stupor of prayer, and his hands were
raised up to heaven, and he went out and closed the door; and he
came [again] at the ninth hour, and found him in the same attitude, and when he came again about the tenth hour, and
found him still in the same attitude, he knocked at the door,
and then went in and found him in a state of silence. And he
said unto him, " What hath happened unto thee to-day, O
" father?" And the old man said unto him, " My son, I felt
" weak and ill"; but the disciple laid hold upon his feet, saying, " I will not leave thee until thou tellest me what thou hast
" seen." The old man said unto him, " Swear to me that thou
" wilt not reveal the matter unto any man until I go forth from
" the body, and then I will tell thee"; and the disciple entreated
him, and the old man said, " I was snatched up into the hea-
" vens, and I saw the glory of God, and I remained there until
" now, when I was dismissed."

221. On one occasion Abbâ Macarius went to Abbâ Anthony in
the mountain, and he knocked at his door, and he went out unto
him, and said unto him, "Who art thou?" And Macarius said unto
him, "I am Macarius," whereupon Abbâ Anthony closed the
door and went inside, and left him outside, but when he saw the
patient endurance of Macarius he opened the door to him, and said
unto him with a smile, " O Macarius, I have been wishing to
" see thee for a long time past, for I have heard about thee";
and having welcomed him he made him rest and refresh himself, through his love for strangers, for Abbâ Macarius had
[come] from great toil. Now when the evening had come, Abbâ
Anthony soaked a few palm leaves in water for himself, and
Abbâ Macarius said unto him, " Give the command, and I will
" soak some for myself," and Abbâ Anthony said, " Soak
" [some]"; and he made up a large bundle for himself, and soaked
it in water, and they sat down from the evening [until the
morning], and they talked together about the redemption of
souls as they plaited the palm leaves, and they threw their
work into the cave through the window. And when the blessed
Anthony went into the cave in the morning, and saw the heap
of palm-leaf work of Abbâ Macarius, he marvelled, and he
seized his hands and kissed them, saying, " Great strength
" hath gone forth from these hands."

222. Abbâ Poemen said, "If a man will throw himself be-

" fore God, and will not esteem himself, and will cast his
" pleasures behind his back, [he will find that] such things are
" the instruments of the work of the soul."

223. The same old man also said, "If a man observeth his
" grade he will not be troubled."

224. The same old man also said, "Make thou the desire
" of thy lust of no effect through the remembrance of God,
" and thou shalt find rest."

225. He also said, "A certain brother went to Abbâ Sîmôn
" to ask him for a word, and although he remained with him
" for seven days the old man returned him no answer; but as
" he was making himself ready to go away he said unto him,
" 'Go, and take good heed unto thyself, for at present my
" 'sins have become a dense wall between myself and God.'"

226. Abbâ Alônîs said, "If I had not hidden (or suppressed)
" myself wholly I should not have been able to build myself."

227. The same old man said, "A man is not able to know
" outside himself the thoughts which are in him, but when
" they resist him from within, if he be a warrior, he will cast
" them out from him."

228. The same old man also said, "A man, wheresoever he
" cleaveth, is built up; look not upon thy mind."

229. The old man often said, "Esteem not thyself, but
" cleave thou to him that leadeth a good life."

230. He also said, "[In] this [life] we do not discern matters,
" and it doth not permit us to profit by the things which are
" good."

231. The old man said, "If a thought about some bodily
" need come to thee and thou cast it forth once, and it come
" to thee a second time, and thou drivest it away, if it come
" to thee a third time, look not upon it, because it is war."

232. A father who was about to die said to his sons, "Dwell
" ye not with heretics, and have no converse with a brother
" who hath a sister, and have no business with the Govern-
" ment, and let not thy hands be spread out to gather in, but
" to give to the poor who are in need."

233. On one occasion Abbâ Evagrius said unto Abbâ
Arsenius, "Since we are without learning according to the
" world, and we have no wisdom whatsoever, [how is it that]
" these Egyptian villagers possess such spiritual excellences?"
Abbâ Arsenius (or Abbâ Macarius) said unto him, "We pos-
" sess nothing whatsoever of the learning of the world, but
" these Egyptian villagers have acquired spiritual excellences
" through their labours."

234. On one occasion Abbâ Arsenius asked an Egyptian old
man about the thoughts, and afterwards another brother said

unto Abbâ Arsenius, "How is it that whilst thou hast so
"much learning, both Greek and Latin, thou askest questions
"about the thoughts of this villager?" Then Abbâ Arsenius
said unto him, "With Greek and Latin learning I am well
"acquainted, but I have not yet learned the alphabet of this
"villager."

235. Now on one occasion when the Archbishop wished to
go to visit him, he sent a message to this effect to him, and
the old man sent him [back] word, saying, "If thou comest I
"will open unto thee, and if I open unto thee I must open
"unto every man, and if I open unto every man I cannot re-
"main here." And when the Archbishop heard these things,
he said, "If I would drive him away I must go to the old
"man, therefore I will not go."

236. On one occasion a brother entreated him to let him
hear a word from him; and the old man said, "As far as it
"lieth in thy power, lead an ascetic life; and work thou that
"secret work which is within, if it be for God's sake, [for] it
"shall vanquish [thy] passions which are external."

237. Abbâ Poemen said, "If there be three [brethren] to-
"gether, and one leadeth a fair life of silent contemplation,
"and the other being a weak man giveth thanks, and the
"other singeth and prayeth with a lowly mind, all three are
"performing work [of equal merit]."

238. A brother asked Abbâ Poemen, and said unto him,
"Tell me: what meaneth it that thou dost not reward evil for
"evil?" Abbâ Poemen said unto him, "In this perception
"there are four divisions; the first is of the heart, the second
"is of the sight, the third is of the tongue, and the fourth is
"that in actions a man returneth evil for evil. If now thou art
"able to overcome the heart, thou wilt not come to the sight,
"but if thou comest to the sight, take heed that thou dost not
"speak with the tongue; but if thou speakest cut it off im-
"mediately, so that thou mayest not actually reward evil for
"evil; and this is the first of the four which a man may cut
"off, and the tongue is the second, and the third is the sight,
"and the fourth is the heart."

239. The old man Anthony used to say also, "If the baker
"did not put a covering over the eyes of [his] animal, it would
"turn round and eat up its hire, and in like manner we also
"have received a covering by the operation of God, so that
"we may first of all be working good deeds without seeing
"them, so that we may not ascribe happiness to ourselves
"and so destroy the hire of our labour. Therefore are we left
"from time to time in unclean thoughts, and we see these
"only so that we may condemn ourselves, and those filthy

" thoughts may become a covering of the few good things
" which we perform. For when a man blameth himself he will
" not destroy his hire."

240. Abbâ Moses asked Abbâ Sylvanus, saying, "Is it possible for a man to make a beginning each day?" And he said
unto him, "If he be a man who is a worker it is possible for
" him to make a beginning every day."

241. A brother asked Abbâ Sisoes, "Why do my thoughts
" not depart from me?" He said unto him, "Because thy
" things are within thee; give them their pledge and they will
" depart."

242. A brother asked Abbâ Theodore, and said unto him,
" If an earthquake were to take place suddenly wouldst thou
" not be afraid, O father?" The old man said unto him, "Even
" if the heavens were to cleave to the earth Theodore would
" not be afraid"; now he besought God formerly that trembling might be removed from him, and it was because of this
fact that he who put the question to him asked him.

243. They used to say that when Abbâ Theodore was a
deacon in Scete he refused to perform the ministrations of
deacon, and that he fled to several places [to avoid doing so],
but the old men would bring him back again, saying, "Thou
" shalt not forsake thy place." Abbâ Theodore said unto them,
" Permit me to make a request unto God, and if He permit me
" I will stand up in my place"; and when he made his petition
to God, he said, "If it be Thy will, O my Lord, for me to re-
" main, permit me [so to do]." Then there appeared unto him
a pillar of fire [which reached] from earth to heaven, and a
voice said unto him, "If thou art able to be like unto this
" pillar, go and perform thy ministrations"; but although he
heard these things he would not consent to minister. And
when he came to the church the brethren fell down before him
and entreated him, saying, "If thou refusest to minister, at
" least hold the cup," but he refused and said, "If ye will not
" allow me [to be] here [as I am], I will depart from these
" places"; and so they left him [there].

244. They used to tell a story about Abbâ Macarius the
Great, who became, as it is written, an earthly God, for as
God overshadoweth the world so also did Abbâ Macarius cover
over the shortcomings which he saw as if he did not see them,
and the things which he heard as if he heard them not.

245. On one occasion a maiden came to Abbâ Macarius to be
healed of a devil, and a certain brother arrived from a monastery which is in Egypt, also, and the old man went out by
night and saw that the brother was committing sin with that
woman, but he did not rebuke him. And he said, "If God

"Who fashioned him seeth [him], and is long-suffering, for it
"He so desired He could consume him, who am I that I should
"rebuke him?"

246. I heard that the blessed man Anthony used to say, "God
"doth not permit wars to wax as fierce in this generation as
"as He did in the generations of old, for He knoweth that men
"are [more] feeble [now], and that they could not bear [them]."

247. Abbâ Macarius used to say to the brethren concerning
the desert of Scete, "Whensoever ye see cells which are turned
"towards the wood, know that the fall thereof is near; and
"whensoever ye see trees planted near the doors, [know] that
"it is near the door; and whensoever ye see young men dwell-
"ing therein, then take up your possessions and depart."

248. Abbâ Muthues used to say, "Satan knoweth not by
"means of what passion the soul may be conquered, but he
"soweth, not knowing whether he will reap; but with the
"thoughts of fornication, and of calumny, and of all the pas-
"sions towards which he seeth the soul incline doth he fight
"against it, and fetter it."

249. When, on one occasion, I was sitting with a certain
old man at Oxyrhyncus, now this old man used to make great
alms and oblations, a widow came to him and demanded a
little wheat, and he said unto her, "Go and bring a measure,
"and I will measure out [some] for thee." And when she had
brought it, and he took the measure in his hand he said unto
her, "This is too large"; and he put the widow to the blush.
And when she had gone, I said unto the Abbâ and priest,
"Wast thou selling the wheat to the widow?" and he said,
"No; I gave it to her in charity." Then I said unto him, "If
"thou didst give all this wheat to her in charity, why didst
"thou act harshly with her, and measure it, and [so] put her to
"shame?"

250. Three of the fathers came on one occasion to an old
man at Scete, and one of them spoke to him, saying, "I repeat
"the Old and the New Testaments by heart"; and the old man
answered and said unto him, "Thou hast filled the air with
"words"; and the other father spoke to him, saying, "I have
"copied the Old and New Testaments"; and the old man said
unto him, "Thou hast filled the cupboards with quires of
paper"; and the third father answered and said unto him, "In
"my fire-place the grass groweth"; and the old man answered
and said unto him, "Thou hast also driven away the love of
"strangers from thee."

251. Abbâ Poemen used to say that Abbâ Isidore used to
twist into ropes a great bundle of palm leaves each night, and
[on one occasion] the brethren entreated him, saying, "Rest

"thyself a little, for thou hast worked too much." And he said unto them, "If we were to burn Isidore and to scatter his "ashes to the winds, he would win happiness, for the Son of "God came to the Passion because of us."

252. A brother said to Abbâ Poemen, "If I stumble and "commit a few minor sins my mind afflicteth me, and blameth "me, and maketh accusations against me, saying, 'Why didst "'thou fall?'" The old man said unto him, "Every time a man "falleth into any shortcoming or folly, if he saith, 'I have "'sinned,' immediately God will receive him."

253. Abbâ Poemen used to say, "It is not right for a man "to be persuaded to the thought of fornication, or to utter "calumny against his neighbour; and he should not in any "way whatsoever incline towards these two thoughts, and he "should not utter them, and he should not meditate upon such "things in his heart. And if he desireth to think about them "and to turn them over in his heart, he will not benefit thereby, "but will rather suffer damage; but if he will act against such "with ferocity, he will subsequently find rest."

254. One of the brethren asked Abbâ Poemen, saying, "Father, what shall I do when the thoughts of fornication "bestir themselves in me, or any other of the evil passions "which are injurious to the soul?" Abbâ Poemen said unto him, "The first time they come upon thee, flee; and the second "time they come upon thee, flee also; and the third time they "come, set thyself against them like a sharp sword."

255. The same old man used to say, "Unless Moses had "been gathering together sheep into the fold he would never "have seen Him that was in the bush."

256. On one occasion the brethren saw that Abbâ Joseph was sad, and that he was greatly distressed, and they asked him to tell them about his sorrow, and what was the cause thereof, but he was unable to speak to them; and they began to say each man among them to his companion, "What are "the suffering and grief which possess the old man, for be- "hold, we have dwelt with him for many years, and we never "before saw him in such grief and suffering as this? Perhaps "we have in some way offended him." Then they threw them- selves on their faces before the feet of the old man, saying, "Peradventure we have offended thee in some matter, O father, "[and if we have] forgive us for Jesus' sake." And the old man made answer to them in a state of grief, saying, "Forgive ye "me, O my brethren, for I am not offended by you, but I am "grieved by myself, because I see that I am going backwards "rather than forwards, and that I am the cause of offence and "loss, not only to myself but also unto all the others. For I see

"that at this present we are trafficking, and are losing in re-
"spect of our souls very much more than we ever gained at
"any time of the profit of the fear of our Lord, because shame-
"lessness and fearlessness have gained dominion over us. For
"in times past when the fathers were gathered together to each
"other they were wont to form bands and ascend into the
"heavens, but we are lax folk, and are dead in our sins.
"Whensoever we draw nigh to each other we come to speak
"that which is hateful about one another, and one by one we
"are raised up that we may descend to the bottom of the deep-
"est abyss. And we do not make to sink ourselves and each
"other only, but also the fathers who come to us, and the
"strangers who gather together to us, and also the people
"who are in the world who visit us as if we were solitary
"monks, and as if we were holy men, and to these last we
"become a cause of stumbling and loss.

"For thus also did Abbâ Sylvanus and Abbâ Lôt say unto
"me: 'Let us not abide here any longer.' And when I asked
"them, 'Why do ye depart from us?' they spake to me as
"follows: 'Up to this day we have benefited by our abiding
" 'with the fathers, but from the time of Abbâ Pambô, and Abbâ
" 'Agathon, and Abbâ Petra, and Abbâ John, the command-
" 'ments of the fathers have been held lightly, and we do not
" 'observe the ordinances and the laws which our fathers laid
" 'down for us. And by assemblies together we suffer loss over
" 'and over again through the useless things which are spoken
" 'among us. And when we sit down at table, instead of doing
" 'so in the fear of God, and with gratitude, and eating that
" 'which God hath prepared for us with praise and thanksgiv-
" 'ing, we occupy ourselves by conversing together and telling
" 'insipid stories; and as we sit at table in this fashion we be-
" 'come so much changed that we do not even hear what is
" 'being read to us on account of the noise of the profitless talk
" 'which we hold with each other. And besides this, after we
" 'have risen up from eating, we converse together with empty
" 'talk. What benefit is it to us to live in the desert, seeing
" 'that we profit nothing thereby?' And Abbâ Lôt said, 'Many
" 'times have I heard from brethren who are strangers, and
" 'from the people who live in the world, and who come to
" 'visit us, that we hold the commandments of the fathers
" 'lightly, and they have said of us, "We should never have
" ' "thought that they were monks!"' And one of the brethren
"who were strangers said, 'I have come to the fathers on
" 'several occasions, and [I see that] year by year they cer-
" 'tainly observe less and less the early rules and conduct of
" 'the fathers.' What now do ye wish? Will ye correct your

" lax behaviour, and observe carefully the commandments of
" our fathers, or must I also depart from you?"

And it came to pass that when the brethren heard these
things, they beat the board for assembling the monks, and the
whole brotherhood gathered itself together, and Abbâ Joseph
spake unto them all the words which are [written] above. And
when all the brethren heard the words of Abbâ Joseph, and learned
the reason of his pain and grief, and that he wished to depart
from them, they cast themselves down upon their faces weeping, and they expressed their contrition to him, saying, "For-
" give us, O father, for the sake of Jesus. We have made God
" angry by our deeds, and we have caused thy holiness grief."
Then each of the fathers said, "Would that thou hadst re-
" buked us on the very first day wherein thou didst hear [about
" us] from the fathers, and that they had not departed from
" us! And would, too, that we had roused ourselves up from
" our slumber and sluggishness! But what are we to do? For
" the old men and the holy men do not teach us, and they do
" not even take their proper places in our congregations, or
" when we sit at meat. Very many of us wish to hear the his-
" tories and commandments of the fathers read, either whilst
" we are sitting at table or between one sitting and the next,
" but we are never able to hear a word of their talk."
And Abbâ Elijah said, "Abbâ Abraham and Abbâ John spake
" much at table, and at the time of reading, and at the time of
" the service; and they began to become excited against each
" other, and the one said, 'Father, such and such a man is ex-
" 'cited,' and the other said, ' Such and such a man maketh us
" 'excited.' Now when Abbâ Joseph saw that the whole brother-
" hood was stirred up, he made supplication unto them, and be-
" sought them, saying, 'I beseech you, O my brethren, to cease
" from your commotion, for God hath called us to peace, and I
" therefore beg you to come and pray, and to make supplication
" unto God that He may make to pass by us the legions and the
" host of the enemy. For, behold, I see them standing up in
" wrath and anger, with their swords drawn, and they wish to
" destroy us all if God doth not stand up to help our wretched-
" ness."

And when he had said these things he was able, with some
difficulty, to quiet them, and Abbâ Joseph himself began to
sing the words of the harpist David, saying, "Their swords
" shall enter their own hearts, and their bows shall be broken,
" and God shall make them like a wheel and as dust before the
" wind. And God shall arise and all His enemies shall be scat-
" tered. O God, deliver me, O Lord, remain to help [me]"
(Psalm xxxvii, 15; lxxxiii, 13; lxviii, 1; vii, 1). And when they

had recited the Psalms of the spirit altogether, and had made
an end of the service, they said, " O holy God, O holy mighty
" One, O immortal holy One, have mercy upon us"; and they
all knelt down in prayer. And as they were praying they heard
the voices of the devils in the air, and the sounds of armour
and of horses, and of many horsemen, and they also heard the
voices of the devils who were saying to one another, " Ye shall
" not have mercy upon them." And again they said, " O luck-
" less monks, why do ye stand up against us?" If we were to
" do [what we could do] to you not one of you would be found
" on the face of the earth! We will never be absent from you,
" and we will never cease from you."

And after the filthy legion had been driven away by the
secret power, and the wicked devils rested from their wickednesses, all the fathers rose up from the earth whereon they had
been poured out in prayer, the earth having been adorned by
their tears, and they all offered repentance unto Abbâ Joseph,
saying, "Forgive thou us, and pray for us that the Lord may
" forgive us, for we have sinned and have provoked Him to
" wrath." Then Abbâ Joseph said unto them: "Rouse ye your-
" selves, O my brethren, and take good heed unto your souls,
" for, behold, ye have heard with your ears the sound of the
" chariots of the Adversary, who threateneth us and seeketh
" to destroy us. Let every man be reconciled to his neighbour,
" and forgive ye every man from his heart the offence [which
" he hath committed]. And bind ye yourselves with the love of
" our Lord, with an urgent mind, and a pure heart, to the
" Lord and to each other. And draw nigh unto God that He
" may draw nigh unto you, and stand up against the Adver-
" sary, who is Satan. If ye wilt observe the commandments of
" the fathers, I will become a surety (*or* pledge) for you that
" Satan shall not be able to injure you, and that the Barba-
" rians shall not come hither; but if ye will not observe them,
" believe me, O my beloved, this place shall be laid waste."

And they offered repentance each to the other, and they became reconciled to each other, and lived in love and in great
peace; and they laid down ordinances among themselves on
that day to the effect that no man should henceforth conduct
himself with negligence and without absence of fear; and that
they should neither do nor say anything at the table which was
alien [to their mode of life]; and that if any man be found here-
after despising and holding lightly the commandments of the
fathers in such a way that he become an occasion of offence
and a cause of loss, first to himself, and next to those who
dwell with him, and then also to the strangers who come to
us, he shall know that he is bringing a punishment upon him-

self, and that he shall become an alien to all the brotherhood.
And Abbâ Joseph sent a brother to bring back Abbâ Sylvanus
and Abbâ Lôt, and when these fathers knew what had taken
place among the brethren, and that they had laid down ordinances to keep the commandments of the fathers, they praised
God, and they rose up, and came, and [when] they saw Abbâ
Joseph they saluted him and wept; and Abbâ Joseph told them
everything which had taken place, and they glorified God
Who had not rejected those who feared Him. And as regardeth
the canons and the ordinances which they had laid down
among themselves, the brethren observed and performed them
all the days of their life; and they died at a good old age,
[after] living lives which were well-pleasing unto God.

257. Abbâ Ammon used to say, "I have spent fourteen years
" in Scete in making supplication unto God by day and by
" night that He would grant me to overcome anger.

258. An old man used to say, "Be like unto a camel when
" thou art loaded with thy sins, and be tied unto and cleave
" unto him that knoweth the way."

259. One of the old men used to say, "Formerly, whenso-
" ever we met each other we used to speak words of profit about
" each other, and we formed companies, and were lifted up
" into the heavens; but now when we are gathered together,
" we come to hateful converse concerning each other, and we
" drag each the other down to the bottom of the deepest
" abyss."

260. Abbâ Achilles came on one occasion to the cell of Abbâ
Isaiah, and found him eating; now there were in the basin
[from which he ate] water and salt, and the old man saw him
hide the basin behind a mat. Then Abbâ Achilles said unto
him, "Tell me, what wast thou eating?" And Abbâ Isaiah
said unto him, "Forgive me, I was cutting some palm leaves,
" and I went up in the heat, and placed in my mouth a mor-
" sel of bread and salt; and my throat was dry by reason of
" the heat, and the food did not go down, and I was pained
" thereby, and I threw a little salt and water into my mouth,
" so that I might be able to eat. But forgive me." The old man
said unto him, "Come ye and see Abbâ Isaiah who eateth
" food which stinketh in Scete; if thou seekest to eat stinking
" food, get thee to Egypt."

261. There was a certain monk who had a brother that lived
in the world, and this brother was poor, and whatsoever the
monk earned by the labour of his hands he used to give to his
brother, but in spite of this the brother became poorer still.
Then the monk went to one of the old men and told him the
matter, and the old man said unto him, "If thou wilt hearken

" unto me thou wilt not give him any more, but wilt say unto
" him, ' My brother, whilst I have anything to give I give it
" ' unto thee, but now thou must bring me some of what thou
" ' earnest by thy labour'; and whatsoever he bringeth unto
" thee, that take from him, and where thou knowest there is
" a stranger, or a poor old man, give it unto him"; and he entreated them to offer up prayer on his behalf. Then the monk
went and did thus, and when his brother who lived in the
world came to him, he spake unto him even as the old man
had told him to do; and the brother went to his house with a
sad mind. And on the first day he brought [to the monk] as
the result of his labour a few garden herbs, and the monk took
them and gave them to the old men, and entreated them to
pray for him; and he was blessed and departed. And the old
man who was in the world returned on another occasion and
brought the monk bread and garden herbs, and his brother
took them, and did [with them] as he did at first. Then he
came a third time, and brought many costly gifts, and wine,
and fish, and his brother saw [this] and wondered, and he
called the poor and relieved them therewith. And the monk
said unto his brother who was in the world, " Peradventure
" thou art in need of a little bread, O my brother?" And he
said unto him, " Nay, my lord, whilst I took from thee that
" which used to enter into my house, I spent everything I had;
" but since I ceased to take anything from thee, God hath
" blessed me and hath had mercy upon me." Then the monk
went and informed the old man everything which had taken
place, and the old man said unto him, " Knowest thou not that
" the labour of a monk is fire, and that wheresoever it entereth
" it consumeth? But it is beneficial for him to shew mercy from
" his own toil, and prayer from the holy men shall be upon
" him, and thus he shall be blessed."

262. On one occasion whilst Abbâ Macarius was passing
through Egypt with certain other brethren, he heard a child
saying to his mother, " My mother, a rich man loveth me, but
" I hate him; and a poor man hateth me, and I love him"; and
when Abbâ Macarius heard [this] he marvelled. And the brethren said unto him, " What is the [meaning of] these words,
" father?" The old man said unto him, " Verily our Lord is
" rich, and He loveth us, and we do not desire to hear Him;
" our Enemy, Satan, is poor, and he hateth us, and we love his
" hateful things."

263. On one occasion, whilst Abbâ Zechariah was dwelling
in Scete, there appeared unto him a vision from God, and he
rose up and came to his father, Abbâ Kîrîôn, and the old man
was perfect, and did not take pains to boast of these things.

And he rose up [and smote him, and said unto him, "They "are of devils"; and when he had thought about the matter a long time, he rose up] and went by night to Abbâ Poemen, and informed him about the matter, and how his thoughts were burning in his heart. Then the old man knew that the matter was of God, and he said unto him, "Get thee to such "and such an old man, and whatsoever he saith unto thee "that do." And having departed to that old man, before he could tell him anything, the old man said unto him, "The "vision is of God; but do thou go and be subject unto thy "father."

264. A certain old man from Scete was dwelling in the mountain of Pîlîsîôn, and there came unto him a man from the palace who had a devil, and he healed him, and the man who had had the devil offered him a bag which was full of gold, but the old man refused to accept it. Now when he saw that he was offended, the old man took the bag itself, which was empty, and he said unto him, "Go [and] distribute the "gold among the poor and the wretched," and he made the bag into a colubium, and wore it; now it was made of hair, and was very stiff, and he wore it for a long time so that he might vex his body.

265. Abbâ Longinus asked Abbâ Lucius three things, saying, "I wish to become a stranger"; the old man said unto him, "If thou dost not hold thy tongue, where wilt thou go? "Wilt thou not become a stranger? Hold thy tongue here, "and behold thou art a stranger." And Abbâ Longinus said unto him also, "I wish to lead a twofold life"; and the old man said unto him, "If thou dost not bend thy neck like a "hook thou art nothing; purify thy wicked thoughts." Abbâ Longinus said unto him, "But I wish to flee from men"; and the old man said unto him, "If thou canst not set thyself "straight first of all with men, thou wilt never be able [to live] "by thyself."

266. A brother asked Abbâ Joseph, saying, "I want to go "out from the monastery, and live a solitary life"; the old man said unto him, "Where thou seest that thou wilt find rest for "thy soul, there dwell." And the brother said unto him, "I "am content to live in the monastery, and I am content to "live alone; what shall I do then?" The old man said unto him, "If thou art content to live in the monastery, and art "[equally] content to lead a solitary life, do this: Weigh thy "thoughts as it were in a balance, and the thought which out- "balances the other, that fulfil."

267. An old man used to say, "What beast is as mighty as "the lion and yet for the sake of his belly he falleth into the

"snare, and all his strength is made weakness? in this wise
"also shall we fall if we be overcome by our bellies."

268. An old man also said, "When the fathers of Scete were
"eating bread and salt they said, 'We must not afflict our-
"'selves overmuch with bread and salt'; and living in this wise
"they became valiant in the works of God."

269. Whilst Abbâ Sylvanus was living on Mount Sinai
brother Zechariah went to the work of the service [i.e., singing and prayer]; and when he had gone the old man said unto
him, "Open out the water [courses] and water the garden."
Then he went forth straightway, and covered his face with his
cloak, and he could see only his feet; and during the time when
he was watering [the garden], a brother came to him, and he
perceived what he was doing, and he went in to him, and made
an apology, and entreated him, saying, "Tell me, O father,
"why thou didst cover thy face with thy cloak and didst in
"this manner water the garden?" The old man said unto him,
"My son, [I did so] that mine eyes might not look upon the
"trees, and that my mind might not be distracted in its work,
"and become buried in the trees."

270. They used to say that, [on one occasion], when a certain old man was sitting in his cell, a brother happened to
come by night to go in to him; and when he arrived at the
door, he heard his voice raised in a dispute, saying, "It is
"sufficient; how long? Get ye gone forthwith." And again he
said, "Come, come to me, my friends." And when the brother
had gone in to him, he said unto him, "With whom wast thou
"speaking, O father?" He said unto him, "I was driving away
"my evil thoughts, and calling my good thoughts to me."

271. There was a certain old man who had a disciple who
dwelt in the desert, and the old man took a piece of dry wood,
and planted it, and he said to his disciple, "Pour a basin of
"water over it every day until this piece of wood beareth fruit."
Now the fountain of water was so far away from them that a
man would set out for it in the evening and return the next
morning. And the disciple did as he had been told, and after
two or three years that wood became alive, and bore fruit, and
the old man took the fruit thereof, and brought it to the church,
and said unto the brethren, "Take ye, and eat the fruit of
"obedience."

272. A certain brother on one occasion found on the road a
piece of wood which had dropped from camels, and he came
to the cell of his Rabbâ bringing it with him; and his Rabbâ
said, "Whence hast thou this piece of wood?" And the brother
said unto him, "From the road." The old man said unto him,
"If it be of the things which are taken from the road bring it

" inside; but if not, go and put it in the place wherefrom thou
" didst take it."

273. They used to say that Zechariah, the disciple of Abbâ
Sylvanus, took certain brethren, and without [the knowledge
of] Abbâ Sylvanus, they broke through the fence of the garden, and enlarged the garden, and then built up the fence again.
And when the old man learned this, he took [his cloak], and
wrapped himself up therein, and went forth, and he said to the
brethren, "Pray ye for me." Now when they saw him, they
fell down at his feet, saying, "Tell us, father, what hath hap-
" pened to thee"; and he said unto them, "I will neither go
" inside [my cell], nor unwrap myself from my cloak until ye
" bring the fence back to its former position"; and [when they
had done so] straightway the old man went into his cell.

274. They used to say that when the old man Rabbâ Magatîs
went forth from his cell, and the thought rose up in his mind
that he would depart from the place, he returned not to his
cell; now he possessed nothing whatsoever of the things which
are required in this world. But he took pleasure in the work
of splitting up the palm leaves which he twisted into ropes, for
he performed sufficient labour each day to provide him with
the very small amount of food which he needed.

275. A brother asked an old man, saying, "If a certain bro-
" ther cometh to me, and saith, 'Perform an act of love, and
" 'come with me here, or go [with me] to a certain place,' and
" I am inconvenienced by the command, what am I to do?"
The old man said unto him, "If thou knowest that without
" offence thou canst fulfil the commandment, go, and it shall
" be accounted unto thee as an acceptable sacrifice; but if thou
" knowest that there will be some offence, thou shalt not go.
" And if thou dost go, take good heed to thy soul."

276. A brother asked an old man, saying, " How is it that
" there are at this present men who labour, but who do not
" receive grace as the early fathers did?" The old man said
unto him, " Formerly love existed, and one brother was raised
" up by the other; but now love hath grown cold, and we each
" drag the other down, and in consequence we do not receive
" grace."

277. They used to say that when Abbâ Theodore dwelt in
Scete, a devil came and wanted to go into him, and the old
man perceived that he wanted to go into [his cell], but he kept
him fettered outside. Then another devil came to go in, and
the old man fettered him also, and a third devil also came, and
finding the other two fettered by the door, he said unto them,
" Why do ye stand outside here?" They said unto him, "He
" who dwelleth within will not permit us to go in"; and the

third devil stirred up strife, and, holding Abbâ Theodore in
contempt, made so bold as to go in. Now when the old man
saw him he fettered him also, and being afraid of the prayers
of the old man, they entreated him, saying, "Set us free." And
the old man accepted their petition, and released them, saying,
"Get ye gone"; and then they departed being ashamed.

278. They used to say that a certain old man had a young
man living with him, and that he one day saw him doing
something which was not beneficial for him; and he said unto
him once, "Thou shalt not do this thing," but the young man
hearkened not unto him. Now when the old man saw that he
would not hearken unto him, he let him alone, and troubled
no more about him; and the young man shut the door of the
place where the bread was kept, and departed from the cell,
and left the old man without bread for three days, and when
he went back, the old man did not say unto him, "Where
"hast thou been?" or, "What hast thou been doing outside?"
Now the young man treated the old man in this fashion, like
a beast. Then afterwards, when one of the old man's neighbours perceived the delay of the young man, he boiled a little
food, and let it down to the old man from the wall, and made
him eat it; and when, by chance, his neighbour said unto him,
"The young man tarrieth a long time," the old man said unto
him, "He hath not tarried, but when he is disengaged he will
"come."

279. A certain brother made a second key and opened the
cell of one of the old men and took his money out of the cupboard, and the old man wrote on a piece of paper, saying,
"Do me an act of love and leave me one half of my money,
"for I have need of it for my necessities"; and he divided the
money (*or* oboli) into two parts, and laid the paper upon them.
And the brother who stole the money came as usual, and he
tore up the paper and took all the money. Now two years
later that brother was forced to die, but his soul was not permitted to go forth from him, and then he called the old man,
and made entreaty unto him, saying, "Father, pray on my
"behalf; it was I who took thy money." Then the old man
said unto him, "Why didst thou not confess this before the
"light became black to thee?" And the old man prayed and
set free the spirit of that brother, and he sold his Book of the
Gospel and made a memorial for him.

280. A certain man used to relate that an old man from
Scete went up to the Thebaïd to dwell there, and according to
the custom with those who are from Scete he made bread
sufficient for his wants for several days. And behold, the men
of the Thebaïd came to him, saying, "How is it that thou

"dost not keep the word of the Gospel which commanded
"men not to care for the morrow?" The old man said unto
them, "What is your custom?" And they said unto him, "We
"work day by day with our hands, and we sell [what we
"make], and buy food for ourselves in the market." The old
man said unto them, "My market is my cell, and whensoever
"I have need I lay down the work of my hands, and take up
"food for myself."

281. An old man used to say, "Discretion is the most ex-
"cellent thing of all."

282. They used to say that certain men came to plead a case
for judgement before Abbâ Ammonius, and the old man paid
no attention to them, but behaved as if he did not hear them;
and behold, a woman said unto her companion, "This old
"man hath no stability." And the old man heard her speaking
thus to her companion, and he called her, and said unto her,
"How many labours have I performed in the desert so that
"I might acquire this instability! Yet, through thee, I have
"destroyed this day."

283. An old man used to say, "Do not eat before thou art
"hungry, and do not lie down before thou art sleepy, and do
"not speak before thou art questioned."

284. A brother asked an old man, saying, "Do I eat too many
"garden herbs?" The old man said unto him, "It will not
"benefit thee [to do so], but eat bread and a few vegetables,
"and thou shalt not go to thy kinsfolk for the sake of things
"[to eat]."

285. An old man used to say, "It is meet that a monk should
"be like the Cherub—all eyes."

286. An old man used to say, "For a man to attempt to
"teach his neighbour, when he hath not been required [so to
"do], is the same as offering him a rebuke."

287. Abbâ Poemen used to say, "Why doth a man distress
"himself to build the house of others, and to overthrow his own?"

288. He also used to say, "Why is it necessary for a man to
"enter by cunning, and not to learn [how to do so] properly?"

289. He also used to say, "Everything which is immoderate
"is from the devils."

290. The old men used to say, "God demandeth nothing
"from Christians except that they shall hearken unto the Di-
"vine Scriptures, and shall carry into effect the things which
"are said in them, and shall be obedient unto their governors
"and the orthodox fathers."

291. An old man used to say, "Whensoever I have been
"able to overtake my soul when I have transgressed, I never
"stumbled a second time."

292. An old man used to say, "The man who setteth death "before his eyes at all times easily overcometh dejection and "littleness of soul."

293. An old man used to say, "Take heed, with all thy "might, not to do anything which deserveth blame, and do "not take pleasure in making thyself acceptable."

294. Abbâ Theodore used to say, "There is no spiritual ex- "cellence so sublime [as that which consisteth in] not despis- "ing a man and treating him with contempt."

295. An old man was asked, "How, and by what means can "the soul acquire humility?" And he made answer, saying, "By examining and enquiring into its own wickednesses only."

296. Abbâ Poemen used to say, "All the spiritual excellences "have entered into this monastery, with the exception of the "one without which in labour [no] man standeth"; and they asked him, saying, "Which spiritual excellence is that?" and he said, "That which maketh a man blame and despise him- "self."

297. The disciple of a certain old man and Rabbâ was at- tacked by the lust for fornication, and he went into the world, and betrothed to himself a wife; and the old man, being greatly grieved, prayed to God, and said, "O Lord Jesus "Christ, do not Thou permit Thy servant to be defiled." And it came to pass that when he was shut up with the bride in the bedchamber he yielded up his spirit, and he was not polluted with the union of marriage.

298. An old man used to say:—"If temptation come upon a "man, and attack him on all sides to such a degree that his "mind falleth into despair, and he murmureth, all his friends "will turn away their faces from him as if by reason of the "temptation"; and he related the following story (in illustra- tion of this statement) and said: "There was a monk in a cell, "and temptation came upon him, and all his friends and be- "loved ones who met him refused even to salute him, and not "one of them would allow him to enter into his cell. If he "lacked provisions, and wanted a man to lend him some, none "would lend him, and he was compelled by reason of his tri- "bulation to go and work in the harvest field; and when he "came back he did not find any bread in his cell. Now it was "the custom among the holy men that every man who went "to work in the harvest field should on his return eat in the "church, but when that brother came on the Sabbath no man "took him and gave him refreshment in the usual way, and "he went to his cell, and he gave thanks unto God without "complaining. Now when God saw his patient endurance, He "abated the temptation in him, and straightway a man came

" and knocked at his door; and he had with him a camel car-
" rying bread which had been sent to him from Egypt; then he
" began to smite himself and to weep, saying, 'I am not
" 'worthy [of this].' And the temptation having departed, all
" the fathers took him, and gave him refreshment, and they
" persuaded him to let them take him to their cells, and through
" his patient endurance he found great benefit."

299. On one occasion certain Greeks came to give gifts of
grace in the city of 'Estarkînâ, and they took with them the
stewards of the city that they might show them what it was
necessary for them to give them, and they took them to a certain brother who had elephantiasis, but he refused to accept
anything, saying, " Behold, I have these few palm leaves, I
" will work at them, and weave ropes, and will eat bread."
Then they carried them to a certain widow, and they knocked
at the door, and her daughter answered from inside, for she
was naked, now her mother had gone out to work, for she was
washing clothes and lived by her labour. And when they saw
that the maiden was naked, they gave her clothes and money,
but she refused to accept them, saying, " My mother will come,
" and say unto me, ' My daughter, God hath willed [it], and I
" 'have found some work to-day, and again we have sufficient
" 'food for this day.'" Then when the mother came, she refused
[to accept the apparel and money], and said unto them, " O ye
" men, I have One Who provideth for me, that is, God, and ye
" seek to take away from me this day Him that hath provided
" for me all my days"; and when they saw her faith they glorified God.

300. A certain man offered gold to one of the aged fathers,
saying, " Take [it] and let it be to thee for expenses, because
" thou hast grown old"; now the old man was an Arian, and he
answered and said unto him that had given [the gold] to him,
" Hast thou come to take away from me Him that hath reared
" me for sixty years? For it is sixty years since I have been
" in this sickness, and I have wanted for nothing because God
" fed me and provided for me"; and he would not consent to
accept anything.

301. One of the fathers told the following story, saying, " I was
" in the room for receiving strangers, and some poor folk came
" to receive charity at eventide on the Sabbath, and there was
" among them only one man who had a mat to lie upon
" when they lay down; and he threw it down under him, and
" then reclined upon it. Now it was exceedingly cold, and
" he took a half of the mat from under him and covered him-
" self over therewith, and he reclined on the other half. And
" I went out during the night and heard him complaining about

" the cold, and then the man turned to himself and said, ' I
" 'give thanks unto Thee, O Lord, because how many are the
" 'rich men, and the owners of possessions who are at this
" 'present moment lying in irons, and in afflictions, and in
" ' prisons, and there are, moreover, others whose feet have
" ' been put in the stocks, who are unable to turn round to any
" ' side, whilst I, like a king, can spread out my feet and lie
" ' down, and besides this, I can go whithersoever I please.'
" And when he had said these things, now I was standing up
" listening to him, I went in and told them to the brethren,
" and they benefited by the words of that poor man."

302. An old man used to say, " Let me think first, and pray
" next, and then let us begin the work, and afterwards let us
" boast ourselves in God."

303. A certain brother asked an old man, saying, " Why is
" it that I feel disgusted when sitting in my cell, and why am
" I sluggish in respect of works of spiritual excellence?" And
the old man answered and said unto him, " Because thou dost
" not keep in mind the rest which those who labour expect,
" and the torments which are laid up for the lazy. For if, in
" very truth, thou wert seeing these things, thou wouldst be
" watchful and strenuous in thy labour."

304. An old man used to say, " The man who maketh a boast
" of the Name of God, and who doeth not the works which
" are suitable to that Name, is like unto a poor man who,
" when a feast cometh, borroweth some clothes and putteth
" them on, and who, when the feast hath passed, strippeth
" them off himself because they are not his own, and giveth
" them to their owners."

305. Abbâ Ammon used to say concerning Abbâ Paphnutius the Simple, who was from Scete, " When I went down
" there I was a young man, and he would not allow me to
" dwell there, saying, ' In my days I will not permit the faces
" ' of young men, which resemble those of women, to dwell in
" ' Scete, because of the war of the Enemy against the holy
" ' men.' "

306. Abbâ Poemen (or Ammon) used to say, " If Nûzardân
" (Nebuzaradan), the chief of the warriors, had never come to
" the land of Judea, he would never have burnt down the tem-
" ple of God which was in Jerusalem with fire"; [now the mean-
ing] of these words is, that if the pleasures of the lust of the
belly had never entered in on the soul the mind would never
have been vanquished in the war of the Adversary.

307. A certain man asked Abbâ Sisoes, saying, " Hast thou
" not even yet arrived at the measure of Abbâ Anthony, our
" father?" And the old man answered and said, " If I had even

" one thought like unto Abbâ Anthony, the whole of me would
" become like unto fire; but I know one man who, even with
" great labour, is able to bear his thoughts."

308. Abbâ Abraham asked Abbâ Agathon, saying, " How
" is it that the devils make war upon me?" And Abbâ Agathon said unto him, "Do the devils make war upon thee? But
" they do not make war against us so fiercely as we ourselves
" do with our own wishes, though they do make war against
" us in proportion as our wishes do. Our desires become devils,
" and they force us to fulfil them. Now if thou wishest to see
" against whom they have made war, [it is] against Moses and
" those who resemble him."

309. A brother asked an old man, saying, "In what condi-
" tion is it meet for a monk to be?" And he said, " Even as I
" myself am, if one may [compare] one man with another."

310. And an old man was also asked, " Why am I afraid
" when I go about in the desert?" The old man said unto him,
" Because thou art still alive."

311. A brother asked an old man, saying, " Why doth my
" spirit go round and round violently?" And he said unto him,
" Because thou hast not yet seen the storehouse of life."

312. And he was also asked, "What is it meet for a monk
" to do?" And he said, "Let him perform all kinds of good
" works in very deed, and let him acquire remoteness from
" every evil thing."

313. And he was also asked, "What is a monk's work?"
" And he said, "He must possess discretion."

314. An old man said, "Unto every thought that riseth up
" in thee say, "Art thou of us, or of our enemies?" And the
thought will always make confession unto thee.

315. Abbâ Agathon used to say, "The crown of the monk is
" humility."

316. Abbâ Isidore said, "When I was a youth and was living
" in a cell, I possessed not the capacity for the service [of
" prayer and praise], for by night and by day there was service
" to me."

317. He also said, "For forty years, I neither leaned upon
" anything nor lay down."

318. He also said, "I was standing forty nights, and did
" not lie down."

319. He also said, "For twenty years I continued to fight
" against one thought—that I might see all men of one mind."

320. An old man was asked, "Why is it that whilst I am
" sitting in my cell my heart wandereth about?" The old man
said to his questioner, "Because thine external lusts feel the
" motions which are in hearing, and in breathing, and in

"taste, for from these, if it be possible for a man, there is
"pure labour, and he should make them to be healthy and
"satisfied within."

321. An old man was asked, "How is it possible for a man
"to live so that he may be seemly in God's sight?" and he
said to him, "[It is possible if a man have an] equable
"[mind]."

322. An old man also said, "Our labour is wood which
"burneth away."

323. Abbâ Benjamin said unto his disciples, "Do these things
"and ye shall be able to live. Rejoice at all times, and pray
"without ceasing, and give thanks for everything.

324. He also said, "Abstinence in respect of the soul con-
"sisteth in making straight its ways and habits, and courses
"of action, and in cutting off the passions of the soul."

325. He also said, "Travel in the path of the kingdom, and
"count the miles, and thy spirit shall not be sad in thee."

326. An old man said, "Thou must be in the same state of fear
"as a man who is going to endure tortures."

327. An old man used to say, "A man shall not trouble, but
"let him like a life of silent contemplation, and hide himself,
"for these meditations (?) are the begetters of purity."

328. An old man used to say also, "Thou shalt desire to be-
"come a eunuch, for this will help thee."

329. He also said, "The giving of thanks maketh entreaty
"on behalf of the feeble before God."

330. An old man used to say, "I do not as yet carry all my
"body so that I may fulfil all my desire."

331. Abbâ Sisoes said, "Exile consisteth in a man living a
"silent and solitary life."

332. One of the fathers said, "I once asked Abbâ Sisoes and
"besought him to speak a word of life to me, and the old man
"answered and said, He who taketh care to guard himself
"against esteeming himself, and against comparing himself
"[with other men] in every work of understanding (*or* discretion),
"is he who fulfilleth the Book."

333. And I asked him also, "In what doth the power of exile
"consist?" And he said unto me, "Wheresoever thou dwellest
"hold thy peace; and about whatsoever thou seest, be it good
"or be it evil, say nothing; and if thou hearest anything from
"a man which befitteth not the upright conduct of the ascetic
"life, say, 'This concerneth me not; I have to do with myself,
"'and myself only.' This is [the power of] exile."

334. One of the old men said, "The love of the work of the
"hands is the ruin of the soul; but the stablishment thereof is
"rest and peace in God."

335. Abbâ Theodore said, "If I did not cut off my soul from "the friends of this world they would not let me be a monk."

336. He also said, "If we seek God He will reveal Himself "unto us, and if we lay hold upon Him He will protect us."

337. On one occasion certain of the old men were sitting and talking about the thoughts, and one of them said, "They "would not appear to be a great matter if a man were to see "his thoughts from a distance."

338. Another [old man] said, "I have never allowed error to "have dominion over me even for an hour."

339. Abbâ Poemen said, "As long as the food which is being "boiled is on the fire the flies will not approach it, but as soon "as it is taken off they cluster round it"; the meaning of this is that as long as our hearts are fervent in the spirit impure thoughts will not approach us, but that if we are negligent and make ourselves to be remote from the converse (*or* occupation) of the spirit they will then gain dominion over us.

340. An old man used to say, "It is necessary to make en-"quiries concerning spiritual works, for through them we ad-"vance in excellence; for it is great labour for us to go forth "from the body in such wise that we do not perform the works "of the body."

341. An old man used to say also, "Affliction and poverty "are the instruments wherewith a monk cultivateth his handi-"work."

342. Certain of the old men used to say, "Whosoever hath "not the instruments of the craft of labour cannot remain long "in his cell, whether they be the instruments of the craft of the "labour of spiritual beings, wherewith he findeth comfort from "God in his inner man in the spirit, or the instruments of "the craft of human labour. He who possesseth not the one "or the other class of instruments cannot remain very long in "his cell."

343. The spirit of God rested upon Abbâ John because of the fear in which he held God; for it is the fear of God which teacheth a man all good works.

344. Abbâ Poemen used to say, "Abbâ Paphnutius was ex-"ceedingly great and mighty, and he ran at all times to minister "unto shortcoming."

345. An old man was asked by a brother, "How should a "monk dwell in his cell?" The old man said unto him, "Let "him dwell by himself, so that his thoughts may be with God."

346. And a brother also asked him, saying, "What shall I "do, for when I am by myself I am greatly afflicted by the "multitude of evil thoughts of all kinds which crowd upon me, "and by the weight of the disgust which troubleth me?" The

old man said unto him, "Give thy soul work, that is to say,
"have a care to pray and have love towards God, and straight-
"way the spirit of Satan will flee from thee."

347. An old man used to say also, "If thou doest something
"which is good, and thou art praised for it, destroy it; guard
"thyself against the thoughts which praise thee, and which
"hold thy neighbour in contempt."

348. Abbâ Isidore's thoughts praised him, saying, "There
"is none like unto thee among the fathers"; and he said, unto
them, "Am I like Anthony or Abbâ Agathon?" And the devils
said unto him, "After all the labours which thou hast per-
"formed thou wilt go to torment"; and he said unto them,
"And ye also will be below me. For a thief through one word
"inherited the kingdom." And Judas also, who wrought mighty
deeds with the Apostles, in one night lost all his labour, and
he went down from heaven to Sheol; therefore let not him that
conducteth himself uprightly boast himself. For all those who
have been over confident about themselves have fallen among
the devils of greed. Retard thou then [thy desire], saying,
"Thou hast had enough; wait a little," and eat thou tem-
perately and slowly. For he who hasteth in his eating is like
unto him that seeketh to eat much.

349. An old man saw sitting among the brethren a brother
who pretended not to be of them, and he said unto him, "How
"canst thou walk in a country which is not thine?"

350. They used to say that Abbâ Poemen never wished to
magnify his word over that of any old man, but in everything
he praised his and belittled his own.

351. There was a certain monk who led a life which was
full of severe ascetic labours, and the Devil laid many plans
and schemes to make him abate them, and to make him to desist therefrom; but the monk would not give him a hearing in
any way whatsoever, but, on the contrary, he played the man
more strenuously than ever, and resisted his wiles and crafts.
Now when the Devil had spent much time in this strife against
him, another devil came to help him; and having enquired of
his companion what manner of war and battle he should set
in array against him, and how it was that the holy man was
abating and making an end of all the things which he was
making [against him], the accursed devil who had come last,
answered and said by the counsel of the Evil One, "Do not
"lift up thyself below him, but raise up thyself above him, and
"in this way thou shalt be able to be stronger than he."

352. An old man asked Abbâ Poemen, saying, "What shall
"I do, father, with my son Isaac, who hearkeneth unto me
"with pleasure?" Abbâ Poemen said unto him, "If thou wish-

" est to be of benefit to him, shew him [an example] by deeds
" and not by words, lest through observing words only he
" be found useless; for if thou wilt shew him by deeds, the
" deeds themselves will abide with him, and he will profit."

353. Certain of the fathers said to Abbâ Macarius the Egyptian, "Whether thou eatest or whether thou fastest, thy body
" hath already dried up"; and the old man said unto them,
" A piece of wood which hath been burned and consumed by
" the fire burneth wholly, and thus also the heart of a man, if
" he be purified by the fear of God, consumeth the lusts from
" his flesh, and drieth up his bones."

354. Abbâ Theodore used to say, "If God imputeth to us
" carelessness in prayer, and the snare in [His] service wherein
" we have been captured, we shall not be able to stand."

355. They used to say of one of the old men that he had
passed twenty years in the church, and had never lifted his
eyes and seen the roof thereof.

356. There was a certain monk whose name was Paul, and
his rule of life and conduct was such that he did not approach
the excessive labour of the work of the hands, nor any trafficking whatsoever, except such as was sufficient to provide for
his small amount of daily food; but he performed one sort of
work of excellence, that is, he prayed continually and ceased
not, and he laid down the rule for himself that he should pray
three hundred prayers each day, and he placed sand in his
bosom, and at every prayer which he prayed, he would lay one
grain of sand in his hand. Now this man asked Saint Macarius,
saying, "Father, I am greatly afflicted"; and the old man
pressed him to tell him the cause of his affliction. Then he
answered and said, "I have heard about a certain virgin who
" hath led an ascetic life for thirty years, and Father Pîôr related
" concerning her that every week she went forth and recited
" five hundred prayers in the day. Now when I heard these
" things I despised myself greatly, for I am not able to recite
" more than three hundred prayers." Then the holy man
Macarius answered and said unto him, "I have led an ascetic
" life for sixty years, and I make fifty prayers a day, and I
" work sufficiently to provide myself with food, and I receive
" the brethren who come to me, and I say unto them what it
" is seemly to say, and I pay my debts, and my mind doth not
" condemn me as one who hath treated [God] lightly; but thou
" who makest three hundred prayers in the day, art thou con-
" demned by thy thoughts? Perchance thou dost not offer
" them with purity [of heart], or thou art able to do more, and
" dost not do it!"

357. I used to know a certain holy man whose name was

Aurelius, and he laboured so hard that he might have been thought to be a shadow because of his disposition to work; during the Forty Days' Fast he used to pass whole weeks [without eating], and in respect of the other days he would eat only once every two or three days.

358. An old man was asked [by a brother], "If I see the sin " of my brother am I to despise him?" And the old man said, " If we hide [the fault] of our brother God will also hide our " [faults]; and if we expose our brother's [faults], God will also " expose ours."

359. An old man was wont to say, "There was a brother whose " name was Timothy, and he used to lead a life of silent con- " templation in a religious house; and a temptation came " upon one of the brethren of that house, and the head of the " house asked Timothy, saying, 'What shall I do to this " 'brother?' Timothy said unto him, 'Expel him'; and when " he had expelled him, the temptation of that brother was sent " upon Timothy, and he cried out to God, saying, 'I have " 'sinned, O my Lord, have mercy upon me.' And he passed " the whole night in a grave of dead men, crying out and say- " ing, 'I have sinned, O my Lord, forgive me,' and the temp- " tation was upon him until he was greatly exhausted. And a " voice came to him, saying, 'Timothy, do not imagine that " 'these things have happened unto thee for any other reason " 'than because thou didst offend thy neighbour in the time of " 'his trial.'"

360. A brother asked an old man, saying, "How shall I be " able to avoid despising my brother?" The old man said unto him, "We and our neighbour are two faces. Now if we pro- " vide the mirror of prayer we shall see the beam in our own " eye, and we shall also see in the mirror the face of our " brother polished and pure."

361. A brother asked an old man and said, "What shall I " do? For there is no feeling in my soul, and I have no fear of " God." The old man said unto him, "Seek thou out a man " who feareth God, and then cling closely to him, and from " him thou shalt learn to fear God."

362. Abbâ Poemen said that Abbâ Athanasius used to say, " Unless a man possess good works before God giveth him a " gift because of himself, it is well known that no one can be " made perfect through the weariness which cometh to him " through himself; but if he reveal [it] to his neighbour, he will " then receive the gift because of his neighbour, and be gratified."

363. A brother asked an old man, saying, "Shew me a word " whereby I may live." The old man said unto him, "Work " with thy hands with all thy power, and give alms."

364. They used to say that Abbâ Copres attained to such a measure [of perfection] that even when he was sick and wanted something, he would cut off his desire from that which his soul asked him [to give it]; and he would give thanks unto God and endure his sickness with joy and without complaint.

365. A brother asked Abbâ Poemen, "What is the meaning " of these words which the Prophet spake, 'My heart shall re- " 'joice in those that fear Thy name'?" (Psalm xxxiii, 21.) And the old man answered and said, "The Holy Spirit spake this " word to man even unto death, and [unto] to-day also."

366. An old man also said, " If a man were to make new " heavens and new earth he would not be able to be free from " care, because the wickedness of the devil is hidden behind " them; but for a man to have no care either for his raiment or " his food is possible."

367. A [brother] also asked an old man, "What shall I do " in respect of that which I love, but which is not profitable to " me?" The old man said unto him, "Approach it not, and " touch it not, and it will of its own accord become an alien " thing unto thee. For David the Prophet wrote unto Joab the " captain of the host, and said unto him, 'Hold fast on the war, " 'and fight mightily against the city until thou dost subdue it' " (2 Samuel xi, 25). Now in this case the city is enmity."

368. Anthony said, " The greatest might of a man is to bring " upon his soul his transgression at all times before God, and " he must expect temptation until the end."

369. An old man used to say, "This is the rule of conduct " which God gave to Israel, that he should remove himself from " that which is outside nature, that is to say, anger, and wrath, " and envy, and hatred, and evil-speaking, and a man must " not judge his neighbour, together with all the other com- " mandments of the olden time."

370. On one occasion certain of the brethren came to Abbâ Sisoes in order that they might hear some profitable words, and when they had spoken much with him, he said nothing unto them about whatsoever they had said, but only, "Forgive me." Then they saw that he was plaiting palm leaves, and they said unto Abraham his disciple, "What are ye doing with these " palm-leaf ropes and mats?" And he said unto them, "We send " them out here and there." Now when the old man heard this he said, "Sisoes eateth here and there." And when they had heard [these things] they were greatly profited, and they departed in great joy because they had seen his humility.

371. Abbâ Copres said, "Whosoever loveth the gratifying " of his own will more than the gratification of the will of God " hath no fear of God."

372. A brother asked Abbâ Amônîs, saying, "How ought a " man to act when he wisheth to begin some [kind of] work, " or when he wisheth to go or to come, or to go from one " place to another, so that action may be according to the will " of God, and may be free from the error of devils?" The old man said unto him, "He must first consider in his mind and " see the motive of that which he wisheth to do, and whence " it cometh, and if it be from God or Satan, or from the man " himself, and then let him do the work [which he contem- " plateth], but let him flee from going and coming, and from " going from one place to another. If he [acteth] not [thus] he " will finally become a laughing-stock for the devils. But after- " wards let him pray and beseech God that that work which " is His he may do, and then let him begin the work, and after- " wards he may boast in God."

373. He also said, "Bear with every man in such a way that " God may also bear with thee."

374. The disciple of Abbâ Ammon told the following story:— One night the old man came out and found me lying down in the courtyard of the cell, and he stood up above me, and with lamentation and tears said, "Where is the mind of this brother " who can thus lie down (*or* sleep) without care?"

375. There was a certain priest in Thebaïs whose name was Dioscurus, and he was the spiritual father of many monks, and at the time when they were about to receive the Holy Mysteries he used to say to the brethren, "Take thought and " see lest any man among you have been snared by the phantom " of a woman during the night, and he be so bold as to receive " the Holy Mysteries. Now the emissions which occur as the " result of a phantom are not caused by the desire of a man, " but take place independently thereof, for they happen natur- " ally, and are due to the excess of matter [in the body], and " they do not, therefore, lead [a man] into subjection to sin. " But the phantoms which arise from the desire are the sign " of an evil wish. For it is meet that the monk should be " superior to the law of nature, and that he should not be found " with the smallest impurity of body, but that he should waste " the body and humble it, and should not permit any super- " fluity of matter to be found therein. Work out plans, then, " that thou mayest cut off [the superfluity of] matter by means " of a long period of fasting, for if we do not thus it will in- " cite the other lusts to come upon us; and it is not meet that " a monk should be occupied with the lusts which rise up in " him daily. And if we do not thus, in what way are we different " from those who live in the world? For we have observed that " men of this kind often make themselves to be remote from

" the desires of their lust, either for purposes of bodily health,
" or for other reasons which are not worth mentioning; how
" very much more, then, should it thus be especially a care to
" the monk for the sake of the health of his spirit, and of his
" soul, and of his body!"

376. They used to say that Abbâ Macarius the Alexandrian
at one time dwelt in a cave in the desert, and that beyond his
cave was another wherein dwelt a panther; one day when he
opened the door of his cave the panther came in and did homage
to the blessed man, and she drew nigh and took hold of the
corner of his garment, and dragged him along gently and went
outside. And the old man answered and said, "What can this
" animal want?" And he went with her until she arrived at her
cave, and she left him outside, and went in and brought out her
young, which were blind, and dropped them at his feet; and
when he saw them, he prayed, and spat in their eyes, which
were opened straightway, and the panther gave them suck,
and took them and went inside. And on the day following the
panther came bringing a sheepskin, and she approached and
placed it before him; then the old man smiled to himself at the
discernment and knowledge which the animal had shewn, and
he took the skin and slept upon it, until it was quite worn out.

377. Now on another occasion, when the door of his cell
was shut, and the old man was sitting in his courtyard, that
panther leaped down into the courtyard from the wall and
came to him carrying one of her young in her mouth; and
when the old man saw that the little panther was blind, he
spat in its eyes, and they were opened, and its mother took it
and departed. And one day later she brought to the blessed
man a sheepskin, and the blessed woman Melania told me,
saying, "I received this same skin from the hands of the old
" man as a gift."

378. A brother asked an old man, saying, "What shall I do
" if when I have given to my brother a little bread or money,
" the devils pollute it, as if [it were given to gain] the approba-
" tion of men?" The old man said unto him, "Even though the
" adulation of men may come, we must give to our neighbour
" that which is necessary," and the old man adduced a proof
of this statement, and said, "Two men dwelt in a certain city,
" and one sowed [a field] and produced a crop of somewhat
" dirty grain, but the other sowed [no field] at all, and pro-
" duced no crop of any kind, neither clean nor dirty; in the
" time of tribulation which of these two men would live [and
" not die] of hunger?" And the brother said unto him, "He
" who produced the crop of dirty grain"; and the old man said
unto him, "Let us then produce a few [good actions], even

"though they be defiled, so that we may not die in the time
"of famine."

379. An old man used to say, "Dainty meats remove [a
"man] from heavenly honours. For satiety, and luxurious liv-
"ing in this world, and the multitudes of lustful habits shut
"the door in our face and prevent us from entering into the
"happiness of God. Consider now the history of the rich man
"and Lazarus; what was it that carried Lazarus into the
"bosom of Abraham? Was it not the immeasurable troubles
"among which he had been brought up? And what brought
"the rich man to Gehenna? Was it not the pleasures and
"lusts which were flaming within his body? Each one of us,
"then, according to his measure, by the nod of the fire of his
"person which is found with him, shall receive his deserts in
"the world which is to come; and each one of us, unless he be
"watchful, shall be shaken up with the wood, and the straw,
"and the stubble. And since it is necessary for us to extin-
"guish carefully the lusts which bestir themselves in us, we
"have need [to drink] water, and not wine."

380. An old man used to say, "True obedience is like unto a
"chaste woman who is betrothed, and who is not drawn aside
"after strange voices; and the ear which turneth away, ever
"so little, from the truth, is like an adulterous woman who
"turneth away from her husband; and the mind which is led
"by every doctrine of error is like unto a harlot, who obey-
"eth every one who calleth her. Let us then rebuke the
"wandering mind which is corrupted by strange voices, and
"which loveth the voice of its seducer instead of that of the
"true bridegroom; for it hath accepted to be called by the
"name of a stranger, and not by that of Christ."

381. An old man used to say, "If thou hast prayed for thy
"companion thou hast also prayed for thyself, but if thou hast
"prayed for thyself only thou hast impoverished thy petition;
"and if thou hast shown that thy brother hath offended thee,
"thou hast also shown that thou hast offended thyself. Those
"prayers, which have not taken their mind with them when
"they have ascended and gone up, stand outside the door, and
"it is love which openeth the door before them. The prayer
"which possesseth not the wings of the spirit to [mount up]
"on high standeth before the mouth of him that prayeth it,
"and thinking that it hath flown away he doth not perceive
"that it remaineth [near him]. Offer with thine offering salt,
"as it is written (Leviticus ii, 13). Let the love of thy Lord be
"salt for thy sacrifice, for the sacrifice which hath not salt
"through His love is despised and rejected before Him."

382. One of the holy men used to say thus:—"I have passed

"the whole period of twenty years in striving so that a strange
"thought might not enter into my heart, and I have seen
"Satan, until the ninth hour, with his bow stretched ready to
"shoot an arrow into my heart; and when he could not find
"an opportunity, he was filled with disgust, and he would
"depart each day, having been put to shame."

383. An old man said, "If thou art a [true] penitent thou
"hast nothing whatsoever to do with these who are in the
"world."

384. There was a certain holy man in Egypt who dwelt in
the desert, and a little way beyond him was an elder (or priest),
who was a Manichean; and this Manichean was obliged to
make a journey and to go to one who was of the same faith as
himself, and as he was going along the road, he arrived at
eventide at the place where the holy man lived, and the Manichean was in great distress, for he had no place near at hand
wherein to enter. Now he was afraid to go to the holy man,
for he thought that he would recognize him, and would not
allow him to enter [his cell]; nevertheless, being sore pressed,
and not knowing where [else] to go, he knocked at the door
of that holy man; and he opened the door, and the Manichean
went in, and the holy man received him with gladness, and he
knew who he was, and he urged him to pray, and he relieved
all his wants, and the Manichean slept, and was refreshed.
And it came to pass during the night that the Manichean came
to himself, and said, "How is it that there is nothing which
"it was seemly to do which this blessed man hath not done
"for me? Verily this is a man of God." Then he rose up and
fell down at his feet, and said, "From this day onwards I shall
"believe as thou believest"; and he turned to the truth, and
he became a friend of the holy man and lived with him always.

385. I have heard that Abbâ Isaac said concerning Abbâ
Muthues his Rabbâ, now they both arrived at the dignity of the
episcopacy, that first of all Abbâ Muthues built his monastery
in the country of the Harbĕlâyê (Herakleans), but that being
much troubled by the multitudes who came to him, he left
that place, and departed, and went to another spot in order that
he might find quietness, and he built a monastery for himself
there. And by the operation of Satan as it were, he found there
a certain brother with whom he was at enmity, and he afflicted
him greatly; and the old man saw [this], and he rose up and
departed to his village, so that the man might not be vexed
through him, and there he built a monastery, and shut himself
in it. Now after a time, the fathers of that place wherefrom
Abbâ Muthues had departed gathered together, and they took
that brother who was aggrieved, and they went to him in order

to entreat him and to bring him to his monastery; and when they
had arrived at the place where Abbâ Sôrîôn used to dwell, they
left their cloaks there, and the aggrieved brother was with
them. And when the fathers had knocked, the old man brought
forward a ladder, and he recognized them, and said unto them,
"Where are your cloaks?" And they said, "They are here
"with us, with such and such a brother." Now when the old
man heard the name of that brother, in sheer joy he took an
axe and opened the door, and he ran to the place where that
brother was, and the holy man fell at the feet of the saint, and
he made entreaty to him, and he kissed him, and saluted him,
and he brought him and the fathers to his cell, and he refreshed
both him and them for three days; and he made ready a meal,
which he was not in the habit of doing, and he rose up and
went with them with great joy. Now afterwards he was called
to the office of Bishop, and he became a worker of signs and
miracles, and he also made his disciple Abbâ Isaac a Bishop,
and he continued to lead a life of spiritual excellence until the
end of his life.

386. They used to say of Abbâ Serapion, the Bishop, that
whensoever a man came to him to receive the monastic garb,
he said these words to him, "When thou prayest say, 'Lord,
"'teach me to do Thy will.'"

387. On one occasion Abbâ Paphnutius was living in a remote desert, and it happened that a certain brother came to
him and found him sick, and the brother took him, and washed
him, and of the food which he had with him he boiled a little,
and brought it to him to eat. And when he saw [this] he
answered and said, "In very truth it had passed from my mind
"that this gratification for the children of men existed"; and
he brought him a cup of cream. Now when the old man saw
him, he wept, and said, "I never expected that, even to the
"day of my death, I should drink wine."

388. One of the fathers told a story, saying: "On one occa-
"sion two brethren according to the body came to the desert
"to a certain monk, and they conducted themselves in an ex-
"cellent manner, and they were praised by the whole brother-
"hood. And it came to pass that one of them fell into a sick-
"ness which lasted not a few years, and his brother ministered
"unto him, and certain fathers came to visit him, and they
"began to praise him that ministered unto him, saying, 'Thy
"'willingness and thy abstinence profit the whole brotherhood.'
"And he answered and said unto them with great humility,
"'Forgive me, O my fathers, for I have not as yet begun to
"'lead a life of rule, but it is my brother who doeth the works
"'of excellence, and that ye may indeed learn that such is the

" 'case, come after me and see.'" Then he took them in to his brother in the cell wherein he lay, and he said unto him, "Father, where is the axe which I gave thee yesterday?" And he began to seek for it. Then he said unto him, "See, O my "brother, do an act of grace and seek for it with me," and the sick brother took it upon himself to be asked for that which he had not taken. And having profited [by his example] the fathers departed from that place.

389. An old man used to say, "Flee from that love which "subsisteth by means of the things which are corrupt, for "with them a man also passeth away and is destroyed."

390. Abbâ Elijah used to say, "The love which a man pos-"sesseth for his neighbour, and which is caused by some "temporal matter is, in the process of time, turned into fierce "enmity."

391. And he also said, "Whatsoever hath its being for God's "sake endureth and abideth for ever with those who are true."

392. On one occasion the priest of Pîlîsîôn heard that certain of the brethren were idle and lazy, and that they were constantly in the city, and that they swam in the baths, and neglected the works of excellence which belong to the life of the monk, and when they came to the congregation he took their monkish dress from them; and having done [this] he was sad at heart, and repented, and he went to Abbâ Poemen and informed him about them. And the old man said unto him, "Hast thou nothing of the old man about thee?" [And he said "Yea."] And the old man said unto him], "Therefore thou thy-"self art like unto them, and thou art nigh unto sin." Then the priest went and expressed his sorrow to them, and he put on them the dress of monks [once more]. Now they were twelve in all.

393. On one occasion tribulation came upon the monks in a certain place where they were living, and they wished to forsake it and come to Abbâ Ammon; and behold, he was travelling in a boat, and he saw them going along by the side of the river, and he ordered the boatmen to bring [the boat] close to land. Then he called these brethren and said unto them, "I am "Ammon to whom ye wish to go"; and he entreated them to go back to their place, and he comforted them, and told them to endure patiently, for there was in the matter no loss to the soul, but only human vexation.

394. On one occasion an old man went up from Scete to the brethren in the mountain, and when they saw that he was a man of great ascetic labours, and that he practised stern self-denial, they entreated him to let them make a meal for him, and they brought him a little wine to drink. Now the people of the country heard about him, and they brought him a man who was afflicted with a devil that he might heal him; and when the devil saw him, he began to revile him, saying, "Hast "thou brought this winebibber to me?" And the old man did not wish to cast him out because of the praise of men, but, because the devil had reviled him, he said unto him, "I believe in "Christ, and I shall not have drunk [this] cup of wine until "thou hast gone forth"; and as he began to drink that devil cried out, and said, "Thou art consuming me": and before the old man could drink that cup [of wine] the devil went forth by the grace of Christ.

395. They used to say that a certain father who was a recluse had a brother, according to the body, who lived in another cell, and that this brother fell ill, and sent to him a message to come and see him before he died; and his brother said, "I am unable to go out for the sake of my brother in the "flesh." And his brother sent him another message, saying, "Come, if it be only in the night, that I may see thee"; and the recluse said, "I cannot do so, for if I did my heart would "not be pure before God." So the brother died, and they did not see each other.

396. They once wanted to make Abbâ Isaac priest in Scete, and when he heard [this] he fled to Egypt, and he went into a field and hid himself among the crop because the fathers were pursuing him, and when they came to that field they began to weary a little; and they turned the ass which they had with them out to feed, but he left the whole field, and went and stood up in that place where Abbâ Isaac was hidden. And in the morning they went out to look for the ass, and they found the ass and the old man [together] and they marvelled; and when they wished to make Abbâ Isaac take an oath [not to run away] he would not allow them [to do so], and he said unto them, "I shall not flee again, for it is the will of God, and "whithersoever I flee I shall come to this thing, for this is a "consecration by God."

397. Abbâ Macarius asked Abbâ Arsenius, saying, "Is it "good for a man not to have any pleasure at all in his cell? "I know a brother who used to have a few garden herbs in "his cell, and to prevent himself from having any gratification "therefrom, he pulled them up by the roots"; and Abbâ Arsenius said unto him, "This is good, but every man [must "do] as he is able, and if he hath not strength to persist in "this perhaps he should plant others."

398. The old men who were in Egypt told Abbâ Elijah that Abbâ Agathon was a great man. And the old man said unto them, "Considering his youth he was a great man in his

" generation, but he was very far removed from the men of old.
" I saw in Scete an old man who was able to hold back the sun
" in his course in the heavens like Joshua, the son of Nun";
and when they heard [this] they marvelled and praised God.

399. A certain brother asked Abbâ Poemen about fornication,
and he answered and said, "[It cometh upon a man] because
" our eyes will not allow us to see the help of God which
" surroundeth a man, for a man is constrained to humility and
" to the fear of God at all times, even as he is constrained [to
" draw] the breath which goeth forth from his mouth."

400. An old man used to say, "If thou wishest to learn to
" know [thy] neighbour praise him more than thou rebukest
" him."

401. They used to say that whensoever one of the fathers
wished to sleep a little, he would sit down in his cell at some
distance from the wall, so that whenever he nodded his head
he became wide awake.

402. And whensoever another of the old men lay down he used
to hold up a book above him, and when he dropped off to sleep
the book would fall down and wake him.

403. Abbâ Besarion said, "I stood up for forty nights and did
" not sleep."

Abbâ Anthony said, "I do not fear God, on the contrary I
" love Him."

404. One of the old men whilst exhorting the brethren to
work of spiritual excellence used to say, "Troubles are hard
" unto those who are not accustomed to them. Troubles are like
" unto dogs; for as dogs bite those who are not familiar with
" them and wag their tails at those who are, so also are
" labours, because they give pain to those who have no ex-
" perience of them, and they are pleasing unto those who are
" trained in bearing them. This exception must, however, be
" made: lusts are wont to produce troubles and adversities,
" but troubles are the cause of pleasure and delights."

405. On one occasion Abbâ Ammon came to cross the river,
and he found that they were making ready a boat to take
[some] men over, and he sat down in it; and behold, there was
another boat which was going to take over some women, and
they cried out to him, "Come thou, father, and cross over
" with us." And he answered and said unto them, "If I had
" not been going to cross over in the public boat I could
" not cross [with you]." Now he had with him a bundle of
palm leaves, and he sat down and plaited mats until that boat
was ready, and then he crossed over the river [in it]. And the
brethren expressed their regrets, saying, "Why hast thou
" done thus?" Then the old man said unto them, "Because I

"do not at all times travel in great haste, and because my
"thoughts are not always in a turmoil." Now this is a proof
that a man should travel on the path of God with a well
ordered mind.

406. One of the old men came to one of the fathers [and
asked him] to go and visit Abbâ Joseph, and he said to him,
"Tell thy disciple to go with us"; and the father said, "Call
"him, and whatsoever thou commandest him, he will do." The
old man said unto him, "What is his name?" and the Rabbâ
of the disciple said, "I know not." The old man said unto
him, "And how long hath he been with thee? Dost thou not
"know his name?" And the father said, "Behold, he hath
"been with me for two years"; then the old man answered
and said, "If he hath been with thee for two years, and thou
"hast not learnt his name, how can I learn it in one day?"

407. A brother asked Abbâ Poemen, and said, "On one oc-
"casion I was distressed, and I begged one of the holy men
"to lend me a certain thing, and he gave it to me as a free
"gift; now if God prospereth me shall I give it to another
"man, or shall I return it to him that gave it to me in the
"time of my tribulation?" The old man saith, "The gift was
"most certainly from God, and it is meet for thee to return it
"to Him, for it belongeth to Him." And that brother said unto
him, "Supposing that I carry it to Him, and He refuse to take
"it, and say unto me, 'Get thee gone, and give it as a free
"'gift to anyone at thy pleasure,' what am I to do?" The
old man said, "The thing still belongeth to Him. For if
"a man bringeth thee something of his own accord and thou
"hast no knowledge about it, in this manner the thing is
"his; but if thou hast borrowed something, either from a monk
"or from a man in the world, and he refuseth to take it back,
"it belongeth to thee and thou mayest do what thou pleasest
"with it."

408. Abbâ Joseph related that Abbâ Isaac said, "I was on
"one occasion sitting with Abbâ Poemen, and I saw that he
"was in a state of great stupefaction, and because I possessed
"some influence over him, I offered entreaty to him, saying,
"'Father, where is thy mind?' And after I had pressed him
"greatly, he answered and said, 'My mind was in the place
"'of the Crucifixion, where the holy woman Mary, the God-
"'bearer, was standing and weeping by the Cross of our
"'Redeemer, and I was wishing that I might at all times
"'feel thus.'"

409. They used to say that Abbâ Sisoes the Theban was
wont to dwell among the reeds of Arsânîâ, where there was,
at some distance from him, an old man who was sick; and

when he heard [of it] he was distressed, for he fasted two days at a time, and that day was the day on which he ought not to eat. And he said in his mind, "What shall I do? For "perhaps the brethren will compel me to eat, and if I wait [to "go to the old man] until to-morrow perhaps he will be dead. "I can only do this. I will go, but will not break the law and "eat"; so he went, and he ate not, and he did not break the rule of life which [he observed] for God's sake.

410. They used to say that Abbâ Netîrâ, who was the disciple of Abbâ Sylvanus, and who dwelt in his cell in Mount Sinai, trained his body, and exercised it in ascetic labours with moderation; but when he was called by force to the episcopacy, he afflicted himself with stern and laborious works. And his disciple said unto him, "Abbâ, when we lived in the "desert thou didst not lead such a life of abstinence and self-"denial as thou now doest"; and the old man said unto him, "There I had the desert, and silence, and poverty, and I only "had to direct my body in moderation so that it might not "become ill; but here I have the world, and I must vex my "body so that it may not be caught by any lust whatsoever, "and that I may not lose my labours."

411. They used to relate that Abbâ Poemen and the brethren at one time worked with their hands, but he could not sell their work; and they were distressed because they had no one to buy their work; and one of the brethren, who was a friend of theirs, went to a certain believing merchant and informed him of the matter. Now Abbâ Poemen [always] refused to accept anything from any man, so that he might not be entreated [for alms] by the multitude. And when the merchant heard [about their need], because he wished to do something for the old man, he made the excuse that he was in need of [the kind] of work [which they did], and he bought a camel and carried away the work as if he had been in need of the same; and the brother who had told the merchant came to Abbâ Poemen, and hearing that the merchant had come and carried away what they had to sell, he said before Abbâ Poemen, "Verily, "O father, the merchant hath taken [the work] away, although "he did not want it." Then Abbâ Poemen said to Abbâ Job, his brother, "Arise, stop the camel, and bring him back, for "if thou dost not do so Poemen will not dwell here with you. "For I do not wish to wrong any man by making him un-"necessarily to suffer loss on my account, and to take my "profit." And the brother departed and brought the camel back with great difficulty, and then Abbâ Poemen was persuaded to stay with them, and when he saw [the camel] he rejoiced as one who had found a great treasure.

412. A certain stranger came to Scete, and brought there much gold, and he entreated the priest that it might be given to the brethren, and the priest said unto him, "It is useless to "them"; and having entreated him many times, and the priest not consenting [to this], the man laid the gold down openly at the door of the church. And the priest said, "My brethren, "if any man hath need let him take [some]," but they refused to touch it, and some of them would not even look at it. Then the priest said unto him, "God hath accepted thy gift, go, and give "it to the poor"; and having been greatly helped he departed.

413. On one occasion the steward of Scete went up to Constantinople, and the Emperor seeing him asked him how the fathers in Egypt were; and the steward did homage, and answered and said to the Emperor, "Behold, they eat each other, "and live." Now when the Emperor heard this, he marvelled, and asked him, "What is the meaning of 'They eat each "'other?'" And the steward said, "The meaning of 'They eat "'each other' is this:—When it happeneth that one of them "is going to die, he commandeth that whatsoever he hath shall "be given to various men according to their needs; and simi- "larly when a man worketh he bringeth [the results of] his "labour, and refresheth all the brethren therewith, and in "this way they live." The Emperor said unto him, "Verily "blessed are ye, for ye are saved and freed from the cares of "the world, and also from the judgement of Gehenna. We, on "the other hand, are troubled by the cares of the world, and "Gehenna is prepared for us because of our sins."

414. They used to say of Abbâ Betimius that, when [the brethren] were coming down from the harvest to Scete, they brought down as a gift for the brethren who were there a jar of oil, which contained the measure of a *kestâ*, and was sealed with plaster. And at the return of the period the year following when they were going to the harvest, they brought everything which was of benefit to the church; and Abbâ Betimius made a small hole with a needle in the vessel of oil, and poured out a little for himself, and thought that he had done some great thing in not having consumed the whole of the oil which was in the vessel. And when the brethren brought their vessels with the plaster coverings intact and the vessels themselves unopened, whilst his vessel had been perforated, he stood there full of shame, just like a man who thinketh that he hath been found [committing] fornication.

415. There was a great and holy man who used to dwell in the inner desert, in a state of glorious ascetic excellence, and the gifts of casting out devils and of healing the sick had been given to him by God, and he used to work great miracles in the Name of Christ, and the beasts also made themselves subject to him at his command. For it chanced on one occasion when he was journeying in the desert that he saw a herd of wild asses feeding, and he said unto them, "In the Name of " our Lord Jesus Christ, let one of you come hither"; and one of them came, and crouched before him very gently, and the blessed man mounted him and sat upon him, and the animal carried him whither he wished to go.

416. One day when the blessed Anthony was sitting in the desert with the brethren about him, suddenly there fell upon him a state of stupor, and he became exceedingly sad and sorry, and he bent his knees and prayed; and when, after a long time, he stood up, he wept and groaned, and the old man began to pluck out his hair, and to throw it away. Now when the brethren saw him weeping they entreated him to tell them what he had seen; and he answered and said unto them, "A "great pillar hath fallen this day from the church." Now he spake concerning that holy man who had fallen from his rule of life. And he sent to him straightway two brethren to see what had happened and to comfort him, and when the holy man saw them, he wailed and cried, and took dust and cast it upon his head, and he fell down before them, saying, "Go ye and say to " Abbâ Anthony, ' Pray for me that ten days may be given me " ' to live, and I believe that I shall repent'"; but he died before five days had passed, and did not remain long enough to offer up repentance for his sin.

417. There was a certain man of noble rank who sold everything which he had, and divided [the money] among the poor and the strangers, and he shaved his head and went and dwelt in a monastery; now there remained to him a remnant of his possessions sufficient for his wants. And after a little time, when he had obtained freedom of speech, he began to be proud and to exalt himself above the other brethren, saying, "They "lack education, and the knowledge of learning"; and the blessed Mâr Basil, the Bishop, sent him a message in a letter, saying, "Thou hast lost the great name which thou hadst in " the world, for thou wast called 'nobleman', and thou hast " not become a monk."

418. Abbâ Gregory made an answer against the thoughts and said to the brethren, "My brethren, inasmuch as we have " passed the measure of children, let us cease from the mind " of children, that is to say, let us free ourselves from the care- "less habits of filthy lusts; for it would be a shameful thing " for us if, since childhood hath passed from us, and old age " hath come upon us, the things of shame had not also passed " away from us."

419. They used to say that when Abbâ Macarius was walking in the desert, he went and found a beautiful spot which was like unto the Paradise of God; and there were in it fountains of water, and numerous palm trees, and trees of various kinds which bore fruit, and when he had come and told the brethren about it, they begged and entreated him to go and settle them there. Then the old men, the aged members of the congregation, who led lives of stern labour, entreated them not to leave their place, and they said, "If pleasure and delight be found in that "spot, and if a man may live therein without vexation and "labour, what pleasure and delight do ye expect to receive "from God? Nay, it is right for us to endure the hardness "of this place wherein we dwell, and to suffer tribulations so "that we may enjoy pleasure in the world to come." And when he had said these things the brethren were restrained and departed not.

420. There was a certain holy man who used to see visions, and he told the following story, saying, "Once when I was "standing up in prayer, I heard a devil complaining in the "presence of his companion, saying, 'I am [suffering] great "'labour and trouble.' And when the other devil asked him so "that he might learn from him the cause of his trouble, he "said to him, 'This is the work which hath been handed over "'to me. When I have carried these monks, who are in Jeru-"'salem and its neighbourhood, to Mount Sinai I have to "'bring those who are in Mount Sinai to Jerusalem, and I "'have no rest whatsoever.'"

421. There was a monk who lived in a cell, far away in the desert, and this monk had a brother who lived in the world, and whose end was nigh, for he had to die; and he sent a message to the monk, saying, "For God's sake do an act of "grace, and come that I may see thee before I die." And when the monk heard [this], he shut the door of his cell, and set out to go to him, and as he was travelling through the desert, he saw an old man sitting on the wayside mending nets; now this old man was the Calumniator, who was making ready his snares to catch in them those who were journeying on the road of spiritual excellence. And he was exceedingly anxious to overthrow that brother, and to trip him up by his snares, for he had not only never allowed his foot to become entangled in the meshes of his nets, but he had also slit in pieces and destroyed his pitfalls through the remembrance of God. Now the monk did not know that the man who was sitting by the roadside mending his nets was Satan, and he said unto him, "Why art thou sitting here in this parched desert? And what "art thou doing here?" The Calumniator said unto him, "I

" am mending my nets wherewith I wish to catch the gazelle
" which are in the desert." And the monk said unto him,
" Make me a net also, for I want to catch with it the gazelle
" which go into my garden and lay it waste." Then that devil
said unto him, "Get thee on thy journey, and I will make a
" net for thee which shall be better than that which thou now
" seest." And when the monk had gone to his brother, he saw
him, and remained with him for two days, and on the third
day his brother died; and he wrapped him up in his grave-
clothes, and buried him with the honour which is due to believing men. And as he was lying there in his brother's house,
his brother's wife rose up by night, and came and lay down
by his side through the agency of the Calumniator, and she
began to say unto him thus:—"God hath sent thee hither to
" provide for thy brother's children, and to bring them up;
"take me, then, to wife, and take care of thy brother's house
" and of his children, and stay here in peace in thine own
" house." And when the monk had heard what she said to
him, he was moved to wrath against her, and he said to her,
" Fie upon thee, O woman! Get thee behind me, Satan!" And
he rose up straightway, and took his staff, and set out to go
through the desert to his cell, and as he was journeying along
the way, he saw that old man sitting in his place and mending
his nets; and the monk said unto him, "Art thou still sitting
" here, O old man? Hast thou prepared for me that net con-
" cerning which I spake to thee?" Then Satan became furious,
and he looked at him in fierce anger and said, "Get thee forth
" from my presence. Yea, thou hast indeed broken the net
" which I made for thee. Didst thou not know that thou wast
" breaking and slitting in pieces during the past night that
" other net which was better than the first one? I am not able
" to make a net which [will catch] thee." And as he was speaking he changed himself into a great serpent. Now when the
monk saw this he understood that it was Satan who had appeared unto him; and he fled from the place in fear, and went
to his cell, and he gave thanks unto God Who had delivered
him from the snare of Satan, who had wished to snare him
and to drag him down into his net through his brother's wife.

422. A certain brother had recently received the garb of a
monk, and he went and shut himself up in a cell, and said,
" I am a desert monk." And when the fathers heard [this], they
came and took him out of his place, and made him to go about
to the cells of the brethren, and to make apologies to them,
saying, "I am not a desert monk, and I have only just begun
" to be a disciple."

423. On one occasion Abbâ Abraham went to Abbâ Arêâ,

and whilst they were sitting talking, a certain brother also came to Abbâ, and repeated the following:—There was a certain rich man in Jerusalem who had become rich by means of fraud, and avarice, and oppression, and wicked acts of various kinds; and when this man came to himself, and understood that there was judgement to come, he drew nigh to a certain teacher, and said unto him, "I beseech thee [to hearken "unto me]. My mind is led captive by worldly care, and by "anxieties which are of the earth; make me whole then, so "that I may not perish." And the teacher gave him to read the Book of the Wisdom of Solomon, and as he was reading [it], he found a verse which said, "He who hath compassion "upon the poor, lendeth to God." Then he shut the book, and gave it to the teacher, saying, "Who is there that is more sure "and more to be trusted than God, Who if I shew compassion "upon the poor, will give me back both principal and in-"terest?" Then he went immediately, and sold everything which he possessed and divided it among the poor, and he left nothing whatsoever of it to himself except four dînârs, which were to be [spent] in burying him; and he fell into want, and became exceedingly poor, and he went about begging, but no man either shewed compassion upon him or gave him food. Finally he meditated within himself, and said, "I will go to "the Lord my God, and will enter into judgement with Him "because He led me astray and made me scatter all my pos-"sessions." Now as he was returning to Jerusalem, he saw two men fighting with each other, and each was striving to take from his companion a certain stone of great excellence, which had fallen from the ephod which was on Aaron, the high priest; now the men did not know what the stone was. Then the man said unto them, "Why are ye fighting and contending with "each other?" And they answered and said unto him, "We "have found a stone, and we do not know what its value is"; and he said unto them, "Give it to me, and take four dînârs," and they gave him the stone gladly. Then the man went into Jerusalem and shewed the stone to a goldsmith, who, as soon as he saw the stone, said unto him, "Where didst thou find this? "For behold, because [of the loss] thereof all Jerusalem hath "been in an uproar for the last three days. But go, and give "it to the high priest, and he will make thee a rich man." Now when he had gone into the temple, the angel of the Lord appeared unto the high priest, and said unto him, "Behold, "a man hath come unto thee, and he hath with him the stone "which was lost; give him, then, gold and silver, and precious "stones according to his desire, and rebuke him and say unto "him, 'Have no doubt whatsoever in thy mind, and restrain

" ' not thyself from lending to God as if thou wert not a be-
" 'liever and a true man, for, behold, I have given unto thee
" 'twofold in this world [for what thou didst lend Me], and in
" 'the world to come life everlasting.'"

424. And the fathers also said:—There was a rich philosopher
in a certain city and he never gave anything to any man, and
the Bishop of the city said unto him, "Dost thou know, O my
" beloved brother, that when we came into this world we
" brought nothing in with us, and that we shall not be able to
" carry anything out with us? But from that which Christ hath
" given unto thee thou shouldst lend in this world, and in the
" next He will reward thee several times over." Then the philosopher said unto the Bishop, "Wilt thou be surety to me that
" if I lend [money] unto Him He will reward me?" And the
Bishop answered and said, "Yea, I will be surety to thee";
and the Bishop having become surety to him, straightway the
rich man began to scatter his possessions, and whensoever he
gave alms to any man he used to write thus: "Behold, I have
" lent to Christ such and such things, Bishop So-and-so being
" security for the same"; and he did thus until he had scattered
all the riches which he possessed. Now when the day arrived
for him to go forth from the world, he commanded his household, saying, "I make you to take an oath by Christ, in Whom
" I have trusted, that this paper shall be laid with me in the
" grave"; and they took the oath even as he made them to do.
And after many days the Bishop came to the city, and he went
to the kinsfolk of the philosopher, and he comforted them and
said unto them, "Did he not give you any commands? And did
" he not make a will?" And they said unto him, "When he was
" dying he made us swear that the paper of indebtedness should
" be laid with him [in the grave], and we did even as he said."
And the Bishop said unto them, "Come ye and shew me his
" grave," and when he had gone and entered into the grave,
he saw the paper laid on the breast of the philosopher, and he
took it, and opened it, and found that there was written in it
thus, "I, the philosopher So-and-so, have gone to Christ, and
" everything which I lent unto Him He hath returned unto me
" many times over; and henceforward I have no claim whatso-
" ever upon Him, except for tranquillity and peace." And every
one who saw and heard [this] praised God, unto Whom all
things are easy.

425. There was a certain rich man in Alexandria whose name
was Dômyânôs, and he fell sick of a grievous disease, and being
afraid that he was going to die he divided thirty pounds' weight
of gold among the poor; and it happened that he recovered,
and then he repented of what he had done. Now he had a rich

friend, who was a chaste and excellent man, and he revealed
to him everything about which he repented, and the friend
answered and said unto him, "Be not sad, O my brother, for
"it is meet that thou shouldst rejoice, because thou hast made
"an offering unto God of thy gold"; but the rich man did not
agree with him. Then he said unto him, "I will give thee
"thirty pounds' weight of gold, and thou must not be vexed,
"but come with me to the temple of Mâr Mînâ, the martyr,
"and say thus: 'It is not I who have given these alms, but
"'this man,' and take that which is thine and go." And having done this, he took thirty pounds' weight of gold, and went
to go forth by the door of the church, and the angel of the
Lord smote him and he fell down straightway, and died. Then
the priests who were in the temple of Mâr Mînâ gathered
themselves together, and they said to the friend, "Take thy
"gold, and be gone." And he said unto them, "God forbid
"that I should take anything from Christ, for I have offered
"it to Him, and it is His, but if it seem [fit] to you let it be
"divided among the poor"; and it was divided according to
his command, and every one who heard feared and glorified
God. My brethren, let us admire the excellence of that friend,
and let us not be sad when we offer alms and oblations unto
God, for we [only] offer unto Him that which is His. And He
Himself hath written that He is the debtor and the borrower,
and hath promised a reward even for a cup of cold water, saying, "Whatsoever ye do unto one of these little ones, ye do
"unto Me" (St. Matthew x, 42; xxv, 40); may He make us
worthy to do His will. Amen.

Here follow the counsels which belong in order to the old
man who spake against the thoughts of fornication, saying,
"Be like unto a man who passeth through a street of taverns,
"etc." (see No. 593, Book I).

426. O man, for thy sake was Christ born, and the Son of
God came that He might make thee to live; He became a babe,
He became a child, and He became a man, being [at the same
time] God in His Nature, and the Son of God.

427. He Who was the Lawgiver became a reader, and He took
the Book in the synagogue, and read, saying, "The Spirit of
"the Lord is upon Me, and therefore He hath anointed Me, and
"hath sent Me to preach the Gospel to the poor"(St. Luke iv, 18).

428. Like a subdeacon He made a whip of cord, and drove
out from the temple all those who sold oxen, and rams, and
doves, *et cetera*.

429. Like a servant He girded a napkin about His loins, and
washed the feet of His disciples, and He commanded them to
wash the feet of their brethren.

430. Like a priest He sat among the priests and taught the people.

431. Like a Bishop He took bread, and blessed [it], and brake, and gave unto His disciples. He was beaten for thy sake, He was crucified for thy sake, and He died for thy sake, yet for His sake thou wilt not even bear disgrace! He rose as God, and He ascended as God. He wrought all things for us, fittingly and in order, that He might redeem us. Let us, then, be watchful, and zealous, and constant in prayer; let us do all things which are pleasing unto Him, and which gratify those who love Him, so that we may be redeemed and live. Was not Joseph sold into Egypt, and was he not in a strange land? And the three Holy Children in Babylon, peradventure they acquired knowledge with man and stood in front of them [of themselves]? Nay, it was because they feared God that He helped them, and made them glorious.

432. An old man, who hath delivered himself unto God, used to say, "The monk hath no will of his own. Now he who "abideth in ministering unto the will of God never wearieth, "but if thou performest thine own will thou becomest weary "and exhausted, because God doth not support thee."

433. The old man also said, "When a soldier entereth the "battle he taketh care for himself only, and so also is it with "the huntsmen; let us then be like unto these, for riches, and "kinsfolk, and wisdom are dung without a correct rule of life "and conduct."

434. The old man also said, "God dwelleth in the man who "worketh with God, for He said, 'I will dwell in them, and "'I will walk in them, and they shall be to Me a people, and "'I will be unto them a God.'"

435. The old man also said, "God saith unto thee thus: If "thou lovest Me, O monk, that which I wish do, and do not "what I desire not. The life of a monk consisteth of:—Good "works, obedience, training, not to blame his neighbour, not "to calumniate any man, and not to complain, for it is written, "'The mercy of the Lord hateth evil things.'"

436. The same old man used to say, "The life and conduct "of a monk are these:—He must not act iniquitously, and he "must not look upon evil things with his eyes, and he must "not hearken with his ears unto things which are alien to the "fear of God, and he must not utter calumnies with his mouth, "and he must not seize things with his hands, but must give "especially to those who are in need, he must neither be "exalted in his mind nor meditate with wicked thoughts, and "he must not fill his belly. All these things he must perform "with intelligence, for by them is a monk known."

437. A certain brother vexed an old man several times by saying unto him, "What shall I do in respect of the wicked "and filthy thoughts of all sorts and kinds which go through "me?" And the old man answered and said unto him, "Thou "art like unto a stagnant pool which is at one time filled with "water, and which at another, when water hath been drawn "up from it, runneth dry. Why canst thou not rather be like "unto the spring which never faileth? Patient persistence is "victory, and victory is constancy, and constancy is life, and "life is kingdom, and kingdom is God."

438. Abbâ Epiphanius used to say, "Whatsoever food thou "wishest to eat with pleasure desire not to give to thy body, "especially when thou art not sick, and that food for which "thou lustest thou shalt not eat. When, however, thou art "eating the things which are sent unto thee by God, give thanks "unto Him at all times, and be grateful unto Him. We have re-"ceived pleasures and delights because of the name of monastic "life, but we perform not the works of monks, and it shall be "that thou art not a monk. What then? Wilt thou not play "the man that, peradventure, thou mayest be clothed in the "apparel which is alien unto thee? Tell me, O brother, how "can a man possess the seal of service unless he posses-"seth humility? For the humble man who seeth another sin-"ning weepeth bitterly, saying, 'This man may perhaps sin "'to-day, but how many times shall I sin to-morrow?' But, if "any man sin before thee, no matter who he may be, con-"demn him not, but consider thyself to be a greater sinner "than he is, even though he be both a child of this world, and "make people to sin against God."

439. He also used to say, "Know thyself, and thou shalt "never fall. Give work unto thy soul, that is to say, constant "prayer, and the love which is in God, before another can give "it evil thoughts; and pray ye that the spirit of error may be "remote from you."

440. He also used to say, "Whatsoever thou doest success-"fully, and makest a boast of, that destroy, for it is not right "for a monk to boast about his good deeds, and if he boasteth "he will fall."

441. "When thou prayest say with a hidden voice unto God, "'Lord, how am I to acquire Thee? Thou, even Thou knowest that "'I am a beast, and that I know nothing. Thou hast brought "'me to the highest point of this life, O redeem me for Thy "'mercy's sake. I am Thy servant and the son of Thine "'handmaiden. O Lord, by Thy wish make me to live.'"

442. The old man is falsehood, and the new man is truth. Truth is the root of good works, falsehood is death.

If the liar, and the thief, and the calumniator, knew that they were to be exposed and made known to all at a subsequent period they would never commit their offences, and it is even thus with those who commit adultery.

443. The sons of Eli, Hophni and Phinehas, were priests of the Lord, but they feared not God, and they and all their house perished.

444. He who layeth hold upon, and bindeth, and taketh to himself the remembrance of evil things, is like unto the man who burieth fire within chopped straw.

445. If thou wouldst talk to a man concerning life, and if thou wouldst say a word unto him with suffering, and with repentance, and with weeping, speak unto him that heareth and doeth; and if thou dost not [do this] speak not at all, lest thou die, and depart without profit from the words wherewith thou didst wish to vivify others. For unto the sinner God saith, "What are the Books of My commandments unto thee, for "thou hast taken My covenant in thy mouth?"

446. Abbâ Epiphanius said, "When the thought cometh to "fill thy bosom, that is to say, thy heart, with vainglory or "pride, say thou unto it, 'Old man, behold thy fornication.'"

447. And he also said, "If we do evil things God will be un-"mindful of His longsuffering; but if we do good things it will "not help us greatly, for in order to increase the profit of free-"dom, and that the merchandise of the will may not be spoiled, "a man must rejoice in contending."

448. On one occasion the brethren entreated Rabbâ Epiphanius, saying, "Speak to us, father, something whereby we "may live, even though thou speakest and we keep not the "seed of thy word because our ground is a salted thing." And the old man answered and said unto them, "He who doth not "receive all brethren, and who maketh distinctions between "them, he who doth this, I say, cannot be perfect."

449. If a man revile thee, bless him, and if he accept the blessing it shall be good for both of you; and if he doth not, he shall receive the reward of his reviling, and thou of the blessing.

450. It is right for a monk to live even as Abbâ Arsenius lived. Take care each day to stand before God without sin, and draw nigh unto Him with tears as did the sinful woman; and pray thou unto the Lord God as if He were standing before thee, for He is near and looketh at thee carefully.

451. He who wisheth to dwell in the desert must be a teacher by his own knowledge, and he must not be in need of being taught, lest, peradventure, he be harmed by devils, and lest he scrutinize his understanding too closely, and lest, in some form or other, he become a laughing-stock to the beings who are above, and to those who are below.

452. The correct rule of conduct for him that loveth God is to be without blame.

453. A certain old man returned an answer against evil thoughts, and said unto the brethren, "Now I beseech you, "O my brethren, that we cease from the ascetic life and its "labours, and that we also desist from the anxieties of evil "thoughts. For what are we? A sound which cometh from the "fine dust, or a sound which cometh from the dust of the "ground. Joseph of Râmâh, having asked to [be allowed to] "take away the body of Jesus, removed it and swathed it with "swathings of fine linen, and then laid it in a new grave. "Now the pure heart is the new grave of the new man."

454. The devils said unto one of the old men, wishing to lead him astray, "Dost thou wish to see Christ?" And he said unto them, "My curse be upon you, and on that which ye say, for "I believe in Christ Who said, 'If they say unto you, Behold, "'here is Christ, or, Behold, there is Christ, believe them not'" (St. Matthew xxiv, 23); and immediately the devils disappeared.

455. What is [the meaning of] the word which the Apostle spake, "To the pure all things are pure?" (Titus 1, 15.) The old man said unto him, "If a man cometh to this word, and "arriveth at this measure, he will see that he himself hath "more shortcomings than any other creature, and that he is "inferior to every being." The brother said unto him, "How "is it possible for me to consider myself more imperfect than "a murderer and inferior to him? Is it possible for me to con- "sider the murderer and the fornicator, whose actions are abo- "minable, better than myself?" And the old man answered and said unto him, "If a man attaineth unto this word, and he "seeth his neighbour committing a murder, or doing some- "thing else which is not good, he will think within himself, "saying, 'This is [only] one sin, and this man hath only com- "'mitted this one sin, but I am at all times a murderer through "'hatred and a wicked will.'"

456. A brother asked Abbâ Job, the brother of Abbâ Poemen, concerning a word which the Apostle spake, saying (Philippians ii, 3), "Esteem every man to be more excellent than thy- "self." And the old man answered and said, "If a man hath "arrived at this measure, and he seeth the offence of his "brother, he will conceal it as if it had never happened."

457. An old man used to say, "I never take a step without "first learning where I am about to put my foot, but I stand "up and look about me carefully, and I am not careless, and

" I do not let [my foot go] until God guideth me, and leadeth
" me on the path to the place which pleaseth Him."

458. An old man used to say, "God giveth a man the op-
" portunity to repent as long as he wisheth to do, and in pro-
" portion as he wisheth, for it is written, 'Speak first thy sins,
" 'and thou shalt be justified."

459. An old man used to say, "Silence is filled with all life,
" but in the speech which is abundant death is hidden."

460. And the old man also said, "Lying and sin are wont to
" lie in ambush in the words which are long and broad."

461. An old man used to say, "Humility never becometh
" angry, and never provoketh a man to wrath."

462. Abbâ Joseph said unto Abbâ Lôt, " Thou art unable to
" become a monk, but thou mayest become wholly like a flame
" which burneth and blazeth fiercely."

463. An old man was asked, "What is humility?" And he
said unto him that asked the question, "If thy brother offend
" thee, and thou forgive him before he can repent and entreat
" thee [that is humility]."

464. An old man also said, " Keep thy conscience with thy
" brother, and thou shalt find rest."

465. Abbâ Paphnutius used to say, "He who esteemeth him-
" self as nothing, whithersoever he goeth, or wheresoever he
" dwelleth, he shall find rest."

466. The same old man said, "During all the days of the
" life of the old men I used to go and visit them twice each
" month, and my cell was distant from them twelve miles,
" and in respect of every thought about which I asked them,
" they never said to me anything except, 'Wheresoever thou
" 'goest esteem thyself as nothing, and thou shalt find rest.'"

467. One of the old men used to say, "Love knoweth not
" how to keep a storehouse [full] of possessions."

468. The same old man also said, " I do not know the actual
" thing whereby, on two occasions, the enemies led me into
" error, and into the committing of sin, and into the trans-
" gression [of the Law]."

469. Certain old men asked John the Less, saying, "When
" thou wast in Crete with the fathers, how didst thou see them
" conducting themselves?" And he said unto them, "By night
" and by day they were performing with all their might the
" work of God, that is to say, [they were reciting] the service,
" and they prayed, and read, and were anxious with divine
" solicitude, and instead of being idle they worked with their
" hands."

470. On one occasion Abbâ Ammon came to the brethren,
and they, whilst expressing regret [for troubling him, asked

him] to say some words of excellence to them; and the old man answered and said unto them, "It is right that we all "should travel the path of God with well-ordered [minds]."

471. Abbâ Anthony used to say, "When we rise up in the "morning each day let us think that we shall not abide until "the evening, and when we come to lie down also let us think "that we shall not abide until the morning; for we know not "the days of our life, but they are known unto God. If we do "this each day we shall not sin, and we shall do nothing "wicked before God, and we shall not lust eagerly for any-"thing belonging to this world, and we shall not be angry "with anyone, but in everything we shall be regarding our "souls, even as men who await death."

472. And he also said, "As fish die when they are drawn "out of the water, even so do monks, who have forsaken the "world, become sluggish, when they remain with the children "of this world or dwell with them; it is then meet for us to "hasten to the mountain even as fish haste to the water."

473. Now they used to say that Abbâ Anthony was wholly [illumined] by the appearance of the light of the spirit, and that he could see what was happening from a distance; now on one occasion he saw the soul of the blessed Ammon being taken up into heaven by the hands of angels, although he was distant from him ten stages.

474. One of the brethren asked him once about the thoughts, and the old man answered and said unto him, "Do not carry "them into effect, but let them settle down and down until "they breed worms and perish."

475. Abbâ Poemen used to say, "If a man pass a hundred "years in the cell he will not understand his departure from "this world and become a monk, unless he attribute sin to "himself at all times, and make himself to be remote, both in "his mind and in his actions, from those things which he "knoweth will separate him from God, and make supplication "unto God at all times through suffering and tears."

476. A brother asked Abbâ Poemen, saying, "What is the "repentance of sins?" And he said unto him, "The repentance "of sins consisteth in a man not committing the sin again "from the moment wherein he repenteth of it; and on account "of this the righteous were called 'spotless,' and because they "had forsaken [their] sins, and had cleansed themselves from "them."

477. And another brother also asked him, saying, "Shew "me a word whereby I may live"; and the old man said unto him, "The first thing of all which the fathers have given us "[to do] is to mourn."

478. Abbâ Poemen used to say, "The passions are four "heads"; and a brother said unto him, "What are they?" The old man said unto him, "Worldly grief which cometh "about many things, the love of money, vainglory, and forni-"cation; and it is meet that we should be on the watch against "these before all other passions."

479. He said also, "If a monk hateth two things he is able "to free himself from the world, and these are," said he, "the "gratifications of the body, and vainglory."

480. The same old man also said, "Wrath is a natural thing "in man, it is his nature, but it must be used to cut off evil "passions. Hunger is natural in a man, but it must be em-"ployed [in satisfying] the want of the body, and not [to gratify] "the feeling of eager lust [to eat], even as the blessed David "said, 'With him whose eye is lofty and whose heart is "'greedy I have not eaten' (Psalm ci, 5; cxxxi, 1). Sleep "too is natural in man, but [it must not be indulged] to "satiety."

481. A brother asked Abbâ Poemen, saying, " Tell me, why "it is that when I offer repentance to a brother who is wroth "with me I do not see him pleased with me?" The old man said unto him, " Tell me truly: when thou offerest to him re-"pentance hast thou not the opinion that thou art not doing "it because thou hast sinned against him, but because of the "commandment?" And the brother said unto him, " It is even "thus." The old man said unto him, " Because of this God "doth not permit him to be pleased with thee, and because "thou dost not offer repentance to him in fulfilment of thine "own desire, but as if thou hadst not sinned against him, but "he had sinned against thee."

482. They used to say that when the disciples of Abbâ Aga-thon were building a cell he remained with them for a period of four months, and when they had finished it, on the first Sabbath on which they dwelt in it, the old man saw in it some-thing which did not afford him profit, and he said unto his disciples, "Arise, let us go away from here." And when they heard [this], they were greatly troubled, and they answered and said unto him, " If thou hadst this thought to depart, why "have we done all this work and built the cell? Moreover, "men will be offended with us, and will say, 'They have left "'this place because they can abide nowhere.'" Now when the old man saw that their souls were grieved, he said unto them, "If some men be offended at us, there are others who will "be edified by us, and they will say, 'These blessed men de-"'parted for God's sake, and they considered nothing [else].' " However, let him that wisheth to come with me come, for I

" shall certainly depart." Then they threw themselves on the
ground, and entreated him to let them go with him.

483. Abbâ Agathon also used to say, " The monk's cloak is
" a sign of the absence of wickedness"; and he also said, "God
" asketh from those who begin the service of the works of the
" fear of God nothing except that they shall order their bodies
" by obedience to the commandments against the passions of
" the lusts."

484. Abbâ Agathon also said, " He who removeth from be-
" fore his eyes accusations, and disgrace (*or* insult), and loss
" (*or* belittlement) is able to live."

485. A brother said unto Abbâ Agathon, " Father, I had the
" order to dwell in a certain place, and I have war there, and
" I want to depart; I would fulfil the command, but I am
" afraid of the war." The old man said unto him, " If it were
" Agathon, he would keep the command, and overcome the
" war."

486. The same old man also said, " If the inner man be
" watchful he will be able to guard the outer man also; but if
" he be not, let us guard the tongue by every means in our
" power."

487. The old man Benjamin was asked by a brother, " Of
" what consisteth the life of a monk?" And he answered and
said, " A mouth of truth, a holy body, and a pure heart."

488. They used to say concerning a certain old man that,
on account of the great humility which he possessed, God gave
him the gift of becoming a seer of visions, and he could see
beforehand when anyone was coming to him, and it was revealed to him concerning it; now the old man was sorry and
did not wish for this thing, and he made supplication unto
God that it might be taken away from him. And he went to an
old Rabbâ, and entreated him, saying, " My brother, labour
" for me, so that this gift may be removed from me"; then
each of them sat down in his cell and made entreaty unto God
concerning this matter, and a voice was heard by that old
man, saying, " Behold, I remove the gift from thee, but when-
" soever thou wishest it is thine." And he went straightway
to the old Rabbâ and shewed him what had been said unto
him, and when he heard [it] he gave thanks unto God.

489. The fathers once asked Abbâ Sylvanus, saying, "What
" work of ascetic excellence hast thou performed that thou didst
" receive the wisdom which thou dost possess, and the gift
" with which is endowed thy face?" And the old man answered
and said unto them with great humility, "[I received these
" things] because I never left in my heart a thought which
" could provoke God to wrath." And they used to say that the

face of the old man Sylvanus shone so brightly, even as did
the face of Moses, with the glorious splendour which he had
received from God, that no man was able to look upon it with
his eyes wide open.

490. Zeno, the disciple of Abbâ Sylvanus, said on a certain
occasion, "Dwell not in a place which is famous, and abide
"not with a man who hath a great name for ascetic ex-
"cellence."

491. One of the brethren asked an old Rabbâ, saying, "Abbâ,
"what shall I do? For whensoever I see the face of a woman
"the war of fornication is stirred up against me." And the old
man answered and said, "My son, guard thine eyes against
"looking on a woman, and behold, henceforth thou wilt have
"no fear." The brother said unto him, "Behold, how very
"often doth a man meet women by chance, without expecting
"to do so!" The old man said unto him, "As far as it is pos-
"sible for thee to do so keep thy watch carefully, both within and
"without; and as concerning that which happeneth by chance,
"and a man meeting women without thinking about it, [in
"that case] passion will have no power to bestir itself. But
"take good heed to thyself that such a thing doth not happen
"unto thee of thine own will, for it is this which the Holy
"Book condemneth, saying, 'Every man who looketh upon
"'a woman to lust after her hath already committed adultery
"'with her in his heart.' For if when thou art not thinking
"about them thou meetest women, and the passion stirreth
"itself up against thee, lift up thy mind immediately to God,
"and He will help thee." Then wishing especially to strengthen that brother, he answered and said unto him, "Behold, my
"son, know thou that thou hast been with me for two years,
"and that I have not as yet seen what manner of face thou
"hast, whether it be good, or whether it be bad, and it was
"this [fact] which urged me to tell thee to guard thine eyes
"from the sight of women." And afterwards he made a prayer
over him, and sent him away to depart to the coenobium, for
that brother used to dwell in the church.

492. They used to say about one of the old men that when
the church was dismissed, he fled straightway and departed to
his cell, and [they said] that he had a devil, but the holy man
was [only] fulfilling the work of God.

493. An old man used to say, "Without prayer thou shouldst
"do nothing, and afterwards thou wilt not be sorry."

494. A brother asked an old man, saying, "If I am in a clean
"place, and the time for service hath arrived am I to return?"
The old man said unto him, "Who, when he remembereth
"riches, will return to poverty?"

495. The old man Theodotus used to say, "Constant hunger "maketh monks to be emaciated and driveth them mad."

496. Abbâ Daniel used to say, "Constant vigil especially "drieth up and maketh the body to diminish."

497. Abbâ Ammon asked Abbâ Sisoes, saying, "When I "read in the Book my mind wisheth to arrange the words so "that there may be an answer to [my] question." The old man said unto him, "This is unnecessary, for only purity of heart "[is required]." From this it ariseth that a man should speak without overmuch care.

498. Abba Theonâ used to say, "Because we put ourselves "out of the sight of God we are led captive by the passions of "the body."

499. Abbâ Poemen used to say, "Temptations are a sure "sign whereby a monk may be known."

500. Abbâ Agathon once fell sick, and another of the old men with him, and as they both were lying in the cell a brother read the Book of Genesis to them; and when he came to the place where Jacob said unto his sons, "Joseph is not, and "Simeon is not, and ye would take Benjamin away that ye "may bring down my grey hairs with sorrow to Sheol," the old man answered and said, "Were not the ten other sons suf "ficient for thee, O Jacob?" And Abbâ Agathon said, "Hold "thy peace, old man, if God holdeth a man to be innocent, "who shall condemn him?"

501. One of the fathers came to Abbâ Theodore of Pîrmê, and said unto him, "O father, behold, brother So-and-So hath "gone back to the world." And the old man said unto him, "Dost thou marvel at this? Wonder not at this, but be sur- "prised when thou hearest that a man hath been able to flee "wholly from the world."

502. If a man thinketh filthy thoughts, doth he himself be- come defiled? Some of the old men said, "Yes, he is defiled," and others said, "He is not defiled, for if he doth it is impos- "sible for simple folk like ourselves to live at all; but [the "truth] is that a man must not carry his filthy thoughts into "deeds."

503. A certain brother went to a strenuous and tried old man, and asked him about this matter, and the old man said unto him, "Every man is required [to do] according to his "ability." Then a brother entreated the old man, saying, "For "our Lord's sake explain these words to me." The old man said unto him, "Behold, supposing that some very desirable "thing were placed here, and that two brethren came in, one "being of great stature and the other of little stature. If now "the mind of him that was of full strength were to say, 'I

" 'wish to possess that thing,' and he did not carry his soul's
" desire into effect, but straightway cut it short, the man would
" not be defiled; if then the man of lesser strength were to
" desire the thing, being incited thereto by his thoughts, and
" he took it not, he also would not be defiled. But, if he de-
" siring it were to take it, he would be defiled."

504. The old man said, "If thou seest a young man going
" up to heaven of his own will, lay hold upon his leg, and
" sweep him away therefrom; for thus will a man help him."

505. The same old man used to say, "If thou criest unto God
" in prayer with a pure heart thy prayer shall not return unto
" thee fruitless."

506. The same old man used to say, "As two words cannot
" be uttered [at the same time] by one voice, and be recognized
" and understood, so is it with the mixed prayer which is
" uttered by a man before God."

507. He also said, "If thou seest the wings of ravens stretch-
" ed out in flight, even so is the foolish prayer of the mind
" which is lifted up."

508. He also said, "If thou art earnest in asking God for
" things, but wilt not pay back as far as thou art able, thou
" must hear the words, 'Thou shalt ask and shalt not receive,
" 'because thou didst accept a loan and didst not pay it back.'"

509. He also said, "The words of the mouth of him that
" prayeth purely before God are a fetter wherewith he shall
" be able [to bind] the devils beneath his feet like a sparrow;
" and, as prisoners tremble before him that is their master,
" even so will they quake at the words of his prayer.

510. He also said, "As the rain when it falleth upon the
" earth taketh the place of a key in the lock thereof, and
" openeth [it] and bringeth forth to sight the growth of the
" seeds and roots which are in it, so are the soul and the mind
" of him that receiveth and tasteth the heavenly droppings,
" for by the words of his lips shall be made known unto man
" his hidden conduct before God, I mean to say, that when a
" man's request and entreaty about everything are made within
" the words of his pure prayer, he openeth the door of the
" treasury of the Trinity, Who is the Lord of treasures, and
" bringeth out therefrom the treasures which are hidden for
" those who are worthy of them."

511. Concerning Abbâ Anthony they used to say:—There was
a man with an unclean spirit which sought to cast him into the
water, and the monks who were with Abbâ Anthony came and
entreated him to pray over the man who was thus troubled,
but he excused himself [from doing so]. And when the demoniac had remained with him for a long time, he smote the

blessed man on his cheek, whereupon the old man made ready the other cheek; and having done this that evil spirit took to flight.

512. A brother asked Abbâ Muthues, saying, "What shall I "do? for my tongue vexeth me. Whensoever I sit among the "brethren I am unable to restrain myself, but I condemn them "in every good work, and treat them with contempt. What "shall I do, then?" The old man answered and said unto him, "If thou art not able to restrain thyself, get thee away, and "stay by thyself, for this is a disease. Now, he who sitteth "among the brethren must not possess four corners, but he "must be altogether round, so that he may move smoothly in "respect of every man." And the old man said unto him also, "I myself do not dwell alone as an example of spiritual excel-"lence, but as an emblem of feebleness, for mighty men are "those who are among the brethren."

513. When the brethren were talking to an old man about the thoughts they said unto him, "Our hearts are hard, and "we do not fear God; whât are we to do so that we may come "to fear God?" The old man said unto them, "I think that if "a man will lay hold in his heart upon that which rebuketh "him, it will bring to him the fear of God." And they said unto him, "What is the rebuke?" The old man said unto him, "In every act a man should rebuke his soul, and say unto it, "'Remember that thou hast to go forth to meet God.' And "let him say also, 'What do I seek with man?' I think that "if a man remain in these things the fear of God will come to "him."

514. Abbâ Timothy said unto a certain brother, "How art "thou?" The brother said unto him, "I destroy my days, O "father." And the old man said unto him, "My son, my days "also are destroyed, and I give thanks."

515. An old man used to say, "The Shunammite woman re-"ceived Elisha because she had no human promise with man; "and they spoke of the Shunammite woman [as] a person of "the soul, and of Elijah [as] a person of the Spirit of God; "when the soul maketh itself remote from commotion and "trouble, the Spirit of God abideth on it, and then it is able "to bring forth, though hitherto it hath been barren."

516. Abbâ Ammon used to say, "I said unto Abbâ Poemen, "'If I go to my neighbour's cell, or he cometh to mine concern-"'ing any matter whatsoever, are we two to be ashamed to "'speak, lest some alien subject of discourse appear between "'us?' The old man said unto him, 'Thou wilt do well, for "'youth hath need of care and watchfulness.' And I said unto "him, 'What do the old men do?' And he said unto me, 'The

" 'old men have been skilled, and have had experience, and
" 'they have arrived at the measure for speech, for in them
" 'there is nothing alien which they can speak with the mouth.'
" And I said unto him, 'And supposing that I have the neces-
" 'sity to talk with a neighbour, wouldst thou that I should
" 'speak with the words of the Scriptures, or with the words of
" 'the old men?' And he said unto me, 'If thou art not able to
" ' hold thy peace it is better for thee to use the speech of the old
" 'men rather than that of the Scriptures, for there is danger
" 'in a man employing the speech of the Scriptures.' "

517. Abbâ Daniel used to say that a man of business once
came to Abbâ Arsenius, and brought him a testament of a
certain kinsman who had left him a very large inheritance, and
having received the deed he wished to tear it to pieces. Then
the man of business fell down at his feet, and said, "I beseech
"thee, do not tear it up, for if thou dost I shall die." And Abbâ
Arsenius said unto him, "I died before he did, though he hath
"only now died, but shall I live?" And he sent the man of
affairs away without having taken anything.

518. A monk went to a nunnery to visit his sister, for she
was sick; now she was a woman who was great with God, and
a firm believer, and she never allowed herself to see the face of
a man, not even that of her brother, lest through her he might
go in among the women. And she sent him a message, saying,
"Go, my brother, and pray for me, that Christ, by His grace,
"may make me worthy to see thee in that world of the king-
"dom of heaven."

519. A brother asked an old man and said unto him, "What
"is the best thing for me to do, so that I may do it and live
"thereby?" And the old man said unto him, "God [alone]
"knoweth which is best; but listen. One of the old men said
"that the mind which rebuked a man was his [best] adversary,
"for it resisted a man who sought to carry out his desires in
"the flesh, and to rebel against God, and not to be obedient
"unto Him, and it would also deliver a man over to his
"enemies."

520. An old man also said, "It is meet that the soul should
"be occupied in the service [of God] by day and night, even
"like Huldah, the prophetess, who used to sit in the house of
"the Lord with supplication and ministration; and also like
"Hannah, who never ceased in her ministrations during a
"period of eighty years."

521. A brother asked an old man, saying, "What shall I do,
"father? For my belly vexeth me, and I am unable to restrain
"it, and therefore I am leading a life of luxury." The old man
said unto him, "If thou dost not throw on it the fear of fasting

"thou wilt never be able to straighten the path. Place before
"it the following parable. A certain man had an ass, and as
"he was sitting upon it and journeying along, the animal would
"not go straight, but went first to this side of the road and
"then to that; and he took a stick and smote it. And the ass
"said, 'Beat me not, and henceforward I will go straight.'
"Now when he had gone a little further on, the man alighted
"from the ass, and placed the stick in [his] cloak-bag which
"was on it, but the ass knew not that the stick was on his
"back. And when the ass saw that its master was not carrying
"the stick, he began to hold him in contempt, and he walked
"among the crops; thereupon his master ran after him, and
"took the stick and beat him with it until he went straight.
"Now the belly of the body is even like unto the ass."

522. A brother said to Theodore of Parmê, "Speak a word
"to me, for behold, I am about to perish." And with great
labour the old man said unto him, "I stand in danger myself,
"and what have I to say to thee?"

523. Abbâ Kêrîôn used to say, "I have performed more
"bodily labours than my son Zechariah, but I have not reached
"his measure of humility and silence."

524. Abbâ Macarius used to say, "Guard thyself against
"freedom of word and deed, for it is meet for a monk not to
"permit his thought to be his judge in anything whatsoever."

525. Mother Sarah used to say to her brethren, "It is I who
"am a man, and ye who are women."

526. A brother asked Abbâ Poemen, "How can it be right
"for me to take good heed to my ways when I am sitting in
"my cell?" The old man said unto him, "For a season I was
"a man who had fallen into the mire up to my shoulders, and
"a basketful of gall hung from my neck, and I was crying out
"to God, 'Have mercy upon me.'"

527. They used to say of the men who were in the cells "that
"their rules were so strict that during the night they slept
"four hours, and assembled for service four hours, and worked
"for four hours; that during the day they worked with their
"hands until the ninth hour, and that after that they pre-
"pared the small quantity of food which they ate, and if any
"man had anything to do in his cell he then did it. In this
"way they filled up their day."

528. A brother asked Abbâ Sisoes, saying, "Why do not the
"passions depart from me?" The old man said unto him,
"Because their possessions are in thee; give them their pledge
"(*or* security), and they will depart."

529. On one occasion the fathers were summoned by the
Archbishop Theophilus, and they went to Alexandria to him

so that he might make a prayer and cleanse a house of idols; and as they were eating with him, flesh of a calf was set before them, and they ate it in simplicity, doubting nothing. And the Archbishop took a piece of meat and gave it to an old man who was near him, saying, "Behold, this piece of meat is very "good, father"; and they all answered and said unto him, "Behold, up to the present we have been eating herbs, but if "it be flesh, we do not eat flesh," and not one of them ate anything more.

530. They used to tell a story of a brother who was the neighbour of an old Rabbâ, and say that he would go into the cell of the old man, and steal whatsoever he found there, and though the old man saw him he never rebuked him, but worked with his hands and wearied himself the more, saying, "Per-"haps that brother is in need"; and the old man suffered much tribulation at the thought, and ate his food in sadness. And when the old man was about to die, the brethren sat round about him, and when he saw in their midst the brother who used to steal from him, he said unto him, "My son, come near "to me"; and when he had drawn nigh to him, he kissed his hands, saying, "My brother, I am grateful to these hands, for "through them I shall enter the kingdom of heaven." Now when that brother heard these things he was sorry, and he also repented, and he became a well-tried monk through the things which he had seen in that old man.

531. On one occasion, when Abbâ Agathon was travelling, and some young men were with him, one of them found a small bag on the road, and he said to him, "Father, dost thou "wish me to take this little bag?" and the old man looked at him in wonder, saying, "My son, didst thou place it there?" And the young man said, "No." Then the old man said unto him, "If thou didst not place it there, how canst thou desire "to take it?"

532. Abbâ Joseph, the priest of Ascalon, told us the following story, saying: There was a certain merchant in Ascalon who borrowed from other people much money, and he hired a ship for himself and put out to sea; and a fierce storm rose up against him, and he lost everything which he had with him; but he himself was saved. And when he returned to the city those to whom he owed money seized him, and they took everything which he had in his house, and sold it, and shut him up in prison; but they left him his wife as an act of charity, so that she might beg for him and feed him. And the woman went about from door to door, and she herself begged for bread for her husband; and one day as she was sitting and eating bread with her husband, one of the chief men of the

city went in to give alms to the prisoners who were there, and he saw the woman and lusted for her, for she was beautiful. And he sent his servant to call her, and she came thinking that he wished to give her alms; but he took her aside, and said to her, " Why hast thou come here? " And she related unto him the whole matter. Then he said unto her, " If I pay " one-third of thy husband's debt wilt thou lie with me this " night? " And that chaste, free woman said unto him, " I have " heard that the holy Apostle said, ' A woman hath no power " ' over her body, but her husband.' I will first ask my hus- " band, and whatsoever he commandeth me that will I do." And having come she told her husband, and he was grieved; and he wept, and said unto her, " Go, and say unto him, ' I " ' have told my husband, and it hath not pleased him, and " ' I have hope in God that He will not forsake us.' " Now there was in the prison-house a certain thief who had been a highway robber, and he was shut up [in a room] inside beyond them, and at that moment he happened to be sitting at a window which faced them, and he heard everything which they were saying; and with tears he said unto himself, " Woe " is me! For although these people are in such great trouble, " they are not willing to deliver over their freedom, and accept " money, and go forth from this place, but they hold their " chastity to be more valuable than riches. What then shall I, " the wretched one, do? For the thought that there is a God " hath never entered my mind, and I never remember that my " evil deeds will be judged, and I have committed many " wickednesses, and many awful murders. And I know that " when the judge cometh here he will kill me without asking " a question, as is just." And he answered and said unto the woman and her husband, " Because I see that ye preserve the " purity of your bodies for Christ's sake, and that ye have " chosen to remain in great tribulation and not to destroy " your chastity, God hath put it into my heart to do unto you an " act of grace which ye deserve, and perhaps God will shew " me mercy through you on the day of judgement. Go ye to " the northern side of the city wall, and dig there in a certain " place, and behold, ye shall find there a large earthen pot, " beneath which is a vessel full of gold. Take it, and pay your " debt, and may a great blessing abide with you so that you may " live upon it; but I beseech you to pray for me continually, " that I may find mercy before God in the day of judgement."

And after three days the judge came to the city, and he ordered them to cut off the head of that thief without [asking any] questions, and after he had been slain, that noble woman said unto her husband, "Wilt thou command me to go and

" see if that which the thief said is true?" And he said unto her, "Go." And she went at the time of evening, and by the indications which the thief had given her, she found the place, and having dug a little she found the money, even as he had told her, and she took it and went to her house, giving thanks unto God. And she brought it out little by little, and she gave it to the creditors, who thought that she brought it to them as the result of her begging, a little from here and a little from there; then when she had paid her husband's debt, he came forth from prison, thanking and glorifying God.

Then Abbâ Joseph said unto us, " Behold these men, O my " brethren! Because they chose to live in affliction, and re- " fused to despise the command of God, God multiplied His " grace unto them without delay. For even if the woman had " hearkened unto that lascivious man he might not, perhaps, have " given her what he promised her; but because they preserved " their chastity which is pleasing to God, God rewarded her " with the whole amount of their debts, and brought them to " a greater state of prosperity than [that which they enjoyed] " at first. And, my beloved, I think thus concerning Adam " when he was in Paradise. Had he kept that little command, " honour greater than that which he had at first would have " come to him; but when he transgressed the command of his " Lord, he fell from and was driven out of the delight and " pleasure wherein he lived. May our Lord make us worthy " to keep His commandments! Amen.

533. On one occasion when Abbâ John and the brethren who were with him were going up from Scete, he who was guiding them lost the way, and the brethren said unto Abbâ John, " What shall we do, father? For this brother hath lost the way, " and peradventure we shall die in wandering about." Abbâ John said unto them, "If ye tell him he will be grieved and " feel ashamed. But behold I will feign to be sick, and will say " that I am not able to go on any further"; and the brethren said, "Father, thou hast well said." And they acted thus, and decided that they would stay where they were until the morning, rather than rebuke the brother who was guiding them.

534. Abbâ Serenus used to say, "I have passed the whole " period of my life in cutting and twisting and sewing palm " leaves, and in spite of it all, had not the hand of the Lord " fed me I should not have had enough to eat. '

Demonstrations which are suitable to Lazy Men and Sluggards, and to all those who take no care for their Souls

535. Those who are in despair, and who have delivered themselves over to the filthy work of their abominable lusts, and who make loose their ways at all times, and who love the lusts which harm them, are like unto the sterile land, and the arid desert, and a house laid waste, and a vineyard without grapes, and an empty vessel, and a body without a soul, and eyes without light, and a dead body without a voice, and hands which are cut off, and knees which are bowed, and a paralytic lying on a bed, and a vessel filled with stinkingness.

536. AGAINST THOSE WHO LOVE VAINGLORY, AND THOSE WHO BOAST OF THEIR ALMS. Those who love vainglory, and those who boast of their fair works and life, are like unto a broken cistern, and a bag with a hole in it, and a tree without fruit, and a naked man, and a moth-eaten garment, and a worm-eaten beam of wood, and unto other things which are consumed by their [false] glory.

537. AGAINST HIM THAT IS NOT CAREFUL (or WATCHFUL) IN RESPECT OF HIS TONGUE. He who is not watchful in respect of his tongue is like unto him whose house door is open, and whose riches are plundered by every man, and he is like unto an uncovered vessel (or unrolled garment), and like that which is unsealed.

538. AGAINST THOSE OVER WHOM EVIL THOUGHTS HAVE DOMINION, AND IN WHOSE MIND WICKED COGITATIONS RISE UP. Those who through their sluggishness give a hand to the thoughts which make a mock of them, and by their negligence help filthy devils to have dominion over them, are like unto an abode which is full of snakes, and a house which is full of evil-smelling things, and a ship which is tossed by the waves, and a poor piece of land which is full of briars and brambles, and unto the thorns that choke it, the end of which is burning.

539. AGAINST HIM WHO DOTH NOT SUPPRESS IN HIMSELF WRATH AND ANGER, AND WHO KEEPETH HIS HATRED AGAINST HIS BROTHER. He who doth not suppress in himself wrath and anger, and who keepeth his hatred against his neighbour, is like unto a savage animal which cannot be tamed, and which goeth along every road, and wandereth about in an erring manner, and unto the man who burieth fire in chopped straw, and like the man who putteth in his bosom the spawn of serpents, and like a den which is full of enraged serpents, and like a cleft in the rock which is full of reptiles which shoot out venom, and a mad dog that barketh at every man, and a wild boar that

gnasheth his teeth as soon as he seeth a man, and like the
evening wolf which goeth about with his mouth wide open to
destroy the simple lambs, and the panther which leapeth upon
the gazelle in the desert, and the ship which saileth on the sea
with an evil spirit for her steersman, and the savage beast
which cannot be subdued, and which walketh on every road
and wandereth about in error without discernment. These
[words] are [directed] to those who are not humble, so that
they may correct themselves and their savage habits, and to
those who are lifted up against their brethren in their pride,
and who do not wish to travel in the path of the humility of
Christ.

540. AGAINST THE CHANGE OF THE EVIL WILL OF THOSE MEN WHO
DENY THE GRACE WHICH IS PERFORMED TOWARDS THEM. One of the
teachers said, "If thou hast made thyself humble, they de-
" spise thee without discernment. If thou hast made thyself
" angry, they hate thee without understanding. If thou hast
" made thyself pleasant, they swallow thee, and thou dis-
" appearest. If thou hast made thyself bitter (*or* cruel), they
" reject thee, and thou art reviled. And if thou hast mingled
" with folk they hold thee to be a liar fair[-spoken], and wan-
" dering. If they have fallen ill, they command thee, and if
" they are despised, they judge thee; if they be visited, they
" abuse thee; and if thou art whole, they leave thee; and if they
" are reclining, they drive thee away; and if aught be required
" from them, they curse thee; and if mercy be shown unto them,
" they oppress thee. Neither grace (*or* goodness), nor justice
" will ever please those who belong to every evil of every
" kind."

Chapter xvi. Questions by the Pupils and the Answers [to the same] by the holy Fathers and Monks

BROTHER. How is love (*or* charity) acquired by men of
understanding?

541. OLD MAN. True and pure love is the way of life,
and the haven of promises, and the treasure of faith, and the
interpreter of the kingdom, and the herald of that which is
hidden.

542. B. I do not know the power of the word.

O.M. If a man loveth not God, he cannot believe in Him,
and His promises are not true [to him], and he feareth not His
judgement, and he followeth Him not. Now because love is not
in him [he cannot] be free from iniquity, and await the life which
is promised, but he performeth at all times the plans of sin;
and this [happeneth] because the judgement of God is [too] ex-

alted in his sight. Therefore let us run after love, wherewith the holy fathers have enriched themselves, for it is able to pay back [what is due] to its nature and its God. This then is praise.

543. B. How doth wisdom dwell in man?

O.M. Now when a man hath gone forth to follow after God with a lowly mind, grace bestoweth itself upon him, and his conduct becometh strengthened in the spirit, and when he hateth the world he becometh sensible of the new conduct of the new man, which is more exalted than the impurity of the human abode; and he meditateth in his mind the humility of the rule of the life which is to come, and he becometh a man of greater spiritual excellence.

544. B. How is love made known?

O.M. By the fulfilment of works, and by spiritual care, and by the knowledge of faith.

545. B. What are the works?

O.M. The keeping of the commandments of the Lord with the purity of the inner man, together with the labour of the outer man.

546. B. Is he who is destitute of work also destitute of love?

O.M. It is impossible that he who is of God should not love, and it is impossible for him that loveth not to work, and it is impossible to believe that he who teacheth but worketh not is a true believer, for his tongue is the enemy of his action, and though he speaketh life he is in subjection unto death.

547. B. And is he who is in this state free from retribution?

O.M. Such a man who speaketh the things of the spirit, and performeth the things of the body, and supplieth his own wants, is not deprived of reward, but he is deprived of the crown of light, because the guidance of the spirit refuseth to rule him.

548. What are fasting and prayer?

O.M. Fasting is the subjugation of the body, prayer is converse with God, vigil is a war against Satan, abstinence is the being weaned from meats, humility is the state of the first man, kneeling is the inclining of the body before the Judge, tears are the remembrance of sins, nakedness is our captivity which is caused by the transgression of the command, and service is constant supplication to and praise of God.

549. B. Are these able to redeem the soul?

O.M. When internal things agree with external, and manifest humility appeareth in the hidden works which are from within, verily, a man shall be redeemed from the weight of the body.

550. B. And what is internal humility?

O.M. The humility of love, peace, friendship, purity, rest-

fulness, tranquillity, subjection, faith, remoteness from envy,
and a soul which is free from the heat of anger, and is far
from the grade of arrogance, and is redeemed from the love of
vainglory, and is full of patient endurance like the great deep,
and whose motion is drawn after the knowledge of the spirit,
and before whose eyes are depicted the fall of the body, and
the greatness of the marvel of the Resurrection, and the demand for judgement which shall come after the revivification,
and its standing before the awful throne of God. [If the soul
hath these things] redemption shall be unto it.

551. B. Is there any man who fasteth that shall not be redeemed?

O.M. There is one [kind of] fasting which is from habit,
and another from desire, and another from compulsion, and
another from sight, and another from the love of vainglory,
and another from affliction, and another from repentance, and
another from spiritual affection; for although each of these
seems to be the same as the other in the mind externally, yet
in the word of knowledge they are distinct. Now the way in
which each is performed by the body is the same, and the way
in which each is to be undertaken is wholly the same by him
who travelleth straightly on the path of love, and who beareth
his burden with patient endurance spiritually, and who doth
not rejoice in his honour.

552. B. Who is the true [monk]?

O.M. He who maketh his word manifest in deeds, and
beareth his passion with patient endurance; with such a man
life is found, and the knowledge of the spirit dwelleth in him.

553. B. Who is the pure habitation?

O.M. He who is destitute of the good things of the body,
and who rejoiceth in the love of his neighbours in the love of
God; for spiritual relaxation is produced in proportion as need
ruleth over the soul.

554. B. With what is a man able to overcome lust?

O.M. With spiritual remembrance. If the desire for the
delights which are to come doth not obliterate that of the
things which are here, a man cannot conquer; for if the ship
of the merchant did not arrive over and over again by means
of hope, he could not endure the storms, and he would go on
his way of tribulation.

555. B. How doth a man go forth from the world?

O.M. By forsaking entirely the gratification of desire, and
by running to the utmost of his power in the fulfilment of the
commandments; for he who doth not act in this way falleth.

556. B. Behold, through what have the men of old triumphed?

O.M. Through the fervour of their supernatural love, and

through the death of the corruptible man, and through the contempt for pride, and through the abatement of the belly, and through the fear of the judgement, and through the promise of certainty; through the desire for these glorious things the fathers have acquired in the soul the spiritual body.

557. B. How can I conquer the passions which trouble me when they are fixed in me by nature?

O.M. By thy death to this world; for if thou dost not bury thy soul in the grave of persistent endurance the spiritual Adam can never be quickened in thee. When a dying man hath departed from this temporary life he hath no consciousness of this world, and all his perceptions are at rest and are abated. Now if thou forsakest that which is of nature naturally, and thou dost not perform it voluntarily in thy person, thou art dead; but if thy desire dieth in repentance, the whole of [thy] nature ceaseth from this temporary life by the death of the spirit just as do the motions of the body at the natural end of time.

558. B. To what extent is a man held capable of revelation?

O.M. To the same extent as a man is capable of stripping off sin, both internally and externally. For when a man dieth by spiritual sacrifice, [he dieth] to all the words and deeds of this habitation of time, and when he hath committed his life to the life which is after the revivification, Divine grace bestoweth itself upon him, and he becometh capable of divine revelations. For the impurity of the world is a dark covering before the face of the soul, and it preventeth it from discerning spiritual wisdom.

559. B. Is he who loveth money able to believe the promises?

O.M. No. If he believeth, wherefore doth he possess [riches]? Perhaps our hope is [set] upon gold, or perhaps the hand of the Lord is too small to redeem [us]? The body of our Lord is given unto us for [our] happiness, and His blood is the drink of our redemption, and He withholdeth from us the loaves of bread and the apparel which groweth old. He who loveth money is divided in his mind concerning God, and he prepareth for himself pleasures before God giveth them unto him; and though he rejoiceth in the promises in [his] word, he maketh them to be a lie by his deed. True indeed is the word of our Lord which He spake, "It is as difficult for the rich man "to enter the kingdom of heaven as it is for a camel to go "through the hole of the needle"; it is impossible to possess in one dwelling both God and mammon. Monks should, then, not belong unto the things which are seen.

560. B. Who is indeed the man of excellence?

O.M. He who crieth out always that he is a sinner, and asketh mercy from on high, whose word is laden with the feeling of discernment, and his senses with the watchfulness of deeds, and who, being silent, yet speaketh, and who, though speaking, holdeth his peace, and whose actions are wholly good fruits for the life of time, and the revelation of Christ.

561. B. What is the way of life?

O.M. The going forth of a man from this world on his entrance into another. But if a man forsaketh his childhood of humility and cometh to the old age of this world in his love, he revealeth the way of life. To go forth truly from this world is to be remote from it.

562. B. And what shall I do in respect of the world which troubleth me?

O.M. This world troubleth thee because its care is in thy mind, and the love of it is in thy body, and its pleasures are in thy heart; forsake the world and it will depart from thee, and root up from thyself all its branches, and behold, the war thereof will die down in thee. For as long as thy body seeketh its gratifications, and its lust is of this world, thou art not capable of life.

563. B. What is pure prayer?

O.M. Pure prayer is little in speech and great in deeds, for if it were not so work would be more excellent than supplication. . . . For if it be not so why do we ask and yet not receive, seeing that the mercy of God aboundeth? The method of penitents is, however, something different, as is also the labour of the humble, for the penitents are hirelings, and the humble are sons.

564. B. From what is the love of money produced?

O.M. From desire, for unless a man desireth he doth not possess. When a man desireth he possesseth, and when he possesseth he hath fulfilled his desire; and when he hath fulfilled his desire, he becometh greedy; and when he hath become greedy he committeth fraud, and when he hath committed fraud his possessions have become many. When his possessions are many his love diminisheth, and when his love hath diminished the remembrance of God is removed from his heart. And when the remembrance of God hath been removed from his heart, the mind becometh darkened, and his understanding is blinded; and when his understanding hath become blinded the power of discernment is darkened, and when the power of discernment hath become dark, the soul loseth its sight. And when the soul hath lost its sight good is rooted out therefrom, and wickedness entereth in, and sin taketh up its rule; and when sin hath taken up its rule the thought of God is blotted out, and the passions of the body are stirred up, and they seek to satisfy their needs. And having taken that which they sought for, it is necessary for much money to be collected, and when money is multiplied, the gratification of the body is fulfilled, and it eateth and drinketh, and committeth adultery and fornication, and it lieth and worketh fraud and oppression, and it transgresseth the covenant, and destroyeth the Law, and treateth the promises with contempt, and the lust for the things which are seen is fulfilled. Let money be an abominable thing in our sight, and let us not love it; but if we perform the lust of the flesh it is an absolute necessity to love money; for money belongeth to the flesh and not to the spirit, even as saith the Apostle, "The flesh hurteth the spirit, and the spirit "the flesh, and both are opponents each of the other" (Galatians v, 17).

565. B. What is the kind of prayer which is not acceptable before God?

O.M. The destruction of enemies, and asking for evil things [to come upon] those who do harm to us, and the health of the body, and a multitude of possessions, and abundance of offspring—prayers for these things are not acceptable before God. But if God beareth with us whilst we are sinners and commit offences against Him, how much more is it right that we should bear with each other? It is not right for us to ask for the things which belong to the body, for the wisdom of God provideth all things.

566. B. What is purity of soul?

O.M. Remoteness from anger and from the error of the remembrance of evil things, and being weaned from the bitter nature, and reconciliation with our enemies, and peace which is beyond troubling, and simplicity of love which is above this world; with these things is the inner man cleansed, and he putteth on Christ and is redeemed.

567. B. What is envy?

O.M. Hatred towards the virtues of other folk, and wickedness towards the good, and a bitter mind towards the innocent, and anger against those who are prosperous in this world, and the cloaking of the upright conduct of those who repent, and vexation with the peace of the lovers of God.

568. B. How ought we to pray before God?

O.M. For the return of sinners, and the finding of the lost, and the bringing near of those who are afar off, and friendliness towards those who wrong us, and love towards those who persecute us, and a sorrowful care for those who provoke to wrath; if a man doeth these things verily there is repentance in his mind, and sinners will often live, and their soul[s] be redeemed in life. For the prayer which our Lord delivered unto us for the need of the body is a word which covereth the whole community, and was not uttered solely for those who are strangers to the world, and who hold in contempt the pleasures of the body. For he in whose dwelling the kingdom of God and the righteousness thereof are found lacketh nothing, even when he asketh [not].

569. B. What is remoteness from the world?

O.M. The thought (*or* mind) which overcometh the love or the body; for if the body be not trampled upon by the feeling of patient endurance a man cannot conquer in his strife.

570. B. Is the soul of a man, which is held fast in the lust of the things which are seen, fair in the sight of God?

O.M. Who is able to live chastely when the body is making demands upon him? Or, in what soul is found the love of our Lord which bestoweth itself upon the things which are seen and which are corruptible? A servant cannot serve two masters, and the soul cannot please God with spiritual excellence so long as the memories of the things which are corruptible are in its mind, for the mind of the flesh cannot please our Lord; and except the world die in the heart humility cannot dwell therein, and except the body be deprived of its lusts, the soul cannot be cleansed from thoughts.

571. B. Why is the mind disturbed at meeting women?

O.M. Because they make use of the lust of nature. For, when the sight hath fallen upon the construction for the production of children and the gratification of the body, that old poison layeth hold upon it, and the law of the desire is confounded; now desire conquereth nature, not by the stirring up of the passions, but by the will, [and] by the fulfilling of works of humility, which, by the might of our Lord, conquer everything by their love, and by the patient endurance of the merit of Christ.

572. B. Who is the mighty man, he who is remote from the world, or he who dwelleth therein?

O.M. The mighty man conquereth in every place, whether he be in the world or without. Nevertheless, the fathers departed to the wilderness, the place which is preserved from the uproar of those who are afraid that as long as they dwell in the body the passions which give trouble will cleave to them. Now, for those who have ended the great strife of their conflict in the world Divine grace hath worked with its power, and it still worketh for the remembrance and benefit of the community, and truly great is the crown of those whose spiritual ship hath not sunk to the bottom of the tossed and troubled sea of this world, and hath not ceased its course heavenwards by the straight road which is full of fear.

573. B. Is it helpful to the soul to make oneself a stranger?

O.M. With perfect thanksgiving it doth help, provided that the soul beareth chastely afflictions, and rejoiceth in our Lord who giveth pleasure; but if it doth not, its good seed is made of no effect because it doth not give fruit beloved of God, and if it endureth and uttereth blessing it hath a reward, but if it lack these things it becometh a mere wandering of the mind, and a sight which is without profit. The best thing of all is the quietness of the mind which is akin to God.

574. B. Since all the creatures of God are holy, why do the fathers make the sign of the blessed Cross over the things which they eat?

O.M. It is true that all the creatures of God were pure [when they came from] Him that created them, but because sin gained dominion everything became polluted; but the advent of our Lord came, and sin was abrogated and righteousness had its rule, and everything was made holy, whether it was in the heavens or on the earth. But because the blessed fathers knew the wiles of Satan, and that they would certainly bring upon them that which would do them harm by means of such things as are employed as food, they signed what they ate with the holy sign of the Great Cross so that they might slay all the craftiness of the Calumniator.

575. One of the fathers said, "On one occasion I was lying "down at night, and I thirsted for water to drink; now there "was near me one of the holy men who lived in a holy manner, "and he saw that I took up the vessel to drink without having "made over it the [sign of] the Cross. And he said unto me, "'Wait, master, wait'; and he made the sign of the Cross "over it, and straightway the Calumniator fell from the vessel "in the form of a flash of fire, and both he and I saw it. And "we wondered at the great might of our Redeemer, and at "the marvellous symbol of His merit."

A variant [reads]:—One of the fathers said, "I was lying "down one night, and I thirsted for water to drink. And there "was with me a certain widow who lived a chaste life, both "when she was with her husband, and afterwards, and she "said unto me, 'Wait, master, wait,' and she made the sign "of the holy Cross over the vessel of water, and straightway "there fell from it the Calumniator in the form of a flash of "fire, and both she and I saw him. And we wondered at the "might of the Redeemer, and at the marvellous symbol of His "merit."

These things were indeed told to us by the blessed mouth which is remote from falsehood; therefore it is required of us necessarily to do this [i.e., make the sign of the Cross] for the protection of our life. Now the Enemy used to wage war openly

against that widow who did these things, even as I have
learned from the chosen ones of our Lord, and one of the holy
men who heard [this] from her own mouth spake thus:—The
blessed woman said as follows:—One day I went to the house
of God, and Satan drew nigh, and said unto me, "Why dost
" thou pray like a man, and say, Glory be to the Father, and
" to the Son, and to the Holy Ghost?" And I said unto him,
" How then shall I pray?" Then Satan said unto me, "Thou
" shouldst pray in this wise, and say, Glory be to thee, Mary,
" mother of Christ." Then I answered and said unto him,
" There is dust in thine eyes, Satan. Why should I forsake
" the Lord and worship a handmaiden?" And he disappeared
from me.

576. And the blessed man said unto me also:—The same
old woman said in my presence:—And again I went to the
church according to [my] custom, and I entered in and prayed,
and then the Enemy came and made blind my eyes, and I
could not see, and I called one of the women, and she carried
me to my house. And after three days he departed from before
my eyes, and he began to go in front of me; then I said unto
him, "There is a thing which thou must do for me. Go thou
" to where thou didst first seize upon me." And we went to the
church, I and he. And I left him where he had seized me, and
went away a short distance, and turning round I looked for
him, and I saw him standing like a shadow; then I went a
little further, and I turned round again, and I [still] saw him.
And I shut the door of the church and went out, and then I
opened it again and went in, and I saw him still standing
there, and he ceased to practise his wiles upon me. Such were
the great things which happened to the blessed old woman.
For the monk must not boast himself over the man who is in
the world, for in it are mighty men; and if such things as these
are to be found in Eve, how much more ought they to be found
in the Adam which hath been redeemed by [the second] Adam?

577. One of the fathers said, "Whilst I was sleeping one
" night, the Enemy came and smote me, and said unto me, ' Go
" 'to the world and work righteousness; why dost thou shut
" 'thyself up like a beast in a cave?' And knowing the wicked-
" ness of the Enemy, who regarded me with an evil eye, I made
" the sign of the Cross, and he fled from me. Then, having
" waited a few days, he came and smote me on the neck in a
" bantering fashion, saying, 'Now that thou hast become a
" 'righteous man, go to the world that I may not destroy thee';
" and when I prayed and made the sign of the Cross over my
" face he departed from me. And after a short time he came
" again, and he took up a seat upon my neck, and then I bade

" my soul to be of good cheer, and stood up, and made the
" sign of the Cross, the symbol of merit, before him, and he
" disappeared again, for he was not able to stand before me."
Now these things took place and happened in this wise in very
truth, and we may therefore know and understand the conduct
wherein God rejoiceth, and there is, even as this [story sheweth],
no reason for fearing the devils and all the evil spirits. Whosoever holdeth in contempt humility, and penitence of the mind,
and the subjugation of the body, and remoteness from the care
for the things which are seen, falleth into the inclination of the
world, and despiseth the good riches of the fear of God, and
his hope for the inheritance of holy men is cut off, and for the
delights of heaven which neither pass away nor are dissolved.
May we, through the grace and mercy of Christ, be held to
be worthy of these things! Amen.

Chapter xviij. Questions and Answers on the Vision of the Mind

A BROTHER asked an old man, saying, In what manner ought a monk to dwell in silent contemplation in
his cell? The old man said, He should have no re-
578. membrance of man whatsoever whilst he is dwelling in
the cell.

579. B. What kind of labour should the heart perform?

O.M. The perfect labour of monks is for a man to have his
gaze directed towards God firmly and continually.

580. B. In what way should the mind persecute abominable
thoughts?

O.M. The mind is unable to do this of itself, and it hath
not the power [to do it], nevertheless whensoever a thought [of
evil] cometh against the soul, it is required of it to flee immediately from the performance thereof, and to take refuge in
supplication [to God], and that shall dissolve the thoughts even
as wax [is dissolved] before the fire, for our God is a consuming fire.

581. B. How did the fathers who dwelt in Scete give
answers to their enemies?

O.M. That service also was great and excellent, but there
was labour therein, and not every man was able to stand firm
therein, and there was in it, moreover, wandering of the
understanding.

582. B. How?

O.M. When a thought hath come against the soul, and the
soul hath, with great difficulty, been able to drive it out,
another thought maketh ready to come, and in this manner the
soul is occupied the whole day long in a war against the

thoughts, and it is unable to occupy itself with the sight of God, and [to enjoy it] continually.

583. B. With what intent, then, should the mind flee towards God?

O.M. If the thought of fornication rush upon thee, seize thy mind and carry it to God immediately, and raise it upwards with strenuousness, and delay not, for to delay is to be on the limit of being brought low.

584. B. If a thought of vainglory rise up in my mind, and it maketh me think that I can be free from the evil passions, is it not necessary that I should contend against it?

O.M. Whensoever thou contendest against it, it will become exceedingly strong against thee, and will act cruelly and sharply, and thou wilt not, as thou imaginest, become strengthened by the Spirit of God; for it is better able to contend against thee than thou art able to contend against it, and thou wilt [not] find thyself, apparently, sufficient of thyself to resist the passions of the thoughts. For as it is with the man who hath a spiritual father, that giveth to him his every desire, and who is without any care whatsoever, and who hath, therefore, no judgement with God, so also is it with him that hath committed his soul to God, for it is, henceforward, unnecessary for him in any way whatsoever to fall into care concerning the thoughts, or to allow a thought to enter into his heart. But if it should happen that a thought hath entered, lift it up strenuously towards thy Father, and say, "I myself know nothing; behold, my Father knoweth." And whilst thou art raising up thy mind, the thought itself will leave it and take to flight half way, for it cannot ascend upwards with thee, and it dare not stand with thee there. There is no service which is superior to this, for it belongeth to confidence, and it hath no care in all the Church.

585. B. How is it that the fathers who dwelt in Scete made use of answers against their enemies, and pleased God thereby?

O.M. Because they worked in simplicity and in the fear of God, and because of this God helped them, and afterwards the service of the vision of God rose upon them, with His help, because of their works of excellence, and because of the mercy of God, and that old man who taught in this wise said, "Once "I went to Scete to visit an old man there who had become "aged in ascetic labours. And having saluted each other we "sat down in silence, and that old man made [me] no answer "whatsoever. Then, whilst I was sitting down, my mind be- "came occupied with a vision of God, and that old man con- "tinued to sit there and to make baskets of palm leaves, and " he neither lifted up his gaze to me, nor did he tell me to eat,

"and for six whole days I ate nothing whatsoever. Now that
"old man was occupied with his work of basket-making the
"whole day long, and when the evening came he soaked some
"palm leaves in water, and worked the whole night through.
"And on the following day, after the ninth hour, he answered
"and said unto me, 'Brother, when hast thou the power to per-
"'form this work of the spiritual vision?' And I answered and
"said unto him, 'Yea, father, and whence hast thou the power
"'[to work thus]? We have accustomed ourselves to learn this
"'from our youth.' And the old man said unto me, 'I have
"'never received teaching of this kind from my fathers. But as
"'thou seest me now, even so have I been all [my] days. A
"'little work and a little meditation, and a little singing of
"'the Psalms, and a little prayer; I have cleansed my thoughts
"'according to my power, and I resist [as far as I can] the
"'thoughts which rush upon me. And in this manner, after-
"'wards, there dawned upon me the spirit of visions, as I
"'learned this [faculty], and I-knew not that any man pos-
"'sessed this gift.' Then I answered and said unto him,
"'I have learned this from my youth up.'"

586. B. How ought a man to see the order of the divine
vision?

O.M. The Scriptures have shown [him how].

587. B. How?

O.M. Daniel saw Him as the Ancient of Days. And Ezekiel
saw Him on the chariot of the Cherubim. And Isaiah saw Him
upon a lofty and glorious throne. And Moses persisted in
being with Him Who cannot be seen, as if he saw Him.

588. B. And how can the mind see that which cannot be seen?

O.M. A king cannot be seen, as far as his exact image is
concerned, when he is sitting on the throne.

589. B. And is it right for a man to depict God in this
manner?

O.M. And what is the better for a man to depict God in
his mind in this manner, or to bow himself down to many
abominable thoughts?

590. B. Peradventure this is accounted as sin?

O.M. No. Only thou must hold according to what the
Scriptures have shown [thee], and the fulfilment of the matter
will come of itself, even as the Apostle said, "Now, as in a
"miracle, we see in parable, but then face to face," the
meaning of which is as if a man were to say, "When the mind
"hath been made perfect, then it will be able to see with ease
"and freedom."

591. B. And is there no confusion in the mind in respect of
this?

O. M. If a man performeth his strife in truth there will be no confusion in the mind, "For," said the old man, "I have "passed a whole week of days without a remembrance of any "human thing having entered my heart." And another old man said, "I was once journeying along the road, and behold, "I saw two angels close to me, one on this side, and one on "the other, and they walked along with me, and I did not "look at them."

592. B. Why?

O.M. Because it is written, "Neither angels nor powers "shall be able to separate me from the love of God, which is "in our Lord Jesus Christ" (Romans viii, 39).

593. B. Can the mind be occupied with, and stay with the divine vision continually?

O.M. Although the mind cannot be occupied with and stay with the divine vision continually, still when it is pressed by the thoughts it can fly to God, and it shall not be deprived of the divine vision. But I say unto thee that if the mind be made perfect in this respect, it shall be easier for thee to move mountains than to bring it down from above. For as the blind man who is shut up in darkness, if his eyes be opened and he go forth into the light, will be unwilling for the darkness to overtake him again, so the mind having begun to see the light of its own person, hateth the darkness, and is unwilling to remember it again. And one of the fathers also said, "I "wished to look upon my mind, saying, Perhaps if I allow my "mind to do so it will go and wander about in the world; but "when I set it free it stood still, and was silent, and did not "know where to go. And again, I lifted it up on high, for it "knew that if it departed and wandered about I had to ad- "monish it; quietness and prayer make strong this class of "service." And the same old man said, "If a man prayeth "continually it will bring correction to the mind immediately."

594. B. How is it possible for a man to pray continually? For the body becometh ill through constant prayer.

O.M. The standing up of a man in his prayer [once] is not said to be prayer, but [he must do so] continually.

595. B. How is [prayer to be made] continually?

O.M. Whether thou art eating, or drinking, or even travelling on the road, or if thou art doing some piece of work, thou shalt not let prayer be remote from thy heart.

596. B. But suppose I be talking with some one, how is it possible for me to fulfil the command, "Be ye praying con- "tinually"?

O.M. Now concerning this the Apostle spake, "In [all "your] prayers, and in [all your] supplications, pray ye at all

" times in the spirit; and when it would be unseemly for thee
" to pray, because thou art speaking with another man, pray
" thou through supplication."

597. What manner of prayer is it necessary for a man to
pray?

O. M. The prayer in the Gospel which our Lord taught His
disciples.

598. B. What limit ought there to be to prayer?

O. M. No measure hath been laid down to prayer; because
He said, " Pray ye at all times, and continually," He did not
lay down any measure to prayer. For if the monk only really
prayeth when he standeth up in prayer, he who is thus doth
not pray with the heart but with the mouth only. Now the old
man said, " It is necessary for the man who is thus to look
" upon all [men] in the same way, and he must be remote from
" all calumny for the love of Christ; to Whom be glory for
" ever! Amen."

599. In another manuscript I have found the following:—A
certain monk who was a foreigner, and was chaste in his conduct, and who came from the city of Antioch, from the monastery which is called Kawsyân, went once to pray in Jerusalem,
and to see the holy places wherein our Lord Jesus Christ went
about, and after he had lived there for a long time, and had
worked a way which was full of every excellence, he wished
to return to his country in peace. Now he lacked food for the
journey and the money which was necessary for his wants,
and he knew not what to do; and when he had gone in to
pray in the great temple of the Resurrection of our Lord, he
prayed, and sat down in sorrow, and he was troubled about
his departure, and the lack of that which he needed. And
having sat down, he dropped into slumber, and slept, and he saw
in his dream our Lord Jesus Christ, Who bade him be of good
cheer, saying, " Arise, be not sorrowful, but go in to the steward
" of My house of the Resurrection, and say unto him, ' Jesus
" 'hath sent me unto thee so that thou mayest give me the one
" 'dînâr of which I am in need, and when He cometh He will
" 'give it [back] to thee for me.'" Now when the monk had
awoke from his sleep, he arose, and prayed first and believed
the vision which had appeared to him, and he rose up and
went to the steward [of the Church] of the Resurrection, as he
had been commanded to do, and he spake to the steward, as
he had been told in the vision. Then the steward said unto him,
" When will Jesus come and repay me?" And the monk said
unto him, " I have told thee what I have heard from Him, and
" as for thee, thou must do what thou wishest." And the
steward said unto the monk, " Give me a paper in thine own

"handwriting for the dînâr, and take [it] and go"; and the monk sat down and wrote thus: "I, John the monk, the "stranger, from Antioch, a city of Syria, and from the holy "monastery of Kâwsyân hereby testify that I have received "from the steward one dînâr for food by the way, and I have, "of mine own free will, set my handwriting thereto saying that "when Jesus cometh He will pay him for me." And after the monk had taken the dînâr and departed, the steward saw that same night in a vision of the night, that a man of splendid appearance came and said unto him, "Take the dînâr which "thou gavest to that monk, and give me the written paper "which he gave thee." And the steward said in the vision, "My Lord, the monk said unto me, 'Jesus will come and re- "'pay me, and will take from thee the paper which I have "'written.'" And the man said to the steward, "I, even I, am "Jesus; take thy dînâr, and give Me the writing which the "monk gave thee. Or, wouldst thou take anything more from "him?" Then the steward took the dînâr from Him, and he laid it in his hand, and gave Him the written paper, and He tore it up.

Now when the steward awoke from his slumber he found the dînâr in his hand, but the written paper had disappeared; and he marvelled and wondered, and praised God. Then he sent some of his people to bring back the monk wheresoever he might be found, and having gone they found him praying, and they said unto him, "Come with us; behold, the steward of the "Church of the Resurrection seeketh thee." And when the monk heard [this], he feared greatly, and said in his heart, "Peradventure he wisheth to take back the dînâr"; and he went with them being troubled and sorrowful. Now when the steward saw him, he said unto him, "For the love of Christ I "entreat thee to eat with me this day," and whilst they were eating, the steward sâid unto him, "What hast thou done with "the dînâr?" and the monk said, "Behold, it is still with me." The steward said unto him, "Mâr Abbâ, take thou as many "dînârs as thou wishest, only give me the paper which thou "didst write [saying] that Jesus would come and repay me." And the monk said unto him, "My lord, forgive me, but I have "received nothing else from thee, for that which I did take was "sufficient for me." Then the steward related unto him that which had appeared unto him, saying, "The dînâr hath been "paid back to me, and the paper which thou didst write hath "been taken by our Lord Jesus Christ from me"; and the steward entreated the monk, saying, "Take from me, if thou "wishest, ten pounds of gold, only write me [a paper, saying], "'Jesus will come and pay thee for me,' and do thou, my lord,

"depart in peace." And the monk said unto him, "Master,
"verily I say unto thee, thou shalt not receive from me another
"jot, and I will not take anything else from thee." And all
those who heard [this story] praised God Who neglected not
those who call upon Him in truth.

600. AN ADMONITION OF THE HOLY FATHERS. Be thou an
enemy unto all folly and sin. Dejection driveth away the fear
of God, captivity [to sin] driveth away the virtues from the
soul. There are three excellences which illumine the mind
always; a man must not see the vices of his neighbours, and
he must do good unto those who do evil to him, and he must
bear with gladness all the trials which come upon him. And
these produce three (*sic*) other excellences, namely, a man must
not look upon the vices of his brother, and this excellence produceth love; and he must bear the trials that come upon him,
and this excellence produceth self-denial. There are three excellences of which the mind hath need, and a man should observe
them always: He should lean away from follies, and he should
not be lax in his service, and he should make strong his heart.
There are three excellences, the which if a man see them with
him he knoweth within himself that he is delivered from devils,
namely, knowledge whereby he will be able to understand and to
discern between thoughts, and the sight of everything before it
cometh to pass, and the power of not becoming entangled with
evil thoughts of any kind. There are three things which gain
dominion over the soul until it arriveth at great weakness,
captivity [to sin], and dejection, and sickness, and these contend against every man's soul, and from them are produced
evil thoughts, and when a man buildeth up they overthrow
[what he hath built]. There are three excellences which benefit and strengthen the soul: mercy, the absence of lust and
long-suffering, and besides these three excellences the mind
hath need to pray without ceasing continually, and a man
must fall down and cry out before God, and hate all evil
passions.

601. And he also said:—The fear of God driveth away all
evil things, but dejection (*or* lowness) driveth away the fear of
God from a man; the wandering of the thoughts driveth away
good works from the soul. There are four things which are
good:—Silence, the keeping of the commandments, humility,
and tribulations. There are four good things which protect the
soul:—Love towards every man, absence of lust, long-suffering,
and a man severing from himself wickedness. And the soul
hath need of the four following virtues at all seasons:—A man
must pray without ceasing, and he should pour himself out
before God continually, and he should declare his own de-

fects in his heart, and he should judge no man, and his own mind should be tranquil. The four following things help a young monk:—Doctrine, the repetition of the Psalms at every moment, and he should not be lax in obedience to fasting, and he should esteem himself to be of no account whatsoever. Through four things the soul is corrupted:—For a man to walk about through the city without guarding his eyes, for a man to have anything to do with women, for a man to have friendship with the rich men of the world, and for a man to love empty talk. Of four things fornication is begotten, namely, by eating and by drinking overmuch, by sleeping overmuch and by idleness, by laughter and by silly words, and by the arrangement of the apparel. By four things the mind is darkened: by a man hating his neighbour, by hating his brother, by crying out evil things, and by uttering them. By four things is the soul laid waste: by a man not keeping silent (*or* tranquil), by loving the works of the world, by trafficking in material things, and by the evilness of the eye. Through four things anger cometh: By a man giving and taking (i.e., buying and selling) in the world, by doing his own will, by loving to teach, and by thinking in himself that he is a wise man. There are three virtues which a man acquireth by weariness (*or* exhaustion): by mourning always, by observing his sins, and by having his death before his eyes every day. He who taketh care to keep these virtues shall be able to be saved by the mercy of God and, to speak briefly, these are necessary for the man who seeketh to live: Faith, and hope, and love, and love of God, and obedience, and humility, and patient endurance, and self-denial, and fasting, and constant prayer, and vigil, and service, and going into exile, and voluntary poverty, and absence of evil passions, and the silence of discretion, and deprivation of various meats. For if a man doth not believe, he can neither hope nor love, nor have affection, nor be obedient; and if he be not obedient, he cannot either be humble, or endure patiently; and if he cannot endure patiently, he cannot practise self-denial, and if he cannot practise self-denial, he cannot draw nigh to fasting. And if he cannot fast, he cannot pray continually, and if he hath no prayer, he cannot keep vigils; and if he keepeth not vigil, service will not be found in him, for he will say and sing the service in a hurried manner. And he who possesseth these things only in a little degree cannot go into exile and become voluntarily poor, and without the love of these things he cannot deprive himself of meats; and a man cannot acquire the silence of discretion when all these things are remote from him. Let us, then, take care to perfect all these things in ourselves with all our might, through the help of God, to Whom be glory for ever and ever! Amen.

602. AN EXHORTATION. Now therefore I have written down for thee all these things so that thy soul may not become sluggish, and so that thou mayest not become the cause of [others] being like unto thee. And because of this I counsel thee to take the yoke of pleasantness upon thy neck, for it will help thee to sit by thyself in silence, and to withdraw thyself from human intercourse, and from cares about the things of this world which will hinder thee. And make thyself as the dust in [thy] humility towards every man, knowing [at the same time] that there is hope [for thee]. And let not weeping cease from thine eyes, for there is the occasion of tears. And make thy cell a hall of judgement of thyself, and a place for striving against devils and evil passions, and let there be depicted therein the kingdom [of heaven], and Gehenna, and death and life, and sinners and the righteous, and the fire which never is quenched, and the glory of the righteous, and the outer darkness, and the gnashing of the teeth, and the light of the righteous, and their joy in the Holy Spirit, and the Passion of our Lord, and the memorial of His Resurrection, and the redemption of creation. And let thy habitation be free from superfluous things, for one of two things will happen unto thee; either through thinking of them thou wilt suffer injury, or in withdrawing thyself from them thy war will be added to and become fiercer. And take heed lest, through [holding in] honour and sparing other folk, thou bring thyself to evil case in the war; whatsoever belongeth to lust and is of the eyes thou shalt not possess, for the wars of thy passions are sufficient for thee. Heal thou and make whole in thy habitation those in whom God hath pleasure; it is He Who knoweth thy sitting down, and thy coming in, and thy going forth. And in all thy conduct be constant in prayer, especially in the night seasons, for [night] is the acceptable time for prayer, as it is written, " Be thou like unto thy Lord, Who prayed to God " continually throughout the night until the rising up of the " Sun." When all voices are quiet do thou fill thy mouth with praise, and thy tongue with glorifying, and whilst others are lying like dead men on their biers do thou depict in thyself the waking of the Resurrection. The night which is darkness unto other folk shall be to thee bright as the day, and instead of filling thyself with wine as other men do, fill thou thyself with the love of God; and in the night season, when silver and gold are stolen, do thou steal the kingdom [of heaven] like a thief. In the night season, when sinners perform their evil deeds to their own injury, do thou labour for the benefit of thine own soul, and take care, continually of all excellences. Then He Who is merciful in His gifts, and rich unto every one who calleth upon Him, will come unto thee quickly and will help thee, and thou shalt smite the Evil One, and shalt bring to naught his crafty acts. And thou shalt make thy mind to shine, and the Lord of All shall place in thee the innocent thoughts of uprightness, and He shall comfort thy mind; then shall the rugged ground become smooth before thee, and the difficult ground shall be as a plain, and thy ship shall anchor in [its] haven. And thou shalt lead beforehand the life which is to come, and thou shalt fulfil the Will of God, according to His Will, both in heaven and on earth; and thy knowledge shall grow and thy joy increase in proportion to thy spiritual conduct, and thou shalt be held to be worthy of the sight of the righteous by the grace and mercy of Christ our Lord, to Whom, with His Father, and the Holy Ghost, be glory now, and always, and for ever and ever! Amen.

603. AN ADMONITION OF ABBÂ MÂR JOHN. Now thou wilt not be able to find a more excellent way than this: He who would repent to Christ of his sins and follies must fall on his face many, many times, [and be sorry for] the sins which he hath committed, and he must make supplication and entreaty to the mercy of God. Moreover, our other fathers have incited [us] to kneel down, and he who continually kneeleth down and prayeth rejoiceth in God. Woe is me, me the man of negligence! Now he who sigheth, and weepeth, and sheddeth tears in prayer, possesseth all excellences together; for if we do not keep watch on and remember always our feebleness, whilst despising ourselves, and holding ourselves in contempt, the devils will lead us astray. Wake thyself up, O my beloved one, and keep in thy remembrance always three moments, and forget them not; the first is the moment of death, with its sorrow, and grief, and trouble, which is immeasurable, that overtaketh every man, when [a man shall stand] before the awful throne of Christ; the second moment is the moment of fear and quaking when men and angels shall rise up, when a man doth not know what command shall come forth concerning him, whether it shall be for life everlasting or for torment everlasting; and the third moment is that when the penalty (*or* decree of doom) shall come forth upon us, with its repentance of soul which shall last for ever, and shall be with us afterwards in the years which shall have no end. At the [remembrance of] these three moments all men fear and quake; may God in His compassion save us from Gehenna and its endless torments! Amen.

I am an apostle, and I cast out devils, and I perform

mighty deeds, but how am I to know that the end of Judas may not be mine, and how am I to know that I shall [not] inherit hanging, and be called by our Lord "Satan" and "son " of perdition"? If thou seest, moreover, a man who is a murderer, and a thief, and an adulterer, and a shedder of blood, thou mayest think whence I shall know [this]; for if this murderer at the end confesseth Christ, he will precede me in the kingdom of heaven, and thou shalt think thus concerning every man. If thou, O man of God, whithersoever thou goest, thinkest these and suchlike things continually, and if thy humility be in proportion to the greatness of thy power, thou shalt never fall. But if a man be neglectful, even for the twinkling of an eye, of his humility, and if pride be mingled in his negligence, he shall be cut off quickly from the height of the love of God, and he shall fall, even as quickly as a glass vessel full of water, which is suspended by a thread of a spider's web, would fall if that thread were to be severed. Now the conduct of humility is thus. If at the beginning, or in the middle, or at the end, or wheresoever it may be, a man first of all layeth hold upon perfect humility, and upon complete contempt of himself, the devils will be unable to approach him, on the contrary, they will flee before him, like flies before smoke, both they and their thoughts; but if a man [doth not] acquire humility, either at the beginning, or in the middle, or at the end of his career, there is nothing which [can stand up] against the strife and contest. As the holy man Evagrius said, "After the vanquishing of [all] the other pas- " sions, there still remain two which will wage war against " the perfect man until death, namely, vainglory and pride." And John, the seer of Thebaïs, used to say, " He against " whom the devil of vainglory still fighteth, wandereth with- " out measure, and is divided [in his mind] to a boundless " degree." The Teacher used to say, "Humility possesseth two " characteristics which are superior to the other excellences of " the spirit, for it seeth to what degree it can abase itself to the " lowest depth, and grace also exalteth humility to God, [and] " to the height which is above; and because grace exalteth it " continually towards God, it acquireth faith at all times, and " strengtheneth confidence. And the second characteristic of " humility is that it feareth not that which opposeth it, that is " to say, it feareth neither devils, nor wild animals, nor evil " men, even as the holy man Evagrius said, 'The man who " 'is proud and wrathful is a timid man, but the humble man " 'is without fear.' And he said, 'Humility by itself van- " 'quisheth both passions and devils, and the labours of the " 'body, and the contests of the mind only serve to strengthen "'humility the more.'"Therefore there is never a time when the monk hath not need of humility. Now it is right for him that dwelleth in silence wishing to arrive speedily at purity of heart, and to take care of [his spiritual] splendour, to guard the three following things:—he must guard his hearing against listening to any word which may strike him and may rouse him up to anger; and he must guard his tongue, not only against rebuking and chiding any man, even though he be a man of no account whatsoever and a man of ignorance, and he must not [attempt] to teach or to admonish. But if a man ask him for a prayer, he must esteem himself to be the servant of him that asketh him, and he must kneel down before the cross and say, " O " Lord, provide for my brethren according to Thy Will, and " according to Thy design, and according as it may be bene-" ficial for them before Thee, and make me, a sinner, worthy " of Thy mercy through my prayers"; let him pray after this example, and it shall suffice. Do not think in thy mind, which may lead thee astray, that thou wilt be able to acquire even one spiritual excellence, no matter which it may be, without afflictions and troubles, whether with or without the desire; for no man who feedeth his body daintily on lusts is able to enter through the door, even as the camel cannot go through the narrow hole of the needle.

Now the pleasures of the body come into being because of unbelief, because the wretched body doth not believe in those good things which are promised unto the hungry, and in the woes which are prepared for those who are filled with food and who live delicately. Therefore he, who believeth in the promises and threats, goeth hungry, and he denieth himself, and he watcheth in prayer, and he humbleth himself, and he layeth hold upon abstinence, and restraineth himself from the gratification of his pleasures, and he inheriteth the purity which is promised to those who are blessed. But if he leadeth a life of sluggishness and pleasure, from it he shall inherit the impurities and the punishments which are prepared for him in Gehenna. Now the desire of the Holy Spirit is thus:—Remoteness from the habitation of men, continual quiet, weeping and sorrowful cries, joyful hymns, the singing of the Psalms, and praises, fasting, and abstinence, and vigil, poor apparel, a humble gait, the cloaking of the thoughts of the passions, the hidden prayer of the mind; know ye that such are the things in which those who are in the desire of the spirit wish to walk, and they never wish to perform the lusts of the flesh. And to speak briefly unto you, O my brethren, fasting, and service, and standing up, and vigil, and abstinence from meats, are the constituent parts of a fair rule of life and conduct, and those who perform them will receive a reward from the true God if they perform them in truth, and if there be no alien pretence in their service. But hearken, O my brethren, for this is the true work of the monastic life, the binding of the understanding which is in God, and the suppression of the alien thoughts which enter his heart; and whosoever hath his heart [set] upon God acquireth for his soul pleasure, and the life which is everlasting. Amen and Amen.

Here end the Histories & the Narratives of the Triumphant Acts of the Holy Fathers and Monks which were composed by the holy and excellent Palladius, Bishop of the City of Helenopolis, & which he wrote to Lausus the Prefect. To God be glory, and honour, and adoration, and worship, and exaltation, for ever and ever! Yea and Amen.

Appendix

Questions of the Brethren, and Answers of the Fathers, which are exceedingly fair and beautiful

THE brethren said:—There were two brethren who were the sons of a merchant, and their father died, and they divided their inheritance between themselves, and unto **604.** each one there came five thousand dînârs. And one of the brethren divided his inheritance among the churches, and the monasteries, and the poor, and he himself became a monk, and he chose for himself a life of continual silence, and fasting, and prayer; now the other brother built a monastery for himself, and gathered brethren to him, and he took care of the strangers, and the poor, and the sick, whom he received and relieved. When the two brothers were dead there was questioning among the brethren about them, and they went to Abbâ Pambô and asked him, "Which manner of life and conduct "was the more excellent and exalted?" And having learned from God, he said unto them, "They are both perfect, and in "my sight they appear to be of equal merit." Explain to us now the old man's words, for how can the man who is destitute, and the man who hath possessions be equal [in merit]? The old man said, "Since the whole conduct of these brethren "was to God, and since whatsoever they did they did it for "God, with an upright aim, and since the aim of each was "the same, they appeared to be in the old man's opinion of "equal merit before God."

605. The brethren asked Abbâ Nastîr, "What rule of life "and conduct should a man follow?"

The old man said, "All rules of conduct are not alike.

" Abraham was a lover of strangers, David was a humble man,
" Elijah loved silence, and God accepted the work of all of them.
" Whatsoever work is of God, if thy soul desireth it, that do,
" and God be with thee."

606. The brethren said:—Abbâ Pambô said, "If there be
" three monks in one place, and one of them live in silence [it
" is] well, and if another be sick and he give thanks in his
" weakness, and if another minister to men and relieve them,
" all three of them are in the same service." Reveal to us now
the mind of this holy man.

And Abbâ Pambô said, "If a man dwell in silence for God's
" sake, and not for the sake of vainglory, or any other human
" thing; and if another, who is sick, give thanks to God for
" his sickness, and he endure him that ministereth unto him
" with longsuffering, he becometh like unto him that is in
" silence; and if he who ministereth unto men doeth it not for
" a reward of this world, but for God's sake, and if he con-
" straineth himself in everything, and doeth the will of those
" who are ministered unto by him in love and gladness, he
" thus becometh like unto him who shutteth himself up in
" silence, and like unto him that is sick, and in this way the
" work of all three is of equal merit. For Abbâ Joseph and
" Abbâ Poemen divided the perfect ascetic life into three
" classes, and therefore Abbâ Nastîr said to that brother, 'If
" 'thou conduct thyself according to any one of the three thou
" 'shalt be perfect.' And this is well known from that which
" Abbâ Anthony said, 'Many have afflicted themselves with
" 'labours and tribulations, and because they had not in them
" 'the power of discernment, they did not know the way of
" 'truth.' And again he said, 'One man might live in a cell
" 'for a hundred years, and yet not know how to dwell therein
" '[rightly] for one day, because he humbleth not himself, and
" 'accounteth not himself a sinner, and a feeble man, and igno-
" 'rant, but he justifieth himself, and blameth others; never-
" 'theless it is right that we should know that, even though
" 'some are sick, and others relieve the wants of men and
" 'minister unto them with an upright aim, those who lead a
" 'life of silence lead a superior life, and follow a line of con-
" 'duct which is more excellent than all the rules of life which
" 'are followed among brethren. And this life is superior in
" 'the same way that the Spirit of God is more exalted than
" 'the holy angels, according to what we have learned from
" 'the history of the holy men Abbâ Arsenius and Abbâ Moses
" 'the Ethiopian. For when one of the brethren went to the
" 'blessed Arsenius [to enquire of him] concerning the love of
" 'a silent life of contemplation, he neither set a table for him

" 'nor gave him refreshment; then he went to the blessed Abbâ
" 'Moses and he both welcomed him and gave him refresh-
" 'ment. And when one of the great fathers heard [this], he
" 'entreated our Lord to reveal to him this matter, saying,
" ' "How is it that one fleeth for Thy Name's sake, and an-
" ' "other welcometh and giveth refreshment for Thy Name's
" ' "sake?" And there appeared unto him on the river two
" 'ships, in one of which were Abbâ Arsenius, and the Spirit
" 'of God Who was travelling along in silence, and in the
" 'other was Abbâ Moses, who was travelling with holy angels
" 'that were feeding him upon honey, with the comb thereof.
" 'And by this the fathers understood that the life of silent
" 'contemplation was as greatly exalted above alms and mini-
" 'strations as was the conduct of Matthew the Evangelist
" 'above that of Zacchaeus the tax-gatherer.' "

607. The brethren said: The brethren asked Abbâ Pambô,
saying, " Supposing that a man who liveth in the world hath
" a wife and children, and supposing that he giveth much
" alms, and setteth free slaves, and redeemeth those in capti-
" vity, and visiteth the sick, and relieveth those who are
" afflicted, and fulfilleth all the things which are proper for
" him [to fulfil], is not such a man equal in labour to one of
" the three classes of monks, that is, to the man that dwelleth
" in silence, or him that is sick, or him that ministereth unto
" the poor?"

And the old man said, "Not altogether."

And the brethren said, " Wherefore?"

And the old man said, " Because, although the man who is
" in the world leadeth a life of righteousness, his whole con-
" duct is outside the body, but all the labour of the monks is
" inside the body, that is, fasting, and prayer, and vigil, and
" hunger, and thirst, and the constraint of the will at every
" moment, and wars, both secret and manifest. And it is well
" known and manifest that the men, who are in the world
" and who are exceedingly excellent in their conduct, are not
" equal to the monks in their labours; for our Lord Jesus Christ
" surnamed the monks ' sons of light,' and those who are in the
" world ' sons of the world.' Now the monks with their mem-
" bers, and with their thoughts, and with their bodies, and with
" their conduct serve God perfectly with stern labours and afflic-
" tions, and they offer themselves up to God as a living, and
" rational, and holy sacrifice, with rational and spiritual ser-
" vice, and they are crucified unto the world, and the world is
" crucified unto them, according to the word of our Lord, Who
" said, ' Whosoever wisheth to come after Me, let him take
" ' up his cross, and follow Me,' that is to say, Let him not

"fulfil his own will, but let him do My will only, and bear
"tribulations of all kinds. And monks shall leave father, and
"mother, and brothers, and sisters, and kinsfolk, and coun-
"try, and in return for these they shall receive a hundredfold,
"and shall inherit everlasting life. And to the men who are
"in the world, He said, 'Acquire for yourselves friends of the
"'mammon of unrighteousness, so that when it hath come to
"'an end they may receive you into their everlasting habita-
"'tions.' For as men who are in the world receive monks
"into their houses, so shall the monks receive those who have
"lived in the world into the kingdom of heaven; and by this
"our Lord shewed that all the good things of God and His
"kingdom belong to the monks who, from their youth even
"to their old age, have laboured to God in the excellent works
"of the ascetic and monastic life. But it is right that we should
"know to what degree the soul is superior to the body. The
"life which is led by the monks in silent contemplation, and
"the works thereof, are as much superior to the life which is
"led by righteous men in the world, as the life and conduct
"of the angels are superior to those of men. And the life and
"conduct of the monks are superior to those of men who are
"in the world, because the latter please God because of their
"love for men, whilst the monks do so because of their love
"for God."

608. The brethren said, "Into how many orders have the
"fathers arranged the monastic life?" And the old man said,
"Into three orders."

609. The brethren said, "What are they?" And the old man
said, "The perfect, those who are half perfect, and the beginners."

610. The brethren said, "Whence canst thou prove to us
"that this is so?" The old man said: "From the words of our
"Lord in the Gospel. For he said, 'The sower went forth to
"'sow. And some [seeds] fell on the roadside, and others fell
"'on the rock, and others among thorns' (St. Matthew
"xiii, 3 ff.) Now these three [kinds of] seed are those who are
"in the world. And as concerning the other seed of which He
"spake, saying that it fell on good ground, and gave fruit,
"some thirtyfold, and some sixtyfold, and some a hundred-
"fold, these are the grades of monks, for the seed which
"yielded fruit thirtyfold is the beginners, and that which
"yielded sixtyfold is the half-perfect, and that which yielded
"one hundredfold is the perfect."

611. The brethren said, "And supposing a man in the world
"conducteth himself in a wholly perfect manner, and accord-
"ing to what is right, is not his labour equal unto that of a
"beginner?" The old man said, "No."

612. The brethren said, "Why [not]?" The old man said, "Although the monk is little and is a beginner, he is still "more excellent than the man in the world who keepeth every "just [demand] of righteousness."

613. "Why did Abbâ Anthony say unto Paule, his disciple, "'Go and dwell in silence that thou mayest receive the temp- "'tations of devils?'" The old man said, "Because the per- "fection of the monk ariseth from spiritual conduct, and "spiritual conduct is acquired by the conduct of the heart, "and purity of heart ariseth from the conduct of the mind, and "the conduct of the mind from prayer which is unceasing, and "from strife with devils; but unceasing prayer, and the con- "tendings with devils, both in the thoughts and in visions, have "no opportunity for existence without silence and solitariness."

614. The brethren said, "What is the meaning of that which "Paphnutius and James the Lame said to Mâr Evagrius, "'Every lapse which taketh place through the tongue, or "'through lust, or through an action, or through the whole "'body, is in proportion to the measure of pride which a man "'possesseth'? Now what is the lapse which cometh through "lust? And what is the lapse which cometh through an action? "And what is the lapse which cometh through the whole body? "Enlighten us about these [various] kinds of lapses." The old man said, "The lapse through lust is the fall which taketh "place inwardly through pride, even as the blessed Maca- "rius said, 'Thou shalt not be lifted up in thy heart and in "'thy mind through the knowledge of the Scriptures, lest "'thou fall into a spirit of blasphemy in thy mind.' And the "lapse through the tongue resembleth that into which one of "the monks once fell through his pride, and he reviled the "holy man Evagrius and the fathers who were in the desert "of Scete. And the lapse through an action resembleth that "into which another monk fell when he became lascivious and "abominable; and the lapse through the whole body resem- "bleth that when, through his pride, one of the brethren was "abandoned to the hands of thieves, and they burned him "with fire."

615. The brethren said:—Palladius said, "Once the blessed "man Diocles said, 'The mind which falleth from God is either "'delivered over to the devil of wrath, or to the devil of forni- "'cation.' And I said unto him, 'How is it possible for the "'human mind to be with God uninterruptedly?' And he said, "'In whatsoever work of the fear of God the soul [is engaged], "'provided that the soul hath due care, its mind is with God.' "What is the meaning of the action of which the old man "spake?"

The old man said, "He calleth [a man's] care concerning
"God's promises 'action of the fear of God,' wishing to say thus:
" —If thou art unable to bind thy thought continually in various
"ways to God, though thou thinkest about His Majesty, and
"His power, and His grace, and thou prayest to Him with-
"out ceasing and without wandering [in thy prayer, thy mind
"cannot be with Him]; but if thou reducest thine understand-
"ing by means of the constant labour of prayer and by the
"thought which is on God, and more particularly through the
"war with devils that [accompanieth] this work, bring down
"thy mind by degrees from the thought which is about God,
"and from prayer, and fetter it with the thought which is
"lower than this, and meditate on the promises of God,
"and think upon His commandments and the correction of
"thyself. And set not free thy mind from spiritual care, and do
"not make it wander and think the thought of possibility, but
"fetter thy mind to some thought of excellence, which will
"make it gain profit. And when it hath rested somewhat, then
"raise it up on high, and make it to labour in the thought
"which is of God, and in pure prayer which hath no wander-
"ing therein. For as the growth of the capacity of those who
"are as yet in the grade of bodily prayer and the reading [of
"the Scriptures] still existeth, even when they are exhausted
"by standing up, and by the singing of the Psalms, and they
"rest their bodies for a little by sitting down and by medita-
"tion upon the reading, and when they have rested their
"bodies and their mind hath become enlightened through the
"reading, they stand up for service and prayer, so also it is
"right for those who have arrived at a correct conduct of the
"mind, and who think continually about God, and who pray
"to Him without wandering, when they are exhausted by this
"severe labour, to bring down their minds from time to time,
"and to relieve it by means of thought concerning some pro-
"fitable subject which is less exalted than the thought about
"God. And this thought must take the place to them of read-
"ing, and they must meditate upon God's promises and com-
"mandments, and upon their straightness which is in God;
"and if some abominable thought knock [at the door of their
"minds] they must quickly make their minds to enter into
"prayer and into the thought which is upon God. And if there
"stir in their heart a thought of passion, as soon as they have
"refreshed themselves by means of thinking about some pro-
"fitable subject, they must make their mind to enter into the
"height of prayer, and they must pray without ceasing, and
"meditate upon God. And from this we know that when the
"soul meditateth with understanding upon some profitable

" subject, or upon some profitable action, its mind is with
" God, even as the blessed man Diocles said. Similarly, when-
" soever a monk thinketh about the passions of sin, or about
" deeds connected with the world, his mind is with Satan."

616. The brethren said, " Why is it that the Divine Light
" did not shine in the hearts of all the monks until a long time
" after they had been cleansed by labours and contests? And
" why is it that the light of grace did shine upon some men
" before they went forth from the world and came to the
" ascetic life, as it did in the heart of Abraham Kindônâyâ
" through the Divine revelation on the day of his feast, and
" straightway he left his feast, and went forth from the world?"
The old man said, " Whensoever this light riseth in its order
" in the hearts of men, according to what the fathers say, it
" cometh in this wise. First of all Divine Grace maketh a man
" hot with the love of God, and he hateth all the glories and
" honours of this world; and next he cometh in a state of
" poverty to this rule of life, and Divine Grace itself first giv-
" eth him the love of labours, and it maketh the things which
" are hard easy to him. And it protecteth him from the fierce
" attacks of the war of devils, so that they may not, whenso-
" ever they wish and will, assault him, but only according to
" his strength, and his capacity, and as is convenient for his
" growth. And thus after many labours and contests, his
" heart is purified with abundant humility, and he shineth
" with the light of grace, and he is held to be worthy to see
" Christ in a revelation of light. And the fathers also said,
" that in proportion as the monk himself travelleth along the
" path of ascetic excellences to meet our Lord by means of
" labours and contests, so doth our Lord advance to meet him
" with light until they meet each other, and then the monk
" remaineth in our Lord by means of labours, and our Lord
" remaineth in him by means of his light, even as Abbâ Isaiah
" said in his interpretation of that which our Lord said, ' Re-
" ' main in Me and I in you.' Thus thou seest, O my brother,
" that He wisheth us to remain in him first of all by the la-
" bours of righteousness, and then He will remain Himself in
" us in purity and in light. And the words, ' The monk travelleth
" ' along the path of ascetic excellences until he seeth Him
" ' and is illumined by Him,' explain the verse, ' My soul
" ' thirsteth for Thee, the Living God,'" *et cetera*.

617. The brethren said, " Why is it that though the holy fathers
" incite us continually to the labours of excellence, and to the
" contending against passions and devils, Abbâ Isidore re-
" strained Abbâ Moses the Ethiopian from works, and from
" contests with devils, saying, ' Rest thee, Moses, and quarrel

"'not with the devils, and seek not to make attacks upon
"'them, for there is a measure [i.e., moderation] in every-
"'thing'; doth this apply also to works and to the labours of
"the ascetic life?"

The old man said, "Because at the beginning Abbâ Moses
"was ignorant of the rule of the ascetic life, and because he
"was healthy of body, he worked overmuch, and he thought
"that he would be able to prevail mightily against devils by
"the multitude of his works alone, and that he would be able
"to vanquish them. Therefore, because the devils perceived
"his object, they attacked him more severely with frequent
"wars, both secretly and openly, but Abbâ Isidore, wishing
"to teach him the truth, and to make him to acquire humility,
"said unto him, 'Without the power of the Spirit which our
"'Lord gave us in baptism for the fulfilling of His command-
"'ments, the which is confirmed in us each day by the taking
"'of His Body and Blood, we cannot be purified from the
"'passions, and we cannot vanquish devils, and we cannot
"'perform the works of spiritual excellence'; thereupon Abbâ
"Moses learned these things, and his thoughts were humbled,
"and he partook of the Holy Mysteries, and the devils were
"conquered, and they reduced their war against him, and from
"that time forward he lived in rest, and knowledge, and peace.
"Many monks have imagined that their passions would be
"healed, and that they would acquire soundness of soul merely
"by their labours and strenuousness, and therefore they were
"abandoned by grace, and fell from the truth. For as he who
"is sick in his body cannot be healed without the physician
"and medicines, however much he may watch and fast during
"the time he is taking the medicine, so he who is sick in his
"soul through the passions of sin, without Christ, the Phy-
"sician of souls, and without the partaking of His Body and
"Blood, and the power which is hidden in His commandments,
"and the humility which is like unto His, cannot be healed of
"his passions, and cannot receive a perfect cure. Therefore,
"whosoever fighteth against the passions and the devils by
"the commandments of our Lord is healed of the sickness of
"the passions, and acquireth health of soul, and is delivered
"from the crafts of the devils."

618. The brethren said, "With what object did those two
"monks say to Abbâ Macarius, 'If thou art not able to be-
"'come a monk like us, sit in thy cell, and weep for thy sins,
"and thus thou shalt be like us?" The old man said, "Because
"they knew that, if a man was able to be a solitary in his
"body, and a dweller in silent contemplation, and a worker
"both in his soul and in his body, who made himself humble

"and who wept each day for his sins, and who cut off from
"himself all memories of every kind of passion and anxious
"thought, and who meditated only upon God and upon his
"own correct behaviour, such a man was a monk (*or* solitary)
"in very truth, even as the blessed Evagrius said, 'The monk
"'who is remote from the world is he who hath cut off from
"'himself all the motions of his passions, and hath fastened
"'unto God all the mind of his soul.'"

619. The brethren said, "Why is it that certain ot the
"Fathers were called Mĕshannayânê [i.e., men who trans-
"ferred themselves from one place to another], since they were
"recluses, and never departed from their cells?" The old man
said, "Because after much silent contemplation, and unceasing
"prayer, and watching of the mind, they were worthy to de-
"part from the earth in their minds, and to ascend unto heaven
"to Christ the King. And they did not do this on occasions
"only, but continually, for whensoever they wished, or when-
"soever they sang the Psalms, or prayed, or meditated upon
"God, straightway their mind was exalted to heaven, and
"stood before our Lord. But there were other [kinds of] 'Mĕ-
"'shannayânê,' that is to say, those who lived with wild
"beasts in the deserts, such as Abbâ Bessarion, and others
"who were like unto him."

620. The brethren said, "What is [the meaning] of the fact
"that when one of the monks saw a brother in the mountain
"he fled from him, and was unable to bear the smell of the
"children of men?" The old man said, "The monk fled be-
"cause he saw that the brother was carrying silver. And when
"the brother saw that the monk fled, he cast off his garments
"and pursued him. And when the monk saw that he had cast
"off his garments, he waited for him, and welcomed him
"gladly, saying, 'Since thou hast cast off the matter which is
"'of this world I have waited for thee. I was not able to bear
"'[the sight thereof] because I myself am naked.' I looked be-
"yond my rule of life and saw that he was carrying a burden
"upon his shoulder like a man who was in the world."

621. The brethren said, "Why did the monk not permit that
"brother who came to him to dwell in the cave by his side,
"but did say unto him, 'Thou art not able to bear up against
"'the attack of devils?'" The old man said, "Because he knew
"his manner of life and works, and also that he possessed not
"the labours and the strenuousness which were sufficient to
"make him strong to resist the fierce assault of the savage
"nature of the devils which make war against the monks. For
"according to the labour of every man, and according to his
"striving, and his rule of life and strenuousness, and accord-

" ing as he is able to bear, so much the greater are the fero-
" city, and the wickedness, and the bitterness, and the craftiness
" of the devils who make war against him. Similarly, when
" one of the brethren entreated Abbâ Apellen to allow him to
" live with him in the desert, he said unto him, 'Thou art not
" ' able to bear the temptation of the devils.' Finally, when
" the brother urged him [to let him do so], he commanded him
" to dwell in a cave by his side. And the devils came against
" him in the night and sought to strangle him, until Abbâ
" Apellen came, and surrounded the cave with the sign of the
" Cross, after which the brother was able to live in the cave.
" For not all monks are able to fight against the devils, but
" only such as are perfect and humble."

622. Why is it that the two Romans who went to Abbâ
Macarius, did not, during the whole period of three years
which they lived [near him] come to him and ask him, or any
other aged man, questions about the thoughts? The old man
said, "Because the elder brother was exceedingly wise, and
" perfect and humble. Had he gone to Abbâ Macarius, or to
" one of the other old men, his perfection would have been
" revealed, and he would have [received] praise throughout
" Scete from the Fathers, who would have wondered, saying,
" ' How is it that a young man hath become perfect in three
" ' years'? It is, however, not right for us to make ourselves
" like unto these two brethren, and to neglect the doctrine of
" the old men. As for the two brethren, the elder was perfect,
" and the younger was humble, and learned from him."

623. The brethren said, "The history of the triumphs of
" Bessarion saith that during all the days of his life he dwelt in
" waste places, and in the desert and in the mountains, and
" among the rocks. Once having come to a certain monastery,
" he stood up by the door like a wandering beggar, and then
" sat down weeping and crying out, even as one who had been
" rescued from a storm. And when the brethren entreated him
" to go in and rest with them, he said, 'Before I find the posses-
" ' sions of my house which I have lost I cannot endure being
" ' under a roof; for thieves fell upon me on the sea, and a
" ' storm reared itself up against me, and I have been robbed
" ' of the riches which I once possessed, and from being a man
" ' of high estate I am become of no account.' Now what were
" the riches which [he inherited] from his parents and lost?
" And what does this [story] mean? Who are parents? What
" does he refer to by the words 'sea, and storms, and waves'?
" Who were the thieves? Are these words spoken of himself or
" of the other persons? The old man said, "These things are
" said of all the monks who are still striving and contending

" against passions and devils, and who are lacking at the pre-
" sent time purity of heart, and fruits of the spirit, and visions
" of our Lord, and they are not spoken of men who are perfect
" as he was. The word 'sea' he applieth to the sea of the mind
" whereon the monk saileth with works of spiritual excellence,
" wherefrom he entereth the haven of impassibility, even as
" the blessed Macarius saith, 'He who wisheth to cleave the
" 'sea of the mind, maketh himself longsuffering.' And he
" calleth temptations 'storms,' and the passions 'waves,' and
" the 'thieves' are devils, and his 'parents' are the Father, and
" the Son, and the Holy Ghost, One God, in Whose image and
" likeness we are made, even as our Creator said, 'Come, let
" 'us make man in our image and likeness,' and also as
" 'our Lord said, ' Be ye like unto your Father, Who is in
" 'heaven.' And He calleth the spiritual excellences, which
" contain likenesses of the similitude of our Father, Who is
" in heaven, and which make us heirs of God, and sons of
" the inheritance of Jesus Christ, by the name of 'riches and
" 'possessions of his parents,' and these are faith, and hope,
" and the love of God and man, and joy, and rest, and peace,
" and graciousness, and pleasantness, and lowliness, and hu-
" mility, and longsuffering, and patient endurance, and in-
" tegrity, and simplicity, and purity, and mercy, and cleanness
" of heart, and the holy light of the mind, and pure prayer,
" and the divine light which riseth on the heart at the hour
" of prayer, and spiritual prayer, and Divine knowledge, and
" the visions and revelations of our Lord. These are the
" possessions of the soul, some of which it acquireth naturally,
" and some by Divine Grace; now those which it acquireth
" naturally are they which the Creator sowed in its nature at
" the beginning of its creation, and those which it acquireth
" by Divine Grace are they which are bestowed upon it by the
" baptism in Christ. And these possessions are lost to a man
" through pleasures, and honours, and lusts, and benefits, but
" they are found and acquired, and the soul waxeth rich in
" them, through tribulations, and revilings, and oppression,
" and hardships. Now although Abbâ Bessarion, and men who
" were as perfect as he was, possessed these things, other
" men lack them and are strangers unto them. [And as re-
" gards the words] ' He once came to a certain monastery,
" 'and sat down outside the door like a wandering beggar,'
" [they mean that] he saw clearly with the secret eye of the mind
" that the greater number of the monks were destitute of this
" spiritual possession, and of the spiritual excellences and gifts
" which have been already mentioned. And being incited there,
" to by the law of affection and of brotherly love, he cried out

" and wept on their behalf, as if it had been on his own, and
" he made supplication to the lovingkindness of God that He
" would make them worthy of the riches of His love, and of
" the possession of His Grace."

624. The brethren said, "What are the nine spiritual excel-
"lences which that holy man possessed, and what did he
"lack?" The old man said, "Although they are not written
"down I think that they were as follows: 1. Voluntary poverty.
"2. Abstinence, 3. Constant evening fasting. 4. Vigil. 5. The
"recital of the whole Book of the Psalms seven times during
"the night and day. 6. The reading of the Holy Books be-
"tween times. 7. Lowliness. 8. Humility. 9. Love of man.
"These are the nine spiritual excellences which he possessed,
"and by means of them he vanquished all passions. By poverty
"he overcame the love of money. By abstinence he conquered
"unbridled appetite and gluttony. By fasting he overcame the
"passion of the love of the belly. By vigil he vanquished
"sleep. By the recital of the Psalms he did away idleness. By
"reading he kept away the converse of evil. By lowliness he
"dispelled wrath and anger. By humility he overcame vain-
"glory and pride. By love of man he conquered hatred, and
"spite, and enmity. Now the spiritual excellence which he
"lacked, and which is the tenth, was the constant fervour of
"the love of God, which is in our Lord Jesus Christ, and this
"can [only] be gathered together, and stablished and ac-
"quired by the secret prayer of the mind, which is unceasing
"and wandereth not, and by the strict and constant suppres-
"sion of the thoughts of the passions, and the incitements of
"devils, when they first begin to bestir themselves in the
"heart. And because among all the works of ascetic excellence
"there is none more difficult [to do] than this, for, even as
"the blessed Macarius said, ' All the fightings and fierce, and
"'crafty, and evil temptations of the devils are set in array
"'against it,' the holy man is not able easily to become per-
"fect in the love of Christ, which is acquired by the concen-
"tration of the mind and by deep thought about God. There-
"fore the blessed Evagrius said, 'If thou canst overcome the
"'wandering of the thoughts, it is the end of all ends; and if
"'thou canst make deep thought about God have dominion
"'in thee, thou canst overcome all passions, and thou shalt
"'be worthy of the perfection of the love of Christ.' By the
"love of man and by the other virtues a monk may, by the
"help of God, vanquish all the passions; but by the love of
"Christ he shall conquer the evil passion of the love of the
"soul, which is the first of all the passions, and which em-
"braceth them all, even as Saint Evagrius said, 'The first of

" 'all the passions is the thought of the love of the soul, and
" 'after it come the following eight.' And again he said, 'Con-
" 'quer the strife of the love of the soul which is in thy bosom,
" 'by that which is towards God.' For until the monk is
" worthy of this love, he is unable to acquire exact consola-
" tion from the remainder of the labours of the other spiritual
" excellences, even though it be that he obtaineth assistance
" from them, as Abbâ Isaiah said, 'Although the children of
" 'Leah were a help to Jacob, yet he loved Joseph most of all,
" 'and when Joseph was born, he wished to leave Laban and
" 'go to his parents,' that is to say, When a monk hath be-
" come worthy, and hath acquired the perfect love of Christ,
" which is stablished by silent contemplation, and the power
" to pray without ceasing, and his soul is at all times rejoicing
" and exulting with gladness, he will not be content to remain
" in this life; but each and every day he will be desiring
" eagerly and longing to depart from the body, and to be with
" our Lord in Paradise, which is the habitation of the spirits
" of just men who have become perfect, and the holy country
" which is exalted above the passions, and devils, and the
" striving of those who cultivate the virtues until the revela-
" tion of our Lord Jesus, Who loveth to make perfect a man
" with the never-ending happiness of His love in a glorious
" kingdom."

625. The brethren said, "Explain to us the course of life
" and labour of the old man [who made] baskets, [and dropped]
" small stones in them." The old man said, "The course of
" life of that old man was one which was of the mind, and it
" was stern, and excellent, and it swiftly brought the monk
" unto purity of heart. And as concerning that which he said,
" 'I set two baskets, one on my right hand and one on my
" 'left,' etc. it doth not [mean] that he sat the whole day with
" his baskets round him, but that his two baskets were set in
" two places. And he himself was occupied with service and
" prayer, and with his toil, and for every thought, good or
" bad, which entered his mind he cast a pebble [into the
" baskets], that is to say, the labour is very severe for the
" man for a certain time at the beginning, because the devils
" are envious at the purity of heart which is acquired by him,
" and therefore they afflicted this old man also for a long time
" with the multitude of evil thoughts which were stirring in
" him, even as he said, 'Many days I have eaten nothing, be-
" 'cause the good thoughts did not outnumber the bad ones.'
" Now he used to afflict his body with the labour of much
" fasting, so that he might do away the evil thoughts, because
" it is not the soul only which feeleth the labours of the body,

"its counterpart through its union with it, but also those
"devils which wage war against the soul, and they feel the
"labours of the body more than doth the soul. For immediately
"the devils see the monk afflicting his body with labours,
"they become afraid, and stagger about, because they are
"more tormented by the labours than is the man who is
"engaged in them. Therefore the blessed Evagrius, when the
"demon of fornication assailed him, stripped off his tunic and
"stood the whole night long, in the season of winter, under
"the open sky, and by these means he made the demon to
"suffer pain, and he fled from him. And again, when the
"demon of blasphemy attacked him, he stood naked under
"the open sky, in the season of winter, for forty days. And
"because the thought of gluttony stirred in the heart of Abbâ
"Zeno, and made him to eat a cucumber by stealth, he cruci-
"fied his soul in the sun, during the season of summer for five
"days. In this wise the holy men were afflicting themselves
"with labours and tribulations, and when the devils were
"stirring up in them the thoughts of sin, the demons were
"afflicted and tortured far more than they thereby. Now the
"demons were afflicted and tormented by the labours of the
"patient endurance of the monks not only in their minds but
"in their persons, through the operation of the holy angels,
"and by the command of God, even as, on one occasion, one
"of the devils was tortured the whole night in the cell of those
"two brethren who were brothers naturally, when he wished
"to separate them from each other. For when the younger
"brother lighted a lamp the devil threw down the candlestick,
"and extinguished the light, whereupon the [elder] brother
"smote him [on] the cheek; and the other brother expressed
"his contrition, and said, 'My brother, have patience, and I
"'will light the lamp [again].' And when God saw the patient
"endurance and humility of the young man, He commanded
"His angel, and he fettered the devil the whole night long in
"their cell; and the devil was tormented therein until the
"morning because of that [blow on] the cheek which he made
"the one brother to suffer from the other through his wicked
"agency; and that wicked devil was fettered and tortured the
"whole night long. And the devils are tortured not only when
"we afflict our bodies with labours, in order that we may not
"consent to the will of devils, but also when they stir up in
"us evil thoughts; if we constrain ourselves a little, and cast
"them from us, at the same time calling our Lord to our
"assistance, straightway the holy angels which cleave unto
"us will constrain the demons, and will drive them away from
"us, and we shall be full of light, and of fervour, and of glad-

" ness. Even as one of the demons said to Abbâ Pachomius,
" 'A certain monk, against whom I wage war, is very strenu-
" 'ous, and whensoever I draw nigh unto him to sow evil
" 'thoughts in him, he betaketh himself to prayer, and I,
" 'though burning with fire, have to depart from his presence
" 'blazing(?) even like iron which hath been thoroughly well
" '[heated] in the fire.' Now monks are, at the beginning [of
" their career] afflicted for a long time, not only by the stir-
" ring up of the evil thoughts themselves, but also by their
" tarrying in the heart; but after a known time a man receiveth
" strength from our Lord, through their tarrying, and also
" after a known time their motion is restrained, and then the
" monk also hath rest from strivings, and he is held to be
" worthy of purity of heart. For at the beginning of the striv-
" ings the devils stir up evil thoughts in the heart mightily;
" sometimes, however, these are destroyed through prayer at
" the very beginning of their movement, and sometimes they
" remain. And afterwards the mind becometh strong against
" them, and doth not permit them to tarry altogether in the
" heart, but it is as yet unable to restrain their violent move-
" ment, and the [tribulation which they cause], even as one of
" the old men said, 'I carried on a strife for twenty years in
" 'order that an evil thought might not enter my heart, and
" 'until the ninth hour I used to see Satan with his bow drawn
" 'to shoot an arrow into my heart. And when he found no
" 'opportunity of doing this, he would become dejected and go
" 'away ashamed each day.' Now the old man [of whom we
" first spake] held fast to his rule in respect of the baskets, and
" though he was afflicted for a long time by the motion of evil
" thoughts, and sometimes even by their tarrying in his heart,
" finally he received power over their tarrying only, for their
" rising up remained for a considerable time. And having
" laboured in striving for twenty years against the motion of
" the thoughts, finally he became strong [enough to resist
" them], and he overcame them. And the devils fled from him,
" and he arrived at a state of purity, and at the haven of im-
" passibility, and he was held to be worthy of revelations."

626. The brethren said, "If the holy men themselves afflict
" themselves with labours of tribulation because of the tarrying
" of the evil thoughts which bestir themselves in them, and if
" they sin against God though not consenting to them, why
" should we toil against the motion of the devils? For behold,
" even as the blessed Evagrius said, 'Whether they fight
" 'against us or not the matter is not in our hands.'" The old
man said, "The perfection of the monks ariseth from a spiritual
" rule of life, and a spiritual rule of life cometh from purity of

"heart, and purity of heart from divine vision; 'Blessed are
"'those who are pure in heart, for they shall see God.' When,
"therefore, a monk laboureth, and afflicteth himself because
"of the motion of evil thoughts, in order to prevent their re-
"maining for a long time in his heart, and when after a con-
"siderable time his heart becometh pure, there remaineth
"disgust only therein, and it vexeth the mind of the monk,
"and preventeth his ascent to God, and cutteth off his journey-
"ing to Him, and doth not allow him to enjoy the vision of
"glory. Now when a monk worketh for a considerable time
"because of the motion of evil thoughts [in him], God hath
"compassion upon his trouble, and not only doth his heart
"become cleansed, and his soul pure from every thought of
"evil, but he is also held to be worthy of the sight of our Lord
"in a revelation of light, and henceforth, the devils never
"again dare to stir up evil thoughts in the heart of him that
"hath been esteemed worthy of this great thing. And should
"it happen that they dare so to do, they suffer pain and burn
"even as he suffereth who is hot, and who kicketh away with
"his feet the piercing goads of iron which glow with heat in
"the fire. During the interval between the beginning of the
"strife against evil thoughts and [the attainment of] purity of
"heart, the devils sometimes vex the monk, and sometimes
"are vexed by him, even as the blessed Evagrius said, 'If
"'those who go down to the conflict afflict [others], they are
"'themselves afflicted'; so the devils afflict us, and they are
"also afflicted by us. They afflict us when we receive their evil
"thoughts, and they are afflicted by us when we, by means of
"prayer and wrath, hide (i.e., suppress) their thoughts. When,
"then, we labour and afflict ourselves for a considerable time
"in order that their thoughts may not tarry in us, we also
"afflict ourselves with labours and prayer so that they may not
"vex and hinder us by [their] violent motion, and afterwards
"power is given unto us by our Lord to lift ourselves up upon
"the necks of our enemies, and thenceforward our heart
"resteth and is at peace, not only from the perception of their
"thoughts, but from all the violence of their motion. And the
"peace and rest of God rule over our souls, and we see that
"there remaineth only the war which is manifest of the visions
"of devils until the time of death merely to terrify us, so that
"we may not be exalted [unduly] and destroy ourselves. And
"should it happen that the devils stir up thoughts in the heart
"of him that hath been made perfect, straightway they be-
"come extinguished, even as fire is extinguished when water
"falleth thereon."

627. The brethren said, "Why do the devils fear the labours

"of the monks, even as the Fathers say, 'If thou wishest the
"'devils to be afraid of thee, despise lusts'?'" The old man
said, "They are afraid because of three things. 1. First. Be-
"cause our Lord treated with contempt three kinds of pas-
"sions, wherein are included and contained all the various
"classes of passions, and these are they: The love of the belly,
"the love of money, and vainglory. By means of these the
"Calumniator fought against our Redeemer, and through His
"constancy in the wilderness, and silent contemplation, and fast-
"ing, and prayer, He overcame Satan; therefore all the monks
"who travel in His footsteps, and who by means of fasting, and
"prayer, and silent contemplation, hide away all the thoughts of
"sin, and who perform their labours in righteousness, our Lord
"maketh to conquer by His strength, and He vanquisheth the
"devils who are their enemies. And as the demons fear and
"tremble, not only by reason of the Crucifixion of Christ, but
"even at the sign of the Cross, wheresoever it be made ap-
"parent, whether it be depicted upon a garment, or whether
"it be made in the air, so also do the devils fear and tremble,
"not only by reason of the labours of our Lord and His con-
"stancy in the wilderness, but also at the existence of the
"monks in the wilderness, and at their silent contemplation,
"and their fasting, and their prayers, and their patient per-
"sistence in the performance of difficult labours, which take
"place for Christ's sake. Therefore on one occasion Abbâ
"Macarius said unto Palladius, 'Speak to the devils which
"'war against thee with disgust, and sluggishness, and
"'despair: if I had no labours of spiritual excellence, neverthe-
"'less for the sake of Christ I would guard these walls and
"'His Name would be sufficient for the redemption of my life.'
"2. Secondly. The war and contest which the devils [wage]
"against the monks possess both rule and system, and they
"are neither irregular nor unsystematic. And as when the
"devils stir up the monks by means of evil thoughts of sin,
"and the monks accept them, and consent to them, and let
"themselves be incited to commit sin thereby, straightway
"their souls become dark, and remote from God, and sorely
"afflicted, and ashamed, and guilty, and weak and miserable,
"so when their souls accept not these thoughts, and they do
"not consent to them, and do not allow themselves to be in-
"cited to sin thereby, but drive them away and cast them out
"as soon as ever they begin to have motion [in them], and
"call upon our Lord to help them, straightway all the former
"things which come against the monks, inasmuch as they do
"not acquiesce in their incitings, are hurled upon the demons
"with greatly intensified force, and they become ashamed,

" and tremble, and are destroyed, even as the blessed Mark
" said, 'As he who breaketh into a house which is not his
" 'own taketh to flight with fear and trembling as soon as he
" 'heareth the voice of the master of the house, so also doth
" ' Satan,' etc. 3. Thirdly. Because without labours and hu-
" mility we who are rational beings are unable to please God,
" and because without them neither men nor angels can en-
" joy His love and His blessings, therefore also the demons and
" devils, which live wholly in a state of pride and laxity, [can-
" not enjoy them]."

628. The brethren said, "Why is it that although the
" Fathers gave the admonition, 'Whensoever a demon ap-
" 'peareth unto a man in any form whatsoever, let that man
" 'make the sign of the Cross, and pray, and that similitude
" 'will disappear,' we see that on several occasions the devils
" still remain, and not in appearance only, but also in terrors,
" which remain for a long time, and in many cases in blows
" and stripes?" The old man said, "The holy Fathers gave the
" admonition because it would apply in the majority of cases.
" For since our Redeemer was crucified for us, and since He
" exposed to disgrace the Rulers and Dominions, which are
" evil demons, and put them to shame openly by His Person,
" even as it is written, from that time onwards, whensoever
" they have made themselves visible to the adorers of Christ
" in divers form [to do them] harm, as soon as a man hath
" made mention of the Name of Christ, and hath signed
" himself with the sign of the Cross, the devils have fled
" straightway, and their forms have disappeared. And this
" happeneth not only in the case of holy men, and perfect men,
" but also in respect of ordinary men who possess short-
" comings."

629. The brothers said, " Why was the blessed Martînyânâ,
" after all the great ascetic practices which he had acquired,
" and the gifts of the spirit which he had received, and after
" he had burned his fingers for the sake of the harlot, still
" afraid of the war of fornication, and why, having gone and
" dwelt in the island in the sea for thirty years, did he not
" stay [for] a season with that woman whom he had brought
" up from the sea, but cast himself in the sea being afraid of
" the contest?" The old man said, "Because the whole strength
" of the demon of fornication was discharged upon him, and
" he was, therefore, properly afraid. For those who have not
" with them this war in all its fierceness imagine that they
" have overcome it, but let them not boast themselves, and
" let them know the truth, that is to say, they have not van-
" quished the demon of fornication, and it is only that he hath

" not waged war against them with all his strength, because
" he hath not been permitted so to do, and he hath not been
" permitted to do so because of their feebleness and laxity.
" For the war of fornication which cometh upon a man only
" attacketh him in the degree which he is able to bear. For,
" behold, the great and famous fathers who endured this war
" in all its severity for a long time were always in a state of
" fear and trepidation, as was also Abbâ Arsenius, who was a
" man eighty years old; and when the noble lady came to him
" and said, ' Remember me in thy prayers,' he did not hesitate
" to say, 'I will pray to God that He may blot the remembrance
" ' of thee out of my heart.' And by means of this which he
" spake, he put to shame the demon of fornication, and shewed
" how great was the hatred for this unclean passion that war-
" reth against the holy men which he possessed."

[The story of Martînyânâ and the harlot is as follows:—
There was a certain monk who dwelt in the desert, and whose
name was Martînyânâ, and he laboured in great works, and
God wrought by his hands many mighty deeds, and he was
applauded by all men. Now when Satan, the Evil One, saw that
he was greatly applauded he became bitterly angry, and he
wished to distract and to withdraw him from his rule of life
and ascetic labours. One day Satan saw that many folk were
glorifying him, and he went and dwelt in a certain harlot, and
he sent her to the blessed man in order to make him fall. So
the harlot took her attire, and placed it in a bag, and went to
the holy man, and when she arrived at his abode it was evening; and she knocked at the door and said, " O Saint Mar-
" tînyânâ, open the door to me, so that the wild beasts may
not eat me." Now the holy man thought that she was a phantom, and he rose up and prayed, and since meanwhile she
ceased not to cry out, he rose up from his prayer, and opened
the door to her, and said to her, " Whence comest thou to
" me, O devil?" And she said, " [My] companions have for-
" saken me on the road, and I wandered about in the desert,
" and have arrived hither"; and he left her [there], and went
into the inner cell, and shut the door thereof between himself
and her. And after the old man had laid down to sleep the
harlot arrayed herself in her attire, and put on her ornaments,
and then sat down; and when the morning had come, the old
man went forth from his cell, and seeing her dressed he said to
her, "Whence art thou? What is thy business?" And she said,
" I am a daughter of people of high degree, and my parents
" are dead, and they have left me great wealth. I heard that thou
" wast a great man, and I have come to thee, and I beg thee
" to come to my house and take me to wife, and we will live

"on thy excellence." Then the old man said unto her, "How "can I forsake my labour and my rule of life, and take thee to "wife, and fall from my covenant?" And she said unto him, "What sin is there in it? Did not Adam and all the Fathers take "wives, and Noah, and Abraham, from whose seed Christ hath "risen?" Now by repeating these and suchlike things, she wellnigh succeeded in leading the holy man away captive, and he said unto her, "O woman, tarry a little so that I may see, lest "peradventure some one may come and see us." And having gone up to the roof to look, he woke up in his mind, and he made a flame of fire and stood up in it, and stayed in the fire until he burnt his toes; and when the harlot saw this, she fell down at his feet and wept, saying, "I have sinned against God "and thee," and she revealed unto him the whole truth, [saying], "I repent." And the holy man sent her to a nunnery, and he remained in his cell until his feet were healed of the burning of the fire. And after he was healed of his sickness, he rose up and went and dwelt in an island in the sea, where there were neither women nor men.]

630. The brethren said, "What is the meaning of that "which one of the old men said, 'If thou seest the wings of "'ravens flying about thou wilt also see the prayer of him "'that is oppressed in mind being exalted?'" The old man said, "As the ravens do not in the course of their flight mount "upwards to the height of heaven like the eagle, but fly close "to the surface of the ground and wheel about [seeking] for "their unclean food, so is the mind of the man who is not fer-"vent in the love of God, and who is continually in a state of "sluggishness and dejection, for when he standeth up for "service or for prayer, his thought will not be exalted to the "height of the love of Christ, but his mind will wander after "evil passions."

631. The brethren said, "An old man said, 'If thou seest a "'young man who, in his desire, ascendeth unto heaven, take "'hold of his foot and sweep him hence, for in this way thou "'wilt help him'; what is the meaning of the words, 'Who in "'his desire ascendeth unto heaven?'" The old man said, "This resembleth that which Isaiah spake, 'If the mind seeketh "'to ascend to the Cross before the feelings cease from feeble-"'ness, the wrath of God shall come upon him because he hath "'begun to do something which is beyond his capacity, with-"'out having first of all cured his feelings.' Now certain of the "beginners in the ascetic life are so silly and bold as to dare "to undertake things which are far above their capacity and "their strength; they do not wish to learn, and they will not "be persuaded by the commands of their Fathers, but, without

" having lived the proper period of time in the coenobium,
" they dare to enter the cell, even as it is written concerning
" one of the brethren in the Book of Paradise, for immediately
" he had received the garb of the monk, he went and shut him-
" self up as a solitary recluse, saying, 'I am a monk of the
" 'desert'; and the Fathers went and brought him out into the
" monastery [again]. There are others, too, who seek to shut
" themselves up for a week at a time, and it in no wise helpeth
" them; and there are others, the children of this world, who
" at the beginning of their careers imitate the exalted rule of life
" of the Fathers, and who imagine that they can imitate the
" rule of the mind, that is to say, of the spirit, when as yet
" they have not fulfilled the rule of the body. Therefore their
" lives and works are not open to the Fathers, and they will
" not receive correction, but they live according to their own
" desire, and they are delivered over into the hands of the
" devils who make a mock of them."

632. The brethren said, "One of the brethren asked Abbâ
" Poemen, saying, ' My body is feeble, and I cannot lead an
" ' ascetic life.' Abbâ Poemen said unto him, 'Canst thou lead
" ' the ascetic life in thy thought, and not permit it to go with
" ' deceit to thy neighbour?' Tell us how the feeble man was
" able to lead the ascetic life in his thoughts." The old man
said, " This question belongeth closely, both in order and
" meaning, to that which a certain brother asked Abbâ Poe-
" men, saying, ' My body is feeble, but my thoughts are not.'
" Now in the former case he spake having regard to those
" who were afraid that through pains and sickness they would
" become negligent of the labours of spiritual excellence, and,
" in a different manner, that they might fall into pains and
" sickness by way of punishment; in the latter case he spake
" having regard to those who had toiled for a very long time
" in the labours of self-denial, and who had finally become en-
" feebled, either through old age, or through pains and sick-
" nesses, and who were ceasing from ascetic labours. Now
" this is what Abbâ Poemen [meant] when he said, ' If thou art
" ' not now able, by reason of thy weakness, to toil in the la-
" ' bours of the body as thou didst formerly, toil in the labours
" ' of the soul, that is to say, the ruling of the thoughts,
" ' which is the ruling of the mind; if thou art unable to fast
" ' from meats, fast from evil thoughts; and if thou art no
" ' longer able, through the weakness of the body, to stand up
" ' and to recite as many Psalms as formerly, make thy mind
" ' to stand up before our Lord, and pray before Him vigi-
" ' lantly with the prayer which is secret and pure, and be
" ' tranquil, and humble, and pleasant, and good, and forgiv-

" ' ing, and merciful; and endure thy sickness and weakness
" ' with praise, and make no man to be sorry by thy tongue;
" ' and judge not, and blame not, and condemn not thy
" ' brother in thy heart. Now these excellences may be culti-
" ' vated in the soul with the labours of the mind, and not
" ' those of the body, and they are not impeded by the weak-
" 'ness of the body.' "

633. The brethren said, ' Why is it that the monks are
" obliged to go round about begging for the meat and rai-
" ment of which they have need, like those who are in the
" world, although our Lord promised them, saying, ' Seek ye
" 'first the kingdom of God and its righteousness, and that
" of which ye have need shall be given to you?'" (St. Matthew
vi, 33). The old man said, "This [saying] is a proof of the
" wisdom and grace of God towards those who are in the
" world, for, in the majority of cases, the righteousness of the
" children of this world consisteth of alms and compassion;
" but the children of light are righteous men and monks who,
" in their persons, and in their members, and in their thoughts,
" serve our Lord. And God hath made the monks to have
" need of the children of this world because of His love, so that
" they may care each for the other, and may pray each for the
" other, that is to say, the children of the world must care for
" the monks, and the monks must pray in love for them. And
" as the children of the world make the monks associates with
" them in the corporeal things of the world, the monks must
" make the children of the world to be associates with them
" in the things of heaven, for our Lord spake to the children
" of the world, saying, ' Make ye to yourselves friends of this
" ' mammon of iniquity, so that when they have become per-
" ' fect they may receive you into their tabernacles which are
" ' for ever ' " (St. Luke xvi, 9).

634. The brethren said, "What is the difference between
" [the words], 'I will dwell in you,' and 'I will walk in you,'
" which God spake concerning the righteous? And what is the
" meaning of 'dwelling,' and 'walking'?" The old man said,
" God dwelleth in the saints through the constant remembrance
" with which they remember Him, as they marvel at Him, and
" His works; but He walketh in them by means of His visions
" and revelations [which He sendeth] upon them as they mar-
" vel at His majesty, and rejoice continually in His love."

635. The brethren said, "With how many, and with what
" names is the meditation upon God called?" The old man said,
"Its names are six, and they are as follows:—1. Hope in God.
" 2. The state of being bound to our Lord. 3. Continuance
" with God. 4. Persistence in all the good works of God.

" 5 Holding fast to God. 6. Dependence upon God. Hope in God
"[meaneth], fix ye your gaze upon Him, and hope in Him, that
"is to say, meditate ye upon Him. Being tied to our Lord
"[meaneth] that we should be bound to our Lord, and should
"fast and pray, until the old man cometh to an end, both
"without and within. Continuance with God is the state of
"being gratified through Him. Persistence [meaneth] that
"we should possess persistence in the Lord in all the good
"works of God. Holding fast to God [meaneth], 'Cut off from
" 'thyself all cares which are not of Him, and let thy mind
" 'fasten its gaze upon God only.' Dependence upon God [mean-
"eth], 'Hang thyself upon God,' to Whom be glory (*or* praise)!
"Amen."

636. The brethren said, "An old man was asked a question by
"one of the brethren, who spake thus:— 'If I am in a state of
" 'admiration of God, and in purity of soul, and the time of
" 'prayer arriveth, ought I to come to prayer or not?'" And the
old man said, "'What man who possesseth riches will make
" 'himself poor?' Explain to us the meaning of the words of
"the holy man." The old man said, "The holy man calleth
" 'admiration of God and purity [of soul]' that to which the
"blessed Mark gave the name 'meditation upon God' and
" ' atmosphere of freedom.' There are some brethren whose
"hearts become pure after labours and great strivings, and
"they become worthy of pure prayer, and their hearts also be-
"come illumined from time to time by the light of Divine Grace,
"and they attain to the meditation which is on God, and to
"the spiritual understandings which are superior to custom.
"The Fathers would not permit the men who attained to this
"capacity, when they were standing in the purity of soul
"of this nature, and in the atmosphere which was free from
"trouble, and when the beater struck the board, and the season
"for prayer arrived, to leave this enjoyable meditation, and to
"stand up and sing the Psalms, but they [allowed] them to remain
"therein until it had come to an end. For a man to sing the Psalms
' and to perform the service could always be found, but such
"meditation and such purity of the understanding, and the
"atmosphere of freedom could not at all times be acquired,
"and a man is neither able nor hath the power to attain to this
"state whensoever he pleaseth, for it is a gift from heaven which
"is given by our Lord from time to time to him that is worthy
"thereof. For this reason one of the Fathers gave the follow-
"ing commandment:—If a man enjoyeth such meditation
"whilst he be standing up at the service, let him not interrupt
"it until it cometh to an end, for such meditation filleth the
"place of the service of the Psalms. See then that thou drivest

"not away from thee the gift of God, and let thy subservience
"(*or* submission) to the same stand firm; but it is right to know
"that certain brethren have not as yet attained to meditation
"of this kind. They have thought that these words were
"spoken for every man and for men of every kind of capacity,
"and although their minds have been illumined somewhat by
"the Psalms and prayers, they have relaxed the fulfilment of
"the canon of their service, wherein are placed their consola-
"tion, and their wages, and their profit, and have occupied
"themselves [with the meditation], but on several occasions
"they have been interrupted in the meditation which hath
"come to them by the devils. It is, therefore, not right for the
"brethren who are beginners in the ascetic life to do this, but
"they should commit their life and works and meditation wholly
"to God, and if it should happen that this meditation cometh to
"them, let them reveal the matter to one of the old men who
"is acquainted with such things, so that the demons may not
"lead them astray and work their destruction."

637. The brethren said, "By what means did the Fathers
"sing the Psalms of the Holy Spirit without wandering [of
"mind]?" The old man said, "First of all they accustomed
"themselves whensoever they stood up to sing the service in
"their cells to labour with great care to collect their minds
"from wandering, and to understand the meaning of the
"Psalms, and they took care never to let one word (*or* verse)
"escape them without their knowing the meaning thereof, not
"as a mere matter of history, like the interpreters, and not after
"the manner of the translator, like Basil and John [Chrysos-
"tom], but spiritually, according to the interpretation of the
"Fathers, that is to say, they applied all the Psalms to their
"own lives and works, and to their passions, and to their
"spiritual life, and to the wars which the devils waged against
"them. Each man did thus according to his capacity, whether
"he was engaged in a rule of life for the training of the body,
"or of the soul, or of the spirit, even as it is written, 'Blessed
"'are the people who know Thy praises, O Lord,' that is to
"say, blessed is the monk who, whilst glorifying Thee with
"praise, collecteth his mind from wandering, and understand-
"eth clearly the knowledge and meaning of the Psalms of
"the spirit, even as it is written, 'Sing ye unto God with
"'praise, sing ye unto our King.' When then a man singeth
"the service in this manner, and payeth attention to the mean-
"ing of the verse, he acquireth daily the faculty of singing a
"song mingled with the meditation of God and with the gaze
"[which is fixed] upon Him. And after the time in which he
"hath arrived at the spiritual rule of life, immediately a monk

"hath begun to sing the Psalms, though one or two sections
"of them become too great for him, he is permitted to sing
"them with understanding and with the meditation which is
"on God, and he refraineth from the customary Psalms, and
"he singeth a song which is superior [to that of] body and
"flesh, and which is like unto that of angels, even as the
"Fathers say."

638. The brethren said, "By means of what thoughts of
"excellence may the children of this world not be offended by
"the monks, when they see or hear concerning the stumblings
"(*or* lapses) which come upon them through the frailty of
"[their] nature, and from the wars of the devils?" The old
man said, "When they consider and look upon the monks as
"frail men, who are clothed with a body which is full of pas-
"sions, and who although they are monks are striving to imi-
"tate the life and deeds of angels, yet owing to the weakness
"of their bodies, and the inclination of their souls, and the
"need which cleaveth unto them, and the strivings of the devils
"against them, the children of the world will see that it is quite
"impossible that the monks should not be snared, involun-
"tarily, by certain weaknesses. For behold, some of the per-
"fect men [mentioned] in the Old and New Testaments were
"caught in snares against their will, through the frailty of
"their nature and the war of the devils, as, for example, the
"blessed and perfect men Moses, and Aaron, and David, and
"Samson, and Hezekiah, and Peter and Paul."

639. The brethren said, "Why do the monks who have led
"a life of hard labour become in their old age silly, and simple,
"and act in a foolish way like children and drunken men?"
The old man said, "Because all the ascetic excellences which
"God hath placed in the nature of their souls, and which ap-
"pear in them from their youth up, perish through the relax-
"ing of the will, and through the love of the body, and the
"war of the devils, and finally through labours and contend-
"ings. Sometimes they receive them from our Lord as gifts,
"even as it is written, 'Except ye turn, and become as little
"'children, ye shall not enter the kingdom of God,' even as
"our Lord said."

640. The brethren said, "What should be the beginning of
"the fight against sin of the man who hath cast all impedi-
"ments out of his soul, and who hath entered the arena, and
"where should he begin the contest?" The old man said, "It
"is well known unto every man that in all the contests against
"sin and its lusts the labour of fasting is the first thing [to
"undertake], and it is so especially in the case of him that
"fighteth against the sin which is within him; and the sign of

" the enmity against sin and its lusts becometh apparent in
" those who go down to this invisible conflict when they begin
" to fast. And next cometh the rising up in the night, and
" whosoever loveth the occupation of fasting all the days of
" his life is a friend of chastity. For as the pleasure of the
" belly, and the laxity caused by the sleep which inciteth to a
" polluted bed, are the head and chief of all the sins which are
" in the world, and all the abominations thereof, so fasting,
" and strict vigil in the fear of God, with the crucifying of the
" body throughout the night against the pleasures of sleep, are
" the foundation of the holy path of God, and of all the spiri-
" tual excellences. For fasting is the strengthener of all spiritual
" excellences, it is the beginning and end of the strife, and it
" is the foremost of all virtues; and as the enjoyment of the
" light cleaveth closely to the eyes which are healthy, so doth
" the desire for prayer cleave closely to the fasting [which is
" observed] with discernment. For as soon as a man hath begun
" to fast, he desireth greatly to converse with God in his mind.
" The body which is fasting cannot continue to lie on [its] bed
" the whole night, for fasting naturally inciteth to wakeful-
" ness towards God, not only by day, but also by night; for
" the empty body is not fatigued overmuch by its conflict with
" sleep, even though it be weak in the senses thereof, for its
" mind is towards God in supplication, and it is better for it to
" cease from labour through weakness than from the weights
" of meats. As long as the seals of fasting lie upon the mouth
" of man, his thoughts meditate upon repentance, and his
" heart maketh prayers to arise; and mildness lieth upon his
" countenance, and abominable motions are remote from him,
" and rejoicing never, in the smallest degree, appeareth in his
" forehead, for he is a foe of lusts and of unprofitable converse.
" The man who fasted regularly and with understanding, and
" whom abominable lust brought into subjection hath never
" been seen, for fasting is the abode of all spiritual excellences,
" and he who holdeth it in contempt disturbeth them all. Now,
" the first commandment which God laid down for our nature
" at the beginning gave [Adam] warning concerning the eat-
" ing of food, and the head of our race fell through eating,
" therefore, at the point where the first corruption took place
" [in asceticism], must begin the building of the fear of God,
" when they lay down the first course for the observance of the
" law. And moreover when our Lord shewed Himself at the
" Jordan He also began at this point, for after He was baptized
" the Spirit took Him out into the wilderness, and He fasted
" for forty days and forty nights; and all those who travel in
" His footsteps lay the beginning of their strife on this founda-

" tion. For who shall treat with contempt, or hold lightly the
" armour which hath been forged by God? If He Who laid down
" the law fasted, who is there among those who would keep
" the law that hath not need thereof? Immediately this armour
" appeareth on a man straightway terror falleth upon the
" thoughts of the chief of the rebellion, that is, Satan; and his
" power is shattered at the sight of the arms which our Cap-
" tain of the host hath placed in our hands, for as soon as he
" seeth the might of this armour on a man he knoweth at
" once that he is ready for the contest. What armour is there
" which is as strong or which giveth such boldness in the
" fight against evil spirits as hunger for the sake of Christ?
" For in proportion as a man is harried and brought low in his
" body, at the time when the phalanx of Satan surroundeth
" him, doth his heart support itself with confidence, and he
" who treateth this with contempt is lax and is a coward in
" respect of other spiritual triumphs, because he hath not upon
" him the armour whereby the divine athletes have gained the
" victory. And at the very beginning the sign of weakness
" appeareth in him, and he himself giveth the opportunity of
" defeat to his adversary, and since he goeth naked into the
" strife it is evident that he will emerge therefrom without
" victory, because he hath cast away from him the strength
" which would stir up in him the divine zeal; for his members
" are not clothed with the flame of hunger, that is to say,
" fasting. As merchants cannot without labour and trouble
" save up riches, so the righteous man without anguish and
" labour for the sake of righteousness cannot expect the crown
" and the reward."

641. The brethren said, "If a man attaineth unto purity of
" heart what is the sign thereof? And when will he know
" himself if the heart is coming to purity?" The old man said,
" When he seeth that all men are fair, and when no man ap-
" peareth to him to be unclean or polluted; whosoever is thus
" indeed standeth in purity. And if this be not the case, how
" can he fulfil the word of the Apostle which saith, 'When a
" 'man standeth wholly in purity, he will think that every man
" 'is better than he in heart and in truth,' unless it be that he
" attaineth to the state of him of whom it is said, 'He whose
" 'eyes are pure seeth not wickedness.'"

642. The brethren said, "What is purity? And to what
" length doth its limit extend?" The old man said, "In my
" opinion purity consisteth in oblivion of the various kinds of
" knowledge which are beyond nature, and which nature hath
" discovered in the world; and the limit thereof is that a man
" should be wholly free from them, so that he may arrive at

" the state of natural simplicity and integrity which he pos-
" sessed at first, and which somewhat resembleth that of a
" child, except in the case of small matters."

643. The brethren said, "Is it possible for a man to attain
" to this state?" The old man said, "Yea. Behold, one of the
" old men attained to this state to such a degree that he was
" in the habit of asking his disciple continually if he had eaten
" or not. And on one occasion one of the saints, who was a
" a very old man, became too innocent and simple, and attained
" to such a state of simplicity and purity that he did not even
" know how to keep watch upon himself so that he might
" partake of the Mysteries, or whether he had done so or not,
" until at length his disciples kept him in his cell, and took
" him that he might partake of the Mysteries, just as if he
" had been a child. Now although he was in this state as re-
" gards the things of this world, he was perfect in his soul."

644. The brethren said, "What are the [subjects of] medita-
" tion and conversation which it is meet for a man to have
" whilst he is living the life of the recluse and passing his time
" in silent contemplation, so that his understanding may not
" occupy itself with casual thoughts?" The old man said,
" Dost thou ask concerning meditation, what shall a man have
" wherewith to put to death the world in his cell? Hath the
" man whose soul is strenuous and watchful any need [to ask]
" the question as to what labour he shall occupy himself with
" when he is alone? What is there for the monk to occupy him-
" self with except weeping? If, then, the monk be unoccupied
" with weeping, and he be able to pay attention to [any] other
" thought, what is the meditation which hath died out of him?
" And if we come to silent meditation, we can also be constant
" in weeping, and therefore let us beseech our Lord most ear-
" nestly with the mind that He may grant this unto us."

645. The brethren said, "Since, then, a man is not sufficient
" for the constant exercise of this faculty, because of the frailty
" (*or* sickness) of his bodily nature, it is right that he should
" have something else besides this which shall be useful for
" the consolation of his mind, so that the passions may not
" attack him through the idleness of the understanding." The
old man said, "The passions cannot attack the soul of the
" monk, whose heart hath been cut off from the world by living
" a solitary ascetic life, unless he hath been negligent of the
" things which it is proper for him to do; and this is so especi-
" ally if he hath, besides the employment [of reading] the
" Scriptures, the helpful thoughts of the man who is occupied
" with spiritual excellence. And living alone and in silence will
" help this [result] greatly, and he will receive in his mind the

" hope of the world which is to come, and the glory which is
" laid up for the saints."

646. The brethren said, "One of the old men said, 'I have
" 'toiled for twenty years that I might see all men together
" '(i.e., alike).' How can a man attain to this measure, and
" when, and by what means? Give us a demonstration con-
" cerning this matter." The old man said, "It is only the per-
" fect men who attain to this measure, and according to what
" the Fathers say, without contemplation in silence, and prayer,
" and great conflicts, and humility, no man can attain thereto.
" And there is a similarity to this demonstration in the case of
" natural parents, for as they regard all their children in the
" same way, and as they love them all equally, and pity and
" spare all of them alike, even though there be among them
" great and small, and healthy and sick, and righteous and
" sinners, and good-looking and bad-looking, so the strenuous
" Fathers after the labours and the contests which they have
" passed through during long periods of time spent in silent
" and solitary retirement, regard all men, both the righteous
" and the sinners, in the same way, and they love them all
" alike and without distinction. And as God maketh the shadow
" to fall upon all men, both upon the righteous and upon sin-
" ners, even though he loveth the righteous for their righteous-
" ness, yet He sheweth most compassion upon the sinners. And
" the coming of our Lord was for the sake of sinners, for [saith
" He], ' I did not come to call the righteous,' &c."

647. The brethren said, "Why was it, when the brother, ac-
" cording to the body, of one of the Fathers who was living the
" life of a recluse, sent to him, when he was about to die, to
" come and see him, that he would not do so, and that the one
" brother died without seeing the other? And what is the
" meaning of the words which he spake, 'If I go forth and see
" 'him my heart will not be pure before God'?" The old man
said, "The holy man was living secluded in a cell, in a habi-
" tation of the brethren, and his brother according to the body
" was also living, like the other brethren in another cell, and
" when the latter became sick unto death, he wished to see his
" brother before he died. Now to the holy man, since he was
" keeping silence in respect of all the other brethren, it did not
" appear to be right to go forth to his brother according to the
" body, and not to go forth afterwards to his spiritual brethren,
" that is to say, to those who dwelt in the monastery with him.
" Had he gone forth to his brother according to the body at
" the season of his death, and had not gone forth to his brethren
" in the spirit, he would not have found freedom of speech with
" God at the season of prayer, but his mind would have passed

"judgement upon him, and his mind would have been dark-
"ened, as if he had held in contempt and treated his brethren
"in the spirit in a dishonourable fashion, and had done more
"honour to his brother according to the body than to them.
"This is the meaning of what he said, 'I cannot go forth, for
"if I do, my heart will not be pure before God.'"

648. The brethren said, "The sage said, 'Whosoever pos-
"'sesseth not the art of labouring, that is, either the things
"'which belong to the labour of the spirit, whereby he may
"'find consolation from God in his inner man in the spirit, or
"'the things which belong to the art of human labour, cannot
"'tarry long in his cell; whosoever doth not possess one or
"'other of these cannot tarry long in his cell.' Explain to us
"the words of the old man." The old man said, "The things
"which belong to the art of human labour are well known unto
"every man; but things which belong to labour of the spirit
"he calleth the following: fasting, vigil, the singing of psalms
"and hymns, the prayers which are said kneeling down, an-
"guish, weeping, tears, and other labours which are like unto
"these. And together with these [there must be the recital of]
"the offices for the seven hours [of the day and night], and
"the reading of the Holy Scriptures and of the [books of]
"doctrine of the old men, and these make the monk to acquire
"patient endurance, and the ability to live the ascetic life alone
"in a cell, and they produce for him joy and spiritual comfort.
"If he be a beginner in the ascetic life and strong, and he toil-
"eth in labours, he will acquire consolation; and if he be a
"feeble old man, or sick, he will labour in the labours of the
"mind, and will find joy. For as all the objects which are of
"gold are wrought by means of anvil, and a hammer, and a
"pair of tongs, so by means of the labour of the body in a
"place of silence and seclusion, and the striving of the mind,
"are wrought all the fruits of the spirit, which the Apostle
"said were love, joy, peace, faith, humility, graciousness,
"pleasantness, long-suffering and patient endurance."

649. The brethren said, "On one occasion, when the bre-
"thren were sitting down and asking questions about the
"thoughts, one of them said, 'It is not a great matter if a
"'man seeth thoughts afar off.' What did he want to say?
"Explain to us the words of the old men." The old man
said, "When the brethren drew nigh to the Fathers and asked
"them questions [wishing] to learn concerning the mode of
"action and thought in respect of the wars of the devils, the
"Fathers did not persuade those among them who appeared
"to possess subtlety of thought, and intelligence, and under-
"standing, and to hate the passions, and to be fervent in the

" spirit, to cast out from themselves straightway the thoughts
" of the passions whensoever they stirred in them, and to make
" them to depart foolishly, but they ordered them to tarry with
" them, and to examine carefully how they arose, and then to
" contend against them; for in proportion as they were trained
" in the knowledge of strivings and contendings against the
" passions and against devils they would benefit not them-
" selves only, but many other people also. And in this wise
" acted also Evagrius, that man of understanding, and Abbâ
" Poemen, and others who were like unto them. Therefore
" Abbâ Joseph said to Abbâ Poemen, ' When the passions rise
" ' up in thee, give unto and receive from them, and understand
" ' carefully their crafty nature, and train thyself to contend
" ' against them.' Now there are certain weak and foolish breth-
" ren whom in no way whatsoever doth it benefit to dally with
" the rise of the thoughts of the passions which are in the
" heart, on the contrary, it is far better for them, immediately
" they perceive the motions of the passions, to cast them forth
" from them by prayer, and with anger and hatred. Therefore,
" when several of the Fathers were gathered together and
" were discussing the conflicts of the thoughts, and whether it
" was right to dally with them because of knowledge [concern-
" ing them], or to suppress them by means of prayer through
" fear [of them], one of the Fathers said, ' Even to understand
" ' the thoughts afar off is a great and excellent work, but it
" ' is a far greater work, and one which maketh a man to ac-
" ' quire practice, for him to understand the thoughts, and to
" ' wage war against them. When he hath gained experience
" ' of their crafty character, then he will suppress them and
" ' make them to disappear by the power of prayer and hu-
" ' mility. Now the meaning of this question is this. When a
" ' man hath laboured in conflict and contest against the pas-
" ' sions for a long time in seclusion, by the grace of our Lord
" ' his heart becometh purified, and rest and peace reign in his
" ' soul, and he hath relief from tribulation, and he rejoiceth in
" ' God at all seasons, and the devils have no power henceforth
" ' to stir up evil thoughts in his soul, because his heart is
" ' filled with divine thoughts, and the understanding of spiri-
" ' tual things, and he is never without the mind which is in
" ' God, and the remembrance of His fear and mercy. And
" ' should the demons dare to stir up thoughts in him, they
" ' will not [succeed] in rousing those which cause anguish
" ' and which bring to naught spiritual excellences, but only
" ' those which are of an ordinary nature, and which impede
" ' the vision, even as Evagrius said.' "

650. The brethren said, " How is it possible for a man to live

" in such a way as to be pleasing to God?" The old man said,
" It is impossible for a monk to rise to the height of the love
" of God, unless he first of all regard with affection and love
" man, the image of God; for this is the end of all the com-
" mandments of our Lord Jesus Christ, even as He Himself
" said, ' If ye love Me, keep My commandments.'"

651. The brethren said, "An old man said, ' If there rise up
" ' in thy mind a thought about the need of the body, and thou
" ' castest it out once, and it cometh to thee a second time,
" ' and thou castest it out, should it come a third time, pay no
" ' regard to it, for it appertaineth to war'; explain to us
" these words." The old man said, "If whilst thou art in seclu-
" sion, and art engaged in spiritual labour, Satan, being envi-
" ous of thee, and wishing to drive thee out of the cell, or to
" impede thy spiritual progress, stir up in thee one of the
" thoughts which goad a man into sin, either to eat before the
" proper time, or to lie down and sleep, or to visit some one,
" or to do something else; and if he sheweth thee thy power
" of discretion [saying], ' It is unseemly for thee to do this
" ' thing'; or again, should some evil devil constrain thee, and
" hinder thee, and wishing to make thee to cease from thy la-
" bour, should mock and scoff at thee; then stand thou up
" quickly, and bestir thyself boldly, and bow thy knee before
" our Lord, and pray, and ask, and entreat for help, and
" mercy, and protection. For that brother who soaked palm
" fibres in water, and who sat down to plait ropes and mats,
" was engaged in a similar war, and a demon roused up in him
" the thought to go and visit one of the brethren; and he cast
" the thought from him twice, and thrice. Now finally, because
" he did not understand that the war was of the Evil One, who
" sought to stop [his work] and drive him out of his cell, he
" was overcome by the war, and he left the palm leaves soak-
" ing in the water, and ran and hurried out in great haste. At
" length the matter was revealed unto one of the holy men
" who was a neighbour of his, and he cried out to him, saying,
" ' Captive, Captive,' and made him to come back to his cell,
" and afterwards the devils cried out with a loud voice, saying,
" ' Ye have overcome us, O monks.' For the demons are so
" wicked, and they are so envious of the monks when they re-
" main constantly in seclusion for our Lord's sake, that on
" several occasions they have, in an irregular manner, driven
" them out of their cells, as if for a good object, but their ob-
" ject was not a good one."

652. The brethren said, "Why was it that Abbâ Ammon
" was not able to overcome the passion of wrath for fourteen
" years, although he said unto us, that he had entreated God,

"with anguish and tears, both by day and by night unceas-
"ingly, to give him the victory over it?" The old man said,
"That passion probably overcame him to an excessive degree
"through the natural constitution of his body, but it is quite
"certain that the passions and the devils waged war against
"him like a mighty man and a warrior. For the devils made
"war upon the Fathers with intense fierceness and violence,
"upon each man according to his capacity, and in proportion
"to their power to triumph, through long-suffering, that is to
"say, through patient and persistent endurance, the battle
"against them was protracted."

653. The brethren said, "Abbâ Dorotheus said, 'Our lack
"'of ability to distinguish between matters will permit us to
"'acquire great excellence in the virtues'; explain to us what
"the old man [intended] to say." The old man said, "He
"wished to say as follows:—'Because of our lack of ability to
"'distinguish between matters we do not make progress in
"'the virtues, and our heart is not quickly purified, and we
"'do not ascend to perfection, because we do not labour with
"'the knowledge and power of discernment which it is right
"'[for us to have]; but [we progress] painfully, and [only] for
"'the sake of vainglory, and as the result of chance circum-
"'stances, and without discretion. And, as it cometh, this re-
"'sembleth that which the blessed Evagrius spake, saying,
"'"As it is not the material foods themselves which nourish
"'"the body, but the power which is in them, so it is not
"'"matters themselves which make the soul to grow, but the
"'"power of discernment which [cometh] from them." And
"'he also said, "As the feeding, and health, and growth of
"'"the body do not come through the actual materials of our
"'"foods, for these are cast out of the body in the draught,
"'"but from the hidden power which is in them, so also the
"'"nourishment and the growth of the soul take place
"'"through the fear of God. And the healthy state thereof
"'"which ariseth through impassibility, and the perfection
"'"thereof which is in righteousness, do not exist through
"'"the labours of the body only, but from the deeds and acts
"'"which [are performed] with knowledge, that is to say,
"'"with a straight object, and from the action of the mind
"'"which hateth passions, and from the prayer which is joined
"'"to humility, and from the mind which is in God."'"

654. The brethren said, "Abbâ Arsenius said unto one of
"the brethren, 'Lead the ascetic life with all the strength that
"'thou hast, and the hidden labour which is within, and which
"'is performed for God's sake, shall vanquish thine external
"'passions'; to what doth he give the name of 'passions'?'

The old man said, "In this case Arsenius calleth the labours
"of the body 'passions.' For labours are also called by the
'name of 'passions,' because they constrain those who toil,
'and make them feel pain, even as Abbâ Macarius said,
"'Constrain thy soul with pains and labours of every kind in
"'ascetic excellence.' And this is what Abbâ Arsenius said to
"that brother, Labour with all thy might in the work of
"righteousness, and toil with the labours of the mind more
"than with all the various kinds of work of the body. For the
"labours of the body only incite and gratify the passions of
"the body, but the labours of the mind, that is to say, the
"thought which is in God, and prayer without ceasing, and
"the suppression of the thought[s] with humility, liberate [a
"man] from all the passions, and they vanquish devils, and
"purify the heart, and make perfect love, and make him
"worthy of the revelations of the spirit."

655. The brethren said, "What is the meaning of that which
"Abbâ Benjamin said, 'Had Moses not been gathering the
"'sheep into the fold he would not have seen Him that was
"'in the bush'?" The old man said, "What he said was
"this:—As the blessed Moses, who was held worthy of the
"vision in the bush, first gathered together the sheep which
"he was tending into one company lest, when going to see
"that wonderful sight, his mind should be perturbed through
"anxiety about the sheep which were [wandering] in the
"desert, so also is it with the monk, for if he wisheth and
"desireth the purity of heart which looketh upon God in the
"revelation of light, it is right that first of all he should aban-
"don every earthly possession, and his feelings, and his
"passions, and he should live in seclusion always, and should
"collect his mind and free it from all wandering and straying,
"and should have one object only to gaze upon, that is God.
"In this manner he will become worthy of purity of heart, and
"he will enjoy visions and revelations concerning Him."

656. The brethren said, "Hieronymus said that the blessed
"Evagrius commanded the brethren who were with him not
"to drink their fill of water, and said, 'There are always
"'demons in the places wherein there is water'; what opinion
"is this?" The old man said, "The blessed Evagrius inter-
"preted these words spiritually, as being suitable to our mode
"of life, and he said that which our Lord said, 'The demon
"'goeth round about in the places wherein there is no water,
"that he may seek for rest, and he findeth it not'; which say-
"ing maketh us to understand that when the unclean devil of
"fornication wageth war against the monk, if the monk
"afflicteth himself by eating food sparingly, and especially by

" drinking water sparingly, Satan will never be able to injure
" him by means of this passion. And the devil will never be
" gratified at the fulfilment of this passion by him, for there is
" nothing which will dry up the arteries, and prevent the
" accident of the night, and make a monk to possess chaste
" and quiet thoughts by day, so much as the restraining of
" the belly by thirst. Some fast the whole day until the even-
" ing, and some fast for [several] nights at a time, yet when
" they break their fast and eat a little food, because they drink
" much water, they benefit in no wise by their fasting and by
" the sparing use of food which they practise because of the
" war of lust. For the drinking of much water filleth the
" arteries [of the monk] with [excessive] moisture, and Satan
" findeth an occasion for exciting him by means of thoughts
" in the daytime, and he trippeth him up by means of dreams
" by night, and he depriveth him of the light of purity. There-
" fore, in another place, Abbâ Evagrius admonisheth the
" monk, saying, ' If thou wishest for chastity make little thy
" food, and restrain thyself in the drinking of water, and then
" impassibility of heart shall rise upon thee, and thou shalt
" see in thy prayer a mind which emitteth light like unto a
" star."

657. The brethren said, " In how many ways doth Divine
" Grace call the brethren unto the life of the solitary ascetic?"
The old man said, " In very many and different ways. Some-
" times Divine Grace moveth a man suddenly, even as it moved
" Abbâ Moses, the Ethiopian, and sometimes by the hearing
" of the Scriptures, as in the cases of the blessed Mâr Anthony
" and Mâr Simon Stylites, and at others by the doctrine of the
" word, as in the cases of Serapion, and Abbâ Bessarion, and
" others who were like unto them. Concerning these three ways
" whereby Divine Grace calleth to those who would repent, I
" would say that Divine Grace moveth the conscience of a
" monk in the manner which is pleasing to God, and that
" through these even evil-doers have repented and pleased God.
" And there is, moreover, the departure from this world by
" the hands of angels, by terrors, and sicknesses, and afflic-
" tions, even as that which took place in respect of the blessed
" Evagrius; and sometimes God Himself calleth from heaven
" and taketh a man out of the world, as in the cases of Paul,
" and Abbâ Arsenius."

658. The brethren said, "Wherefore is it that the beginning
" of the doctrine of the old men is laid down in the books from
" the choice (*or* election) of Abbâ Arsenius, and on [his] com-
" ing forth from the world into a monastery, and from a monas-
" tery of the brethren into the seclusion which is in a cell?'

The old man said, "Because he was called by God to the
"monastery, and from the monastery to the cell, and because
"it is certain that these two calls were according to the Will
"of God, well was it that the beginning of the doctrine of the
"old men [was derived] from the history of this holy man."

659. The brethren said, "Explain unto us these two calls of
"Abbâ Arsenius. What is the meaning of that which was said
"in the first call, 'Flee from the children of men and thou
"'shalt live,' and what is the signification of that which was
"said at the second call, 'Flee, keep silence and live a life of
"'contemplation in silence, for these are the principal things
"'which keep a man from sinning?'" The old man said, "The
"meaning of 'Flee from the children of men, and thou shalt
"'live,' is this:—If thou wishest to be delivered from the
"death which is in sin, and to live the perfect life which is in
"righteousness, leave thy possessions, and family, and country,
"and depart into exile, that is, to the desert and mountains
"to the holy men; and cultivate with them My command-
"ments, and thou shalt live a life of grace. And the meaning
"of 'Flee, keep silence, and live a life of contemplation in
"'silence' is this:—Since when thou wast in the world thou
"wast drawn towards anxieties about the affairs thereof, I
"have made thee to come out from the world, and I have
"sent thee to the habitation of monks, so that after a short
"time of dwelling in the coenobium thou mayest be drawn, first
"to the cultivation of My commandments openly, and secondly
"to contemplation in silence. And now that thou art trained
"in the former sufficiently, thou mayest flee, that is to say,
"get thee forth from the monastery of the brethren, and enter
"into thy cell, just as thou didst go forth from the world, and
"didst enter into the monastery. And the meaning of 'Keep
"'silence, and lead a life of contemplation in silence,' is:—
"Having entered into thy cell to contemplate in silence, thou
"shalt not give the multitude an opportunity of coming in to
"thee, and talking to thee unnecessarily, except on matters
"which relate to spiritual excellence; if thou dost not do this
"thou wilt benefit by sitting in silent contemplation. For
"through the sight, and the hearing, and the converse of the
"multitude who shall come in to thee, the captivity of wander-
"ing thoughts will carry thee off, and thy silence and thy con-
"templation will be disturbed. But do not imagine that the
"mere fact of having left the brethren in the monastery, or
"not bringing other men into thy cell to be disturbed by them
"will be sufficient to make thy mind to be composed, or to
"enable thee to meditate upon God, and to correct thyself,
"unless thou dost take good heed not to occupy thy mind

"with them in any way whatsoever when they are remote
"from thee. For until a man arriveth at a state of impassi-
"bility, and overcometh by striving both the passions and the
"devils, whensoever a monk remembereth any man in his cell,
"he remembereth him in connexion with some passion, that
"is to say, with desire (*or* lust), or with anger, or with vain-
"glory. And if it should happen that the mind wandereth in
"respect of ordinary things (*or* means), unless he cutteth them
"off from him, his wandering inclineth through absolute neces-
"sity towards a remembrance which is allied to some passion.
"And it is also thus in the case of a neophyte, for whensoever
"during his contemplation in silence he remembered women
"he falleth into the lust of fornication; and whensoever he
"remembereth men, he is either wroth with them in his
"thoughts, and he maketh accusations against them, and
"blameth them, and condemneth them, or he demandeth from
"them vainglory, and he inclineth to passibility. Therefore
"when Abbâ Macarius was asked, 'What is the right way for
"'a brother, who is a neophyte, to live in his cell?' he said,
"'Let no monk when he is in his cell have any remembrance
"'whatsoever of any man, for he cannot profit in any way in
"'restraining his feelings from the conversation of men, ex-
"'cept he take care to withhold his thoughts from secret in-
"'tercourse with them.' This is the meaning of the words,
"'Flee, keep silence, and contemplate in silence.'"

660. The brethren said, "What is the meaning of the words
"which one of the old men spake, saying, 'He who dwelleth
"'with men, because of the commotion of worldly affairs is un-
"'able to see his sins; but if he dwell in the silent repose of
"'the desert he will be able to see God in a pure manner?'"
The old man said, "The excellences which are cultivated in
"the world, and to which our Lord, speaking in the Gospel,
"ascribed blessing, are lovingkindness, peace-making and
"the other commandments which are like unto them, and it
"is quite possible for such virtues to be cultivated in the world
"by certain strenuous persons. But the purity of heart which
"seeth God, and to which our Lord ascribed blessing, saying,
"'Blessed are the pure in heart, for they shall see God,' can-
"not be acquired without dwelling in the desert, and solitary
"and silent contemplation, and the monk must acquire it in
"the following way. First of all a man must go forth from
"the world, and dwell in a monastery, and after his training
"in a monastery and having gone into his cell, he must die
"through contemplation in silence, and through the other
"labours of his body, and through striving against the pas-
"sions, and through conflict with devils. Then through the

" tranquillity of mind [which he will acquire] in silent contem-
" plation, he will remember his sins, and when he hateth his
" passions, and hath petitioned for the remission of his sins,
" and hath suppressed his thoughts, and hath become constant
" in pure prayer, and hath cleansed his heart from odious
" thoughts, then shall he be worthy to see in his heart, even
" as in a polished mirror, the light of the revelation of our Lord
" [shine] upon it, even as the Fathers say. Well, then, did that
" holy man say to those brethren, Visit the sick, reconcile the
" men of wrath, for he who cultivateth spiritual excellences in
" the world cannot, by reason of the commotion of the affairs
" thereof, see his sins; but if he continue in silent contempla-
" tion and prayer he shall see God."

661. The brethren said, "What is [the meaning of] that
" which Abbâ Sisoes said to Abbâ Ammon, ' Freedom of my
" ' thoughts in the desert is sufficient for me?'" The old man
said, " Sisoes was a great and a perfect old man, and he dwelt
" all the days of his life in the remote desert, and after he had
" become old, and was exceedingly feeble, the Fathers brought
" him to the monastery of the brethren, who used to go in
" and visit him each day, for the sake of some profitable dis-
" course and helpful prayer. And because he was unaccustomed
" to feel comfortable in the presence of many folks, his mind
" began to wander about in remembering the brethren, and
" to meditate upon many things, and he was unable to find
" that dominant freedom for the continuous, secret prayer of
" the mind, which is superior to every influence that would
" make it decline, and is free from every [other] attraction,
" and he was, therefore, rightly grieved. Now one day, Abbâ
" Ammon went to visit him, and he saw that he was sorry
" about his coming from the desert, and he said unto him,
" ' Father, it is not right for thee to be sorrowful because thou
" ' hast drawn nigh to the place where the brethren dwell, for
" ' thy body hath become feeble, and thou art unable to per-
" ' form those works wherein thou wert wont to labour in the
" ' desert.' Now when Abbâ Sisoes heard these things, he
" looked at Abbâ Ammon sternly, and he answered him with
" indignation, saying, 'What sayest thou to me, Ammon?
" ' Was not the freedom of the thoughts which I had in the
" ' desert sufficient to take the place for me of all labours?
" ' And as regards thyself also, O Ammon, who art conscious
" ' of the life and acts of the freedom of the mind, and who art
" ' not subject unto the constraint of wandering and disturb-
" ' ance of the mind, and who art not impeded by old age and
" ' infirmity, tell me what thou art able to do in the desert at
" ' thy great age? Even if I be unequal to the labours of the

" ' body, because I have become infirm through old age, I am
" ' better able to perform the labours of the mind than I was
" ' in the time of my early manhood. Or, perhaps in thy opinion
" ' the clear shining of the mind, which a monk acquireth by
" ' a life of contemplation in silence, and the constant inter-
" ' course with God, and the prayer which is without ceasing,
" ' and the remembrance of Christ, and the constant gazing
" ' upon Him, and the exultation of the soul in Him, and the
" ' favour of His love, and the affection for His command-
" ' ments, and the desire for His good things, and the medita-
" ' tion upon His glory, and the thought about His excellence
" ' and His majesty, and the admiration of His humility, are
" ' matters which are small and contemptible? All these labours
" ' of the mind, and many others which are like unto them,
" ' neither old age nor infirmity impedes, but they are pre-
" ' vented, and brought low, and, by degrees, are destroyed,
" ' by converse with the children of men, and by seeing many
" ' people, and by care about worldly affairs.' "

662. The brethren said, "They used to say that when the ser-
" vice in the church was over, Abbâ Macarius was wont to flee
" to his cell, and that the brethren said, 'He hath a devil, but
" ' he doeth the work of God.' Now who were those who said
" that he had a devil? And what was the work of God which
" he used to do?" The old man said, "Those who said that
" he had a devil were the lazy brethren. Whensoever Satan
" seeth the monks who are leading a life of spiritual excellence
" in the monastery, the devils stir up the lazy brethren to wage
" war against them, by means of abuse, and revilings, and
" backbiting, and calumny, and by means of the trials which
" they bring upon them. Now the work of God which Abbâ
" Sisoes did when he fled [to his cell] was this: Prayer ac-
" companied by weeping and tears, according to the exhorta-
" tion of Abbâ Isaiah, who said, 'When the congregation is
" ' dismissed, or when thou risest up after eating, sit not
" ' down to talk with any man, either concerning the affairs
" ' of the world, or concerning matters of spiritual excellence;
" ' but go thou into thy cell, and weep for thy sins, even as
" ' Abbâ Macarius the Alexandrian said unto the brethren who
" ' were with him, "Brethren, flee." And the brethren said,
" " " Father, how can we flee more than [in coming] to the
" " " desert?" and he laid his hand upon his mouth, and said
" ' unto them, "Flee ye in this manner"; and straightway
" ' every man fled to his cell and held his peace.' "

663. The brethren said, "Abbâ Anthony said, 'As a fish
" ' dieth when it is lifted up out of the water, so doth the monk
" ' [die] if he remain long outside his cell'; explain these words

"to us." The old man said, "Because the remembrance of
"God is, in our Lord Jesus Christ, the life of the soul, which
"the Fathers call the 'repository of life,' and 'the breath of
"'the life of the soul and of the mind,' when the monk tarri-
"eth in the cities, and in the sight and converse of the child-
"ren of men, he dieth in respect of the breath of life which
"is in God, that is to say, he forgetteth God, and the love of
"Christ groweth cold in his heart, the love which he hath ac-
"quired by many labours, and he forgetteth his virtues, and he
"becometh lax in respect of [his] liking for tribulations, and
"he loveth pleasures, and hath an affection for lusts, and the
"sincerity of his heart is troubled through the disturbance
"which entereth into his senses, that is, seeing, and speaking,
"and hearing, which are indeed the strength of the soul; and it
"happeneth also that he falleth into great passions, wherefrom
"may Christ God save us! Amen."

664. The brethren said, "The excellent man Hieronymus
"said in the history of the triumphs of the blessed Isidore, the
"archimandrite, that he had in his monastery one thousand
"monks, and that they all lived within the gate of his habita-
"tion, and that none of them ever went outside it until the day
"of his death, except two brethren who only set out therefrom
"to sell their handiwork, and who brought in only such things
"as were required for their absolute needs. How is it that in
"an assembly of our early Fathers, that is, a congregation
"containing one thousand brethren, two men only were suffi-
"cient [to provide for] their ministrations? In our generation
"if there was a congregation of five and fifty monks, only five
"would lead a life of ascetic excellence in seclusion, and the
"[other] fifty would be going out and coming in ceaselessly
"and without rest to supply them with what they needed."
The old man said, "Concerning the love for labours, and the
"watch which the early Fathers kept [on themselves], and
"concerning the love of pleasure, and the laxity of ourselves
"who belong to a later time, if it be right to tell the truth, we
"ought to speak most concerning the laxity and ignorance of
"the governors of monasteries. In former times the brethren
"who lived lives of contemplation and seclusion and loved
"spiritual repose were many, and those who went out on to
"the high roads, and entered the cities, and performed outside
"labours were few; but in our days, in a congregation which,
"as ye have said, containeth five and fifty monks, five will lead
"a life of spiritual repose inside the monastery, and the other
"fifty will toil ceaselessly in the works which are outside it,
"and during the whole time they will complain and blame the
"five who are inside, because they do not go out and serve

" even as do they. And through the words of these foolish and
" insolent men all the spiritual excellences which are cultivated
" in the monastery will perish and come to an end. And accor-
" ding to what I say, if the Fathers set the life of contempla-
" tion in silence against the whole of the labour of the ascetic
" life, and if it be more excellent than it all, who would blame
" him that loveth spiritual contemplation and repose, and the
" quiet of the cell?"

665. The brethren said, "On one occasion a congregation
" of monks assembled on the great festival of the Resurrec-
" tion, and there were gathered together in the monastery all
" the Fathers, and all the recluses, and other monks, and all
" the old men in the congregation were asked, Which is the
" mightiest and most severe war which can come upon monks?
" And they all agreed that no war is harder or more cruel
" than that which maketh a man to leave his cell and depart,
" and that when that war is fought down, all other contests
" may be easily reduced. Explain to us the meaning of these
" words." The old man said, "Constant spiritual repose in a
" cell hath hope closely bound up in it, but going out there
" from is united to despair. As long as a man liveth in spiri-
" tual repose, and loveth the quiet of the cell, little by little he
" goeth forward, one step at a time, according to the order of
" succession; and he hath hope that in our Lord he will van-
" quish each of the passions, and that through his repose and
" labours he will acquire spiritual excellences and the grace of
" Christ. But if the life becometh tedious to him, and he go
" forth and leave his cell, and wander about, he will neither
" vanquish the passions, nor acquire spiritual virtues, but he
" will incline to despair, and to utter destruction. Therefore
" the Fathers have well said that no war is more cruel than
" the war of wandering."

666. The brethren said, "Abbâ Theodore and Abbâ Lûkî
" passed fifty years in being harassed by their thoughts which
" urged them vexatiously to change [their] place [of living];
" and they said, 'When the winter cometh we will change.'
" And when the winter had come, they said, 'We will change
" 'in the summer'; and thus they continued to do till the end
" of their lives. Reveal to us if it were the devils who were
" urging these famous Fathers to go forth from their cells for
" a period of fifty years, that is, until their death." The old
man said, "The devils urged the great Fathers to wander and
" to go forth from their spiritual repose because they well
" knew the benefit which accrued to them therefrom, and these
" holy Fathers were urged by the devils also, but did not leave
" their cells. To-day, however, in this generation, the same

" devils harass the monks, and drive them out of their cells
" by this war of departure, and therefore the great Fathers
" who have felt this war of wandering and of departure have
" said, ' There is no war which is more cruel to the monk than
" ' this; may Christ help us and deliver us from it.' "

667. The brethren said, "Abbâ Anthony used to say, ' He
" ' who dwelleth in the desert is free from three wars, that is,
" ' from speaking, hearing, and seeing'; explain these words to
" us." The old man said, "The old man did not speak [thus]
" because the strife of him that dwelt in spiritual repose in the
" desert was less fierce than that of him that wandered about
" and mingled with men, but that he might show how much
" more hard and laborious was the war of devils which taketh
" place in the heart of those who dwell in spiritual repose
" than that which cometh in the heart of those who dwell with
" brethren. And because of this the fathers pursued after a life
" of contemplation in silence, lest when the wars of speaking
" and seeing and hearing were added unto that which was
" already in their heart, they would fall by reason of their
" severity, even as actually happened on one occasion, for a
" woman came to the monks who were living a life of silent
" contemplation, and there was added to the war which was
" already in their hearts the wars of seeing, and hearing, and
" speaking, and they would have been vanquished by the
" severity thereof had it not been that the grace of our Lord
" supported them. That the war which taketh place in the
" senses of the soul against the monks who live a life of silent
" contemplation is mightier and fiercer than that which taketh
" place in the senses of the body, is well known from the words
" which the blessed Evagrius spake, saying, Against the
" monks who lead a life of silent contemplation the devils in
" person wage war, but against those who lead a life of spiri-
" tual excellence in a general assembly of brethren, the devils
" only stir up and incite the lazy brethren; but the war which
" ariseth from the sight, and the hearing, and the speech is
" much less fierce that that which is waged against the monks
" who dwell in silent solitude."

668. The brethren said, "What is the meaning of that which
" Abbâ Anthony said, ' A monk's cell is the furnace of Baby-
" ' lon, and it is also a pillar of light'?" The old man said,
" There are two things peculiar to the cell; the one warmeth
" and setteth on fire, and the other giveth light and rejoicing.
" To neophytes it is oppressive and troublesome, by reason of
" the many wars and the dejection which are therein, but it
" rejoiceth the perfect and maketh them glad, with purity of
" heart, and impassibility, and revelations of light; and it is

" even thus with those who begin to live in silent contempla-
" tion, for although at the beginning they are for a consider-
" able time afflicted by the wars of the passions, and by devils,
" they are never forsaken by the help of Divine Grace. For our
" Lord Himself, the Son of God, Jesus Christ, cometh to them
" secretly, and he becometh to them a helper and a companion,
" and after they have overcome both passions and devils, ac-
" cording to systematic order, He maketh them worthy of the
" happiness which is in His perfect love, and the revelation of
" His glorious light."

669. The brethren said, "Abbâ Moses the Ethiopian was on
" one occasion reviled by certain men, and the brethren asked
" him, saying, 'Wast not thou troubled in thy heart, O father,
" ' when thou wast reviled?' And he said unto them, 'Although
" ' I was troubled, yet I said nothing.' What is the meaning
" of the words, 'Although I was troubled I spake not'?" The
old man said, " The perfection of monks consisteth of two
" parts, that is to say, of impassibility of the senses of the body,
" and of impassibility of the senses of the soul. Impassibility of
" the body taketh place when a man who is reviled restraineth
" himself for God's sake and speaketh not, even though he be
" troubled; but impassibility of the soul taketh place when a man
" is abused and reviled, and yet is not angry in his heart when
" he is abused, even like John Colobos. For on one occasion
" when the brethren were sitting with him, a man passed by
" and upbraided him, but he was not angry, and his coun-
" tenance changed not; then the brethren asked him, saying,
" ' Art thou not secretly troubled in thy heart, O father, being
" ' reviled in this fashion?' And he answered and said unto
" them, ' I am not troubled inwardly, for inwardly I am just
" ' as tranquil as ye see that I am outwardly'; and this is per-
" fect impassibility. Now at that time Abbâ Moses had not
" arrived at this state of perfection, and he confessed that al-
" though outwardly he was undisturbed, yet he was waging a
" contest in his heart, and he maintained silence and was not
" angry outwardly; and even this was a spiritual excellence,
" although it would have been a more perfect thing had he not
" been angry either inwardly or outwardly. And the blessed
" Nilus made a comparison of these two measures of excellence
" in the cases of the blessed men Moses and Aaron. The act of
" covering the breast and heart with the priestly tunic which
" Aaron performed when he went into the Holy of Holies re-
" presented the state of a man who, though angry in his heart,
" suppresseth his wrath by striving and prayer; and the state
" of a man not being angry at all in the heart, because he hath
" been exalted to perfection by [his] victory over the passions

"and the devils, Nilus compared to that which is said of the
"blessed Moses, saying, 'Moses took the breast for an offer-
"'ing, because the soul dwelleth in the heart, and the heart
"'in the breast.' And Solomon said, 'Remove anger from thy
"'heart,' and concerning Aaron the Book saith, 'He was cover-
"'ing his breast with the ephod and tunic,' and this teacheth
"us monks that it is meet for us to cover over the wrath which
"is in the heart with gentle, and humble, and tranquil thoughts,
"and that we should not allow it to ascend to the opening of
"our throat, and that the odiousness and abomination thereof
"shall be revealed by the tongue."

670. The brethren said, "Why is it that, although all the
"fathers used to admonish the brethren to ask the old men
"questions continually, and to learn from them, and to reveal
"to them their thoughts, and to live according to their direc-
"tions, one of the old men said to one of the brethren, 'Go,
"'sit in thy cell, and thy cell shall teach thee everything'?"
The old man said, "There is no contradiction in these words
"of the Fathers, and what the old man said hath an object,
"the meaning of which is well known. The old man who ad-
"monished the brother that he should learn like a beginner
"was great and famous, and to that brother who asked him
"the question he spake thus:—In the early days when thou
"goest to thy cell lay hold upon the habits (or orders) of the
"neophytes, and live according to them for a considerable
"period, that is to say, with fasting, and vigil, and reading,
"and reciting the offices, and all the other things, until at
"length, after the lapse of time, the life of contemplation in
"silence shall give thee the order which befitteth thy seclusion,
"and will add those things which are seemly, and will diminish
"those which are not. This is the meaning of that which was
"said by the holy man, 'Sit in thy cell, and it shall teach thee
"'everything.'"

671. The brethren said, "One of the old men used to say,
"'A man shall have no care, and he shall contemplate in
"'silence, and shall cover up himself; three meditations shall
"'teach purity.' What is the meaning of these three words?"
The old man said, "'A man shall have no care' means that
"he shall not care concerning the shortcomings of others, and
"that all his anxiety shall be concerning his own shortcomings.
"And, 'He shall contemplate in silence' means that he shall
"not speak even concerning matters of spiritual excellence
"if it will trouble any man or condemn him. And 'He shall
"'cover up himself' meaneth that he shall not reveal his
"life and deeds, but as far as possible, he shall be un-
"known and unhonoured. Now by these things is esta-

"blished the purity of heart which seeth God in a revelation
"of light."

672. The brethren said, "How is it possible for a monk to
"die every day for the love of Christ, even as the blessed Paul
"said, 'I swear by your boasting, my brethren, that, in our
"'Lord Jesus Christ, I die daily, and the world is dead unto
"'me, and I am crucified unto the world, and the world is
"'crucified unto me, and I live, yet not I, but Christ liveth in
"'me'?" The old man said, "A man [can do this] if he con-
"template in silence at all seasons, and perform the other
"works of the body, I mean fasting, and vigil, and the recital
"of the books of the Psalms, and prayers, and genuflexions,
"and groanings, and pain, and weeping, and tears, and sighs,
"and the reading of the Holy Scriptures. And he must espe-
"cially take care concerning the works of the mind, that is,
"the constant remembrance of God, and meditation upon Him
"and His blessings, and upon His commandments and His
"threatenings; and his gaze must always be on our Lord, and
"his prayer must be without ceasing and without wandering,
"and the odiousness of the passions must be away from the
"heart, and he must suppress with keenness the thoughts of
"the devils which arise at their prompting. And he must
"possess that excellence which is the first and most important
"of all the spiritual virtues, and of all the labours of the ascetic
"life of the mind, that is to say, death in respect of all the
"anxieties and cares of this world. And a monk must have no
"care, and no anxiety, and he must not think about anything,
"or seek anything, or desire anything, or lust for anything,
"except for the time when he will attain to the perfect love of
"God in our Lord Jesus Christ. And he must fulfil at all times
"the command of the blessed Paul, and his admonition to us
"wherein he said, 'Love ye your Lord, rejoice in your hope,
"'pray without ceasing, be fervent in spirit, endure your
"'tribulations, be not anxious about anything, cast all your
"'care upon the Lord; and let all your prayers, and all your
"'requests, and all your petitions be made known unto God,
"'to Whom be glory for ever and ever! Amen.'"

673. The brethren said, "How can love be acquired by men
"of understanding?" The old man said, "True and pure love
"is the way of life, and the haven of promises, and the trea-
"sure of faith, and it sheweth [the way of] the kingdom, and
"it is the expositor of the judgement, and the preacher concern-
"ing what is hidden."

674. The brethren said, "We do not know the power of the
"word." The old man said, "If a man doth not love God he
"will not believe in Him, and His promises are not certain to

" him, and he feareth not His judgement, and he goeth not
" after Him ; but, because love is not in him, so that he may flee
" from iniquity, and wait for the life which hath been pro-
" mised, he is always performing the work of sin. And he doth
" this because His judgement is raised too far above his eyes.
" Therefore let us run after love, wherein the holy fathers
" were rich, for it is able to reward its nature and its God, and
" this is its praise."

675. The brethren said, " In what way doth wisdom live in
" a man?" The old man said, " Now when a man hath gone
" forth to follow God with a sincere mind, grace taketh up its
" abode in him, and his life and deeds are strengthened in the
" Spirit, and he hath taken a hatred to the world, for he per-
" ceiveth that new spiritual life which is in the new man, and
" which is exalted above the impurity of human life, and in
" his mind he thinketh upon the humility of the life and works
" which are to come, and which are [more] excellent than those
" here."

676. The brethren said, " By what is love made known?"
The old man said, " By the fulfilment of work, and by spiri-
" tual meditation and by the knowledge of faith."

677. The brethren said, " What are works?" The old man
said, " The keeping of the commandments of God in the purity
" of the inner man, together with the [performance of] labours
" by the outer man."

678. The brethren said, " Is every man who is destitute of
" works also destitute of love?" The old man said, " It is im-
" possible for the man who is in God not to love and it is
" impossible that he who loveth should not work; and it is incre-
" dible that he who teacheth and doth not work is indeed a
" believer, for his tongue is the enemy of his actions, and al-
" though he speaketh life, he is in subjection unto death."

679. The brethren said, " And is he who is in this state de-
" stitute of reward?" The old man said, " The man who
" speaketh the things of the spirit, and who performeth the
" things of the body is not destitute of reward, and that which
" he needeth is fulfilled for him, but he is deprived of the crown
" of light, because he desireth not that the rule of the spirit
" shall have dominion over him."

680. The brethren said, "Fasting and prayer: what are
" they?" The old man said, "Fasting is the subjugation of
" the body, and prayer is converse with God, vigil is the war
" with Satan, abstinence is the being weaned from meats,
" standing up is the humility of the primitive man, genuflexion
" is the bowing down before the Judge, tears are the remem-
" brance of sins, nakedness is our captivity through trans-

"gression, and [reciting the] service is constant supplication
"and the praising of God."

681. The brethren said, "Are these things able to redeem
"the soul?" The old man said, "When the things which are
"within agree with the things which are without and the hu-
"mility which is manifest appeareth in the hidden works
"which are within, in very truth a man is redeemed from the
"heaviness of the body."

682. The brethren said, "And what is internal humility?"
The old man said, "It is humility of love, peace, concord,
"purity, restfulness, gentleness, subjection, faith, remoteness
"from envy, [and it is] the soul which lacketh the fervour of
"anger, and is remote from the lust of arrogance, and is
"separated from vainglory, and is filled with patient endur-
"ance like the great deep, and whose motion is drawn after
"the knowledge of the spirit, and before whose eyes is de-
"picted the departure from the body, and the great marvel of
"the Resurrection, and the call to judgement, which [shall come]
"after the quickening, and its standing before the awful throne
"of God, and the being redeemed."

683. The brethren said, "Is it possible for a man to fast and
"not to be redeemed?" The old man said, "There is a fasting
"which is a matter of habit, and another which is of desire,
"and another which is of constraint, and another which is of
"the sight, and another which is of vainglory, and another of
"tribulation, and another of repentance, and another of spiritual
"love; and although each one of them is the same outside the
"mind, yet in the word of knowledge they are distinct. Now
"although the manner of each in respect of the body is the
"same, yet each should be undertaken with thorough pur-
"pose, and a man should journey straightly along the way of
"love, and should bear his burden with spiritual patience, and
"he should not rejoice in his honour."

684. The brethren said, "Who is the true [monk]?" The old
man said, "He who maketh his word manifest indeed, and en-
"dureth his pain patiently; with such a man new life is found,
"and the knowledge of the spirit dwelleth in him."

685. The brethren said, "Who is he that liveth purely?" The
old man said, "He who is free from the delights of the body,
"and who rejoiceth in the love of his neighbours in the love of
"God; for in proportion as need hath rule over the soul is
"spiritual repose produced [therein]."

686. The brethren said, "With what can we vanquish lust?"
The old man said, "With the remembrance of the good things
"of the spirit; for, if the desire for the good things which are
"to come doth not abrogate the lust for the delights of this

"world, a man cannot overcome at all. Except the merchant's
"ship be laden with manifold hope it will not be able to endure
"the storms, and will sail on the path of tribulation."

687. The brethren said, "In what way doth a man go forth
"from the world?" The old man said, "He doeth this when he
"forsaketh the gratification of all his lust, and when, so far as
"it lieth in his power, he runneth to fulfil the commandments;
"the man who doth not do this will fall."

688. The brethren said, "Through what did the men of old
"triumph over nature?" The old man said, "Through the
"fervour of their love which was above nature, and through
"the death of the man which is corruptible, and through con-
"tempt of arrogance, and through abatement of the belly, and
"through the fear of the judgement, and through the sure and
"certain promise; through the desire of these glorious things
"the Fathers acquired in the soul a spiritual body."

689. The brethren said, "How can we vanquish the passions
"which afflict us, since they are placed in our nature?" The old
man said, "Through your death to the world, for except a man
"burieth himself in the grave of continence the spiritual Adam
"can never be quickened in him. For when a dead man de-
"parteth from this temporary life, he hath no perception of the
"world, and all his senses are at rest and they are useless. Now
"if that which appertaineth to thy natural body thou dost for-
"sake naturally, and thou dost not do the same voluntarily in
"respect of thine own person, thou wilt die; but if thy desire
"dieth through repentance, [thy] nature will cease from this
"temporary life in the death of the spirit, even as the natural
"emotions of the body ceased through its natural end."

690. The brethren said, "To what extent is a man held to be
"worthy of revelations?" The old man said, "To the same
"extent as he is held to be worthy to cast off sin inwardly and
"outwardly. For when a man dieth through spiritual slaughter
"to all the conversation of this temporary life, and when he
"hath committed his life to the life which is after the quicken-
"ing, Divine Grace alighteth upon him, and he is held to be
"worthy of divine revelations; for the impurity of the world is
"a dark covering to the soul, and it preventeth it from dis-
"cerning spiritual meanings."

691. The brethren said, "Can the man who loveth money be
"faithful to the promises?" The old man said, "If he believeth
"why doth he possess [anything]? Is our hope fixed upon
"gold? Or is the hand of the Lord too short to redeem? He
"gave us the Body of our Lord for happiness, and His holy
"Blood as a drink unto our redemption; and hath He kept back
"from us the loaf of bread and the apparel which grow old?

" He who loveth money hath a doubt in his mind concerning
" God, and he prepareth [the means of] life before God giveth
" them unto him; and, although in his words he rejoiceth
" in the promises, he maketh them to be a lie by his deeds.
" True is the word of our Lord, Who said, ' It is as difficult for
" ' a rich man to enter into the kingdom of God, as for a
" ' camel to go into the eye of a needle' (St. Matthew xix, 24);
" to possess both God and mammon in one abode is impossi-
" ble. Now those who follow the ascetic life do not belong to
" the things which are seen."

692. The brethren said, ' Who is truly the man of ascetic ex-
" cellence?" The old man said, ' He who at all times crieth out
" that he is a sinner, and asketh mercy from the Lord, whose
" speech beareth the sense of discretion, whose feelings bear
" the excellence of works, who though silent yet speaketh, and
" who though speaking yet holdeth his peace, and whose acts
" and deeds bear good fruit to his temporary life and the mani-
" festation of Christ."

693. The brethren said, " Which is the way of life?" The old
man said, " That whereby a man goeth forth from this world
" in his entrance into the other; but if a man forsaketh his
" childhood of humility, and cometh to the old age of this
" world in his love, he revealeth the way of life. Now the true
" departure from this world is remoteness therefrom."

694. A brother said, "What shall I do to this world when it
" troubleth me?" The old man said, " The world troubleth
" thee because the cares thereof are in thy mind, and love
" therefor is in thy body, and its delights are in thy heart. Let
" the world depart from thee, and tear out from thee all the
" roots (or branches) thereof, and lo, the war thereof will
" cease from thee. For as long as thy body seeketh [its] plea-
" sures, and its lust is of the world, it is impossible for thee to
" live."

695. The brethren said, " What is pure prayer?" The old
man said, " That which is of few words and is abundant in
" deeds. For if [thy] actions be not more than thy petition, thy
" prayers are mere words wherein the seed of the hands is
" not; and if it be not thus, why do we ask and not receive,
" since the mercy of Grace aboundeth. The manner of the peni-
" tent is one thing, and the labour of the humble is another;
" the penitent are hirelings, but the humble are sons."

696. The brethren said, " By what is the love of money pro-
" duced?" The old man said, "From lust, for except a man
" lusteth he will not possess [money], and if he doth not pos-
" sess [money] he will not lust. When a man lusteth he pos-
" sesseth [money], and having acquired it he fulfilleth his lust;

" and having fulfilled his lust, he becometh greedy, and having
" become greedy he committeth fraud; and having committed
" fraud his possessions increase, and when his possessions
" have increased love becometh little in him. And when love
" hath diminished the remembrance of God is wanting in the
" heart, and the intelligence becometh darkened, and his power
" of discernment becometh blinded, and when the power of
" discernment hath become blinded, the power of distinguish-
" ing is darkened, and when the power of distinguishing hath
" become darkened, the soul goeth blind. And when the soul
" hath become blind goodness is rooted out therefrom, and
" wickedness entereth in, and sin hath dominion; and when
" sin hath obtained dominion the thought of God is blotted
" out, the passions of the body are roused up, and they seek
" for the means for working out their needs. And when they
" have obtained that which they seek it becometh necessary
" for much money to be gathered together, and when money
" hath multiplied the pleasure of the body is fulfilled, and a
" man eateth, and drinketh, and committeth adultery and forni-
" cation, and he lieth and acteth fraudulently, and transgresseth
" the covenant, and he destroyeth the Law, and despiseth the
" promises, and lust is fulfilled, and God is wroth. For if the
" lust for the things which are seen be hated in our sight, we
" shall not love money, but if we perform the lust of the flesh
" it is necessary to love money, because it belongeth to the
" flesh and not to the spirit, even as the Apostle said, 'The
" 'flesh hurteth the spirit, and the spirit the flesh, and both
" 'are opponents each of other'" (Galatians v, 17).

697. The brethren said, "What kind of prayer is that which
" is not acceptable before God?" The old man said, "[The
" prayer for the] destruction of enemies. When we ask that
" evil things [may come] upon those who do harm to us, and
" for bodily health, and abundance of possessions, and fertility
" in respect of children, these requests are not acceptable be-
" fore God. If God beareth with us, who are sinners and who
" offend Him, how much more is it right that we should bear
" each with the other? It is, then, not meet that we should
" ask for the things which concern the body, for the wisdom
" of God provideth everything [necessary]."

698. The brethren said, "What is purity of soul?" The old
man said, "Remoteness from anger, and the error of remem-
" brance of evil things, being weaned from a bitter disposition,
" friendliness towards our enemies, peace which is superior to
" troubling, and sincere love which is above the world; by
" means of these the hidden man is purified, and he putteth on
" Christ, and is redeemed."

699. The brethren said, "What is envy?" The old man said, "Hatred towards the virtues of others, and wickedness to-"wards the good, and a bitter disposition towards the innocent, "and anger against those who are prosperous in this world, "and the concealment of the upright acts and deeds of the "penitent, and vexation at the peace of the friends of God."

700. The brethren said, "In what way ought we to pray "before God?" The old man said, "For the repentance of "sinners, and the finding of the lost, and the drawing nigh of "those who are afar off, and friendliness towards those who "do us harm, and love towards those who persecute us, and "sorrowful care for those who provoke God to wrath. And if "a man doeth these things truly and with a penitent mind, "the sinners will often gain life, and the living soul will be "redeemed. Now the prayer which our Lord delivered to us "as to the needs of the body, is one which applieth to the "whole community, and it was not uttered for the sake of "those who are strangers to the world, and with whom the "pleasures of the body are held in contempt. He in whose "habitation (*or* life) the kingdom of God and His righteousness "are found lacketh nothing, even when he asketh not."

701. The brethren said, "What is remoteness from the "world?" The old man said, "The thought which vanquisheth "the love of the body, for if the body be not trodden down by "the lust of patient endurance, a man cannot conquer in the "fight."

702. The brethren said, "Can the soul of a man who is held "fast in the love of the things which are seen be pleasing unto "God?" The old man said, "Who is able to live in chastity "when the body is making demands upon him? Or, how can "be found the love of our Lord in the soul which hath its "abode with the things which are seen and are corruptible? "No man can serve two masters, and the soul cannot please "God with spiritual excellence so long as the remembrances "of corruptible things are in its mind, for the mind of the "flesh is not able to please God; except the world dieth out "of the heart humility cannot live therein, and except the body "be deprived of its lusts, the soul cannot be purified from "thoughts."

703. The brethren said, "Why is the mind disturbed at the "meeting with females?" The old man said, "Because they "are employed in the fulfilment of the lust of nature. When the "gaze falleth upon the structure which [is intended for] the pro-"duction of children, and for the pleasures of the body, the "poison of olden time seizeth upon a man, and the law of his "will becometh confused; now the will conquereth nature, not

333

" by the stirring up of the passions, but by the fulfilment of
" works. The humble by the power of our Lord conquer
" everything by their love through the patient endurance of
" the merit of our Lord."

704. The brethren said, "Who is the mightier man? He
" who is remote from the world, or he who dwelleth therein?"
The old man said, "The mighty man, wheresoever he dwell-
" eth, conquereth whether he be in the world or out of it. Now
" the Fathers departed to the desert place which was free from
" noise and tumult, because they were afraid that so long as
" they abode in the body the passions which afflicted them
" would cleave unto them; but those who have completed the
" great strife of their contest in the world [have performed] an
" act of grace the power whereof hath worked, and still work-
" eth, for the help and benefit of the community. And verily
" their crown shall be a great one, because into the disturbed
" and troubled sea of the world their spiritual ship, which was
" on its way to heaven along the straight path which was full
" of fear, hath not gone down."

705. The brethren said, "If a man maketh himself a stranger
" to the world, is it helpful to his soul?" The old man said,
" If it fulfilleth with praise it is helpful, and if it endureth tri-
" bulation in chastity, and rejoiceth in our Lord, it is benefi-
" cial, but it is not, if it doeth away the good seed and pre-
" ventethit from producing beloved fruit unto God. If it beareth
" and is blessed, it hath a reward, but if it lack these things
" it becometh a wandering to the mind, and a sight which is
" profitless; but best of all these things is the tranquillity
" of the mind which is nigh unto God."

706. The brethren said, "Since all the creatures which
" God hath made are holy, why were the Fathers in the habit
" of making the sign of the blessed Cross over such of them
" as they ate as food?" The old man said, "Verily, all God's
" creatures are pure, through the Grace of Him that created
" them, yet, because sin obtained dominion, every one of
" them became polluted; then came the advent of our Lord
" and abrogated sin, and righteousness obtained dominion,
" and everything became sanctified, whether it was in the
" heaven or on the earth. But because the blessed Fathers
" knew the harmful disposition of Satan, who even by means
" of such things as are used as food carrieth on a war to our
" injury, they sealed their foods with the holy sign of the Great
" Cross, that they might bring to naught all the crafts of the
" Calumniator. For one of the old men said, 'On one occa-
" ' sion, when I was lying down at night, I thirsted for water
" ' to drink. And there was near me a holy man who lived

" ' chastely, and he saw me take up a vessel of water to drink
" ' without having made over it the sign of the Cross. And he
" ' said unto me, "Wait, master, wait," and he made the
" ' sign of the Cross over it, and straightway there fell from
" ' the vessel the Calumniator in the form of a flash of fire; and
" ' both he and I saw this, and we marvelled at the great power
" ' of the Redeemer, and at the wonderful sign of His merit.' An-
" other version of the story reads:—And one of the Fathers said,
" On one occasion I was lying down at night, and I thirsted for
" water to drink. And there was near me a certain widow, who
" led a chaste life, both when she was with her husband, and
" afterwards, and she said to me, 'Wait, master, wait,' and she
" made the sign of the Holy Cross over the vessel of water, and
" straightway the Calumniator fell from the vessel in the form of
" a flash of fire; and both she and I saw it, and we marvelled at
" the great power of our Redeemer, and at the wonderful sign of
" His merit. These things were indeed spoken by that holy mouth
" which was remote from falsehood. Therefore we must neces-
" sarily do this (i.e., make the sign of the Cross over our food)
" for the protection of our life. For against this holy woman
" who did these things, the enemy waged war openly, ac-
" cording to what I have learned from a certain saint, a chosen
" man of God, who heard the matter from her own mouth,
" and he spake thus:—The blessed woman spake unto me,
" saying, One day I went to the house of God, and Satan
" drew nigh, and said unto me, Why dost thou pray like a
" man, and say, Glory be to the Father, and to the Son, and
" to the Holy Ghost? And I said unto him, If I am not to
" pray thus, how shall I pray? And the blessed woman said,
" Satan said unto me, Pray thus, and say, Glory be unto thee,
" O Mary, mother of Christ. Then I answered and said unto
" him, [There are] ashes in thine eyes, O Satan. Why should
" I forsake the Lord and adore the mother? And Satan disap-
" peared. And the blessed man also said unto me, This same
" old woman said unto me:—On another occasion I went to
" church according to custom, and I knelt down and prayed,
" and then the Enemy came and made blind mine eyes, and I
" could not see, and I called to one of the women, and she led
" me to my house. After three days Satan departed from be-
" fore mine eyes, and he began to go away from before me,
" and then I said unto him, There is something which I must
" make thee do. Go thou to the place where thou didst seize
" upon me; and we went to the church, both he and I, and I
" left him where he seized upon me. Then I went away a short
" distance, and when I turned and looked at him I saw that
" he was standing like a shadow; and I went on again, and

"then turned, and still I saw him. And I shut the door of
"the temple and went forth, and then I opened it again and
"went in, and I saw him still standing [there], and at that
"time his wiles ceased from me. Such were the great things
"which happened to that blessed old woman. For the monk
"must not boast himself over the man who liveth in the
"world, for there are mighty men in the world; for if such
"qualities are found in Eve, how much greater ones should be
"found in the Adam which is redeemed by Adam?"

" One of the Fathers said unto me, 'One night whilst I was
" 'sleeping, the Enemy came and smote me, and said unto
" 'me, "Get thee into the world and cultivate righteousness,
" ' "for why dost thou shut thyself up like a beast in caves?"
" 'And knowing the wickedness of the Enemy, who was look-
" 'ing at me with an evil eye, I made the sign of the Cross in
" 'his face, and he fled from me. Then he waited a few days,
" 'and came and smote me on the neck, and said unto me
" 'mockingly, "Now thou art a righteous man, rise up, and
" ' "get thee into the world, that I may not destroy thee"; and
" 'having prayed, and made the sign of the Cross over my
" 'face, he departed from me. And a little while afterwards he
" 'came again, and sat upon my neck; then I made myself
" 'bold, and stood up, and made the sign of the Cross, the em-
" 'blem of merit, before him, and again he disappeared, for he
" 'was unable to resist me. For all these things took place,
" 'and happened in very truth, and we may therefore know
" 'and understand that there is no rule of life in which
" 'God so much rejoiceth, or which is so terrible unto the
" 'devils, and unto all evil spirits, as the rule of humility,
" 'and penitence of mind, and the subjection of the body, and
" 'remoteness from the things which are seen. Whosoever de-
" 'spiseth these things will fall into the mire of the world; and
" 'whosoever holdeth in contempt the good riches of the fear
" 'of God, shall have his hope of the inheritance of the saints
" 'cut off, and of the delights of heaven, which never pass
" 'away and never end. May we all be held worthy of these
" 'through the grace and mercy of our Lord Jesus Christ, the
" 'True God, to Whom, with His Father, and the Holy Spirit,
" 'be glory, now, and always, and for ever and ever! Amen.'"

INDEX
TO TEXTS FROM SCRIPTURE

Index to Texts from Scripture

INDEX

Index

Chaereus, I, 70
Charity, Sayings on, II, 88ff
Cherubim, II, 273
Children, the Three Holy, II, 244
Christ, efficacy of His Name, I, 44
Christians, I, 59, 63, 66, 108, 151, 154, 198, 238, 239, 280, 381
Chronius, I, 196, 379; II, 66, 193
Chronius of Phœnix, I, 175
Chrysoroan, I, 244
Chrysostom, John, Saint, I, 90
Church, persecution of, I, 39
Colluthus, I, 154
Constans, I, 65
Constantine the Great, I, 65, 184
Constantine the Less, I, 150, 151
Constantinople, I, 106, 163, 165, 172, 223; II, 72, 104, 237
Constantinus, I, 163
Constantius, I, 65, 150, 151
Copres (Kopres), I, 364ff; II, 63, 69, 133, 226
Corinthians, I, 154
Cornelius, the martyr, I, 197
Cosmas, of Sinai, I, 270
Crete, II, 248
Crocodiles, I, 375
Cronius, of Nitria, I, 192
Cross, the, I, 60, 61, 62, 64
Cross, the Name of the, I, 43
Cross, the Sign of the, I, 10, 16, 44, 156, 278, 322; II, 23, 106, 144, 269, 270, 299, 300, 334, 335, 336
Cucumber, II, 62
Cûsh (Nubia), I, 99
Cyprus, II, 119
Cyzicus, city of, I,

D ÂBHÂ (i.e., Wolf River), I, 50
Dagon, the idol, II, 193
Dalgâw, desert of, I, 334
Dalmatia, I, 162
Damanhur, city of, I, 89
Daniel, Abbâ, Sayings of, I, 273; II, 22, 30, 54, 71, 78, 85, 105, 128, 157, 161, 177, 188, 253, 256
Daniel, the Prophet, II, 26, 83, 196, 273
Daniel, Parnâyâ, II, 159
Dathan, I, 286
David, King of Israel, I, 43, 56, 228, 375; II, 16, 116, 194, 208, 226, 250, 284, 307
Dead Sea, the, I, 187
Decius, Emperor, I, 90

Demetrius, Bishop of Pessinus, I, 90
Devil, appears in the form of an Indian, I, 11; as an ass, I, 112
Devils, the, and Pachomius, I, 290; attack Anthony, I, 13; described, I, 22
Didymus, Abbâ, I, 95, 106, 378
Dîkâpôlîs (Decapolis?), I, 379
Diocles, the wandering monk, I, 180, 181; II, 287
Diogenes, the philosopher, I, 85
Dioscorus (Dioscurus), Abbâ, I, 103, 105, 106, 156, 363; II, 18, 227
Dogs, worship of, I, 344
Dômnîn, I, 191
Dômyânôs, II, 242
Dorotheos, Abbâ, II, 315
Dorotheos of Thebes, I, 91, 92, 144, 180
Dosphoria, wife of Heronion, I, 166
Dracontius, uncle of Origen, I, 103
Dropsy, I, 106
Dulas, Abbâ, disciple of Bessarion, I, 243

E DESSA, city of, I, 182, 228
Eggs, I, 107
Egypt, I, 82, 159, 162, 211, 224, 236, 238, 264, 340, 374; II, 18, 20, 37, 70, 72, 91, 98, 99, 110, 124, 149, 244
Egypt, Inner, I, 4; worship of idols in, I, 344
Egyptians, I, 128, 194, 198, 351; II, 20, 110
Elephantiasis, II, 218
Eli, the high priest, II, 28, 246
Elijah the Great, the Prophet, I, 13, 109, 142, 197, 202, 336, 339; II, 85, 159, 189, 199, 255
Elijah, Abbâ, II, 208, 232, 233
Elijah of the Cave, I, 187
Elisha, the Prophet, II, 29, 255
Elpidius, the Cappadocian, I, 185, 186
Embalming, I, 382
Emeralds, I, 97, 98
Epiphanius, Abbâ, I, 26, 27; II, 28, 77, 119, 246
Epiphany, the, I, 118, 375
Ephraim of Edessa, I, 182, 183
Esau, I, 165, 179
Espîr, a place in the Red Sea desert, I, 192
'Estarkînâ, city of, II, 218

343

The Paradise of the Holy Fathers

Petarpemotis, I, 364ff
Peter, Bishop of Alexandria, I, 40
Peter, St., I, 51, 185, 374; II, 307
Peter the Egyptian, I, 174
Peter the Monk, I, 214
Petra, Abbâ, II, 207
Petronius, I, 285, 286
Pharaoh, I, 224, 344, 369
Philagrius, II, 35
Philemon, I, 379, 381
Philistines, II, 193
Philosophers, their visit to Anthony, I, 59
Phinehas, II, 28, 246
Physicians of Nitria, I, 100
Piamon, the virgin, I, 152
Pierius, the author, I, 106, 160
Pîlîsîôn (Pelusium), II, 232
Pinianus, husband of Melania, I, 161, 162
Pîôr, Abbâ, I, 104, 218; II, 43, 116, 224
Pirme, II, 253
Piterius, of the Porphyry Mountain, I, 148
Pitêroum, Abbâ, I, 148
Pithyrion, I, 374
Plato, I, 85
Poemen, Abbâ, I, 265, 266; II, 7, 9, 10, 13, 19, 22, 23, 26, 29, 31, 33, 34, 38, 39, 44, 47, 51, 52, 56, 58, 59, 60, 63, 64, 65, 66, 69, 75, 82, 83, 85, 86, 87, 99, 102, 103, 108, 112, 116, 119, 120, 121, 122, 123, 124, 125, 127, 129, 130, 131, 139, 140, 143, 144, 145, 151, 164, 165, 166, 171, 172, 173, 174, 175, 176, 179, 180, 183, 184, 185, 188, 189, 190, 192, 194, 196, 197, 198, 201, 203, 205, 206, 212, 216, 219, 222, 223, 225, 226, 232, 234, 235, 236, 247, 248, 249, 250, 253, 255, 257, 284, 303
Poemenia, I, 173
Polycratia, I, 52
Pomegranates, I, 107, 119
Pontus, I, 223
Possidonius, I, 173, 174
Porphyrites, I, 147
Poverty, Maxims about, II, 35ff
Prayer, Constant, II, 24ff
Prophets, I, 202
Proverbs, Book of, I, 135
Psalms, Book of, I, 43, 46, 96, 100, 135, 228, 270, 288, 289, 349, 365; II, 5, 278, 305, 306

Psalms, service of, II, 24ff
Ptolemy, the Egyptian, I, 135, 176
Publicola, I, 159
Pûrpûrînê, II, 145
Pûrtê, II, 172
Pyramids of Gîzah, I, 380
Pythagoras, I, 85

RABBÂ of Tabenna, I, 283ff
Raisins, I, 107
Râmâh, II, 29, 247
Raven, I, 185
Red Sea, I, 128, 192
Reeds, II, 4
Reîth, II, 61
Resurrection, I, 62, 73, 150; Festival of, I, 118
Rumnîn, I, 191
Rîtheaôn, II, 139
River, the Wolf, I, 50
Romans, I, 82, 351
Rome, I, 75, 90, 123, 156, 158, 159, 190, 191, 197, 224; II, 57, 119, Rufinus, I, 106, 157; martyrdom of, I, 106

SABAS, I, 187
Sabinus, I, 233
Salt, I, 12
Samson, II, 307
Samuel, I, 56
Sârâ (Sârâh), Emmâ, or Mother, II, 46, 61, 63, 99, 127, 173, 257
Sarânîs, II, 174
Sarmâtâ, II, 5, 140
Sarnaos, II, 22
Satan, I, 31, 34, 35, 46, 55, 96, 124, 131, 179, 208, 210, 211, 214, 220, 227, 234, 237, 247, 261, 262, 274, 310, 356, 373; II, 18, 48, 54, 82, 85, 94, 107, 176, 239, 240, 281, 297, 299, 301, 321, 335
Satan and Macarius, II, 161
Satan as a dog, II, 25; as Gabriel, II, 162; as Christ, II, 163
Sayings of the Fathers, the 10,600, I, 106
Scete, I, 114, 118, 120, 129, 134, 135, 156, 176, 209, 216, 217, 234, 240, 260, 267, 268, 270; II, 5, 6, 7, 8, 16, 18, 19, 33, 35, 36, 37, 41, 45, 46, 49, 53, 55, 62, 63, 64, 71, 92, 99, 102, 106, 107, 115, 116, 121, 122, 124, 128, 130, 132, 141, 143, 145, 152, 157, 158, 159, 166, 176, 177, 182, 185, 186, 187, 191,

348